PHENOMENA

ALSO BY ANNIE JACOBSEN

Operation Paperclip

Area 51

The Pentagon's Brain

PHENOMENA

THE SECRET HISTORY OF THE U.S. GOVERNMENT'S INVESTIGATIONS INTO EXTRASENSORY PERCEPTION AND PSYCHOKINESIS

ANNIE JACOBSEN

LITTLE, BROWN AND COMPANY

New York • Boston • London

Little, Brown and Company
Hachette Book Group
1290 Avenue of the Americas, New York, NY 10104
littlebrown.com

First Edition: March 2017

Little, Brown and Company is a division of Hachette Book Group, Inc. The Little, Brown name and logo are trademarks of Hachette Book Group, Inc.

The publisher is not responsible for websites (or their content) that are not owned by the publisher.

The Hachette Speakers Bureau provides a wide range of authors for speaking events. To find out more, go to hachettespeakersbureau.com or call (866) 376-6591.

ISBN 978-0-316-34936-9
Library of Congress Control Number: 2016959021

10 9 8 7 6 5 4 3 2 1

LSC-C

Printed in the United States of America

For Kevin, Finley, and Jett

CONTENTS

PART III
THE DEFENSE DEPARTMENT YEARS

PART IV
THE MODERN ERA

PHENOMENA

There are but two powers in the world, the sword and the mind. In the long run the sword is always beaten by the mind.
—Napoleon Bonaparte

There are two ways to be fooled. One is to believe what isn't true; the other is to refuse to believe what is true.
—Søren Kierkegaard

Prologue

This is a book about scientists and psychics with top-secret clearances. It is about the U.S. government's decades-long interest in anomalous mental phenomena, including extra-sensory perception (ESP), psychokinesis (PK), map dowsing, and other forms of divination, all disciplines the scientific community rejects as pseudoscience. Across recorded history these disciplines have been called magical, mystical, supernatural, and occult. Today they are called paranormal. Those who practice them have been lionized, vilified, and burned at the stake. And then, just a few years after the end of World War II, the U.S. government determined anomalous mental phenomena to be effective military and intelligence tools, and began to investigate their possible use in classified operations. This book tells the story of this post-war endeavor and its continuation into the modern era.

The real action began in 1972, when a small group of promising young scientists was approached by the Central Intelligence Agency to embark upon a research program involving psychics, or "sensitives." The work took place at Stanford Research Institute, the second-largest Defense Department–funded independent research facility in the nation. The CIA challenged the

scientists to first determine whether extrasensory perception—
the ability to perceive things by means other than the five known
senses—and psychokinesis—the ability to perturb matter with
the mind—could be demonstrated and repeated in the laboratory. If so, the CIA wondered, how might these disciplines be
best deployed against the enemy to win the Cold War?

The results of the CIA program were spectacular. "A large
body of reliable experimental evidence points to the inescapable
conclusion that extrasensory perception does exist as a real phenomenon," the CIA concluded in 1975. Focusing on the results,
the military and the intelligence services wanted in. This included
the Navy, the Air Force, the Army (including its Intelligence and
Security Command and the Development and Readiness Command), the Coast Guard, the Defense Intelligence Agency, the
National Security Agency, the Drug Enforcement Administration, the U.S. Customs Service, the Secret Service, and the Joint
Chiefs of Staff. Over time, numerous presidents, congressmen,
and members of the National Security Council were briefed.

When a theoretical understanding of the phenomena could
not be found, grave tensions arose. In the postwar age of advancing technology, science has taken an aggressively hostile attitude
toward supernatural, or paranormal, beliefs. Extrasensory perception and map dowsing are just modern names for divination:
the practice of seeking knowledge of the future or the unknown
by supernatural means. Psychokinesis was based upon a protosci-
entific tradition not unlike alchemy, the fabled supposition that,
using magic, man could affect matter. How could the U.S. government condone such things?

In 1942 Dr. Gertrude Schmeidler, an experimental psychologist with a PhD from Harvard, conducted an experiment on the
subject of anomalous mental phenomena with psychology students at City University of New York. In her questionnaire, she
explored individuals' beliefs about ESP and PK. Her analysis of

the data led her to create the term "sheep" to refer to individuals who were confident about the possible reality of ESP and PK, and "goats" to refer to those who doubted the existence of any so-called anomalous mental phenomena. This explicit difference, between believers and disbelievers of mental phenomena, has existed in the upper echelons of the U.S. military and intelligence communities since World War II. This book tells their story.

The sheep–goat divide also exists across America, but with a clear minority of goats. Gallup polls and Pew Research Center studies reveal that a majority of Americans alive today harbor paranormal beliefs: 73 percent say they have had a supernatural or paranormal experience, and 55 percent believe in psychic or spiritual healing. Many Americans also believe in extrasensory perception or telepathy (41 percent); believe that extraterrestrials have visited Earth (29 percent); or say they've seen a ghost (18 percent). A minority 27 percent do not believe in anything supernatural. This group includes scientific skeptics, who are also an important part of this story.

Were the government's psychics gifted seers or skilled magicians? And are the scientists who studied them, many of whom continue to study these phenomena today, on the brink of discovery? Are they modern-day scientific revolutionaries akin to Galileo, Louis Pasteur, and Madame Curie, each of whom solved scientific mysteries that baffled scientists for millennia? Or is ESP and PK research a fool's errand, nothing more?

How do scientists—people of reason—approach such enigmatic subject matter? And what about the psychics themselves? Who were the individuals hired by the U.S. government for these top-secret programs, and how do they explain their military and intelligence work? To research and report this book I interviewed fifty-five scientists and psychics who worked on government programs, including the core members of the original group from Stanford Research Institute and the CIA, the core group on the military side, defense scientists, former military intelligence officers and government psychics, physicists, biologists, neurophysiologists, cyberneticists, astrophysicists, a general, an admiral, a Nobel Laureate, and an Apollo astronaut. These are their stories.

—

PART I

THE EARLY DAYS

The cause is hidden; the effect is visible to all.
—Ovid

CHAPTER ONE

The Supernatural

supernatural: unable to be explained by science or the laws of nature; of, relating to, or seeming to come from magic, a god, etc.

—Merriam-Webster dictionary

It was May 10, 1941, a day during World War II remembered in the history books for its bizarre links to the supernatural. Rudolf Hess, the deputy führer of the Third Reich, woke up in his villa in the Munich suburb of Harlaching and, on the advice of his astrologer, chose this day to make his secret move. The six planets were in Taurus and the moon would be full, the star chart allegedly said. Hess ate breakfast, had a brief conversation with his wife, and asked his driver to take him to the Messerschmitt aircraft facility in Augsburg. Shortly before 6:00 p.m., he climbed into a Bf 110 fighter-bomber and flew north. Flying low so as to avoid radar, Hess made his way down the Rhine River, across the Dutch coast, out over the North Sea and toward

Scotland. Roughly five and a half hours after taking off, he bailed out of his aircraft and parachuted into a field at Floors Farm, near Eaglesham, a village south of Glasgow.

His intention, Hess later said, was to make his way to Dungavel Castle and barter an alliance with England using as an intermediary the Duke of Hamilton. Instead, the deputy führer of the Third Reich was arrested and taken into custody. The interrogation that followed remains classified by British intelligence until 2041, but stories and theories about what really happened abound. Had Hitler's obsessively loyal second-in-command really betrayed the Nazi cause on the advice of an astrologer? Or had British intelligence constructed an elaborate web of deception to catch Hess, using his belief in the supernatural as bait?

Years later, while serving a life sentence in Spandau prison, Hess allegedly revealed his motivation to Albert Speer, the Reich's former minister of Armaments and War Production. "Hess assured me in all seriousness that the idea had been inspired in him in a dream by supernatural forces," Speer wrote in *Inside the Third Reich*. Two of Hess's personal astrologers, Karl Krafft and Ernst Schulte-Strathaus, were reported to have constructed the star charts that aided Hess in believing the tenth of May to be cosmically suited for his rogue flight.

But there exists another version of the story, one that was revealed by the British Broadcasting Corporation in 2002. "Britain's most famous witch," a woman by the name of Sybil Leek, had been recruited by British intelligence "to provide phony horoscopes for the Germans who believed in Astrology," according to the BBC. "She apparently wrote a chart which convinced the Nazi Rudolf Hess to fly to England, where he was captured." In other words, Leek's star charts were instruments of black propaganda inserted into the deputy führer's inner circle to influence his behavior and help foster certain beliefs. "Mum stayed silent about the Hess affair all her life," says her son, Julian Leek, a Florida resident. "It's still officially classified and the individual who revealed the story [in 2002] has moved to South America and [apparently] doesn't answer email."

To the Third Reich, Rudolf Hess's rogue flight was a supreme embarrassment. Adolf Hitler declared Hess legally insane and responded with Special Action Hess, the mass arrest of more than 600 astrologers, fortune-tellers, clairvoyants, faith healers, and other German practitioners of the supernatural or the occult. Artifacts of divination, including tarot cards, scrying mirrors, and crystal balls, were confiscated, as were entire libraries of mystical texts. "The circulation of all occult literature was forbidden," wrote Wilhelm Wulff, an astrologer ensnared in Special Action Hess. A decree was issued making it illegal to "predict future events, the divination of the present or the past, and all other forms of revelation not based on natural processes of perception...to include the reading of cards, the casting of horoscopes, the explanation of stars and the interpretation of omens and dreams." Practitioners of magic, including Wulff, were interrogated by agents of the Gestapo and many were sent to concentration camps.

Meanwhile, inside the Third Reich, reliance upon the occult continued—not on the orders of Adolf Hitler but because Heinrich Himmler, Reichsführer-SS and the man *Time* magazine called "the Police Chief of Nazi Europe," relied upon the supernatural as a power source himself. At least one account suggests Hitler was embarrassed by Himmler's belief system.

"What nonsense!" the Führer told Albert Speer, as recounted in *Inside the Third Reich*. "Here we have at last reached an age that has left all mysticism behind it, and now he [Himmler] wants to start that all over again. We might just as well have stayed with the church."

In a postwar account by Wilhelm Wulff, Himmler's personal astrologer, astrology was "*privilegium singulorum*. It is not for the broad masses." For the Reich to control the war message, explained Wulff, powerful belief systems that lay outside the Nazi creed needed to be curtailed. But not entirely. The Nazis' head of foreign intelligence, SS-Brigadeführer Walter Schellenberg, made an important point to Wulff about the power of mystical belief systems. They were "a suitable vehicle for the propagation of political concepts and for the political control of a nation," Schellenberg said, meaning astrology could be used for great effect in a propaganda campaign.

The same kind of manipulation was occurring in the United States. In the summer of 1941, a German-born Hungarian named Louis de Wohl was preparing for a speech at the annual convention of the American Federation of Scientific Astrologers, in Cleveland, Ohio. De Wohl, a plump, bespectacled British citizen, was one of the highest-profile astrologers in the Western world. His admirers in London included Lord Halifax, who was Britain's Foreign Secretary, and the Duke of Alba, the ambassador from Spain. In honor of the astrology convention that year, the *Cleveland News* profiled de Wohl on its front page under the banner "Astrology has too many quacks." De Wohl's mission in America was to remove the occult stigma from stargazing and to elevate it into the realm of "astro-philosophy," he said.

War was raging across Europe, and in de Wohl's syndicated American column, "Stars Foretell," emphasis was always on the Nazi threat. "Hitler's chief jackal is moving into the house of violence," he predicted, "Seer Sees plot to Kill Hitler." Starting in June 1941, just one month after the Hess affair, de Wohl's predictions became unusually specific, and things he predicted started to come true. "A strong collaborator of Hitler who is neither German nor a Nazi will go violently insane," he foretold. "He will be in South or Central America, probably near the Caribbean Sea." Three days later, U.S. newswires reported that the Vichy High Commissioner of the French West Indies, Admiral

Georges Robert, had gone crazy and had to be restrained by staff. The *New York Post* reported that newspaper editors across America "besieged de Wohl with requests for exclusive stories."

As de Wohl's popularity escalated to meteoric heights, the Federal Communications Commission made a bold move. In August 1941 it lifted its long-standing ban against astrologers and aired an exclusive interview with the man hailed "The Modern Nostradamus." Then, for the first time in U.S. history, an astrologer was filmed for a U.S. newsreel. "On August 28, Pathé News released the newsreels' first plunge into prophecy with a nationwide audience of 39,000,000 sitting as judge jury and witness," declared a press release issued by de Wohl's manager. Except none of it was true. De Wohl's successful American career was a product of British intelligence, and his so-called manager was none other than the spymaster Sir William Stephenson, a man whom Winston Churchill famously called Intrepid. SS-Brigadeführer Walter Schellenberg was correct when he stated that astrology was a vehicle for the propagation of political concepts.

Louis de Wohl was a committed astrologer but he also worked for British intelligence through its operational arm in America, the British Security Coordination Office. According to de Wohl's declassified intelligence file, his columns, the interviews, and the predictions were all part of an elaborate black propaganda campaign designed "to organize American public opinion in favor to aid Britain." Even the American Federation of Scientific Astrologers and its 1941 convention had been fabricated by MI6. The way it worked was masterful: the British spy agency first fed information to de Wohl, which he would write up in his column, "Stars Foretell." The British spy agency then fed the bogus information to the U.S. press, which—unable to fact-check with the Reich—the press would report as real. For example, the Vichy High Commissioner of the French West Indies never went insane.

According to the CIA's Office of the Historian, de Wohl's handler worked with U.S. spy chief Colonel William Donovan to coordinate and "oversee U.S. intelligence collection and analysis efforts," this before the Office of Strategic Services, precursor to the CIA, even existed. British intelligence believed England needed America to join the war in Europe in order for the Allied forces to beat the Nazis. De Wohl's phony predictions were intended to help sway public opinion away from the prevailing U.S. isolationist views. The ruse was effective. In one declassified memo, Stephenson wrote of de Wohl, "An ever-growing audience [is] becoming convinced of his supernatural powers."

Three months later the Japanese bombed Pearl Harbor and the U.S. declared war on Japan. On December 11, Hitler declared war on the United States. America had entered World War II, and it was time for Louis de Wohl to head home to England.

For the next few years, de Wohl was used by the Allies as a countermeasure to Heinrich Himmler's use of astrology and the occult. Under the direction of master propagandist Sefton Delmer, de Wohl wrote seemingly authentic astrology charts that predicted the demise of certain Nazi admirals and generals, and stated that Hitler would be betrayed by his inner circle. These fake star charts and horoscopes were included in near-perfect replicas of a banned German astrological magazine called *Zenit*, to be smuggled into Germany for underground distribution. The idea was to make it look as if *Zenit* was being secretly published in Germany by German occultists working in defiance of the astrology ban. Instead, the counterfeit magazines were seized by the Gestapo in the port city of Stettin, as detailed by Wilhelm Wulff in his postwar memoir *Zodiac and Swastika*.

Occult interests in the public domain are for the most part a leisure pursuit. When entwined with the Nazis' national security apparatus, they became potent and consequential. As Reichsführer-SS, Heinrich Himmler promoted quasi-science projects that helped foster the myth of the superior German Übermensch, or Superman. Himmler had been fascinated with the occult since his college days, and when he became a Nazi Party district leader, in 1925, he hired a sixty-six-year-old retired army colonel named Karl Maria Wiligut to advise him on these matters. Wiligut, an expert in runes and Teutonic symbols (he designed the SS death's-head ring, *Totenkopfring*) was a seer, or medium, who claimed to be able to channel a tribe of ancient Aryans from AD 1200. Elevated to the position of SS-Brigadeführer, Wiligut remained on Himmler's personal staff until SS intelligence officers discovered that between the wars, in 1923, Wiligut had been committed to a mental institution and declared legally insane. In 1936 he was removed from the SS command structure, but Himmler continued to meet with him privately until at least 1941, as indicated in Himmler's diaries, which were captured by the Allies after the war.

By the time Wiligut was removed Himmler had already created a vast Nazi science academy called Das Ahnenerbe, or the Institute for Research and Study of Heredity, of which he was president and overlord. The mission of Ahnenerbe, according to Allied intelligence, was "to prove that the Nazi ideology was directly descended from ancient Teutonic culture and was therefore superior to all others." To demonstrate this link, Himmler leaned on the mystical and the occult.

Ahnenerbe scientists were dispatched across the continents to excavate prehistoric sites attached to mystical and supernatural ideas. From Istanbul to Iraq, they searched the globe for lost lands like Atlantis and fabled items like the Holy Grail and the Lance of Destiny, the spear said to have pierced Christ in the ribs as he hung on the Cross. On Himmler's orders, SS officers scoured Germany's occupied territories, raiding libraries of the occult and looting artifacts related to magic. Entire museum collections of mystical texts in Poland, Ukraine, and Crimea were crated up for

Ahnenerbe possession. Among the items said to be most coveted by Himmler were artifacts of ancient Germanic magic that had miraculously survived three centuries of witch hunts.

The Ahnenerbe was vast and well funded. It had fifty subsidiary branches covering broad natural science fields such as archeology, geology, and astronomy. But it also operated highly specialized divisions, like one for geochronology, the dating of rock formations and geological events, and speleology, the study and exploration of caves. One branch, called Survey of the So-called Occult Sciences (*Überprüfung der Sogenannten Geheimwissenschaften*), was where research on extrasensory perception, astrology, map dowsing, spirit channeling, and other forms of anomalous mental phenomena and divination was pursued. And it was from the official Ahnenerbe documentation on these unusual subjects, captured separately by the United States and the Red Army, that the psychic arms race between the Soviet Union and the United States first got under way.

Now it was July 1945, and World War II was over in Europe. The Nazis had been defeated, their ideas vanquished. Some fifty million people were dead. But between the Americans and the Soviets—former allies—the competition over the spoils of war had only just begun. The end of World War II marked the beginning of a new war, called the Cold War, and with it would come an arms race of colossal proportions. During World War II, the Nazis had managed to create some of the most technologically advanced weapons in the world. That they mixed magic and the supernatural with science and technology was, in 1945, only vaguely understood. But the Reich's supernatural secrets would soon become part of the Cold War arms race.

For ten weeks now the Russians had ruled Berlin. Members of an elite U.S. scientific intelligence effort, called Operation Alsos, had been trying to gain access to a bombed-out villa in Dahlem, a formerly affluent suburb where numerous Nazi science institutes once stood. The villa in question was located at 16 Pücklerstrasse, and "The Gestapo scientists had all cleared out before our arrival," recalled Samuel Goudsmit, a nuclear physicist and the leader of the group, "some of them leaving sufficient clues in their deserted homes for us to track them down later." This villa was not a home but the former headquarters of Himmler's Ahnenerbe Institute.

The Alsos group was only vaguely familiar with the Ahnenerbe's research. Only weeks before had it come to light that through a division called Applied War Research, the Ahnenerbe had supplied the Luftwaffe and other military services with living victims from the concentration camps to be used in human experiments. How Heinrich Himmler used the supernatural and the occult as part of the Nazi war effort was not yet understood by Alsos. "Because the activities of this strange academy were shrouded in [a] mystery that just might have concealed something really important, we [needed] to make a thorough investigation of the organization," Goudsmit later explained in discussing the Ahnenerbe.

Goudsmit made his way down into the basement of the villa, where he came across a small cache of Ahnenerbe relics. "Remnants of weird Teutonic symbols and rites," he recalled. "Strange dummies which at first looked like bodies of victims, a corner with a pit of ashes in which I found the skull of an infant." Had Heinrich Himmler been a practitioner of black magic, Goudsmit wondered? What had been going on here?

As macabre and mysterious as these Nazi artifacts were, they did not pose an immediate threat. Alsos was on the move, with more pressing matters to deal with. Huge Nazi weapons caches, including V-2 rockets and chemical weapons like sarin and tabun gas, were being secreted out of the country by the Americans for exploitation back home.

For Goudsmit and the Alsos team, the most critical aspect in dealing with a mystery like Ahnenerbe science was to make sure that the information did not fall into Soviet hands. For what would soon become evident was that as much as the Allies were gathering scientific intelligence, so too were the Soviets. By war's end, the Reich's most treasured and most promising weapons programs had been carted up and transported east into occupied territories like Poland, where they remained out of range of the Allied bombing campaigns. This new competition between Russia and the United States—between east and west, between communism and capitalism—was a contest of one-upmanship, the technique or practice of gaining a feeling of superiority over another. The absolute goal in this Cold War began as a relative one: simply to stay ahead of the new enemy in rank, knowledge, and weapons technology. In 1945, the long-term goal to outperform the Soviets in every action had not yet come to pass. And so, the Ahnenerbe relics were crated up and sent to U.S. Army headquarters in Frankfurt. Alsos moved on.

Immediately after World War II, the governments of both the United States and the USSR began investigating new ways to influence and control human behavior. And here was where Ahnenerbe science first appeared outside Nazi Germany. Leading the charge in the United States was the newly formed Central Intelligence Agency. One of the CIA's early programs sought to develop a truth serum, an age-old quest that touched upon ideas of magic potions and sorcerers' spells. In consort with U.S. Army scientists at the Army Chemical Center in Edgewood, Maryland, this classified program was first called Bluebird, then Artichoke, and finally MKULTRA. For these and other programs like them the CIA hired magicians, hypnotists, and even Sybil Leek, Britain's famous white witch.

One of the men running these controversial programs for the CIA was Morse Allen, a deception and polygraph expert promoted to serve as the director of Project Artichoke in 1952. It was Morse Allen's job to search the globe for the most potent drugs in existence so that the Agency could exploit them for intelligence use. The Nazis' Ahnenerbe Institute had begun this kind of research in the concentration camps, pushing human physiology to extremes in order to allow Nazi scientists to measure and monitor results. Now the CIA and the KGB would conduct similar experiments, each side arguing that the other side's programs required countermeasures to defend against them.

In October 1952, Morse Allen learned about a Mexican field mushroom that put humans in an altered state. The fungal growth, called teonanáctl — God's flesh — gave certain "sensitive" or psychic people supernatural abilities, at least according to ancient Aztec legend. "Very early accounts of the ceremonies of some tribes of Mexican Indians show that mushrooms are used to produce hallucinations and to create intoxication in connection with religious festivals," Morse Allen told his program officers in a rare surviving Project Artichoke memo. In some cases, teonanáctl apparently endowed man with the power of divination, the ability to access information about the future or the unknown. In other men, the mushroom acted like a truth serum and made them confess to things against their better judgment or free will. "The literature shows that witch doctors, or 'divinators,' used some types of mushrooms to produce confessions or to locate stolen objects or to predict the future," Morse Allen wrote.

In early 1953 the CIA dispatched one of its scientists to Mexico on a hunt to gather samples. But God's flesh was elusive. The mushroom grew in remote canyons, and only in the hot summer months after it had rained. The scientist came back empty-handed, but Morse Allen was confident the CIA would ultimately prevail. He instructed his agents to keep searching while he personally traveled to the mushroom capital of America, a farming town in Pennsylvania called Toughkenamon, where he secured a contract with the town's top mushroom grower. Once the CIA had located teonanáctl samples, it planned to mass-produce the hallucinogenic mushroom for classified intelligence agency use.

The quest for God's flesh was renamed MKULTRA Subproject 58. Two years passed without success. Then, in the late summer of 1954, Morse Allen learned that an Army captain at the Army Chemical Center, one of the CIA's military partners in MKULTRA, was also on the hunt for the hallucinogenic mushroom said to endow men with divinatory powers. His name was Henry Karel "Andrija" Puharich, and in addition to being an Army captain, Puharich was a research scientist, a medical doctor, and a trance-state specialist.

Since 1947, Dr. Puharich and a well-funded, prizewinning staff of scientists, doctors, and technicians had been conducting a wide range of unusual research at a privately funded facility called the Round Table Foundation, located in rural Maine. Puharich was also a longtime believer in mental phenomena, even claiming a personal childhood experience with telepathy. When Captain Puharich was called in for a briefing, it came to light that he knew more about magic, mystical, supernatural, and occult research than just about any other scientist living in the United States at the time. Dr. Puharich was granted a higher security clearance and briefed on classified Army Chemical Center efforts to locate drugs that could produce altered states and enhance psychic functioning.

Now, with government interest piqued in multiple agencies and the potential of a game-changing drug seemingly close at hand, the real race could begin.

CHAPTER TWO

The Puharich Theory

Henry Karel "Andrija" Puharich was born in Chicago on February 19, 1918, the son of poor Yugoslavian immigrants. His brutal, violent father had come to America as a stowaway. His mother, a housewife, nurtured and protected her only son as best she could. Growing up in the Chicago slums, Andrija worked as a milk delivery boy for Borden's Dairy Farms, and it was in this context that he had his first experience with what he would call extrasensory perception, the ability to perceive things by means other than the five senses. One day on a milk run a vicious guard dog cornered him. Fearing that the animal was about to tear him to shreds, Puharich panicked, but there was nowhere to run. "So I sent out feelings of calmness and peace," Puharich later recalled. Remarkably, the dog calmed down, then sat, leading him to believe that mind-to-mind telepathy had "stopped the attack." Entranced and empowered by this experience, Puharich vowed to become a medical doctor and solve the biological circumstances behind this mysterious force of nature called ESP.

When Puharich was a teenager, his parents divorced and he and his mother went to live on a farm in Garter, Illinois. There, he worked nights and weekends in the farmer's orchards, driving a mule team and tending to the fruit trees. Puharich was a bright, curious boy, unusually observant, and the natural world cast a spell over him. In plants and animals he saw deep meaning. Like so many research scientists before him, the natural world was his first laboratory.

In high school, Puharich excelled. He served as president of the student council, sang in the glee club, and played quarterback on the varsity football team. When it came time for college, Northwestern University College of the Liberal Arts offered him three scholarships to attend. As an undergraduate he majored in philosophy and premedical studies, then went on to Northwestern's medical school. To earn money, Puharich worked for the university as a tree surgeon, trimming dead branches and plugging holes made by insects. He saw the human nervous system as similar to the root system of a tree, he later wrote. He scoured the works of medieval physicians like Alessandro Benedetti, a pioneer of postmortem examination, gathering a historical understanding about the science of the brain. And he began developing his own ideas about the biology of the human mind. Why does man think certain thoughts? What is consciousness? What is the difference between the brain and the mind?

"I would venture to say that nobody really knows another's mind thoroughly," he wrote in his journal in 1942, "and I would further venture that very few people really know their own mind." What makes man think certain thoughts, he wondered, from a biological point of view? How does perception work? Does consciousness come from within or from without? And how to explain energy between people? "We all know that there are people who can thrill and exhilarate one, and that there are others who simply bore and fatigue one." What, he wondered, was this intangible force?

Puharich combed through great works of medicine, literature, and science seeking answers. He could find nothing that satisfied him. "It would certainly be a great step forward for [mankind] if we could sit down and untangle the jungle that is our mind," he wrote. In medical school, he began to explore the biological processes by which a man thinks. "Understanding the nature of man's consciousness," declared Puharich, "is my lifelong quest."

Like so many young men of his generation, World War II introduced Puharich to military life. In 1943, while still in medical school, Puharich was commissioned as a second lieutenant in the U.S. Army Medical Corps. A chronic middle ear infection exempted him from being sent overseas to the war. He met and married Virginia "Jinny" Jackson, a War Department secretary and the daughter of a prominent Wisconsin physician. In 1947 he finished his medical degree and began working alongside some of the top medical men in Chicago. His mentor, Dr. Andrew C. Ivy, was one of the most famous physicians in America, having riveted the nation with searing testimony at the Nuremberg Doctors' Trial in Germany.

Puharich did his residency at the Permanente Research Foundation in Oakland, California, publishing numerous papers on the effect of various drugs on the brain. He formulated his first major theory, on nerve conduction and an unknown energy force, which he called the Puharich Theory. "The brain and the nervous system [are] linked to cells, and instructions [in the form of] energy flows between them," Puharich wrote. "The point that I am trying to establish is that the brain is an area wherein is localized the cell energy of the body. I shall label this cell energy 'dynamics.'" Puharich believed this energy force, present in all animals and insects, radiated somewhere on the electromagnetic spectrum but that man had not yet invented technology to measure or record it. The Puharich Theory was embraced by the nation's top doctors, "heartily received and critically reviewed." When, a few months later, two Yale University scientists, Lloyd H. Beck and Walter S. Miles, first reported that the olfactory nerve of the bee radiated energy in the infrared spectrum, one of Puharich's theories was proved right. And the medical community wanted to hear more of what he had to say.

Puharich's own energy was boundless. He was strikingly handsome and charismatic, by all accounts easy to talk to. With his close-cropped black hair and deep-set blue eyes, he looked like Gary Cooper in a lab coat. Women adored him, and men did too. He could engage in conversation the shyest person in the room as easily as he could command the attention of a Nobel Laureate. This was elemental to his character and his charm, said his friends.

One night at a party, on December 9, 1947, he met Dr. Paul De Kruif, the legendary microbiologist and author of *Microbe Hunters,* one of the most popular science books of the day. De Kruif told Puharich he was "keenly interested in the important implications of the [Puharich] theory," and suggested Puharich travel east and deliver it as a lecture to the nation's top physicians and scientists.

Over the next few weeks, the two men exchanged a series of letters. In addition to his support, De Kruif issued a prescient warning. "All creation, including science, is a war against precedent. Science, to be vital, must grow out of competition between individual brains, foils one to the other, each man mad for his own idea." Conformity was a scientist's death knell, said De Kruif. "Beware the Establishment!" he warned.

On the advice of his new friend, Puharich traveled east, lecturing on the Puharich Theory to colleagues at Harvard and Yale. From the podium he spoke freely about his ideas, which merged philosophy, mysticism, and science. "What is the nature of the process that enables man to reflect, and to reflect upon, the universe in a range that now encompasses the phenomena that lie between God on the one hand, and nuclear energy on the other?" he asked. Did inspiration, imagination, and Einstein-like thinking come from within, or was initiative an external force? He urged his colleagues to go out into nature and to observe. "Watch long trails of birds in migration, the unerring return of the homing pigeon, the struggle of the fish going upstream to spawn, the orderly movement of armies of ants, the pecuniary nature of the bee," he said, for in nature, the mysteries of the universe are revealed. As for man, "The answer to these many questions, I am convinced, lie in the nature of the nervous system," Puharich declared, "a sensitivity to forces, some of which we already know, and most of which are unknown." Puharich's ideas were a merging of medicine and mysticism. "I have wondered at the clairvoyance of the mind that can break loose from the shackles of conformity and 'facts' and can give us the philosophy of Plato, the universe of Newton, the spirit of Christ, and the psychological insight of Henry Thoreau, Walt Whitman, William James and Khalil Gibran. The deep study of this problem is my life's work."

Among those in attendance who were enchanted by Puharich's Theory and ideas were two wealthy benefactors, Joyce Borden Balokovic and Zlatko Balokovic. Joyce was a primary shareholder of the Borden dairy fortune; Zlatko was a world-renowned Yugoslavian-born virtuoso violinist who owned one of the world's largest collections of Guarnerius and Stradivarius instruments. The Balokovics took an immediate interest in Puharich and suggested they work together on a future project. "After the Harvard lecture, [I] accepted an invitation to visit friends in Camden, Maine," Puharich wrote in his journal. The new friends were the Balokovics.

Camden was a place unlike anything Andrija Puharich—a boy raised in the Chicago slums and then on a farm—had ever experienced. This magnificent coastal community was a summer colony for an elite group of America's ruling class, children of Golden Age industrialists who earned their money the old-fashioned way, by inheriting it. Here in Maine the summer cottages were 10,000-square-foot homes with gatehouses, carriage houses, boathouses, and stables. Days were spent yachting. Evenings were passed in wicker chairs on wooden verandas, sipping cocktails and admiring the environs. Nights were spent in the salon or library discussing ideas: great works of literature, national security, world religions—and in the case of Joyce Borden Balokovic, extrasensory perception. She suggested Puharich create a research laboratory in Maine dedicated to the study of the Puharich Theory. She and Zlatko would be happy to donate, she said, and so would many of their friends. To demonstrate, Joyce introduced Puharich to a friend she was certain would also want to become a benefactor, Alice Astor Bouverie.

Alice Astor Bouverie was an heiress, a philanthropist, and the only daughter of John Jacob Astor IV, of the Astor dynasty. Alice was just ten years old when her father, one of the richest men in the world, died in the sinking of the RMS *Titanic*. Astor left his daughter $5 million, roughly $120 million in 2017. Like Joyce Borden, Alice was interested in ESP, and in mental telepathy in particular, a notion she learned about from her father. John Jacob Astor IV was a world-class businessman, investor, and real estate tycoon, but he also wrote science fiction novels about ESP. In *A Journey in Other Worlds: A Romance of the Future,* published in 1884, Astor's space-traveling protagonists communicated telepathically with one another. "Do tell me how you were able to answer my thought," one character says to another. "I see the vibrations of the grey matter of your brain as plainly as the movements of your lips; in fact, I see the thoughts in the embryonic state taking shape," comes the reply. In 1948, Alice Bouverie became the first among many wealthy individuals to personally finance Dr. Puharich's work. Bouverie's initial check was for $106,000, more than $1 million in 2017. With this investment, Puharich started his first research foundation.

A third female patron was introduced to the growing circle: Marcella Miller du Pont, of the chemical and weapons production conglomerate. Like Joyce Borden and Alice Astor, Marcella du Pont was passionate about ESP and willing to finance Puharich's research efforts in this area. The three wealthy women helped Puharich come up with the name for his new foundation. In homage to the legend of King Arthur, Merlin the Magician, a sword, a stone, and the Holy Grail, it would be called the Round Table Foundation. At Puharich's Round Table, there was no chivalric order; men and women were equals. It was not as much an antiestablishment foundation as it was a secret society of elites. Alice Bouverie became the organization's first vice president. Joyce Borden Balokovic served as treasurer. Marcella du Pont went by the honorary title "mother of magic."

Documents from the Library of Congress, previously unreported, reveal that it was du Pont who first brought the attention of top-tier government officials to the Round Table Foundation, including Admiral John E. Gingrich, the powerful director of security and intelligence for the Atomic Energy Commission. In a letter to her brother du Pont wrote, "my great friend Admiral John Gingrich [is] interested in using some of the significant facts for the Navy that [will] come out of these [Round Table] experiments." Gingrich served as the chief of Naval Material Command from 1953 to 1954 and was responsible for all Navy procurement activities. Another Navy man, Rexford Daniels, a Yale PhD, former lieutenant commander in Navy intelligence, and current member of the U.S. Navy Reserve, would stop by for drinks on the porch at the Round Table Foundation. Daniels, who had a summer home in neighboring Camden, advised military officials on radio frequency and microwave technology, which was still in its infancy in the late 1940s. He was interested in ESP as a possible means of long-distance communication in submarines. As a member of both the military establishment and the East Coast aristocracy, Daniels would soon become a liaison for Dr. Puharich between these worlds.

Money poured in. One wealthy benefactor after the next joined the Round Table Foundation, including Ruth Forbes Young, of the Forbes family of bankers, and her husband, Arthur Middleton Young, the Princeton University mathematician–philosopher, cosmologist,

and astrologer who famously designed Bell Corporation's first heli-
copter, the Model 30, in 1942. Congresswoman Frances Payne
Bolton, granddaughter of oilman Henry B. Payne and the first
woman elected to Congress from Ohio, was a supporter and patron.
Henry Belk of the Belk department store fortune came on board,
flying up to Maine in his private jet for foundation meetings. Henry
Cabot Paine, a Boston Brahmin, became involved, and so did John
"Jack" Hays Hammond Jr., son of the diplomat and mining magnet
John Hays Hammond Sr., and himself the inventor of the Navy's first
torpedo, the Hammond torpedo.

In this way, the members of the Round Table Foundation were
a unique mixture of old-money philosophers and scientists, diplomats and weapons designers, poets and mystics. They all had deep
pockets and nonconformist ideas. But their common bond began
via an interest in extrasensory perception. Was it elemental to
human consciousness? A product of nerve conduction? Or some
other unknown energy force? The quest of the Round Table
Foundation was to conduct experiments to find out and to fund
the research that would allow the Puharich Theory to advance
from conjecture to hypothesis to scientific theory.

With the remarkable influx of cash from his new friends and
associates, Dr. Andrija Puharich moved his family from California
to Maine, into a seaside mansion in Glen Cove. Jinny, Puharich's
wife, had just given birth to their first child. It was here, starting
in 1949, that work began in earnest. Meanwhile, six hundred miles
to the south, in Washington, D.C., the Central Intelligence Agency
Act of 1949 was passed, broadening the Agency's authority and
power. Soon the civilian pursuits at the Round Table Foundation
and the national security goals of the CIA would entwine.

The opulence of Puharich's new home and laboratory facility,
called Warrenton Estate, was part of its mystique. The main house

was designed by the famous Beaux-Arts architect Stanford White. Warrenton had forty-five rooms, eight fireplaces, and twelve baths. There were wraparound porches, a soaring three-story entrance, a library, a salon, and a billiard room. From third-floor turrets guests enjoyed sweeping views of Owl's Head Bay, of seagulls and swans and sailboats on the sea. The sixty-five-acre property featured manicured lawns, boxwood hedges, vegetable and flower gardens. There was a footpath leading from the main house down to a private beach on Penobscot Bay. The adjacent two-story steepled barn would become home to Puharich's impressive laboratory, where a staff of research assistants worked on experiments relating to the five known senses and a quest for the elusive sixth sense. The plan of action at the Round Table Foundation was to establish itself as a trailblazer in ESP and related research, then garner blue-sky research grants from national science foundations, corporations, and the government.

Dr. Puharich began conducting experiments involving audio waves and human hearing. The normal threshold for hearing in humans is 20 Hz to 20 kHz, but Puharich knew of cases in which certain individuals could hear well beyond that range. Puharich wondered, was there an analogy in ESP? To assist him in this quest, the foundation hired an ear surgeon from New York named Samuel Rosen. Dr. Rosen had a theory that hereditary deafness might be curable if only he could figure out how to redirect certain sound waves in the ear canal. In New York City, Rosen conducted traditional surgeries related to human hearing and the ear canal. During his fellowship at the Round Table Foundation, he performed experimental surgeries on goats and dogs with Puharich acting as his assistant. The work was informative, but soon it was time for Dr. Rosen to return to his medical practice in New York.

Some months later, during a routine operation on a patient who was legally deaf, Rosen accidentally hit a tiny, stirrup-shaped object called the stapes bone, located in the middle ear. When the surgery was over, a most remarkable thing had happened: the deaf patient could now hear. An accident had changed medical history. To Puharich's eye, this was serendipity at work. This groundbreaking surgical procedure, now called the "Rosen stapes" operation, has since restored hearing to tens of millions of deaf people around the world. For the foundation to be affiliated with Dr. Rosen was a fortuitous milestone. Puharich, though not directly responsible, took credit. Grants from major donors flowed in to the Round Table Foundation, including ones from General Foods Corporation and the Kettering Foundation. The monies, earmarked for traditional research, kept the foundation afloat. Meanwhile, Dr. Puharich's mystical and supernatural beliefs began to deepen.

One of the more influential people in his life during this period was Jack Hammond Jr., the wealthy American inventor and ESP advocate, who was twenty years Puharich's senior. Hammond held more U.S. patents than any other living American at the time, including a lucrative one for his eponymous torpedo, the first radio-controlled underwater missile in use by the U.S. Navy. The concept was based not on an original idea of Hammond's but on one from his mentor, the futurist, physicist, and inventor Nikola Tesla. Equally noteworthy was that Tesla had been but one of Jack Hammond's influential mentors decades before. Born into a wealthy family of industrialists and diplomats, and owing to these powerful family connections, Hammond had been mentored by three of the most famous inventors of the nineteenth century: Thomas Edison, Alexander Graham Bell, and Tesla.

Jack Hammond was rich, well respected, and confident in his mystical and supernatural convictions. He lived in a medieval-style seaside castle in Gloucester, Massachusetts, filled with ancient artifacts collected from around the world. He practiced astrology and mental telepathy and believed in ghosts. And he seamlessly balanced success as a scientific inventor with numerous unorthodox ideas. Over discussions at the Warrenton estate, the bond between the men grew. "Jack became my mentor, teaching me more subtleties of life than any book can capture," Puharich wrote in his journal. "He taught me the art of invention, how all his ideas came to him in dreams, in reveries."

Jack Hammond, like Nikola Tesla before him, believed scientific inspiration could come to a man from an unknown energy force, in the form of a dream. There was precedent for this idea, including personal accounts from two Nobel Laureates and a founding father of modern organic chemistry, August Kekulé. At a science symposium in Germany in 1890, Kekulé, who discovered benzene, revealed that the idea had come to him in a dream in which he imagined a snake eating its own tail, like the ancient symbol of the ouroboros. In 1920, Frederick G. Banting, an unknown Canadian surgeon at the time, woke up from a dream telling him to "surgically ligate [tie up] the pancreas of a diabetic dog in order to stop the flow of nourishment," he later said. The discovery, that diabetes could be treated with insulin injections, won him the Nobel Prize in Medicine in 1923. Otto Loewi, the German pharmacologist who discovered acetylcholine (a neurotransmitter involved in dreaming) woke up in the middle of a dream, jotted down a few notes on paper, and went back to sleep. Loewi's dream led to the discovery that nerve cell communication is chemical, not electrical, and for this he won the Nobel Prize in Medicine in 1936.

At Warrenton in the late 1940s and early 1950s, Puharich and Hammond spent many nights in front of a roaring fire discussing Tesla's theories. Science was about searching and researching, the two men agreed, which is why it was called research. One of Hammond's research ideas was to try to determine whether ESP worked on a kind of mental radio channel, transmitted between individuals like radio waves. Tesla, who wrote in his memoirs that he'd experienced extrasensory perception as a child, had originally shared this idea with Hammond, wondering whether ESP might travel on extremely low frequency (ELF) waves. ELF waves were extraordinarily long, as in thousands of miles long. In nature, ELF waves are generated by thunderstorms, lightning, and natural disturbances in Earth's magnetic field.

In an effort to expand on Tesla's ideas and test them scientifically, Hammond and Puharich built a floor-to-ceiling box, made entirely of metal and lined with copper mesh, called a Faraday Cage. The cage shielded anyone seated inside from all electrostatic and electromagnetic waves except ELF waves. Puharich and Hammond then hired world-famous psychics and tested them inside the cage at Warrenton. They called their psychic experiments Project I.

The first psychic hired was Eileen Garrett, an Irish medium famous among the New York City parapsychology set. Garrett came to live at the Round Table Foundation, and for weeks at a time Puharich's researchers tested her psychic abilities in and out of the Faraday Cage using a set of five traditional ESP test cards called Zener cards, each with one of five basic symbols (circle, square, wavy lines, cross, star) printed on one side. When inside the cage, Puharich wrote, Ms. Garrett's extrasensory perception "was increased by a healthy margin over those scores obtained under ordinary conditions," suggesting electronic shielding had a positive impact on psychic functioning. These results encouraged the scientists to expand their tests at the foundation to include a wide array of psychic phenomena, such as mental telepathy, map dowsing, astrological predictions, and palm reading.

Meanwhile, Puharich continued his laboratory experiments with audio waves. He was fascinated by audio aberrations in sane individuals: people who claimed to "hear things" inside their minds but who did not otherwise test for psychosis. In search of one of these individuals to use as a test subject, Puharich reached out to his friend and colleague Warren S. McCulloch, who worked with doctors and patients at Bellevue Psychiatric Hospital in New York City. As one of the founders of the cybernetics movement (defined as the science of control and communication in the animal and the machine), McCulloch was a powerful establishment scientist and CIA asset. He served as chairman of numerous conferences of the Macy Foundation, a secret funding conduit for the CIA's MKULTRA program. It is likely that this work with McCulloch regarding audio aberrations placed Puharich on the CIA's radar.

Puharich asked McCulloch to find him a patient at Bellevue who'd been committed for the first time to the psychiatric ward for hearing voices. McCulloch located a machinist whose psychiatric medical profile was completely normal other than a sudden audio aberration. Before the voices appeared, the machinist had displayed no symptoms of insanity. Whereas many a 1950s doctor would have written the man off as crazy, Puharich and his foundation had another theory to pursue. They believed the man might be hearing voices that were traveling on a radio wave, that the machinist was somehow "tuned in" to a specific radio frequency that other individuals could not hear. "We found out that his job was the key to the diagnosis," Puharich wrote.

In the machine shop where the man worked, the machinist's daily routine was "grind[ing] metal casings against carborundum wheels" for hours at a time. At the foundation facility, Puharich's research team gave the man a dental examination, "which showed that his metal fillings were coated with carborundum dust," or silicon carbide, a semiconductor. The carborundum "behaved like the crystal rectifier in the old crystal radio sets of the 1920s," wrote Puharich. When the subject was placed inside the Faraday Cage, all electrical and radio signals were eliminated. "We found that his voices ceased," Puharich confirmed. "His teeth were cleaned and he was cured of the 'psychiatric' problem." The man was never crazy to begin with. "Rather, we found that he was precisely tuned to radio station WOR in New York City." It was another medical breakthrough for the Round Table Foundation.

The Round Table's work soon caught the attention of the *New York Times*. In the summer of 1951, the newspaper dispatched one of its most famous reporters to investigate. Arthur Krock, a Pulitzer Prize–winning columnist and the former Washington bureau chief, was impressed by what he saw at Puharich's foundation. "General Foods seeks Puharich's assistance in discovering the physiology of taste and the Guggenheim foundation has its eye on other projects," Krock wrote, lending an air of credibility and intrigue to the secretive organization. Dr. Andrija Puharich was a "pragmatic dreamer," Krock wrote, a true American public servant, whose "devotion to ideals [could be] the salvation of Governments as well as of men. The secrets he pursues concern extrasensory perception—the tangibles felt by man and beast that cannot be traced to any one of the five senses." It was the fall of 1951, and ESP was being written about in the *New York Times* without contempt. Even more remarkable, Krock compared Puharich's quest to that of Louis Pasteur, the French chemist and microbiologist whose contributions to germ theory changed medicine and who discovered the principle of vaccination. Krock was also the first person on record to reveal that Puharich was working with the U.S. government, specifically with the Navy.

At the Pentagon, interest in Dr. Puharich's esoteric work was on the rise. In the summer of 1952, Lieutenant Colonel John B. "Jack" Stanley of the Army's Office of the Chief of Psychological Warfare traveled to Maine to meet with Puharich. The government's new psyops organization, created only months before, had been designed to counter psychological warfare threats from communist forces working in the Soviet Union, China, and North Korea. Declassified records reveal that Stanley also served as the Army liaison to the CIA. While Puharich may have been antiestablishment in his scientific theories, he was conservative when it came to honoring security agreements with the federal government. All he ever publicly stated about this meeting was that Colonel Stanley was "quite interested in a device which we had been developing in order to increase the power of extrasensory perception." Nothing more.

But so much more was going on behind closed doors, in black programs and classified projects that would take decades to see the light of day. Three months later, on November 24, 1952, Puharich traveled to Washington, D.C., to deliver a classified briefing to the members of the Office of the Chief of Psychological Warfare. Then, just two weeks after his return to Maine, Puharich received a letter from the Army calling him back into military service. This was a major turning point in the life of Dr. Andrija Puharich. Many of his pursuits at the Round Table Foundation were esoteric and nonconformist, existing far outside the bounds of scientific oversight or stringent laboratory controls. "Beware the Establishment!" Paul De Kruif had warned. And yet here, now, Puharich was being called back into government service, and there was nothing he or any of his wealthy benefactors could do.

The very next week, a strange event occurred, one that Puharich would later attribute to fate, to some kind of a supernatural force beyond his control. With hindsight it was in this timeframe that Dr. Puharich's life took a dangerous turn, one many ESP proponents fall victim to. Cognitive scientists and psychologists call it confirmation bias, or myside bias, the tendency to search for, interpret, or favor data that confirms a deeply held, preexisting belief.

As Puharich prepared to depart the Round Table Foundation on Army sabbatical, he traveled to New York City to attend a party for the Irish psychic Eileen Garrett. There, he met a Hindu scholar and mystic named Dr. D. G. Vinod, who was visiting America as part of a lecture series for the Rotary Club. "At that time, [Vinod] surprised me by asking permission to hold my right ring finger at the middle joint with his right thumb and index finger," wrote Puharich. "He said that he used this form of contact with a person to read his past and his future." Intrigued, Puharich listened. Dr. Vinod held Puharich's finger this way for about a minute, "whistling between his teeth as though he were trying to find a pitch. He leaned back in his chair and for an hour, told my life story with utter precision, as though he were reading out of a book. His accuracy about the past was extraordinary," Puharich wrote. Puharich was transfixed, smitten by one of the oldest forms of divination, chiromancy. (Whereas knowledge of the future is precognition, knowledge of the past that could not have been learned by normal means is called retrocognition.)

Puharich vowed to bring Dr. Vinod to the Round Table Foundation before he returned to the U.S. Army. On December 31, 1952, the two men flew in a small airplane from New York to Maine. They landed in Augusta, where Puharich's administrator, a man named Henry Jackson, picked them up. "We drove over the country roads in the snow," Puharich recalled, "chatting all the way." When they arrived at the Warrenton estate, Dr. Vinod entered the great hall of the laboratory without saying a word or even taking off his winter coat. "Hank and I followed him," Puharich later wrote, and when he sat down, "we realized he had gone into a trance."

It was New Year's Eve, and the estate's main house was empty. Puharich and Jackson stared at Dr. Vinod, who remained silent, seated, and still. "At exactly 9:00 p.m. a deep sonorous voice came out of Vinod's mouth, totally unlike his own high-pitched, soft voice with its distinctly Indian accent," wrote Puharich. Jackson and Puharich scribbled notes, eager to create a record of what Vinod said. After ninety minutes of speech, Vinod emerged from his purported trance state, claiming to have no memory of what had just happened. Setting objectivity aside, Puharich decided that

Dr. Vinod had channeled a supernatural force. When pressed for a name, Vinod identified the force as a group of entities called "the Nine Principles and Forces."

Dr. Puharich summoned his wealthy benefactors and asked Dr. Vinod to again lead the group in a séance. Participants included Alice Bouverie, Marcella du Pont, and Ruth Forbes and Arthur M. Young (mathematician, philosopher, and the inventor of the Bell helicopter). During this session, the supernatural force allegedly reappeared to discuss a wide array of mystical concepts, Puharich wrote, from ESP and psychokinesis to the possibilities of teleportation and alchemy. The nine entities also referred to Einstein, Jesus, atomic weapons, and cosmic rays. In letters housed at the Library of Congress, Marcella du Pont refers to having participated in this séance with Dr. Vinod.

If Puharich's wealthy benefactors saw the Hindu scholar's performance as perhaps something mystical or metaphorical, Puharich took what Dr. Vinod said literally. The experience would begin to obsess him and to shape his research ideas. When Puharich started the Round Table Foundation in 1949, the premise of the Puharich Theory was that a mysterious, unknown energy force existed inside the human nervous system. Now, three years later, on the eve of his return to the Army, Puharich had convinced himself that this energy force was something outside the human body, some kind of extraterrestrial intelligence. Puharich had taken the concept of confirmation bias to an irrational extreme. If he were not about to begin two decades of work with the Department of Defense and the CIA, Dr. Andrija Puharich could easily be written off as a man of eccentric, illogical ideas. Instead he was headed on a lecture tour in service of the Pentagon, discussing his hypothesis in a series of classified military and intelligence community briefings throughout America, from Maryland to Texas.

He would pursue this hypothesis to the gates of death.

CHAPTER THREE

Skeptics, Charlatans, and the U.S. Army

In 1952, with the publication of the book *Fads and Fallacies in the Name of Science,* science writer Martin Gardner single-handedly jump-started the modern scientific skepticism movement. The skeptics' goal, Gardner declared, was to expose cranks, crackpots, and charlatans in the modern age. "Since the bomb exploded over Hiroshima, the prestige of science in the United States has mushroomed like an atomic cloud," Gardner wrote in praise of science. "More students than ever before are choosing some branch of science for their careers. Military budgets earmarked for scientific research have never been so fantastically huge." On the downside, he lamented, the "less informed general public" and "untold numbers of middle-aged housewives" were falling for pseudoscience, "sensational discoveries and quick panaceas. German quasi science paralleled the rise of Hitler," Gardner warned.

Gardner did not mention Dr. Puharich in his book; he had

no way of knowing that the Defense Department had hired the neurobiologist to deliver classified lectures on ESP to high-ranking officials at the Pentagon. Instead, the book surveyed a group of popular beliefs parading as science, including the Flat Earth Doctrine of Wilber Glenn Voliva, the World Ice Theory of Hanns Hörbiger, and Dianetics by L. Ron Hubbard. The book reintroduced readers to the eighteenth-century term "pseudoscience" (originally used to describe alchemy, the magic-based, medieval forerunner of chemistry), which Gardner said aptly described a collection of beliefs not based on the scientific method, and therefore not science.

Since the seventeenth century the scientific method has remained a pillar of research science, a body of techniques used and relied upon for investigating phenomena. There are five basic steps in the scientific method: observation, hypothesis, prediction, experimentation, and conclusion. In the scientific method, if an experiment is not repeatable, then the original hypothesis must be refined, altered, expanded, or rejected. Herein lies the central organizing claim against ESP experiments, a claim that would continue to plague military scientists working in the milieu for decades to come. Repeatability of an experiment is central to the scientific method. Skeptics reject claims that ESP and PK are so-called fickle phenomena.

James Bank "J.B." Rhine, the father of modern American ESP experiments, first popularized ESP in the 1920s. Inside his Duke University Parapsychology Laboratory, Rhine and his wife, Louisa, conducted tens of thousands of ESP tests, mostly using Zener cards and dice. The study of ESP became so fashionable that by the 1940s, Rhine's work was included in the Psychology 101 course at Harvard University. But in 1952, Martin Gardner devoted the last chapter of *Fads and Fallacies* to debunking Rhine's work, which he concluded was the product of "an enormous self-deception."

Important to this story are three claims Gardner leveled against

Rhine's research and ESP research in general. They were 1) loose laboratory controls; 2) the skewing of data; and 3) the premise that the attitude of the scientist conducting the experiment can negatively influence the subject or psychic. Claim three, Gardner noted, always seemed to be used by psychic researchers to bolster an argument for the mercurial nature of the phenomena. To borrow from Dr. Gertrude Schmeidler's concept of sheep and goats, psychic researchers often claimed that psychics were negatively impacted by the presence of goats (nonbelievers). Gardner quoted J. B. Rhine to make his point. "The subtlest influences seem to disturb the operation of these [psychic] abilities," Rhine wrote in a research paper published in 1949. "If the scientist is a disbeliever it will upset the delicate operation of the subject's [psychic] abilities." In the scientific method, there was no room for this interpretation. Instead, Gardner concluded, "ESP and PK can be found only when the experiments are relatively careless, and supervised by experimenters who are firm believers." This is not science, he said. It is merely a scientist convincing himself of a deeply held, quasi-science belief.

What Martin Gardner did not know was that J. B. Rhine, like Puharich, was working on numerous classified ESP research programs with the Department of Defense at the very time the public was reading Gardner's book. Declassified documents reveal that in 1952 the Army initiated a secret program with Rhine's Duke University Parapsychology Laboratory involving ESP and animals. Army commanders wondered, "Could dogs locate land mines buried underwater, under conditions that gave no normal sensory clues?" After forty-eight tests carried out on a beach in Northern California, scientists at the Engineering Research & Development Laboratories at Fort Belvoir initially expressed surprise. "There is [presently] no known way in which the dogs could have located the under-water mines except by extrasensory perception," the Army's scientists concluded. But a second set of eighty-seven trials delivered results shown to be "explainable by chance." And a three-day follow-on program proved "an utter failure," with a "rather conspicuous refusal of the dogs to alert."

Still, the mixed results of the dog program led to additional Army research programs, also overseen by Rhine. In an effort to study "The Phenomenon of Homing in Pigeons," Rhine led a joint pilot experiment with the world's leading ornithologist, Dr. Gustav Kramer of the Max Planck Institute in Germany. The client was the U.S. Army Signal Corps Pigeon Center at Fort Monmouth, New Jersey. Declassified documents indicate that the central question being asked in this program was "How does the homing pigeon do it?" How does the bird find its way home over extremely long distances? And "Why do some pigeons get lost?" Kramer, Rhine, and a team of researchers spent two months working on the problem, only to conclude that "it is not known how the pigeon does it." The Army's response was patience and more experimentation: "cracking Mother Nature's mysteries, which evolved over millions of years," would take time, Army scientists wrote. (In 2017, the mystery of homing in pigeons remains unsolved. There is still no general theory agreed upon by ornithologists.)

Rhine's third animal ESP research program with the Defense Department involved domestic cats. This study was conducted by Dr. Karlis Osis, a Latvian-born PhD whose area of expertise was deathbed visions. In the 1940s, Dr. Osis spent four years traveling across America and northern India interviewing thousands of doctors and nurses whose patients said they'd experienced apparitions shortly before they died. After completing his study, Osis hypothesized that the Indian patients, whose belief system allows for reincarnation, were far more likely to experience visions before death than the American patients, whose belief system more likely did not support this doctrine.

The cat experiment was designed to determine whether man

could communicate telepathically with a cat. Two dishes of food were set down, the goal being an attempt to mentally direct a cat to a specific dish. "In the first [experiment] the effort was made by the experimenter to influence the cat," reads the report. After two hundred trials, Rhine determined that Dr. Osis's results were "very elusive and delicate...not spectacular." Still, Rhine encouraged his Defense Department partners not to give up on ESP. "There is a wide range of military uses of basic [research] programs," Rhine wrote, "not only in intelligence but in other applications [and] capacities in men and animals under the heading of extrasensory perception."

As for Dr. Andrija Puharich, removed from the utopian conditions at the Round Table Foundation in Maine, Defense Department work was a shock. In late January 1953, he traveled to San Antonio to deliver a classified briefing on extrasensory perception to officers with the Medical Field Service School of the U.S. Air Force. In February, he traveled to Washington, D.C., to the Pentagon, where he delivered a second briefing to the Advisory Group on Psychological Warfare and Unconventional Warfare. Declassified CIA and Defense Department documents confirm that these meetings took place, though further details remain lost or classified. In March 1953, Dr. Puharich arrived at the Army Chemical Center in Edgewood, Maryland, where he would remain for the next two years.

What is known is that at Edgewood, Puharich ran the post dispensary, overseeing soldiers' general heath. In nearby laboratories, Army scientists worked on a variety of classified efforts to weaponize chemical agents that could degrade or alter human behavior and perception. Puharich was cleared for at least one of these programs. Declassified documents indicate that he worked on a research project described as an effort "to locate a drug that might enhance ESP." Like the CIA's quest for a truth serum to make captured enemy spies talk, the Army wanted a drug to turn ESP on and off like a light switch.

In program discussions with Army supervisors, Puharich was challenged "to find [a] drug that could bring out this [ESP] ability, to allow normal people to turn it on and off at will." It is not known whether or not he was privy to the CIA's ESP programs. Declassified documents indicate that it was around this time that the CIA gave its hallucinogenic mushroom program a new code name. From now on it would be called MKULTRA Subproject 58.

One thing is clear from Andrija Puharich's journals. It did not take long for him to become discontented with Army life. He missed the Round Table Foundation, its esoteric work, its camaraderie, and its spirit of nonconformism. The Army was rigid and conventional, always following the chain of command. Puharich missed his wealthy, eccentric friends, whose lives were unfettered by financial restraint. Adding turmoil to his situation, Puharich had a personal secret to conceal. His wife suffered from severe depression, and her symptoms were getting worse. Puharich feared that Jinny was mentally ill. Then, on June 17, 1954, fifteen months into his Army contract, Puharich received a telephone call from Alice Bouverie that would soon offer him a way out of Army life. An incident had happened the night before, Bouverie said, during a dinner party at her New York City residence. She'd found a channeler with powers similar to those of Dr. Vinod. The man's name was Harry Stump, and he was a sculptor from Holland. Puharich had met him at a dinner party at Alice Bouverie's house a few months before and remembered him; he'd demonstrated mental telepathy and other forms of extrasensory perception for the guests.

"He and his [girlfriend] were here for dinner last night," Bouverie told Puharich. "Being a sculptor, I thought he'd be interested in some of my pieces." Bouverie was referring to the collection of museum-quality jewelry she'd inherited from her late father. When handed a 3,400-year-old scarab-shaped necklace engraved with Egyptian hieroglyphs, Stump had "staggered around the room a bit, and fell into a chair." Worried that the sculptor was having an epileptic fit, Bouverie told Puharich she had rushed to the kitchen to get Stump a glass of water while the other dinner party guests tended to him. "When I got back he was sitting rigidly upright in the chair and staring wildly into the distance," she said. "He asked for a paper and pencil, and began to draw Egyptian hieroglyphs."

In a guttural voice Stump alternated between English and an unrecognizable foreign language, as if channeling an entity from ancient Egypt, Bouverie said, and in this trance state he spoke of "a drug that would stimulate one's psychic faculties." Puharich asked to see the drawings. Bouverie concurred and, even better, she said, revealed that one of her guests had transcribed what Stump said during the spontaneous séance. Bouverie agreed to send Puharich the documents right away.

At Edgewood, Puharich made his doctor's rounds, all the while thinking about the telephone call. At day's end he walked across the base to his Army-issue apartment. Edgewood was ugly and uninspiring, the antithesis of the Warrenton Estate. He hated being here, a cog in the Army's Cold War military machine. He collected Jinny and their three young daughters and headed over to the Edgewood pool for an evening swim. Back at their apartment after dinner, the doorbell rang. It was a courier from New York City carrying a special-delivery package for Captain Puharich from Alice Bouverie.

Puharich opened the large envelope and settled down into an easy chair to read. He told Jinny to go to bed without him. Flipping through the pages, he marveled at the strange symbols the Dutch sculptor had produced in his trance. Harry Stump had spoken of stone temples, dog-headed statues, and an ancient medical procedure involving "termites with pincers on their heads." And he drew a picture of the drug he said could stimulate psychic functioning. It was a simple mushroom rendered with spots on the cap and the word "mushroom" written neatly underneath.

It was wildly serendipitous, if not suspicious. Puharich had been asked by his superiors to locate a drug that turned ESP on and off; at a dinner party hosted by a wealthy friend, a guest delivered instructions about this mysterious drug while in a somnambulistic trance. But it's important to note that in 1954 the hallucinogenic mushroom had not yet been identified by American botanists nor the CIA scientists who were actively searching for it. Given Puharich's propensity to interpret any and all events as the work of a supernatural force, it would be easy to discount the story as apocryphal—except for the fact that the Dutch sculptor had just provided the CIA with a key lead in its yearlong, unsuccessful quest to locate the drug teonanáctl.

The more Puharich learned about Harry Stump's channeling abilities, the more his fixation with Stump grew. And so did his obsession with the hallucinogenic mushroom. Puharich wrote to the Boston Mycological Society, in Massachusetts, and learned that the mushroom Stump referred to was the *Amanita muscaria,* first identified by Swedish botanist Carl Linnaeus in 1753. This was the poisonous mushroom so often referred to in Nordic and Germanic fairy tales, and likely the reason for its association with magical potions, witches, goblins, and trolls. Puharich vowed to find out more about this mushroom. When his case was solid, he would bring the story of the Dutch telepath to his Army Chemical Center bosses, he later wrote. He enlisted Alice Bouverie to help.

Bouverie journeyed to the rare book collection at the New York Public Library, where she netted a serendipitous lead. While she was searching the botanical section in the Arents Tobacco Collection room, a librarian recognized Bouverie as one of the city's major philanthropists and asked whether she needed help.

Bouverie said she was interested in a certain type of field mushroom; the librarian told her that there was another person in New York City who apparently shared this same interest and who had recently visited the collection with the same request. That person was R. Gordon Wasson, the librarian said, vice president of the J.P. Morgan & Company bank.

Puharich and Alice Bouverie arranged to meet Gordon Wasson at Bouverie's home. Wasson and his wife, Valentina, a pediatrician, had been investigating a mushroom cult in Mexico, Wasson explained. The mushrooms were difficult to locate but he was determined to find them. He'd traveled to Mexico twice and was planning a third expedition. Perhaps Dr. Puharich wanted to come along? The Mexicans believed that the mushroom was a pathway to the supernatural, Wasson said. These were not just hallucinogenic mushrooms, they were alleged to have divinatory powers. Numerous shamanistic tribes around the world believed in the mushroom's supernatural qualities, he explained, allowing human consciousness to separate from the physical body and for a brief time operate independently of the body. This out-of-body experience, sometimes called traveling clairvoyance, had been written about in mystical literature since the dawn of recorded history, he added. He confirmed that the mushroom he was talking about was called teonanáctl, God's flesh.

Where Wasson saw shamanistic ritual, Puharich saw opportunity. "The idea that a human could [psychically] travel to a remote location, obtain information, and return with this intelligence" had profound implications for the Army, he wrote. In a series of extraordinary coincidences, Puharich had found exactly what the Army and the CIA were searching for. Now confident that he could make a solid case to his military superiors, Puharich asked Wasson if he would share this information. Citing patriotism, Wasson agreed. In August 1954, Captain Puharich briefed his Army superiors on the teonanáctl mushroom, emphasizing how rare this information was. "Mr. Wasson assured [me] that to the best of his knowledge, which had been world-wide and covered many years, the Mexican sacred-mushroom ritual had not with certainty been known to exist before his discovery," Puharich said he told his supervisors. "It is true that there were some scattered references to its existence in obscure journals [and] ancient manuscripts, but no one had ever proven that there was substantial fact behind the legend" of the sacred mushroom.

The Army was interested, and Puharich was given a higher security clearance for a classified "psycho-chemical research program." He was told there was another research program going on, also involving mushrooms, but he would have to wait for an even higher clearance to be granted in order to learn more. The program Puharich's superior was likely referring to was the CIA's MKULTRA Subproject 58, Morse Allen's unsuccessful effort to locate teonanáctl.

By 1954, the CIA's two-year effort was still floundering. Allen had assigned a young chemist named James Moore the job of infiltrating East Coast mycology groups with the goal of finding out where in Mexico the elusive teonanáctl mushroom grew. As shown in surviving MKULTRA documents, Dr. Moore, posing as a deep-pocketed professor, was in fact backed by funding from the Geschickter Fund for Medical Research, in Washington, D.C., a principal funding source for the CIA's brain warfare program. Moore told the various mycology groups he wanted to fund private mushroom-hunting expeditions to locate the legendary teonanáctl. Dr. Moore "maintains the fiction that the botanical specimens he collects are for his own use since his field interest is natural-product chemistry," wrote the CIA's chief of the Technical Services Division, Sidney Gottlieb. Excited to be posted to a classified ESP project on which he'd already invested so much personal time, Puharich waited patiently for his security clearance to be granted, but his expectations were misplaced. When the

CIA learned from the Army Chemical Center about Puharich's meeting with Gordon Wasson, the Agency chose to bypass Puharich and approach Wasson directly through their shill, Dr. James Moore. Andrija Puharich was no longer needed, and his security clearance never came.

Privy to none of this, Puharich remained obsessed with Harry Stump and what he believed were the sculptor's supernatural powers. Puharich spent his weekdays working with patients at the Army Chemical Center in Edgewood, and on weekends he traveled to Alice Bouverie's home in New York City to conduct ESP experiments on the Dutch psychic. Privately, at his own home, Puharich's personal life was spiraling out of control. Jinny's mental illness was getting worse, and, according to his journals, in 1954 she was sent to an unnamed hospital for psychiatric treatment. During this low point in American medical history for the treatment of the mentally ill, Jinny Puharich was given insulin shock therapy, a cruel procedure whereby the patient is injected daily with large doses of insulin to induce comas over a period of several weeks and sometimes for up to two months. Save for a few references in Puharich's notes and journals, little else is known about this hospitalization.

In his professional life, Puharich saw himself as a man at a crossroads. His two-year Army commission was coming up for review and he was being recommended for a promotion. Puharich told his superiors he was interested only in pursuing "medical work and research in extrasensory perception." The Army was equally candid with him, he recalled, and "explained to me that it was very difficult for the military to engage in the kind of research we had been discussing [because] anyone who was interested in this subject was automatically branded as a crackpot."

Puharich presented Alice Bouverie with a proposal. What if Harry Stump agreed to work at the Round Table Foundation, full-time? Stump could live on the Warrenton estate, be tested in the laboratory, and still have plenty of time to sculpt and paint. Bouverie thought the idea was brilliant, and told Puharich she was willing to finance it.

At the Army Chemical Center, Puharich met with his superior officer. "I spoke to my commanding general and informed him that I was no longer interested in the Army proposal made earlier," Puharich wrote. "I felt I could pursue my studies with greater ease in Maine than I could with restrictions of Army military life. Such studies were incompatible with the demand for conformity imposed upon government personnel." On April 1, 1955, Puharich signed separation papers, officially parting ways with the U.S. Army. With funds in hand from Alice Bouverie, he packed up Jinny, now released from the hospital, their three daughters, and their cat. The family set out on a weeklong drive from Edgewood, Maryland, to Glen Cove, Maine.

Puharich was thrilled. He could finally refocus his research efforts on ESP experiments full-time. He could continue his search for the unknown energy force he believed powered extrasensory perception. Harry Stump, the Dutch sculptor, would follow just a few weeks later.

★   ★   ★

Written accounts of individuals who claim to channel disincarnate spirits, or communicate with the dead, can be found across recorded history. Not all mediums are charlatans or intentional deceivers; many believe in what they do. In the late nineteenth century automatic writing as a by-product of channeling became a popular conceit. One of the most famous cases involved a Frenchwoman named Catherine-Elise Müller, who went by the pseudonym Hélène Smith. Examination of her story reveals more about Andrija Puharich than he was willing to admit in his private journals or published memoirs. From 1894 to 1898, a psychology professor named Théodore Flournoy studied Hélène Smith at the University of Geneva, in Switzerland. In a self-imposed trance, or autohypnotic state, Smith would describe to him in great detail events from the lives of historical figures, including the poet Victor Hugo and Marie Antoinette. Hélène Smith spoke in Italian, French, Hindi, and other languages that were unidentifiable. Even more colorfully, Smith claimed to be able to psychically travel to Mars, whose landscapes she painted and whose language she said she could speak and write. The odd Martian glyphs she penned were reproduced in Flournoy's book, *From India to the Planet Mars,* a 447-page account of his exhaustive study of Smith, one of the most famous mediums of that age.

The professor's conclusion was that she exhibited cryptomnesia, a word he invented that has since been recognized by legal scholars, skeptics, and the American Psychological Association. Flournoy believed that the content produced during Hélène Smith's séances came from her "subliminal imagination, derived largely from forgotten sources, for example books read as a child." The brain was capable of astonishing feats, Professor Flournoy said, including knowledge of foreign languages heard only briefly, sometimes decades before. As for the Martian-speak, Flournoy attributed it to an age-old condition called glossolalia, or speaking in tongues, a concept discussed by Paul in First Corinthians to describe divinely inspired speech: "For if you have the ability to speak in tongues, you will be talking only to God, since people won't be able to understand you." Of his findings, Professor Flournoy declared, "Science has disclosed a hidden subliminal work within each individual being." His popular book sold more than 100,000 copies, a significant number in 1899.

In the years that followed, cryptomnesia was used as a defense in two high-profile plagiarism cases, whereby the plagiarist was said to have unconsciously taken intellectual property from another author and subliminally "remembered" it as their own. The most famous case involved Helen Keller, who in 1892, at the age of twelve, was accused of plagiarizing a short story she'd written in braille called "The Frost King." In what became a very public investigation, Keller was accused of stealing parts of Margaret T. Canby's "The Frost Fairies," published earlier in a book of stories called *Birdie and His Friends*. Passages in Helen Keller's story were indeed identical to ones in Canby's story. Mark Twain leapt to Keller's defense. "She was subconsciously retelling a story that had somehow successfully embedded its plot into her being and, in the retelling, she came too close to the original," said Twain. "How a deaf-blind child could so closely replicate the intricate plot details of a story and make it her own is a marvel in itself." Margaret Canby agreed. "Under the circumstances, I do not see how any one can be so unkind as to call it a plagiarism; it is a wonderful feat of memory."

In 1903, a similar case was discovered and described by Carl Jung in his paper "Cryptomnesia." This time the accused was the German philosopher Friedrich Nietzsche. While reading Nietzsche's *Thus Spoke Zarathustra,* which famously deals with the mystical concept of eternal recurrence, Jung recognized a four-page section lifted verbatim from a book published fifty years before. He wrote to Nietzsche's sister, Dr. Elisabeth Förster-Nietzsche (Nietzsche had already gone mad and died), who remembered reading the passage with her brother, she told Jung, when they were children. This, Jung wrote, "shows how the unconscious layers of the mind work," and propelled him to develop his own ideas about man's collective unconscious.

Thirty years before Puharich published writings about Dr. Vinod channeling a group of supernatural entities called the Nine Principles and Forces, a British adventure writer named Talbot Mundy had published a novel called *The Nine Unknown*. Originally serialized in *Adventure* magazine in 1922, Mundy's fictional story, set in ancient India in 270 BC, tells the tale of a group called the Nine Unknown who make up a secret society during the reign of the Emperor Ashoka, a historical figure of the Mauryan dynasty. Mundy's nine fictitious characters are contacted by a supernatural force and told it is their job to act as guardians of a book containing secret and powerful knowledge. The mission of the Nine Unknown is to preserve and develop this secret knowledge and to keep it from evil forces that are actively trying to destroy it.

Was Puharich a deceiver? Delusional? Had he plagiarized another man's work and claimed it as his own? Was he suffering from cryptomnesia? It is impossible to know. What is known is that, now released from Army obligations, Dr. Andrija Puharich was free to do as he pleased. His wealthy benefactors encouraged and supported his hypothesis that a supernatural force was responsible for all things related to anomalous mental phenomena.

If things had been different, Puharich might have exited the narrative here, having earned an anecdotal place in the annals of the U.S. government's ESP and PK research. But this is not what happened. Instead, as indicated in his declassified FBI file, the Federal Bureau of Investigation was assigned to observe and keep track of Puharich's ongoing ESP experiments at the Round Table Foundation in Maine.

CHAPTER FOUR

Quasi Science

With his return to the Round Table Foundation in Maine in April 1955, life on the breezy, sea-swept coast offered idyllic work conditions for Dr. Andrija Puharich. "The pungency of pine and spruce, the damp salt smell of the sea, the boom of Owl's Head foghorn" were inspiring, he wrote. During the coldest winter months the foundation had briefly closed its doors, but now, after a few weeks of spring cleanup, the laboratory was up and running again. Jinny Puharich appeared to be doing well in the new environs, and Puharich began spending time with his family again. They enjoyed picnics in the blueberry fields and took hikes along the old Mohawk Indian trails. The birch and hemlock forests were filled with porcupines, woodchucks, and deer; the rocks covered with bright green moss. There was an air of majesty and mystery to things.

At the CIA, Dr. James Moore was still posing as a professor, still trying to ingratiate himself with R. Gordon Wasson, still without success. Puharich, however, remained in close contact with Wasson as the banker-turned-ethnomycologist prepared for his third expedition to Mexico in search of the sacred mushroom called God's flesh. On June 29, 1955, Wasson, accompanied by a New York society photographer named Allan Richardson, arrived in the remote village of Huautla de Jiménez, in Oaxaca. A local guide took them to a deep ravine awash in teonanáctl mushrooms after a spring season of heavy rain. "Allan and I were the first white men in recorded history to eat the divine mushrooms," Wasson later wrote. Wasson reported hallucinating intensely, but stated that no divinatory powers were revealed. After the mystical experience was over the two New Yorkers packed up a cardboard box full of fungi and returned to the United States. Upon arrival, Wasson sent a cache of mushrooms to Puharich at his laboratory in Maine.

Inside the Round Table laboratory, Puharich performed a chemical analysis of the mushrooms' toxicity. Three chemicals produced the hallucinogenic effects, he learned: muscarine, atropine, and bufotenin. Armed with this information, he set out to create an antidote. Puharich's plan was to drug Harry Stump to learn whether the legend was true, whether God's flesh could produce divinatory powers in certain men. But first Puharich decided to try the hallucinogenic mushroom himself. So, apparently, did Alice Bouverie and a few other "individuals" from the lab. There is no record of how these personal drug experiments turned out. Puharich was not the first scientist to experiment on himself. Isaac Newton test-tasted arsenic, Nikola Tesla allowed 250,000-volt electrical shocks to course through his own body, Sigmund Freud took copious amounts of cocaine. In Puharich's case, whatever laboratory controls that might have been in place at the Round Table Foundation before drugs entered the mix were now likely thrown to the winds.

For the teonanáctl mushroom experiment with Harry Stump, Puharich sought out a special witness, someone he believed would understand what it was that he was trying to accomplish. The person he chose was his friend Aldous Huxley, the famous author of the dystopian classic *Brave New World*. Like Puharich, Huxley was interested in the trance state as a means of gathering unseen information about the natural world. Huxley had studied and written extensively about shamanistic people, and he had also conducted a drug-induced trance experiment on himself, at his home in Los Angeles in 1953. Under the supervision of British psychiatrist Humphry Osmond, Huxley had ingested four-tenths of a gram of mescaline, the principal hallucinogenic agent in peyote, and recorded the eight-hour experience on paper. The result was *The Doors of Perception,* published in 1954. A mere sixty-three pages long, the book met controversy and criticism, most notably from Huxley's literary friends. Thomas Mann called it escapism. Christopher Isherwood labeled it a "deadly heresy." Philosopher Martin Buber called Huxley's taking drugs and writing about it an "illegitimate...fugitive flight" from reality. Jim Morrison named his band The Doors after reading it. The book has sold hundreds of thousands of copies and has never gone out of print.

Huxley arrived at the Round Table Foundation in August 1955. As a child in turn-of-the-century England, he suffered from an eye infection that left him practically blind for nearly three years. For the rest of his life, he was half-blind in one eye. Having been deprived of one of the five known senses made Aldous Huxley keenly interested in the idea of a sixth sense, he said. During his three-week visit, he wrote several letters. To his brother Julian he noted that he was staying at "a most beautiful place, where my young friend Dr. Puharich heads this foundation for research into ESP and the physical, chemical, and psychological means whereby the psi [psychic] faculties may be intensified."

Huxley was intrigued by the odd mix of people present, whom he referred to as "the strange household assembled by

Puharich [with] various psychics doing telepathic guessing remarkably well." He wrote about "Mr. Narodny, the cockroach man, who is preparing experiments to test the effects of human telepathy on insects," and he noted discord between "Alice Bouverie and Mrs. Puharich, behaving to one another in a conspicuously friendly way." The foundation member he best related to, Huxley wrote, was Harry Stump, "the Dutch sculptor, who goes into trances in the Faraday cage and produces automatic scripts in Egyptian hieroglyphics." The feeling was mutual between the two men. In an unpublished memoir, Harry Stump wrote that he and Huxley enjoyed "walking around the property, communicating without sound."

According to Puharich's notes, on August 7, 1955, Harry Stump was in the middle of a telepathy demonstration for Puharich and Huxley when he "slipped into a deep trance." The "Egyptian persona" emerged, and Puharich decided it was time to drug Stump with the teonanáctl mushroom. The results were nothing close to what Puharich had hoped for. "Harry fell asleep briefly, then woke up abruptly," noted Puharich. "He looked at Aldous and myself and weakly asked if I had given him some alcohol." Stump appeared drunk and confused. The symptoms became alarming, with Stump "staggering around as though he were heavily intoxicated with alcohol." Huxley called out for Puharich to give Stump the antidote. "While I busied myself with drawing some atropine into a syringe, Aldous watched him closely," Puharich wrote. But by the time the antidote was ready Stump had calmed down, and Puharich decided to go ahead and test him to see whether enhanced psychic functioning could be achieved.

Puharich started with an experiment he called sightless reading. He placed a small, suitcase-sized box draped in fabric on the table between Huxley and Stump. Inside the box numerous items were concealed. According to Puharich, Stump correctly identified the hidden items in record time. But if Puharich was hoping for contact with the supernatural, none came. Huxley now insisted to Puharich that drugging Stump without his knowledge was unethical and that it was time to give Stump a shot of the antidote. When Puharich did, Stump's trance state quickly wore off. Upon returning to a normal state of consciousness, Stump appeared not to remember being in the hypnotic state.

Huxley returned to California. Harry Stump's psychic powers began to wane. The Egyptian persona rarely appeared. The following month, on September 8, 1955, according to Puharich, Stump went down to the seashore to fish and went into a trance for the last time on record. A foundation member found him sitting on the beach, staring out at the sea. He'd apparently located a piece of charcoal and scrawled Egyptian hieroglyphics on the coastal rocks. Puharich said he had the message translated by a professor of Egyptology at Brown University, and that it read: "Eternity is Watching. The Doors are opened for the soul. All is well." The accuracy of this is anyone's guess; Puharich is the only source.

But all was not well at the Round Table Foundation. Jinny Puharich's mental health was on a downward spiral again. Puharich accepted an invitation from his benefactors Joyce and Zlatko Balokovic to move Jinny into their private guesthouse, hoping that the solitude might do her some good. But her condition worsened, and in March 1956 she was sent to live with her parents in Madison, Wisconsin, where her father was a chief of staff at a local hospital. Alice Bouverie arranged for a twenty-two-year-old Dutch au pair named Bep Hermans to come take care of the Puharichs' three young children, who remained at Warrenton. Hermans arrived in late March 1955, and almost immediately Puharich began having an affair with her. Meanwhile, Harry Stump became depressed. His trance powers now vanished. He tried drawing hieroglyphs in a waking state but could not. His traditional sculpture and painting work suffered under his gloomy mood.

During a visit around this time, one of Puharich's investors, the department store tycoon Henry Belk, happened upon a *Paris Match* magazine article that gave him an idea. The article profiled a forty-seven-year-old former house painter and World War II concentration camp survivor named Peter Hurkos who was taking Europe by storm with his psychic abilities. Hurkos had recently solved cases for Scotland Yard and the Paris metro police, wrote *Paris Match*. Fifteen years before, in July 1941, Hurkos had been painting a building in The Hague when he fell off a third-floor balcony and suffered a traumatic brain injury. For three days Hurkos lay in the hospital in a coma; when he woke up, he possessed extrasensory perception, he said. Hurkos's specialty was psychometry, the act of divining information from an object through touch. Belk's idea was to bring Hurkos to the Round Table Foundation and test him in the lab. In the fall of 1956 Peter Hurkos arrived at the Warrenton estate.

"Hurkos gave Harry [Stump] a confidence he never had before," the former au pair, Bep Hermans, recalled. "Whereas Harry was quiet in nature, Peter was loud and rambunctious." Hurkos was a huge man, six-foot-three and full of vitality. "He was always good-humored, loved to tell jokes, especially dirty ones. In spite of their conflicting natures, Peter and Harry got along famously and forged a great telepathic team," Hermans remembered. She witnessed Hurkos's psychometric talents and was amazed by them. While blindfolded, "when given an object, like a watch or a ring, he could tell in great detail about the person to whom the object belonged."

Despite the personnel challenges, work at the Round Table Foundation was on the upswing. Money flowed into the foundation's treasury. A second Faraday cage was built. Puharich's ESP experiments with Hurkos and Stump delivered "groundbreaking results," wrote a visiting reporter from *Parade* magazine. The foundation hired two new scientists and a researcher. An administrative assistant wrote quarterly progress reports. Then— betrayal. In the spring of 1956 Puharich learned that the CIA had bypassed him and contacted the banker and mushroom hunter Gordon Wasson directly, and had infiltrated his group. Puharich was furious and became paranoid, Bep Hermans recalls. "He felt the CIA was after his research."

Since Puharich's departure from the Army Chemical Center, the CIA had not let up in its quest to locate an ESP-enhancing drug. Still posing as a professor, and with $2,000 in financial incentive, James Moore had finally managed to persuade Gordon Wasson to take him along on a mushroom-hunting expedition. An official CIA invoice for MKULTRA Subproject 58, dated March 21, 1956, indicated payment "in support of an expedition...for the purpose of studying and collecting hallucinogenic species of mushrooms of interest." The expedition to the secret ravine in Oaxaca where the teonanáctl mushrooms grow "will take place between June and July 1956." By the time Puharich found out about the CIA's involvement, the expedition was well under way.

Ironically, the mission proved to be a traumatic experience for the CIA's Dr. Moore. "He was like a landlubber at sea," Gordon Wasson later recalled. "He got sick to his stomach and hated it all." At one point, the group's small airplane was deemed too heavy for flight and had to make an unscheduled stop in order to lighten its load. The pilot decided to leave Moore roadside, in the care of a group of local Indians, promising to come back for him. The pilot did eventually return, but by then Moore had developed diarrhea and a bad case of nerves. "Our relationship deteriorated," Wasson recalled. Moore managed to fulfill his CIA mandate and returned from Mexico with a bag of teonanáctl mushrooms for the Agency to analyze in its lab. The Director of MKULTRA, Sidney Gottlieb, expressed approval. From these mushrooms, Gottlieb wrote, the Agency could conceivably create "a completely new chemical agent," provided the hallucinogen could "remain an Agency secret."

This was wishful thinking on the part of the CIA. After Wasson returned from the expedition, he struck a publishing deal with *Life* magazine and authored a twelve-page account of the experience under the heading "Seeking the Magic Mushroom." Wasson left out any mention of the CIA's involvement but highlighted the part about the mushroom's alleged ability to access and enhance ESP. "The Indians believe that the mushroom holds the key to what we call extrasensory perception," Wasson wrote. Like an oracle, the mushroom could answer questions about the future and the unknown. "One may consult the mushroom about a stolen donkey and learn where it will be found and who took it," Wasson asserted, and if a person's loved one had disappeared, the mushroom eater "will report if [that person] still lives or is dead, whether he is in jail, married, in trouble or prosperous." Seeing as how this was the first mushroom trip recounted by a white man, someone who just happened to be a vice president at the J.P. Morgan & Co. investment bank, the article caused a sensation, rendering null and void the CIA's desire to keep the drug a secret psychic weapon under military intelligence control. Pleasure seekers flocked to Mexico to eat God's flesh.

At the Round Table Foundation in Maine, things had taken a dark turn as drugs began to take hold. When Wasson returned from his expedition, he sent Puharich another package of hallucinogenic mushrooms. Puharich began regularly dosing Peter Hurkos with the drug, using himself as the so-called control. Hurkos became fixated on outer space and took to roaming around the estate late at night, scanning the sky. One night, he said he saw a flying saucer touch down on Owl's Head beach. It did not take long for the extraterrestrials to appear, described by

Hurkos as "very small [and] very old, with young bodies...No word was spoken...They just looked at me." Then Hurkos started seeing ghosts and having premonitions.

According to a journal entry dated July 17, 1956, Hurkos had ventured down to the Warrenton kitchen to make himself a sandwich and a pot of coffee, and was returning to his room upstairs when he saw a poltergeist. "As it went by me, I could feel a cold breeze on my face," Hurkos said. "I was so frightened, I spilled the coffee all over the tray." The following morning, the telephone rang. It was Alice Bouverie's son calling with tragic news. His mother had unexpectedly died the night before, in her sleep.

Puharich fell apart. Alice Astor Bouverie was dead, his financial lifeline severed. He was now convinced that ghosts were real. "He became paranoid about who he could trust," Bep Hermans recalls. "He took up drinking and smoking and had outbursts of anger and distrust." Harry Stump quit, and Puharich and Hurkos packed their bags and left for Mexico, determined to locate more of God's flesh.

Puharich was like a cat with nine lives. He and Hurkos returned from Mexico with more tales and more mushrooms. And yet through all of it, Puharich somehow managed to keep the foundation's coffers full. By spring 1957, the Round Table Foundation was again bustling with activity, with more than a dozen scientists and psychics in residence at the Warrenton estate. Experiments included telepathy, map dowsing, palmistry, and eyeless sight.

Then, on August 27, 1957, yet another remarkable event occurred, this one grounded in reality. Two Pentagon employees arrived at the foundation for a visit, and the shadowy life of Dr. Andrija Puharich took a perplexing new turn. Documents from Puharich's FBI file reveal that the government agents were from the Department of Defense. One was Dr. Harvey E. Savely, director of the U.S. Air Force Office of Scientific Research (AFOSR). The second man, William J. Frye, was head of biophysics research at the Army Laboratory at the University of Illinois. The men stayed at Warrenton for two nights and three days, holding private discussions with Puharich. One month later, the Round Table Foundation abruptly shut down.

Puharich and Bep Hermans, now officially a couple, moved briefly to New York City, then to California. A Freedom of Information Act request, granted in 2015, reveals that Puharich was hired by the U.S. Army to work as a "consultant on mushroom toxicology" at the Fort Ord Station Hospital Laboratory in Monterey, California. Jinny Puharich remained in Wisconsin, her mental health in steep decline. In late 1957 she agreed to a divorce. On December 20, 1958, Andrija and Bep were married in Las Vegas, en route to Fort Ord. The following month, on January 24, 1959, Virginia Jackson Puharich walked out onto the roof of the seven-story Methodist Hospital where her father served as chief and leapt to her death.

Andrija Puharich grew his hair long and put on fifty pounds. He located a wealthy new benefactor to finance his ongoing ESP research on a private ranch located ten miles south of the Army base in Carmel Valley. He started taking more drugs. Whereas in Maine he had been a maverick among East Coast conservatives, with their straitlaced social mores, in California there were no such societal bounds. Bep Hermans recalls what life was like in Carmel during those strange days. "One time, when Andrija and Paul [his benefactor] had organized a mushroom binge for a select group of people, I was invited to participate as an observer and to take notes. Entering the room where they had gathered, I saw that the party was already in full swing. I was startled. Without any shame, a middle-aged couple—both psychiatrists—was copulating wildly. The woman's legs thrashed in the air while she shouted that love would save the world from destruction. Paul was violently ill, throwing up all over the place. Another man, whom I had never seen before, was singing an aria from the opera *Aida*." Hermans, now pregnant with their first child, threatened to leave if Puharich didn't pull it together.

Puharich ignored his wife's wishes and embarked on another mushroom hunting trip, this time to the remote village of Juquila, Oaxaca, two hundred miles south of Mexico City. The original expedition was made up of nine people, but after four weeks of violent illness everyone but Puharich returned. Puharich had pushed on alone, his wife was told, determined to find a witch doctor to test for divinatory powers. A Freedom of Information Act request granted in 2015 reveals that the trip was sponsored by the U.S. Army Chemical Corps. A second trip, the following year, was financed by the Department of Pharmacology at the University of Washington. For that effort, Puharich led a fourteen-man scientific expedition back to Juquila, this time with an ABC camera crew filming the journey for the paranormal-based television show *One Step Beyond*.

By 1961, Bep, now pregnant with their second child, gave her husband an ultimatum: he had three months to figure out a way to settle down or else she'd leave him and take the couple's children back to Europe with her. "It was a complete surprise when he announced one evening in May [1961] that a group of New York businessmen had invested $300,000 in [some] hearing aid research" he was working on, she said. Declassified documents reveal that the financiers were not businessmen but officials from the Atomic Energy Commission, Medical Research Department. Puharich had sold them on an ESP research project he called "skin reading" but which the AEC identified as "skin as an organ of sensory communication beyond the tactile."

With a new influx of cash, Puharich purchased a large house at 87 Hawkes Avenue in Ossining, Westchester County, and moved his family back to New York. With its ten bedrooms, multiple fireplaces, wraparound porch, and beautifully landscaped property, the Ossining home was a mini version of the Round Table Foundation. But gone were the wealthy benefactors dedicated to esoteric research unfettered by financial constraints. The U.S. government was a different kind of patron.

Puharich's handler on the classified AEC contract was Paul S. Henshaw, a medical doctor who'd been involved with U.S. atomic weapons and nuclear energy programs since the Manhattan Project. Dr. Henshaw was interested in numerous aspects of Puharich's ESP work related to unexplored areas of human biological potential. "If biologic memory involving information is stored at molecular levels in cells, then perhaps biologic communication can be transmitted and received by living things, through skin," Henshaw wrote, citing Puharich's proposal.

It was a radical idea in 1961, with the discovery of the double-helix structure of DNA just eight years old. In sixty years time, this kind of hypothesis would be far more commonplace but in 1971 it was inconceivable to most professionals. Still, Henshaw arranged for the AEC to finance Puharich's radical research idea, making no up-front claims as to the results. "Because of [the] newness of the claims being made by Puharich, the writer doubts the validity," Henshaw observed. Yet after working with the eccentric neurobiologist on an experiment, Henshaw became convinced that Puharich's results were legitimate. Declassified documents indicate the experiment involved two deaf women, one age sixteen and one age thirty-six. Both women could read lips but neither of them could hear sounds. In his laboratory, Puharich played musical notes for the test subjects and, according to physiology tests, neither of them registered hearing sound. But after Puharich attached electrodes to the test subjects' skin, in a predetermined location near the jaw, when musical notes were sounded, the women could seemingly hear. Indeed, it appeared that biological communication could be transmitted and received by humans, through skin.

There was a hitch. Henshaw advised his AEC colleagues that he had no way to certify the experiments against fraud. "The women could have been cued," he wrote, "possibly part of some financial scheme." To solve this issue, Henshaw requested authorization to bring his own deaf person into Puharich's lab, someone Henshaw knew personally and was certain was deaf. Puharich agreed, the AEC provided funds, and Henshaw brought to Puharich's lab a deaf man named Robert Case (the son of a colleague who happened to be president of Boston University, he wrote). With Case as Puharich's test subject, Henshaw became convinced. "Based on demonstration, this doctor is no longer skeptical," Henshaw wrote. "It is biologically possible for people to hear with their skin." The AEC then provided Puharich with a new round of funding. America's nuclear weapons agency was "interested in phenomena of how the skin, under certain conditions, can function like an ear."

Andrija Puharich was like a sphinx, an enigmatic and inscrutable person. Mysterious, unreadable, impossible to fully comprehend. He was full of inventions and ideas that were far ahead of his time. And yet as fascinating as this concept of skin hearing is, it is equally difficult to discern why the Atomic Energy Commission was pursuing it. Further documentation on Puharich's work remains classified. In the years that followed, from his laboratory in Ossining, Andrija Puharich continued to work on secret government contracts involving anomalous mental phenomena. These included assignments from the National Aeronautics and Space Administration's Biotechnology and Human Research Office and from the Air Force Systems Command, Rome Air Development Center. With the Dutch psychic Peter Hurkos, he traveled to the Sixth Naval District Personnel Conference in

Charleston, South Carolina, to demonstrate ESP and psychometry (token object reading) to submariners.

But government-sponsored research could hold Puharich's
attention only for so long. He was much more interested in
quasi-science pursuits. In early 1963 his longtime financier,
Henry Belk, arrived at the Ossining estate with an enticing
research proposition, this time centered in the jungles of Brazil.
It involved a so-called psychic healer named Arigo who was
reportedly able to perform major surgeries with a pocketknife,
without anesthesia, without the need for stitches or antibiotics
and without causing any pain. Puharich said he was in. Unwilling to tolerate this lifestyle any longer, Bep Hermans packed up
the children and left for Europe. Belk and Puharich left for
Brazil.

Over the next seven years Puharich shuttled between Ossining and Brazil, sometimes with Belk, sometimes without. Convinced that Arigo's psychic surgeries were authentic, Puharich
studied the controversial faith healer to the point of obsession,
documenting his "surgeries" on 8mm film. Determined to get
one of his military clients interested in sponsoring his Arigo
research, Puharich wrote numerous proposals outlining the potential "for psychic healing on the battlefield." No government
sponsor took the bait, but he persevered. One evening in Ossining in the summer of 1970, Puharich set pen to paper to define
his future research goals. There were two. One was to develop a
"theoretical basis for all extrasensory perception research." The
second was to search the world for supernatural healers like Arigo
and "to test them under laboratory controls." If only he could get
government-sponsored data on these so-called "supernormals"
his efforts would be legitimized.

In the fall of 1970 Andrija Puharich participated in a conference in Rye, New York, entitled "Exploring the Energy Fields of
Man." Also present at the conference were several of Puharich's

former colleagues from the Round Table Foundation, including Arthur Young and Charles T. Tart. CIA asset Dr. José Delgado, famous for his research in mind control through electrical stimulations of surgically implanted brain chips, was the featured dinner speaker. During the three-day event Puharich attended a lecture given by Itzhak Bentov, an Israeli rocket scientist, biomedical engineer, and author who wrote about "the mechanics of consciousness." In his lecture, Bentov spoke of a twenty-three-year-old Israeli man purported to have extraordinary powers of psychokinesis and mental telepathy. During a demonstration at Israel's University of Technology, this man had stopped and started broken watches, moved the needle on a stationary compass, and bent metal by thought alone, Bentov said.

Puharich was intrigued. After the lecture, he asked Bentov to share more information with him about this young man and his extraordinary powers. Puharich learned that the individual was a former Israeli paratrooper who lived in the port city of Jaffa, outside Tel Aviv. His name was Uri Geller. Now Puharich had a new obsession. If he could figure out a way to meet this man and test him under laboratory conditions, Puharich was confident he could secure a government research contract, he told Bentov. The agency Puharich had in mind for this endeavor was the CIA.

Not only was Puharich's call taken seriously, it escalated to the top of the command structure, to the office of CIA director Richard Helms.

CHAPTER FIVE

The Soviet Threat

U.S. government military efforts to explore psychic phenomena remained mostly out of the public eye until December 1959, when an article about a secret government ESP program appeared in a French magazine called *Constellation*. The article, entitled "Thought Transfer, Weapon of War," was written by journalist and former French resistance spy Jacques Bergier. Bergier had strong ties to the intelligence community and an interest in the supernatural. He was working on a book about prophecy, conspiracy, and the Nazi obsession with the occult.

In his article Bergier reported that ESP tests had been conducted aboard the world's first nuclear-powered submarine, the *USS Nautilus,* the year before. The *Nautilus* was also the first vessel to reach the North Pole, a feat accomplished by sailing under the polar ice cap. The purpose of the experiment, wrote Bergier, was to see whether long-distance telepathic communication could be achieved through barriers that included thousands of miles of seawater, thick polar ice, and the metal walls of a submarine. According to Bergier the ESP experiment involved simple sender-receiver trials using Zener cards. The sender was a sailor onboard the *Nautilus,* isolated inside a cabin during the experiments; the receiver was a technician on land, at the Westinghouse Friendship Laboratory on America's East Coast. Bergier identified the man overseeing the joint-service ESP experiment as Air Force Colonel William H. Bowers, director of the Biological Department of the Air Force Research Institute. Bergier's story stated that starting on July 25, 1958, the sender and the receiver communicated telepathically over a sixteen-day period.

Initially, "Thought Transfer, Weapon of War" garnered little attention outside France. Then, in February 1960, an expanded version of the story was published in France's top science journal, *Science et Vie,* under the heading "The Secret of the Nautilus." There were no authors identified, but editor Gérald Messadié said multiple sources had confirmed the story on condition of anonymity. J. B. Rhine of the Duke University Parapsychology Laboratory, with whom the Defense Department had conducted ESP and animal experiments in the early 1950s, was identified as the civilian scientist assigned to the project, and it was reported that "about 75% of the telepathic tries are said to have been successful." The Navy's response was that the story was a hoax.

Whether the story was true or fabricated remains a debate. But in 1960, real-world consequences were a result. The most significant turn of events was how the Soviets used the news story to their strategic advantage. "In Leningrad the Nautilus reports went off like a depth charge," states a declassified Defense Department document. "Soviet parapsychology research was actually stimulated by the 1960 French story concerning the US atomic submarine *Nautilus.*" Years later, the Soviets falsely claimed they had begun their ESP research programs only after they learned of the *Nautilus* tests from the French science journal. U.S.

intelligence analysts monitoring the situation knew this was Soviet propaganda, as indicated in statements made in April 1960 by Dr. Leonid L. Vasilev, Russia's leading ESP researcher. "We carried out extensive and until now complete unreported investigations under the Stalin regime," Vasilev told a group of top scientists gathered in Leningrad. "Today the American Navy is testing telepathy on their atomic submarines. Soviet scientists conducted a great many successful telepathy tests over a quarter of a century ago. It's urgent that we throw off our prejudices. We must plunge into the exploration of this vital field."

The prejudices to which Vasilev referred could be summed up in the story of one man: Grigori Rasputin. In Soviet Russia, all twentieth-century forays into the mystical, magical, or supernatural were framed by his cautionary tale. Rasputin was a Russian monk said to have swayed men, women, and nations with the power of his eyes. In 1910, Czar Nicholas II took the mysterious faith healer from Siberia into his court after Rasputin allegedly stopped the bleeding in the czar's hemophiliac son. From there, Rasputin began advising the czar on affairs of state, including battle plans during World War I. Rasputin's ability to survive assassination attempts added to his mythical status, but eventually he was done away with by a group of unidentified conspirators who poisoned him (twice), shot him, and then drowned him in the icy Neva River as if to make sure he was dead. After the Communist Revolution of 1917, healers and sorcerers were outlawed by the new ruling party, and research into extrasensory perception went underground.

Marxist doctrine considered mysticism, like religion, an opiate of the masses; science and technology were productive forces. Determined to outpace the Americans in the field of ESP research, in a 1963 Kremlin edict the Soviet minister of defense, R. J. Malinosky, declared telepathy to be science- and technology-based, and ordered the creation of the Special Laboratory for Biocommunications Phenomena at the University of Leningrad. The man in charge was Dr. Leonid L. Vasilev. The goals of the laboratory, wrote a Defense Department analyst, were to establish "scientific proof of telepathic communications" and "to identify the nature of brain energy that produces it." For this, a partnership was established with the Bekhterev Brain Institute in Moscow, in order to study and "to harness the possibilities of telepathic communication." That the Soviets were looking at the brain as a secret weapon made the Defense Department take note. "The discovery of the energy underlying telepathic communication will be equivalent to the discovery of atomic energy," proclaimed Vasilev. The prevailing hypothesis put forth by Russian scientists in 1963 was that "telepathic impulses are radiated along the lines of bits of information in a cybernetic system," according to declassified documents.

It all sounded very scientific, which was the point. As in the 1963 edict, the Soviet nomenclature around ESP was rewritten to sound technical, thereby severing all ties with ESP's occult past. Mental telepathy was now "long-distance biological signal transmission." Psychokinesis was "non-ionizing, in particular electromagnetic, emissions from humans." When the phrase "psychotronic weapons" started appearing under the rubric of biocommunications phenomena, U.S. intelligence analysts were baffled. Psychotronic weapons were described in Soviet science journals as electromagnetic weapons involving "the generation of high-penetrating emission of non-biological origin."

At first it seemed as if the research was bifurcated, divided into separate disciplines. One branch involved traditional ESP and PK research programs, and another involved a radical new kind of weaponry that truly was high-technology based. Not until 2011 would the reason these two programs were originally entwined be revealed as originating in the Nazi SS Ahnenerbe documents captured by the Soviets at the end of the war. "Both the first and second programs had open [unclassified] and closed [classified] parts," explains Professor Serge Kernbach, director of Cybertronica Research, Advanced Robotics and Environmental Science at the University of Stuttgart. Both programs stemmed from Ahnenerbe research on the "psycho-physiological effects of microwave emissions [that] were actively investigated during the NS [National Socialist] regime." In the Soviet laboratories, if ESP and long-distance telepathic communications were proven to be scientific fact, they would be classified as augmented perception and cognition in humans. Electromagnetic weapons, which are designed to degrade or destroy perception and cognition in humans, would be useful countermeasures. To this end, defense minister Malinosky ordered the Secretary of the Central Committee of the Communist Party, P. N. Demichev, to establish a special commission for "paranormal human abilities and biological radiation studies." In 1962, one of the lethal Soviet electromagnetic weapons programs appears to have been moved out of the research laboratory and into the battlefield. The target was the U.S. embassy in Moscow.

In 1962, American military engineers were conducting a security sweep of the U.S. embassy in Moscow, searching for listening devices, when they discovered a strange electromagnetic signal. The first analysis by American scientists was that this was some new means of eavesdropping. But further investigation revealed that the Soviets were using multiple frequencies to transmit a series of widely fluctuating and irregularly patterned microwave beams aimed primarily at the upper floors of the central wing of the embassy, where the ambassador and top intelligence officials had their offices. The CIA had reason to believe that the Soviets were developing an electromagnetic weapon designed to adversely affect the behavior of embassy personnel.

Military engineers determined that the microwave beam was coming from a source inside a tenth-floor apartment inside a building located roughly 100 meters to the west, across Tchaikovsky Street; it affected the west facade of the embassy building, with highest intensities between the third and eighth floors. The signal (determined to have a power density between 2.5 and 4.0 GHz) was given the code name MUTS, or Moscow Unidentified Technical Signal, and had apparently been in use since 1956. The Pentagon got to work on a counterstrategy and assigned the Advanced Research Projects Agency (ARPA) the job of initiating a classified program to duplicate the effects of the Moscow Signal.

Declassified documents reveal that scientists with Johns Hopkins University's Applied Physics Laboratory were assigned to oversee the research. An elaborate facility was constructed inside the Walter Reed Army Institute of Research, Forest Glen Section. There, inside an anechoic chamber (an echo-free room designed to completely absorb reflections of either sound or electromagnetic waves), primates were irradiated with microwave beams with a power density similar to that of the Moscow Signal. ARPA's Richard S. Cesaro was in charge of what was called Project Pandora. Within a few months of beaming the signal at the monkeys, Cesaro became convinced of its harmful nature, deciding that it adversely affected the internal organs of primates, including the brain. "In our experiments we did some remarkable things. And there was no question in my mind that you can get into the brain with microwaves," Cesaro later said. It was later determined that the microwave beam produced Alzheimer's disease.

In Moscow, U.S. embassy personnel were not told anything about the mysterious electromagnetic beams. Instead, the State Department set up a classified endeavor, or "cytogenic testing program," code-named the Moscow Viral Study, to secretly conduct genetic testing on embassy personnel. The physician in charge was Dr. Cecil Jacobson. By collecting blood samples from individuals exposed to the Moscow Signal, the State Department would have a control group whose white blood cells could be analyzed for chromosomal damage. Employees were told they were being tested for a simple viral infection going around Moscow. Not for two years were senior civilian officials briefed on the Moscow Viral Study. When these individuals expressed serious concerns about the secret testing of employees, the program was terminated. The State Department was told that the best countermeasure it could take was to turn the ten-story embassy building into a giant Faraday cage. In a declassified memo dated April 3, 1965, a consultant suggested a "selection of suitable copper screening and mandatory coverage of all window openings."

A vicious debate ensued among defense scientists, with accusations of hysteria and malfeasance being hurled back and forth. One of the Navy's top scientists, Dr. Samuel Koslov, led the charge of those who insisted that the Moscow Signal was harmless. "The actual physical results were nonexistent, but the real psychological trauma (in this case in a group of well-educated and dedicated people) was sad and startling," Koslov later wrote in the Applied Physics Laboratory alumni digest.

ARPA's Richard Cesaro and others vehemently disagreed. Based on the evidence that the electromagnetic beam could penetrate the human nervous system, Cesaro argued that it was necessary to determine exactly what kind of weapon this was and "whether the Soviets have special insight into the effects and use of athermal radiation on man." In 1969, the Defense Department quietly expanded ARPA's Project Pandora to include "the human." Highly classified studies code-named Big Boy and Project Bizarre now projected microwave beams at unwitting sailors stationed in the Philadelphia Naval Yard. The experiments would remain secret for seven years.

Throughout the 1960s, as a result of the escalation in the ESP wars, electromagnetic weapons were having lethal real-world consequences, certainly on U.S. embassy personnel and Navy sailors. During this same time frame Soviet efforts in psychokinesis were also gaining momentum and garnering attention within the Defense Department and the CIA. One Russian individual commanded the Pentagon's attention more than anyone else, and that was a pretty forty-four-year-old woman named Ninel Kulagina, who was purported to be able to move matter with her mind.

Born in Leningrad in 1926, Kulagina's parents named her after Vladimir Lenin, the founder of the Russian Communist Party and leader of the Bolshevik Revolution. Ninel, a popular girl's name, is Lenin spelled in reverse. (In the West she was erroneously identified as "Nina," and the name stuck.) Kulagina, a decorated war hero, had been a front-line soldier for Mother Russia during World War II. At the age of fourteen she joined a Red Army tank regiment along with her father, brother, and sister before the Nazis invaded Leningrad the following year. For her service as a tank radio operator, Kulagina was awarded the Military Merit medal. She left the army in 1946 and married a naval engineer. She'd always had psychokinetic abilities, Kulagina told *Science News,* which first manifested themselves when she was a child; sometimes when she got angry, objects around her spontaneously moved.

Starting in the mid–1960s, Kulagina's mysterious ability to move matter with her mind became the subject of a state-run TV program called *Science Films,* produced by Leningrad Studios.

Kulagina was filmed using psychokinesis to move objects sealed inside a glass aquarium, including metal salt shakers, matchsticks, and cigar canisters. In the United States, skeptics cried fraud. But the CIA and the Defense Department were not so sure, declassified documents indicate, owing to a film of a classified experiment in a research laboratory at the Ukhtomskii Military Institute, in Leningrad, on March 10, 1970. In the film, Kulagina was shown to be able to stop a frog's heart with her mind. One explanation, analysts wrote, was that trickery or fraud was at play, and that the film was part of a Soviet disinformation campaign to trick U.S. defense officials into thinking Kulagina could actually accomplish this. An alternative explanation was that she had psychic powers. What is certain is that the film caused uproar within the American defense community.

Seated beside Kulagina was Genady Sergeyev, the Soviet military doctor in charge of the experiment. After roughly twenty minutes of mental preparation, Kulagina indicated she was ready to begin. On the table in front of her a technician placed a ceramic jar. Inside it was a small lump—the frog's heart—still beating. The organ had been surgically removed from the animal's body and set in Ringer's solution, which can keep the heart of a small animal beating for roughly one hour. Thin wires and electrodes attached the heart to an electrocardiogram machine, allowing scientists to track the heart's beats per minute. Kulagina's physiology was similarly monitored. Sergeyev instructed her to start. With both hands in front of her on the table, she began concentrating with the "purposeful intent" of stopping the frog's beating heart. According to the declassified documents, Kulagina's heart rate rose to 240, her blood pressure became elevated, and "heightened biological luminescence radiated from her eyes."

"In the first of the experiments the electrocardiogram (EKG) indicated [heart] activity ceased about 7 minutes after Kulagina began concentration on 'stopping the heart,'" wrote a Defense

Department analyst. After the measurement was recorded, Kulagina then "reactivated" the heart so that it began beating again. A second test followed. "In a second experiment, with [another] heart in a metallic container, heart activity ceased after 22 minutes," wrote the Defense Department analyst. In both experiments, "Kulagina was 1.5 meters [4.9 feet] from the 'target' hearts."

A separate experiment followed. "Kulagina attempted to increase the heart rate of a skeptical physician" who'd been hooked up to a separate EKG machine. "Abrupt changes were noted in both people [Kulagina and the skeptical physician] within one minute after the experiment began," the analyst wrote. "After 5 minutes, [Dr.] Sergeyev judged the heart activity of the physician had reached dangerous levels and the experiment was terminated." Disbelieving defense analysts argued that this was further proof of a Soviet disinformation campaign, that the ruse of the so-called skeptical physician was gilding the lily, so to speak. Others were not so sure. "This is perhaps the most significant PK test done and its military applications, if true, are extremely important," cautioned an official with the Medical Intelligence Office of the U.S. Army.

In response the Defense Department called for a joint intelligence assessment of "the Soviet psychoenergetic threat," a term invented by the Pentagon to include all matters related to Soviet anomalous mental phenomena research and electromagnetic weapons programs. The task fell to the Medical Intelligence Office of the U.S. Army, Office of the Surgeon General. During the Vietnam War this office had been moved to the newly formed Defense Intelligence Agency, where it assessed everything from a foreign country's medical capabilities to its infectious diseases. In 1970, the office was transferred back to the Surgeon General's office. Because it was the mandate of the Medical Intelligence Office to assess foreign biotechnical developments of military medical importance, assessing the Soviet psychoenergetic threat was its job.

The two-year effort resulted in a 174-page classified report called *Controlled Offensive Behavior—USSR,* published in 1972. "This study is a review and evaluation of Soviet research in the field of revolutionary methods of influencing behavior," stated the author, Captain John LaMothe, "intended as an aid in the development of countermeasures for the protection of US or allied personnel." Evidence indicated that the Soviets were rapidly developing "methods of controlling or manipulating human behavior through subtle, non-identifiable means," LaMothe found, with influencing techniques including psychopharmacology (i.e., drugs), subliminal messaging, and electromagnetic weapons. With regard to extrasensory perception and psychokinesis research, LaMothe wrote, "Communist state authorities, the military and the KGB display an unusual, disproportionate interest in parapsychology," and that "Military involvement in psi [i.e., psychic] research [is] confirmed."

LaMothe broke down the danger into four categories of existential threat. Soviet agents with psychoenergetic abilities hypothetically could 1), "Disable, at a distance, US military equipment of all types, including space craft," 2), "Know the contents of top secret US documents, the movements of our troops and ships and the location and nature of our military installations." 3), "Mold the thoughts of key US military and civilian leaders, at a distance," and 4), "Cause the instant death of any US official, at a distance." In essence, wrote LaMothe, through the use of targeted extrasensory perception and psychokinesis, a Soviet agent could disrupt military technology, access state secrets, influence the action of national leaders, and assassinate U.S. officials. These threats were what U.S. military and intelligence scientists needed to focus on, he wrote.

Citing scientists and experts, LaMothe saw an immediate need to create a program to mirror the Soviets' psychic warfare undertakings. "I am really disturbed," Oliver J. Caldwell, a former Office of Strategic Services officer who was known to run operations for the CIA, told LaMothe, "because if the United States does not make a serious effort to move forward on this new frontier, in another ten years it may be too late." Sybil Leek, whom LaMothe identified as a "noted astrologer and author," warned that "there is a great danger that within the next ten years the Soviets will be able to steal our top secrets by using out-of-the-body spies." Dubbed England's "Most Famous Witch," Leek advised the CIA on witchcraft and the supernatural. LaMothe's report raised issues that merited further inquiry, but the alarmist nature of his text limited its distribution. To those in the know, LaMothe's sources were biased in favor of ESP research programs.

The classified report circulated through the military and intelligence communities. It was the CIA, not the Defense Department, that took action first. If the Soviets were putting this much effort into psychic and psychotronic research, the United States needed to be one step ahead, and also needed to send that message back over the Iron Curtain. This was the nature of the Cold War, a contest of one-upmanship and the mandate to outperform the enemy in knowledge and weapons technology. The alarm bell had been sounded. The psychic warfare race with the Soviets had begun.

PART II

———

THE CIA YEARS

The chessboard is the world; the pieces are the phenomena of the universe; the rules of the game are what we call laws of nature. The player on the other side is hidden from us.

—Thomas Huxley

CHAPTER SIX

The Enigma of Uri Geller

It was the summer of 1970, and inside the Zahala, Tel Aviv, home of Moshe Dayan, Israel's minister of defense, a twenty-six-year-old former army paratrooper named Uri Geller sat huddled over a map. Dayan, with his signature black eye-patch, was the most famous general in the world, having recently overseen the capture of East Jerusalem during the 1967 Six-Day War. Geller, with his boyish good looks and boundless charisma, was the most famous psychic in Israel. Soon he would be the most famous psychic in the world.

Unknown to most, General Dayan had an illicit pastime that involved digging up archeological treasures across Israel and the Sinai, without a license or scientific oversight. His process, he later explained in his memoir, was to drive around the country-side looking for possible ancient dwelling sites to pilfer. "Bull-dozers preparing ground for construction and cultivation brought to light remains of ancient settlement[s]," wrote Dayan. Other times target sites came to him as "visions," early in the morning after he woke up. "I am not superstitious," said the general. "Nor am I a believer in the prevision of dreams... It may be that what I had dreamed was [an ancient site] I had passed earlier in the week." Following this intuition, Dayan would then drive to the site, comb through the earth, and bring home whatever Canaanite or Philistine relics he found. After cleaning them off and sometimes gluing pieces together, he would put the relics on display in his home. It was dangerous work. In 1968, while looting ancient artifacts from a cave in Azur, Dayan was badly injured by a landslide. He spent three weeks in the hospital recovering.

At his Zahala home, the general's gardens were filled with massive stone artifacts from antiquity: wishing wells, vestibules, cornices, and columns. Inside the study was where the smaller treasures were on display, including tiny statuettes and magic talismans dating back to the time of Eglon and the book of Judges. It was here, in the presence of this museum-quality collection, that Uri Geller recalls first using his "powers" to help Dayan find buried treasures, using an ancient form of clairvoyance called map dowsing. "I spent hours over the maps," Geller recalled in 2016. "Moshe Dayan utilized my powers to help him locate ancient artifacts and archeological finds illegally. I was young and naïve at the time. Here I was, talking to *the* Moshe Dayan."

Dowsing is the ability to locate water, minerals, or man-made objects buried underground by means of a divining rod, usually a forked twig, but also a pendulum or one's hand. Few divinatory practices have incensed modern skeptics as much as dowsing has. In *Fads and Fallacies,* Martin Gardner pointed out that dowsing was decreed to be satanic by the Inquisition in 1701, only to become "a common and respectable practice" later in the eighteenth century, during what was supposed to be the Age of Enlightenment. Then, in 1917, the U.S. Geological Survey declared "the matter of water-witching to [be] thoroughly discredited."

"Some of the most famous dowsers have been illiterates," quipped Gardner, "completely puzzled by their odd ability and offering no explanation for it." Dowsing was pure pseudoscience, he said, suspect in every way. "Far from a harmless and inexpensive superstition," Gardner wrote, "an untold number of dowsers throughout the world were being paid handsomely for their services," and to men of science that seemed unacceptable and wrong. While Geller was not being paid for his map dowsing services in 1970, eventually he would command extraordinary fees for his locating services. In 1986 the *Financial Times* of London reported Geller's map dowsing fee to be £1 million per job (GBP).

The most common form of dowsing involves a divining rod or forked stick, believed to be the source of inspiration for the archetypal magic wand. Drawings of men with divining rods have been found in prehistoric cave paintings in North Africa and Peru, dating to 6000 BC. Egyptians, Scythians, and Persians adapted the practice to include swinging pendulums above maps. In medieval Germany, miners used dowsing forks to locate mineral deposits in gold and silver mines. When German miners were imported to England in the 1500s, they brought the art of dowsing with them. In America, dowsing became common in the late 1800s as a means to help homesteaders and farmers locate water and drill wells.

The first known use of dowsing techniques by the U.S. military in battle occurred during the Vietnam War. In the winter of 1967, Marines used dowsing rods to locate tunnel systems built by the Viet Cong. The man in charge of training the Marines was Louis J. Matacia, a former topographical surveyor with the Army and a longtime dowser. This classified project was briefly made public on March 13, 1967, when an article appeared in *The Observer,* a government publication for U.S. forces in Vietnam. Under the headline "Shades of Black Magic: Marines on Operation Divine for VC Tunnels," a journalist reported that "an old-fashioned method of locating water in arid areas, the divining rod, has been updated and put to military use in Vietnam."

Marines using what was identified in the article as "Matacia's Wire Rudder" were skeptical at first, the reporter was told, until they "did locate a few Viet Cong tunnels." Private First Class Don R. Steiner explained, "Marines operate the divining rod by holding one in each hand, level with the ground, pointing in the direction of their movement. As the carrier [of the two wires] moves over, under or along a hidden structure, the wires will swing into alignment with the structure" hidden underground. Steiner said that when he was out on patrol, he watched his rods spread apart as he passed by a Vietnam hut. "Upon checking inside the building, Marines discovered a tunnel that led to a family bunker underneath the trail, right where the rods had reacted," Steiner said. The reporter could not locate anyone who could explain how the rods worked and surmised that their action depended—at least in part—on belief. "In this day of nuclear powered devices, it may seem there is still room for the old, if you happen to be a believer," the reporter wrote.

In a 2016 interview for this book, Louis Matacia, age eighty-five, explained that in his opinion, "Dowsing is human intelligence. No one knows why it works, only that it works [in] all kinds of situations but not all the time." (Matacia shared photographs of his time spent at Camp Lejeune, North Carolina, teaching dowsing techniques to Marines with the Counter Guerrilla Warfare Command, using coat hangers as divining rods to locate booby traps, punji pits, and underground weapons depots, as described in the *Observer* article.) Next Matacia traveled to Marine Corps Base Quantico, in Virginia, to demonstrate dowsing techniques for commanders with the Special Warfare Agency and ARPA. Here engineers had constructed a replica of a Vietnamese village, complete with tunnels and traps, waterways and bridges, and twenty structures, some of which had false ceilings and double walls. In this simulated environment Matacia used a divining rod to demonstrate how he could locate tunnels, traps, weapons caches, and more. The skill, he said, "could be taught to any open-minded Marine."

But the commanders were skeptical, Matacia remembers, and declassified documents confirm that the Marine Corps did not go forward with a program involving his dowsing techniques. "The cause of an effect is just as important as the results produced in order to formulate doctrine," a declassified memo states. "The Marine Corps will again become interested in dowsing only when it can be conclusively demonstrated that the average Marine can employ the technique without regard to his personal convictions, confidence level, or subconscious development." In the age of science and technology, the Corps was unwilling to endorse a technology that was based on something other than the scientific method.

In Israel, Moshe Dayan's map dowsing endeavors with Uri Geller came to an end in 1971, after a group of twenty Israeli archeologists signed a petition urging the minister of defense to give up his "legally questionable hobby." In his 1978 memoir, *Living with the Bible,* Dayan discusses his illegally acquired collection and how the "archeology of the Holy Land" can be used as a way "to reinterpret familiar Bible stories in a new light." He does not mention using Geller as a map dowser. In 1971, Geller had plenty of other work to keep him busy. He was quickly becoming one of Israel's most popular entertainers, bewildering audiences with his mysterious powers of extrasensory perception and psychokinesis. But he was a man at a crossroads, about to be transformed from an obscure Israeli citizen to one of the most scrutinized entertainers in the Western world. The fierce controversies over the authenticity of Geller's powers would become their own hall of mirrors.

Born in Israel in December 1946, Uri Geller came into a world informed by war. His parents, Jews living in Budapest, Hungary, had fled Nazi persecution in the late 1930s and taken up residence in the British Mandate of Palestine. In 1946, as Israel fought for independence, sniper fire and street fighting were commonplace. In a BBC television interview in 1987, Geller's mother, Manzy Freud, described the exterior of the family's Tel Aviv apartment complex as being pockmarked with bullet holes. Once a stray bullet flew into her son's bedroom where he lay sleeping, she said. It narrowly missed the boy and lodged in the wall.

The original manifestations of Geller's strange abilities revolved around instruments that measured time, his mother once told the BBC. The first watch he ever wore, a gift from his father when he was seven years old, stopped working a few hours after the young Uri Geller had strapped it on his wrist. His second watch, a replacement, also stopped working after he put it on, his mother said. The family was poor, and life was a struggle, Geller recalls. His mother was a hardworking seamstress; his father a career soldier with a wandering eye. "His infidelity devastated my mother," Geller says. His parents divorced when Uri was ten, and he was sent to live on a kibbutz. In this strange new environment he felt odd and alone. His ability to stop the hands on a watch disappeared.

In 1957, Geller's mother married a man named Ladislas Gero, and the family moved to the Mediterranean island of Cyprus, where Gero ran a small hotel in Nicosia. Like Israel, Cyprus was marked by violence, its Turkish and Greek inhabitants warring against one another and also against their British occupiers. When Geller was sent to a Catholic boarding school in Nicosia, his

unusual abilities returned. "He astonished friends with his amazing feats [like] bending forks," his former teacher, Julie Argrotis,
told a British newspaper in 1975.

On weekends and holidays Geller lived in the attic of his
stepfather's hotel at 19 Hera Street. One of the hotel's residents at
the time was a grain trader from Israel named Yoav Shacham.
Tough-looking and powerfully built, in the afternoons Shacham
practiced martial arts in the hotel garden. Geller, now fourteen,
was intrigued by the man and his warrior poses. In an effort to
impress the grain trader, Geller says he demonstrated to Shacham
how he could bend metal spoons and keys. Shacham was
impressed and offered to teach Geller martial arts. A bond grew
between the two of them. One day, Geller confided in Yoav
Shacham: "I said, 'Yoav, I can read your mind and I know you
are an Israeli spy,'" Geller recalls.

The way Geller remembers the story, Shacham was stunned,
his cover compromised by a fourteen-year-old boy. Geller swore
that he wouldn't say a word about it. The reason he'd told Shacham this, he said, was because he dreamed of growing up and
becoming a spy for Israel's intelligence agency, the Mossad. Geller
says that Yoav Shacham presented him with a challenge. "He told
me that when I came of age I was to join the Israeli Army as part
of the paratroopers. I was to work hard. I was to become the best
soldier I could possibly be. Attend officer training school. Then
find him." Then and only then, Geller recalls, "he said he would
get me into the Mossad." This undertaking gave Uri Geller a
sense of purpose he had not known before.

Geller made a commitment to himself. One day he would
work for the Mossad. Determined to succeed, he did precisely
what Yoav Shacham told him to do. When he turned eighteen
he moved back to Israel and volunteered for the paratroopers. In
1965 he became a soldier in the Israeli army. He went through
weapons training and learned how to jump out of airplanes. After

eleven months, he was accepted into a class for Officer Training School. But his dream was shattered in the second week of November 1966. A national newspaper reported that Major Yoav Shacham had been killed in action during a skirmish in a Jordanian border town. "I became overwhelmed with grief," Geller recalls. Sorrow turned to despair. "I was so sad and depressed that during the night [watch] I fell asleep on the [military] post. I woke up to a kick in the ribs." Officers do not fall asleep on watch, Geller was told. "They said I was not officer material and told me to go home." Geller's opportunity to do secret government work for Mossad died with his friend. Or so he believed.

He returned to his paratrooper unit, unsure of his future and feeling ashamed and insecure. On June 6, 1967, his unit was called to fight in the Six-Day War. He was sent to Ramallah, north of Jerusalem. "We were under tremendous attack by Jordanian Patton tanks," Geller recalls. In search of cover, the unit took shelter in a graveyard. Israeli aircraft were bombing the enemy. There was mortar fire and explosions all around. The company commander, Captain Ehud Shani, was killed instantly. Geller's best friend at the time, Avram Stedler, had his leg blown off and bled to death in front of him. From behind a rock a Jordanian soldier stood up and raised his weapon at Geller. "I raised my Uzi," says Geller. "He looked into my eye. I looked into his eye." Geller shot first and killed the man.

Geller became lost in thought, trying to process what had just occurred. He'd killed a man, an enemy soldier roughly his own age, who just as easily could have killed him. For a few moments he became oblivious to his surroundings, he says, and did not hear the incoming mortar. There was an explosion, and Geller was knocked unconscious. When he woke up, he was in Hadassah Hospital in Jerusalem with shrapnel wounds and a crushed elbow.

After surgery, the Israeli army sent him to a rehab center to recover. Unfit to return to active duty, Geller was assigned the job of supervising teenagers at a government-run summer camp.

To entertain them, he performed telepathy demonstrations. Among the children at the camp was a thirteen-year-old boy named Shimshon "Shipi" Shtrang who became mesmerized by Geller's abilities. "It was a long time ago but I was totally amazed by what Uri could do," Shtrang recalls in 2016. "I'd never seen anything like that before." Shipi asked Geller if he had any other tricks. Geller said they weren't tricks; they were real. He showed Shipi how he could bend a metal spoon by placing two fingers near the neck, concentrating hard, and saying, "Bend, bend, bend," like a magical incantation from a storybook.

Geller's first paid appearance was a performance at Shipi's middle school the following year. Word spread. Soon Geller was being paid to perform at dinner parties. Next came small nightclub bookings. Geller's magnetic personality and amazing abilities dazzled audiences, and soon he was selling out 300-seat theaters in uptown Tel Aviv. He was earning real money now, and he bought his mother a state-of-the-art Grundig television set. Stories about Geller began appearing in the press. Who was this Uri Geller? In one interview after another, Geller insisted he was not a stage magician, that his powers were real. Houdini was an illusionist and escape artist who could free himself from shackles, handcuffs, and chains; Henry Blackmore Jr. was a stage magician who made the illusion of sawing a woman in half famous. Geller's own demonstrations were not sleight of hand, he told reporters. He didn't know why he had the powers he possessed, he said, and he often pondered this conundrum himself. But he never wavered from his stated conviction: his powers were real.

One day in late 1969 or early 1970, the legal scholar Amnon Rubinstein heard about Uri Geller. Rubinstein was the host of a popular TV talk show called *Boomerang*. "We'd just done a show on psychics," Rubinstein explained in 2016, in an interview in Tel Aviv. "I was skeptical of psychics in general. That was the premise of the show. My wife told me we'd been invited to a party where Uri Geller was performing and we had to go and see him. On the way there, I said to her, I am a one hundred percent rational man. I do not believe in this," Rubinstein recalled. At the party, Rubinstein was standing with a group of guests when the charismatic young Geller walked up to him. "He looked me in the eye and said with great conviction, 'Pick a number between one and one hundred thousand. Any number at all.' I chose a number and said it aloud. [Geller] opened his palm. There, on the palm, in black ink, it was *written*. The number I had in my mind."

Rubinstein, known as the founding father of Israeli constitutional law, recalls being astonished. "Uri has the unusual power of influencing other people's thoughts," he says. Still, Rubinstein wondered whether what had happened was some kind of extraordinary luck. And so, after that first meeting, he tested Geller in his own home, in what he says ended up being countless sessions. "He could write something down ahead of time on a piece of paper and hide it, and would then tell me, my wife, or my children to write whatever we wanted. Any number, any name, or any capital city, and almost without exception he was always right," says Rubinstein. "He could somehow plant a thought right in our mind. To me this is so much more significant than spoon bending. This is a single phenomenon that casts doubt on many of the foundations of our rational world." Of Geller's critics Rubinstein says, "Sure, there are critics, but I'm not one of them. This is the one debate I'm unwilling to have: whether or not Uri Geller's powers are real."

Amnon Rubinstein was not the only high-profile Israeli who took an interest in Geller. Across Israel, newspapers began reporting that Geller had admirers in the uppermost echelons of government. Geller had met privately with Brigadier General Aharon Yariv, the head of military intelligence, reported *Haaretz*. He bent a spoon for Meir Amit, the former chief of Mossad, and was photographed at a function speaking with General Ariel Sharon, according to *Maariv*. In the summer of 1970, he was seen having lunch with Israel's famous defense minister, Moshe Dayan, at the White Elephant Restaurant in Zahala. It was during this lunch that Dayan invited Geller to his house, set the maps in front of him, and asked him to use his powers to locate architectural sites buried underground.

With his increasingly high profile, Geller's popularity was on the rise. But it was an event in the fall of 1970 that elevated him to international fame. Geller was giving a telepathy demonstration at the Tzavta Theater in Tel Aviv when he became physically ill and had to sit down. "Is there a doctor in the house?" he asked. A man came forward and took Geller's vital signs. His pulse was racing between 160 and 170 beats per second, the doctor said. Geller apologized to the audience for the disruption, then made an official-sounding proclamation. The reason he'd become ill, he said, was because a historic event was about to happen or had just occurred. Geller claimed that Gamal Abdel Nasser, the president of Egypt—Israel's sworn enemy at the time—"had just died or is about to die."

A journalist in the audience named Ruth Hefer ran to a pay phone to call her contact at Israel Radio International. There was no news about Nasser coming in over the wires, Hefer learned. When the journalist returned to the theater, she found Geller still seated on a stool, looking ill. Audience members were filing out, some demanding that their money be returned. Twenty minutes had passed when someone ran into the room shouting. Radio Cairo had just announced that President Nasser was dead. At 6:00 that evening, he'd suffered a heart attack and died. With this news, Uri Geller's reputation skyrocketed. At a New Year's Day press conference, Prime Minister Golda Meir was asked what lay in store for Israel in the coming year. "Don't ask me," she was quoted as saying, "Ask Uri Geller."

That first moment of national fame did not last long. "After that, I fell off the map," Geller recalls. "Israel is a small country. It was as if everyone had seen my act. I did telepathy, stopped and started watches, bent spoons. People wanted more. They wanted magic. But I'm not a magician. I could not add or invent new tricks." Geller watched with dismay as his audiences began to thin. "I moved into smaller theaters," Geller recalls. "And even smaller theaters after that."

Then one night an American scientist named Andrija Puharich showed up at a nightclub where Geller was performing. Uri Geller's life would soon take another radical turn.

The nightclub Zorba was located in the old quarter of the ancient port town of Jaffa, and on the night of August 17, 1971, Uri Geller was backstage, getting ready for a telepathy demonstration. It was a barn of a place, decorated with crepe paper lanterns and strings of holiday lights, a favorite Israeli summer spot. A rock band played on a large stage. During intermission jugglers entertained the audience. Finally it was time for the evening's main attraction.

"Ladies and gentlemen, please welcome Uri Geller," said the announcer. The tall, charismatic Geller emerged from backstage as the crowd went wild with applause. With his thick mop of black hair, hip dress, and lanky body, Geller looked more like a member of an English rock band than a telepath. He picked up the microphone and made a modest announcement. "With the cooperation of the audience," Geller said, "I am going to try to demonstrate simple telepathy and psychokinesis. I hope I will succeed."

He sat down on a stool facing the audience. His assistant, the now seventeen-year-old Shipi Shtrang, blindfolded Geller as a freestanding chalkboard was wheeled onstage. First, said Geller, he would perform a mind-reading act. With Shtrang's help, audience members would come forward to write three-digit numbers on the blackboard, which faced away from Geller. Before Geller made a guess, he asked everyone in the audience to concentrate hard on what had been written on the board, because his powers were enhanced by audience participation. "Eyeless sight" was a basic form of mental telepathy, Geller explained, the ancient ability to "see" without using one's eyes. Among various divinatory practices, the term "seeing" was used to connote insight, augury, or interpretation. The word "seer" comes from the verb "to see," and it appears in the Bible, but in basic telepathy, or eyeless sight, it was literal, Geller said.

Audience members lined up to participate. In one instance after the next, Geller would take a few moments to concentrate before writing a three-digit number on a notepad in his lap. Still blindfolded, he would hold up the notepad for the audience to see, and say aloud what he'd written in this alleged demonstration of eyeless sight. This night, as most nights, he was correct roughly ninety percent of the time. Next, he moved on to a similar set of trials, this time guessing the names of capital cities, with similar results.

After the show a man approached Geller. He was middle aged and eccentric looking, with a frizzy mop of unkempt hair and a thick mustache like the one Albert Einstein wore. The man spoke with an American accent and introduced himself as Dr. Andrija Puharich. The two had spoken briefly on the telephone a few weeks before, Puharich reminded Geller. He was the American research scientist and neurophysiologist interested in examining Geller from a medical point of view.

Geller agreed to meet Puharich the following day at the Tel Aviv home of an Israeli army officer. When Geller arrived at the address, he marveled at the scientist's gadgetry. "The room was filled with equipment," Geller recalled in 2016. "Thermometers, compasses, clocks, watches, a reel-to-reel audio recorder and a Konica 8mm film camera, which was very state-of-the-art back then." Puharich did not tell Geller that he was keeping track of the experiments as part of a CIA research proposal he was working on, one that he would title "A Research Program Whose Goal Is to Unambiguously Resolve the Question as to Whether or Not Direct Brain Perception and Direct Brain Action Exist."

In declassified documents obtained as part of a 2015 Freedom of Information Act request for this book, Puharich told the CIA that he and an Israeli army officer named Simcha Shilony had witnessed Uri Geller "Breaking a gold ring held in another person's clenched fist; Concentrating on a pair of bimetal-type thermometers, and selectively making the temperature rise 6 to 8 degrees Fahrenheit on one or the other instrument; Starting broken clocks and watches solely by concentration; Moving the hands of a watch forward or backward without any physical contact with the watch," and, "telepathy...with 90% accuracy in telepathy tests where Dr. Puharich would think of a 3-digit number."

After spending two weeks testing Uri Geller in the summer of 1971, Puharich was convinced that Geller's abilities would be of interest to the CIA. From his contacts in the intelligence world, Puharich suspected the Agency was looking for its own Nina Kulagina to test in a lab. Puharich did not tell Geller about his plans involving the CIA. Instead he simply told Geller that his extraordinary powers should not be wasted in Israeli nightclubs, but that he should be tested in a laboratory setting in the United States. Geller asked Amnon Rubinstein for advice. "I told him absolutely he should go be tested in America, at a serious research institute like Stanford," remembers Rubinstein.

Puharich returned to the United States after telling Geller he'd be in touch soon. From his home in Ossining, he put together a research proposal and submitted it to his CIA contact for review. "The situation was sensitive," recalls Dr. Kit Green, the scientist who ran the CIA's Life Sciences Division at the time.

Green would soon become Uri Geller's handler, and was interviewed at length for this book. "The [report] was escalated to the top. In fact the decision to test Geller was a decision made by CIA director Richard Helms, which I know because I am the one who received his call," confirms Green.

Except there was a hurdle to overcome. The CIA wanted Geller, but they also wanted to distance themselves from Puharich. In declassified documents, CIA analysts describe Puharich as a potential liability "with whom many unsavory reports have been linked." A shell entity needed to be created through which Geller-related funds could flow and Puharich could be paid—ideally an organization or a person of solid repute. Puharich knew exactly the right person. His name was Edgar Mitchell, the astronaut and Apollo 14 crew member.

CHAPTER SEVEN

The Man on the Moon

A pollo astronaut Edgar Mitchell became fascinated by the idea of mental telepathy in 1967, while reading a book about mind-to-mind experiments conducted by the polar explorer and decorated war hero Sir Hubert Wilkins. These experiments gave Ed Mitchell an idea. He'd just begun astronaut training and decided that if he were chosen to voyage to the Moon, he'd conduct his own mental telepathy experiments on the way. In Wilkins's book *Thoughts Through Space: A Remarkable Adventure in the Realm of Mind,* the aviator described ESP experiments he carried out while searching for a group of lost Russian explorers whose airplane went down over the North Pole in 1938. "It's a remarkable story by a remarkable man," Mitchell recalled in a 2015 interview at his home in Florida. "A shame most people have forgotten about him. People forget history, and that's the way it is."

Mitchell related to Wilkins because Wilkins was a voyager of the first order, one of the world's most famous explorers of the modern era. He was a larger-than-life individual whose daring feats commanded respect wherever he went. In 1926 he became the first man to fly from North America to the polar regions of Europe, proving there was no continent under the Arctic ice. He led multiple expeditions to the Arctic and Antarctic, and in 1931 attempted to reach the North Pole in a surplus World War I submarine. After his death in November 1958 the U.S. Navy took his ashes to the North Pole aboard the nuclear submarine *USS Skate* and scattered them in the majestic Arctic as the great explorer had requested.

Now, as Ed Mitchell prepared for his Moon voyage, his interest in extrasensory perception grew. All his life he'd been a rule follower, a naval officer and an aviator, a test pilot and an aeronautical engineer. But then, in 1961, while getting his PhD in aeronautics and astronautics at the Massachusetts Institute of Technology, he began studying topics that expanded and altered his worldview, including quantum mechanics, galactic evolution, and star evolution. "These were abstruse subjects," Mitchell later recalled. "No one knew the answers to the questions they posed." Studying these concepts, he found himself increasingly interested in what science had not yet figured out. "I would lie awake at night wondering about the meaning of life and man's place in the universe," Mitchell recalled. Selected for astronaut training, he began practicing meditation and yoga. "Meditation produces qualitative and beneficial shifts in psychophysiological conditions," he said. And as he prepared for the voyage into outer space, he started to contemplate the meaning of inner space, or human consciousness. What does consciousness mean? And how do outer space and inner space align?

At 4:02 in the afternoon of January 31, 1971, there was no more time to wonder what it would be like in outer space. Apollo 14 was minutes from launch, and Ed Mitchell braced himself for what was about to unfold. Here on a tiny spit of land off the coast of Florida, Ed Mitchell, Alan Shepard, and Stuart Roosa were about to leave planet Earth. The clock was ticking, and from a technical standpoint the danger on board this rocket ship was rising. Training helps an astronaut master extraordinary human functioning: an unusual degree of control over what transpires within his or her body. At any given moment in space a myriad things can go wrong, and to exist in this state for an extended period of time requires immediate focus and attention. "We'd spent ten percent of our time studying plans for the mission and ninety percent learning how to react intuitively to all the 'what ifs,'" Mitchell later recalled.

To prepare for space travel and for landing on the Moon, the Apollo astronauts cultivated extraordinary human functioning, Mitchell says. They learned to develop intention techniques. To get to the Moon and back, they would have to function in an extremely hostile environment for more than 200 consecutive hours, on very little sleep. Whereas another man's adrenaline might spike to dangerous levels, astronauts trained their minds to keep their bodies calm. This is not something that can be faked. Every breath and every heartbeat of each of the Apollo astronauts would be monitored by aerospace doctors on the ground, in real time. "The mind has to convince the body all is well. Through training, this can be done," Mitchell said. On land, they had rehearsed for every contingency they could face on the mission, including how to withstand g-forces, how to maneuver in zero-gravity conditions, and how to scale craters and climb hills in environments that mimicked the Moon's.

It was now just a few minutes to blastoff and Ed Mitchell sat buckled into a small seat inside the cone-shaped spaceship, attached near the top of the Saturn V rocket. The rocket was taller than the Statue of Liberty and weighed 6.2 million pounds. It was in this quiet moment anticipating blast and fury that Mitchell accepted there was nothing for him to do but sit still. Here was the moment when "the mind [could be] called upon to keep the body calm," Mitchell recalled in 2015. The scientist in him knew that inside the lower portion of the rocket there were more than 66,000 gallons of liquid hydrogen fuel. In a matter of seconds a small pyrotechnic device would deliver a spark, ignite the fuel, and cause the massive explosion necessary to generate thrust. If everything went right, the three men would be on their way to the Moon. If anything went wrong, they would die instantly, in an inferno. Twenty seconds passed. There were now fifty seconds to go. The upper-access arms connecting the space capsule to the scaffolding released and swung away.

"Initiate firing command," boomed a voice. NASA computers took charge.

Inside the space capsule Ed Mitchell listened to the rushing sounds of liquid as thousands of gallons of propellants sped through the rocket's fuel lines. He could hear the turbo pumps spinning as the countdown continued. "Ten...nine...eight." Kerosene and liquid oxygen hurtled into the combustion chambers of the first-stage engine of the Saturn V. Next came ignition, then fire and flames. Pad 39A trembled in an explosion of fuel. Computers indicated to NASA technicians that there was sufficient power to launch. The clock reached 0 and the rocket's massive hold-down arms fell away. Apollo 14 lifted off the launch pad, headed for the Moon.

The Moon. Earth's only natural satellite. A subject of mystery and mysticism since the dawn of recorded history. The Moon is thought to have formed some 4.5 billion years ago, its origins inextricably linked to the earliest evolution of Earth. The Apollo 14 voyage to the Moon was for NASA a pivotal moment in its attempt to understand these origins. This was the first lunar landing mission to focus on science and geology rather than space-travel techniques. Ed Mitchell and Alan Shepard would collect rock samples from a meteor impact site called Cone Crater and bring these samples home. Geologists believed that this data could provide a view of the ancient aftermath of the cataclysmic impact believed to have left debris across the Moon's surface one billion years before.

Hours passed. Time and motion took on an exceptional dimension, Mitchell later recalled. As Apollo 14 made its way to the
Moon, the spacecraft rotated slowly so the side facing the sun
wouldn't get too hot. Mitchell closed his eyes and experienced
the sensation of standing still. He took a pen from his bag and
released it, then marveled as it floated through the air in front of
him. Out here in space there appeared to be no up or down.
He reached for the telescope and used it to look out the window
at the stars. In 1595, the microscope opened up the world of
small-scale science, of biology. Thirteen years later, in 1608, the
telescope opened up wide-scale science, the world of cosmology.
What twentieth-century instrument would open up the study of
consciousness, Ed Mitchell wondered, the unsolved mystery that
is the human mind?

The Apollo 14 astronauts ate their freeze-dried dinner, went
to the bathroom, and brushed their teeth. Now it was time to
sleep. Each astronaut pulled down his nearest window shade(s) to
shut out the bright light of the sun. Each was allowed to bring
along personal reading material and music to help him fall asleep.
After some minutes of quiet time, the schedule indicated lights-out.

"I did not intend to fall asleep immediately," Ed Mitchell
recalled in 2015. He had an alternative plan in place. He was
going to conduct a secret experiment that had been arranged
with three civilian colleagues back on Earth, two physicians and
a Swedish-born psychic named Olaf Johnson. Just as Sir Hubert
Wilkins had done three decades before, Ed Mitchell intended to
conduct a long-distance mind-to-mind telepathy experiment right
here in outer space. Mitchell would act as the sender, Olaf Johnson as the receiver. Two of Mitchell's physician friends, Edward
Maxey and Edward Boyle, would act as witnesses, sitting with
Johnson in his Chicago apartment. Doctors Maxey and Boyle
had helped train Mitchell in extraordinary human functioning
techniques by teaching him advanced scuba diving techniques.

Mitchell reached into his bag and pulled out a clipboard and a secret set of five Zener cards, now a staple in modern ESP experiments. On each card was a symbol: circle, square, star, cross, three wavy lines. He flipped the cards over so he couldn't see the symbols, then shuffled the deck. He chose a card at random and turned it over. Staring at the symbol, he concentrated for fifteen seconds. With his pen, he noted on his clipboard the precise time it was on Earth and the symbol he'd been staring at. He repeated this effort twenty-five times, each time with a new Zener card randomly chosen from the five. The process took approximately seven minutes. When he finished, he put his things away and went to sleep.

Eighty hours passed. Edgar Mitchell grew a beard. He longed for a bath and a slice of his mother's apple pie. From one of the craft's five windows, he looked back and forth between the Moon's mysterious surface and a map in his hands. Men have been making maps of the Moon since the days of cuneiform writing. This particular map had been made by NASA and was the product of data collected on previous flights. Ed Mitchell was an expert navigator and map reader, and it was his job to take this map with him when he and Shepard got to the surface of the Moon.

"The Moon looks huge," he told Houston control. Their target, Cone Crater, was getting closer. Almost visible now. Mitchell could see the upper end of the Sea of Fertility and noted how much darker it was than everything around it. "There's Theophilus," he told Houston. "The craters look fresh. Vivid." He saw the Descartes site. The Albategnius Crater. Herschel's west wall. He marveled at the long shadows and the rugged landscape. Finally, he located the eastern edge of Fra Mauro, their designated landing site. Remarkably, as long as everything went according to schedule, their destination was just a few hours away.

The *Kitty Hawk* command module was orbiting the Moon now, at an altitude of roughly ten miles. "This scale is so deceiving,"

Mitchell said. "We could be five hundred feet in the air, the way this terrain looks," he told NASA. "Tracking the landmarks is rather phenomenal."

After ten rotations around the Moon, it was undocking time for the *Antares* lander. Mitchell and Alan Shepard prepared for their landing; Stu Roosa would remain inside *Kitty Hawk,* in orbit for two days until rendezvous and the return journey back to Earth. Mitchell and Shepard readied themselves, then squeezed down into the tunnel that connected the command module to *Antares.* A deep breath. A leap of faith. Ready, set, go. Shepard opened the hatch. Out they went, and into the lunar module. *Antares* was their lifeline to the Moon and back.

Before their final descent to the surface, Shepard and Mitchell were required to fly the lunar module around the backside of the Moon two more times. Each orbit took between ninety minutes and two hours. Mitchell felt an incredible psychological tension in the lunar module, he said, and he wondered whether his fellow astronauts had felt this strain too. He looked at the map of the Fra Mauro landing site and compared it with the visuals out the window. "Looks just like the map," he told Houston optimistically. He felt excitement as energy coursed through his body. Time passed. Now there was one last trip around the Moon. "As Al and I orbited only a few thousand meters above the highest lunar peaks, the familiar gray landscape became recognizable," he recalled in his memoir. "There were mountains and valleys, a sun in the sky. For the first time in three days there was a relative up and down; the tiny Earth in the distance appeared as a satellite of the Moon." But this time, as the two Apollo astronauts emerged from the backside of the Moon, something technical went terribly wrong. On the instrument panel an Abort signal flashed. In outer space Abort is not a nuanced word. Abort indicates halt, discontinue, terminate. This signal flashed again and again, indicating that there was something catastrophically wrong with the computer guidance system.

Mitchell's mind scanned through various scenarios, he recalled in 2015. He had to stay focused on the solution. He could not allow his mind to think negatively, to consider that they may have come 240,000 miles only to be told to turn around and go home. He could not allow himself to think about Apollo 13, which suffered a technological failure that canceled its Moon landing and very nearly killed the astronauts on board. "Keep the mind focused," Mitchell said to himself. Consider "the mysterious cadence of serendipity." A voice from Houston interrupted his thoughts. "Ed, I wonder if you could try tapping the [instrument] panel," someone said.

Mitchell tapped the panel. My God, he thought. The light actually went off. Filled with an enormous sense of relief, Mitchell took a deep inhale, then exhaled. Then the Abort light came back on. With detached acceptance, Mitchell says he wondered again whether they had really traveled all this way to turn back without landing on the Moon.

"Try tapping the panel a bit again," Houston said.

"Okay," Mitchell agreed, and tapped it.

"You tapped it again, right?" someone in Houston asked.

Yes, he'd tapped it. This time nothing happened. The Abort light continued to flash red. He and Shepard waited to hear what Houston said next. The silence was agonizing, he later recalled. Houston suggested that they make another rotation around the Moon. Do not think about this as rotation unlucky number thirteen, Mitchell told himself. Houston would work on the problem while the two astronauts were on the far side, or "dark side," of the Moon, where there is no communication or signal line back to Earth. Have faith. Believe in serendipity, Mitchell repeated to himself, like a Mantra.

Back in Houston it was 2:00 a.m. At the Johnson Space Center, NASA engineers and technicians had little choice but to try to figure out how to bypass the Abort command. This meant calling a man named Don Eyles, in Cambridge, Massachusetts. Eyles, age twenty-seven, was the computer scientist who had designed the guidance system on *Antares*. When NASA called, Eyles was at the instrument laboratory at MIT, watching the Apollo 14 mission on TV. He needed to design a workaround that would cause the spaceship's computer to override its own Abort signal, and he had less than two hours to do it. "We deceived the program by telling it an abort was already in progress," Eyles recalled in 2016. It was a sixty-one-keystroke solution.

Houston relayed these sixty-one keystrokes to Ed Mitchell on *Antares,* who copied them down on a notepad. After they emerged from the far side and were in the first few seconds of their initial-descent engine burn, Mitchell entered these critical keystrokes into the computer—in an exact order and at precisely the right times—while simultaneously preparing to land. But now there was another problem. Dealing with the Abort signal had lengthened the mission. The new danger was that fuel was running out. The astronauts had to get down to the surface without delay. Shepard ran calculations. Based on the amount of fuel they had remaining in the landing tanks, even with a flawless landing the astronauts would have only seconds to spare before they would run out of fuel.

Mitchell focused his mind on landing. He could not allow his thoughts to linger on danger or fear. Never mind that the Abort signal had been turned off manually. This meant that if the astronauts really did need to abort for safety reasons, there would be no indicator alerting them to take that action. The need to abort was now going to be a manual call.

Mitchell and Shepard were readying for their descent onto the surface when a flashing light indicated a new problem: the landing radar was malfunctioning. *Antares*'s landing radar system allowed the craft to sense proximity to the surface as the module descended. Without this radar there would be no way to safely touch down. The target area on Fra Mauro was littered with boulders and meteor impact craters. The radar was designed to allow the craft to land on flat ground. Neither manual nor visual sensing was possible because the astronauts were facing upward during descent. If *Antares* landed on an incline, there was considerable risk that the module could tip over. And if it tipped over, it could not be righted by two men. The astronauts would run out of oxygen and die on the Moon.

Mitchell could feel his adrenaline soaring. Time was running out. Fuel was running low. As the lunar module pilot, landing was up to him, but this new code he'd just typed into the onboard system had somehow interfered with the landing radar. According to mission control rules, without landing radar there could be no landing on the Moon. At NASA, rules were rules. In 2015, Mitchell recalled Alan Shepard looking over at him and shaking his head in solidarity and disbelief.

What was going to happen? Had they really come this far to abort before they set foot on the Moon? If they were unable to land, surely this would be the end of the entire Apollo program. Mitchell took a deep breath. The communication channels were loud with static, he recalled. With all the noise, it was hard to hear. Unable to come up with anything else to do, he commanded the radar to obey.

"Come on, radar," he said aloud. "Lock on!" An excruciating moment. Then another. "And just like that," said Mitchell, "in the nick of time, the radar started up and locked in."

The astronauts looked at their instrument panel. Shepard looked out the window. They were exactly where they were supposed to be.

"Right on the money," Mitchell told Houston.

"Right on the money," Shepard agreed.

"You are go for a landing," said Houston.

"Shoot for the Moon," Shepard said.

Mitchell read his position to Houston: they were at "2048 feet, coming down a little fast. 1500 feet. 500 feet. 100 feet. Starting down. 90 feet. 50 feet. 40. 20."

Mitchell felt a bump. The footpads of *Antares* hit the Moon. "We're on the surface," Mitchell said. Mitchell had made the most precise landing to date, approximately eighty-seven feet from the targeted landing point.

"It felt tremendous," he later recalled.

So little was known about this place. Only four explorers had been here before, on Apollo 11 and Apollo 12. The total time humans had spent on this lunar landscape was just 53 hours and seven minutes.

No one knows for sure how the Moon was formed, only that it was most likely once part of Earth. The prevailing theory is that the Moon was formed when the formerly larger Earth, called the protoearth, was impacted by a Mars-sized object that hit Earth with such force that it ejected debris that later formed our Moon. One thing was certain. Earth, with its moving plates and erupting volcanoes, was very different from the Moon, in that Earth destroys its own record over millions of years. The airless Moon is different. It appears to have no moving plates, and for this reason scientists believe the Moon's surface has likely preserved a record of its history since it first formed. The idea that humans could learn more about Earth's origins by investigating what remains on the Moon, by collecting rock samples from inside and outside the craters and bringing the samples back to Earth, was guiding the mission that lay ahead. Mitchell and Shepard were to collect rock samples from the 1,100-foot-wide, 750-foot-deep Cone Crater. That was the target.

At last *Antares* was on the Moon. It hadn't crashed. It also hadn't landed on level ground, so it tilted to one side. The unsettling feeling that the craft might tip over was not something Mitchell could allow his mind to linger on. Before the astronauts could leave *Antares* and step onto the Moon's surface they had four hours of duties to perform. They consulted their checklists, performed their tasks, and sent status reports to Houston. Mitchell affixed a 16mm camera, the Maurer data acquisition camera, to his side of the module and pointed it out the window to record terrain and engineering data for future missions. After completing the work on their checklists, the astronauts began procedures to open the hatch.

Finally the time had come. Alan Shepard went first, Ed Mitchell right behind. As he made his way down the ladder, he heard Houston say, "Okay, Ed, we can see you coming down." A camera mounted on the lower part of the module was recording their descent and broadcasting the images back on Earth. Mitchell jumped past the last step and landed on the surface. "I stepped over a few craters that were filled with dust," he later recalled. "Then I looked up at the sky. It was inky black without a star in sight, and I couldn't see the Earth at all." He stood for a moment, gazing "at this amazing new place." Then he got to work.

Looking around, Mitchell realized they were in the middle of a large boulder field. "It covers perhaps as much as a square mile," Shepard told Houston as they began the first of two four-and-a-half-hour excursions on the lunar surface. They erected a flag and assembled TV equipment. They set up a miniature thermonuclear station designed to power monitoring equipment for years to come. They took photographs and shot film. Then they rested inside the module and prepared for the second excursion, to their target: Cone Crater.

For their journey the astronauts would take with them three ancient tools: a wheelbarrow in which to carry things; a gnomon to check and measure shadows; and a map with which to navigate. Mitchell carried the map. They took turns dragging the wheelbarrow across the lunar surface, which reminded Mitchell of a tractor moving through a plowed field. They set down the gnomon and photographed its shadows. They took samples and trudged on. Then, back in Houston, a devastating realization emerged: "They aren't where they think they are." They were on the Moon, and they were lost.

Scientists and engineers in Houston calculated, then recalculated, and then concurred. The astronauts were overestimating the rate of their progress by as much as a factor of two. Disagreements followed. Mitchell and Shepard had entirely different interpretations of where they were in relation to Cone Crater. They argued. Then Houston piped in, to try to help problem-solve. Mitchell expressed his anger with the geologists. This was their fault, he said; they were far too preoccupied with rocks. While the astronauts endeavored to determine their location, back in Houston the engineers drew their own conclusions. "They think they have completed a little under half their journey," said one scientist, when in reality they had completed "only about a third."

Mitchell told Houston that the bubble of his space suit was distorting his vision. He said his perception was off and was messing with his ability to accurately process information. There were "craters hidden behind other craters," he said. As he struggled to get his bearings, he reported seeing car-sized boulders on a rim. His primary problem in navigation was the surprising roughness of the terrain, he said. Everything looked closer than it was.

Mitchell summoned his astronaut training and focused his attention on the task at hand, he later recalled. Keep moving, he told himself. Gaze out, not in.

At Johnson Space Center scientists and technicians examined charts and Moon maps.

On the Moon, Shepard was having as difficult a time as Mitchell was. "There's hardly a level spot anywhere," Shepard said. He lost his footing and fell. Mitchell hurried to his side and helped him to his feet.

"One or both of them is breathing heavily," Houston noted.

Mitchell eyed a boulder. "Strange," he noted aloud. Embedded in the boulders Mitchell reported seeing huge chunks of glass. He began to perspire. Frustration affects physiology, and Mitchell's metabolism rose to a rate higher than it had been at any time on this journey. "I'm going on medium cooling," he told Houston, adjusting the cooling system on his portable life support system. His heart rate rose to 100 beats per minute. Houston told both astronauts to sit down.

"Why don't we pull up beside this big crater," Mitchell said to Shepard. "Take a break, get the map, and see if we can't find out exactly where we are?"

They rested; Mitchell consulted his map. Finally the two men stood up, having agreed to make another go at it.

"I think I know where we are," Mitchell said.

In Houston, the flight surgeon noted that Shepard's heart was now beating at 120 beats per minute.

"Putting the map away," Mitchell said.

The astronauts resumed walking. The grade was getting steeper. Shepard sounded winded. Mitchell took photographs with a Hasselblad Electric Data Camera, with its specially designed lens and glass plate that placed reference crosses on each image to help determine distance and height. Shepard's heart rate rose to 150 beats per minute; Mitchell's slowed to 115, then raced back up to 128. The flight surgeon instructed the men to stop and rest again.

"Our positions are all in doubt now," Mitchell said.

"Perhaps you can think with us, if you want," Shepard suggested to Houston.

"Distance became plastic," Mitchell later recalled, enhanced by the "unreal clarity of the airless scene." He ordered his mind to stay focused. "Now that we were on the lunar surface, our estimates in distance were in error by one hundred percent, as objects typically appeared one-half as far away as they really were," he later said.

Pause; regroup; keep moving, in that order, Mitchell told himself. Get to Cone Crater. That is the goal. Then came the moment: Shepard suggested they turn around. Mitchell considered what was being said. Shepard was older and wiser. Ten years earlier, in 1961, he had become the first American in space. Now, age forty-seven, he struggled for breath as he labored across the surface of the Moon. "No. Let's keep going around this crater," Mitchell insisted.

"We can't stop without looking into Cone Crater," he told Houston. That was the goal. They could not come all this way without getting to the target. Ed Mitchell was not prepared to fail. Houston gave them permission to leave their wheelbarrow behind. They were given a thirty-minute extension to reach the rim.

His breathing labored, Mitchell said, "Let's take a look at the map." More bad news. He realized he was looking at a very distinct map marker, and that it was a landmark he thought they had already passed. "This was terribly, terribly frustrating," Mitchell recalled.

On Earth, a decision was made. This was it, the turning point. The final call. Turn back now, Houston said.

The astronauts turned around. They saw *Antares* in the distance, slightly tipped. "We kangaroo-hopped our way back down the slope, taking giant leaps through the void that is the lunar atmosphere," Mitchell recalled. Shepard took his famous golf shot. Mitchell performed a javelin throw. After spending four hours and thirty-five minutes on the lunar surface and setting a new distance-traveled record (of approximately 9,000 feet), the astronauts arrived at *Antares* and climbed inside. They stowed their lunar samples and prepared for takeoff. With the push of a computer key *Antares* blasted off the Moon. After approximately one hour and forty-seven minutes they succeeded in rendezvous-ing with Stu Roosa in the *Kitty Hawk* command module.

On the way back to Earth his disappointment was profound, Mitchell recalled. They had come all this way and failed to get to the target. Peering out the spacecraft window, Mitchell stared down at planet Earth. He thought about his family. He thought about his country. He thought about his life in the military and the current war in Vietnam. And he became overwhelmed with a thought he'd never considered before. "Particular scientific facts about stellar evolution took on a new significance," Mitchell explained, stellar evolution being the birth of stars, when time began. "This was not religious or mystical, but something else," he said. Sitting there in the command module, he experienced what he later described as a "flash of understanding. Its full mean-ing somehow obscured." It was "silent and authoritative," he recalled in 2015. But with simple clarity, he said, he understood one universal truth: "Man is connected to other men through consciousness." That was the link between inner space and outer space. He felt a peacefulness he had never experienced before. Later he would identify this feeling as "savikalpa samadhi," a term from ancient Sanskrit that means perfect oneness with the universe. Mitchell looked over at his fellow astronauts, wonder-ing whether they were experiencing this too.

Time passed. Mitchell pulled out his five Zener cards and twice repeated his mind-to-mind telepathy tests with the two physicians and the psychic Olaf Johnson in Chicago. These were tests that all parties had agreed to keep secret. He couldn't wait to get home.

After the astronauts landed they were quarantined for ten days. One morning during breakfast Shepard was reading the newspaper when a headline caught his eye: "Astronaut does ESP experiment on Moon flight," it read. "Al Shepard doubled over with laughter," Mitchell recalled. Shepard showed the article to Mitchell and made a comment about how journalists had no shame, how they were willing to fabricate stories just to sell newspapers. There was an awkward moment of silence, remembered Mitchell. Then he told Shepard, "I did it." Someone from his small group must have leaked the story.

Shepard looked nonplussed, Mitchell remembered. "He silently returned his attention to his breakfast plate. The subject was never brought up again."

Around the world, Mitchell's ESP experiments became a kind of running joke. The headline in *Maariv,* Israel's leading newspaper, read, "Captain Edgar D. Mitchell, the Uri Geller of the Astronauts."

It did not take long for the press to get hold of the data from Mitchell's outer space ESP tests. Out of 200 attempts to communicate telepathically, the psychic in Chicago got 51 correct hits, roughly the same as chance would predict. When Mitchell tried to defend the failure as a product of timing—he said his astronaut workload delayed his telepathic transmission time by roughly one hour—skeptics had a field day. But the world's ridicule did not matter to Ed Mitchell. He was a changed man. For six months after his return from the Moon he honored his obligations to NASA, shaking hands with prime ministers and presidents, kings, congressmen, and high school students. But his worldview had shifted. He redirected his focus toward an understanding of what consciousness was. "The topic of consciousness," he said, "is as vast as the cosmos and as close to us as sleep." The reason he'd performed ESP tests in space was because "Telepathy demonstrated that there is an information linkage between people that goes beyond the laws of science as they are presently understood." From now on, he was interested only in pursuing "subjects that purport to examine or explain man's purpose" on this Earth. "Man's attempt to understand himself and the nature of the universe," he declared, "is the ultimate frontier."

His thoughts about society took a negative turn. "I began thinking that there was something wrong with ideas such as nation and state. From this viewpoint it is only logical to make war on other countries and on the countryside," he said. There had to be another way. "The denial of the nonmaterial aspect of life, its sacred participation in the miracle of existence," he wrote, "this leaves people with no source of meaning and direction" in life. Ed Mitchell had gone to the Moon and come back—and he was profoundly disappointed by what he returned to. "The resulting view may be stated thus: I am simply a prisoner," he said. The only hope for happiness was to seek a higher understanding of consciousness. This was his new quest.

Mitchell began spending all his time with people who shared his ideas about consciousness and mental telepathy. He made new colleagues and friends. He left NASA. He divorced his wife. In November 1971, at a convention in Houston, he met Andrija Puharich. The two men became fast friends. Puharich interested Mitchell in a research idea. He had recently traveled to Israel, Puharich said, where he'd tested a young man named Uri Geller who had extraordinary mental powers. Not only was Geller telepathic, Puharich reported, he had psychokinetic abilities that allowed him to stop and start watches, and to bend metal with his mind.

Puharich was preparing to bring Uri Geller to America, he said, to be studied in a laboratory here. Perhaps Ed Mitchell wanted to collaborate on a Geller project with him? Mitchell needed no time to think about the proposition. The answer, he told Puharich, was yes. The Apollo astronaut was on board.

CHAPTER EIGHT

The Physicist and the Psychic

Inside a laboratory at the Northern California think tank Stanford Research Institute (SRI), a young physicist named Harold ("Hal") Puthoff sat down to write a letter. It was March 1972. Puthoff was an expert in quantum electronics and electron beam devices. At age thirty-five he was a bit of a prodigy, having already coauthored the university physics textbook *Fundamentals of Quantum Electronics,* published twenty-three papers, given fourteen national symposium lectures, and registered two patents, one for a tunable infrared laser. The letter Puthoff was writing was addressed to a New York City man named Grover Cleveland "Cleve" Backster, a former CIA analyst whose area of expertise was detecting deception. This letter would alter the course of Hal Puthoff's life.

Puthoff was on a quest to answer one of physics' great unsolved questions. "I was interested in questions like 'What is life?' but also in questions like '*Why* is life?' Was physical theory as we knew it capable of describing life processes?" Puthoff explained in 2015. Cleve Backster had recently performed an experiment that Puthoff thought might point him in an interesting new direction on this quest. "I wanted to obtain a small grant for some research in quantum biology," Puthoff recalled.

In 1972, Puthoff was a rising star at SRI, the second largest Defense Department research institute in the country after RAND Corporation, and located in the heart of Silicon Valley. Founded in 1946, SRI performed a broad spectrum of scientific research with an annual operating budget of $70 million (roughly $400 million in 2017). Of its staff of 2,600, more than 400 had PhDs. Puthoff was slight in build, thoughtful and soft spoken. Because he often appeared in the lab with baggy circles under his eyes, some colleagues described him as a Mick Jagger look-alike but with a larger derriere.

Before working as a laser scientist Hal Puthoff had worked for U.S. Navy intelligence. As a young lieutenant in the Naval Reserve he was loaned out to the NSA to work on a classified code-breaking program called Project Lightning involving ultra-high-speed supercomputers. Top-secret work was interesting, Puthoff found, but he decided that a traditional career in the military was not for him. He began focusing on quantum physics, on esoteric concepts including quantum entanglement, zero-point energy, and how quantum theory might account for biological life processes—hence the question, *Why* is life?

The year 1972 was a unique time to be an American physicist with links to the Defense Department. The 1950s hard-science approach to defense problems was beginning to thaw. "In the aftermath of World War II, science became swept up in a wave of technology," says Puthoff. "Everything was about mechanization, about apparatus-based, inanimate physics. In general, any kind of philosophizing about physics dropped away," he recalls. "Most scientists followed the Feynman dictum 'Shut up and calculate.'" In the late 1960s metaphysics—with its interest in abstract concepts such as knowing, being, identity, cause, time, and space—began to make a comeback. "Physicists began thinking about life processes again," Puthoff says. Questions about biology, or what Puthoff calls "animate physics," were back on the chalkboard. Physicists like Puthoff began to ask the age-old question, Where does human energy come from?

"Quantum physics has yet to explain basic life forces in biological systems," Puthoff says, "starting with, Why does a cell divide? I wondered, are there fields and forces involved that we are not seeing in regular physics?" He began searching the literature coming out of the world's top research labs. This led him to the work of Yakov Terletsky, chairman of theoretical physics at Moscow University and winner of the Laureate of the State Prize, and Gerald Feinberg, a physics professor at Columbia University. Both men were working on hypotheses involving a subatomic particle called a tachyon. In America, scientists had recently proven the existence of numerous previously unknown subatomic particles, including the neutrino, the muon, and the quark. "The tachyon is proposed to be superluminal, faster-than-light but not forbidden by quantum physics," says Puthoff. "I wondered, could it be—maybe—that in the tachyon flow, that was where there was the extra field?" That field, or force, physics can't see. It was in pursuit of the elusive and theoretical tachyon that Puthoff sat down to write his letter to Cleve Backster.

Backster was not a scientist. He was a deception researcher and interrogation expert, a man rooted in the intelligence community, where he had worked for more than twenty-five years. He had earned his stripes in World War II, in the Army's Counter Intelligence Corps, where he conducted narco-interrogations of enemy forces, early attempts to get POWs to reveal military secrets using so-called truth serums. After the war Backster joined the CIA, where he cofounded the Agency's polygraph program.

The polygraph, or lie detector, works on the assumption that deception can be detected by measurable changes in human body functions, including pulse, respiration, and perspiration. In most people, the fear of being caught in a lie produces anxiety, which in turn causes these individual levels to change. Backster authored the CIA's infamous "lifestyle issues" test, a series of questions that asked of each prospective CIA employee things like "Are you a homosexual?" and "Do you take drugs?" For over a decade, Backster administered these tests, monitoring applicants' reactions with a polygraph. Eventually he moved to New York City and founded the Backster School of Lie Detection. There he began training FBI agents and state police detectives the art of detecting deception. He quickly became an expert witness for law enforcement, testifying in courtrooms and before congressional committees. Colleagues liked to say that Cleve Backster could always spot a liar, but he saw the situation from a different point of view. "I like to think of the polygraph as a truth detector," he said.

Then, on the night of February 2, 1966, a single experience changed the direction of Backster's lifework. The way he told the story, he'd been up late working in his office on a hard-to-crack FBI case when his eyes landed on a new houseplant his secretary had recently purchased for the office. He wondered what would happen if he administered a polygraph to a plant? Are plants aware? Backster attached the polygraph's sensor pads to the plant's leaves, set the levels on the machine, sipped his coffee, and thought about what to ask the houseplant. Then he got an even better idea, he recalled. Why not try to elicit a more direct, potentially anxiety-producing effect? He decided to set the plant's leaves on fire and see whether the polygraph recorded a measurable change.

Something remarkable happened, he said. As he prepared to strike the match against the matchbox's ignition strip, the lie detector readings spiked dramatically. It was a eureka moment for him. Plants had consciousness, he was convinced. And even more interesting, he later explained, was his next realization: his experiment suggested that plants had extrasensory perception and could communicate with other life-forms. The plant perceived that it was going to be burned by Backster's lit match and reacted with a measurable change, he said. He wrote up his findings as "Evidence of a Primary Perception in Plant Life," which was published in the *International Journal of Parapsychology* in 1968. He called the results of his experiment the Backster Effect. His work would eventually become the subject of the bestselling book *The Secret Life of Plants,* by journalists Peter Tompkins, a former OSS officer, and Christopher O. Bird, a CIA operative.

Skeptics and scientists tore the Backster Effect to shreds, starting with the fact that plants lack a nervous system. Backster's methods were amateurish, naïve, and irresponsible, they said. Backster was not a scientist, and his experiment did not adhere to scientific method. As of 2017, no other scientist has been able to repeat the experiment under strict laboratory controls. But the idea of plant sentience inspired others to consider the possibility. Indeed, Charles Darwin, who studied plants all his life, once observed that the root tip, or radicle, "acts like the brain of one of the lower animals." Undeterred by his critics, Backster stood by his experiment. "Such high resistance to new ideas does not concern me," he said. "I have a truly wonderful ally: Mother Nature."

By the time Hal Puthoff wrote his letter to Backster, the former CIA polygrapher had broadened his experiments on plant sentience. In a follow-on experiment he cut a houseplant in two, then moved the halves into different rooms, where he burned the leaves to see whether distance affected the polygraph response. His conclusion, that a plant's ability to register fear and read minds was not limited by distance, was the experiment that caught Hal Puthoff's attention.

"I wanted to do a similar, long-distance experiment," remembers Puthoff. For over a year he had been tracking the work of international scientists who were on the tachyon hunt. "Physicists were doing all kinds of experiments in search of the tachyon," says Puthoff. "Cosmic ray experiments, accelerator experiments, but they were all apparatus-based, inanimate physics experiments. The one place no one had looked was in biological organisms, in animate physics." Which is how Cleve Backster fit in. "My idea was to grow an algae culture, split it, then separate the cultures by a distance of five miles. Then I'd zap one culture with a laser, burn it, see if the sister culture responded." Puthoff's experiment would attempt to answer two questions. "The first question was, Do living organisms really interact at a distance? If the answer was yes, then the second question was, Could the existence of tachyons provide the answer as to how the organisms communicate?"

Puthoff wrote Backster and included a copy of his proposed algae culture experiment. He wanted to know what Backster thought of his idea. The letter arrived at Backster's lab in March 1972. By then, Backster had moved on to a new series of extrasensory perception experiments involving humans and plants. His human research subject was an artist and a psychic named Douglas "Ingo" Swann.

Ingo Swann, by his own account, had been considered odd since the age of three. As a boy growing up in Telluride, Colorado, he was not just "doubly or triply" strange, he said of himself, "I was quadruply freaky." He experienced premonitions and saw the auras of people around him. When he closed his eyes and went into a dream state, he could leave his body and travel to other places, a situation understood and accepted by his maternal grandmother, who was also "sensitive." Swann's family encouraged him to study hard at school, develop his art, and channel his "spontaneous shifts in perception and awareness" into his work. In 1955, he graduated from Westminster College, in Salt Lake City, with a double major in biology and art. He had plans to become a scientist and to get a PhD in genetic research, but instead enlisted in the U.S. Army and served three years in Korea.

After he left the Army, in 1958, Swann moved to New York City determined to pursue a career in art. To pay the bills, for the next twelve years he worked as a clerk in the office of the United Nations Secretariat. But at night and on weekends he worked on his passion and his craft, and it was in the New York City art scene that he met a legendary woman, a painter, muralist, and high-society entertainer named Buell Mullen.

Mullen moved in a circle of the powerful. She had painted portraits of world leaders including President Eisenhower and Madame Chiang Kai-shek. "She loved to give large, sit-down dinner parties in her glamorous studio on Central Park South, its tall windows facing on Central Park," Swann wrote in an unpublished autobiography. "One of her favorite topics was psychic phenomena." Swann found this amazing, he said. "For the first time in my life, I was able to witness the actual but hidden extent of the demand for psychics among the wealthy, among politicians, Wall-street types, cultural gurus and even among the very powerful." Swann was even more surprised to learn that many of these individuals financed ESP experiments; Cleve Backster was one beneficiary. This was reminiscent of the way Alice Astor Bouverie, Marcella du Pont, and Joyce Borden Balokovic had financed Andrija Puharich's work two decades before.

At one of Buell Mullen's parties Ingo Swann met Cleve Backster. The two men hit it off. Swann asked Backster if he could come to his lab. "What I wanted to do was see plants responding to human thoughts," Swann later recalled. He was also at a turning point in his life, having recently left his day job at the UN to focus on his artwork. In order to support himself he'd taken a job as a guinea pig for psychic research. Most of the work came from the American Society for Psychical Research (ASPR), the oldest such organization in the United States, founded in 1885 by the philosopher and physician William James. Despite its fancy offices inside a beautiful brownstone at 5 West Seventy-third Street, behind the Dakota apartment building, Swann generally disliked working at the ASPR. In his opinion most of the PhDs in residence were small-minded and "snobbish," fueled by bureaucratic pettiness and self-righteous indignation about who was psychic and who was not.

At ASPR, Swann had been working with the director of research, Karlis Osis, the Latvian-born PhD who specialized in deathbed visions. This was the same Dr. Osis who'd participated in the U.S. Army's classified ESP tests with cats, starting in 1952, back when Osis worked as a researcher at J. B. Rhine's Parapsychology Laboratory at Duke University. Now, Osis was using Swann for a series of experiments purported to involve out-of-body experiences (OBEs), also known as traveling clairvoyance. The Osis-designed OBE experiment had Swann seated in a lounge chair inside an office at ASPR and wired up to a refrigerator-sized machine called a Beckman Dynograph, which recorded his physiological signals on magnetic tape. Across the room was a tray suspended from the ceiling. Osis's assistant, Janet Mitchell, would enter the room carrying a box with an object hidden inside. She'd ceremoniously climb a ladder and, out of view of Swann, place the box on the tray. When she was ready, she'd indicate to Swann that the experiment had begun.

"I was expected to practice floating up out-of-the-body to the ceiling and utilize my out-of-body 'eyes' to spy down on the targets hidden on the suspended trays," wrote Swann. "Take your time," Janet Mitchell would say. "Don't feel nervous because that raises your blood pressure and distorts the brainwave feed-outs," Swann recalled being told. Very quickly Swann said he could "see" what was hidden in the box. The problem, he said, was that he had great difficulty trying to articulate what he saw. Osis found this unacceptable and got mad. Swann's description of the items was inadequate, he said. Swann asked for a pen, and instead of trying to say what he saw, he drew what he saw. Osis and Mitchell were thrilled with the results—so thrilled, they said, they planned to repeat these experiments under tightly controlled laboratory conditions and submit the results to the Psychology Board of America for review.

Ingo Swann was fascinated by the tray test results, but for a different reason. "There [was] a myth or legend in psychical research and parapsychology that psi subjects [i.e., psychic people] need time to gather their wits and for their impressions to start coming in," he wrote, as if target identification required time. Throughout history there existed the conception of mediums rubbing their temples or gazing into a crystal ball, concentrating and waiting for the phenomenon of extrasensory perception to occur. "I was finding this anticipated slowness not true at all regarding the experiments at the ASPR," Swann noted in his journals. "I found, or eventually noticed at any rate, that the moment I set my attention onto the target—well, there it was.... Instantaneously," he wrote. "I first noticed this on the [earlier] informal, long-distance experiments. When Janet said she was ready to record the brainwaves, my attention went to the target [without any] delays. I then noticed this had also been true in the case of the OOB experiments as well, and with all of the other kinds of experiments, too."

The Osis experiments helped Swann identify something he'd not considered before. Psychic functioning occurred at light speed, metaphorically at least. Swann decided to call this concept the "speed or velocity of psi signals," or "instantaneous connection to the psi signals." He'd mentioned this idea to some of the PhDs at ASPR, and they'd dismissed it. After all, he was not a scientist and lacked a PhD, they said. "No one knew what I was talking about," said Swann. Except Cleve Backster, who told Swann that he'd recently received a copy of a research proposal from a physicist named Hal Puthoff, who was pursuing a related hypothesis at the Stanford Research Institute.

Swann wrote a letter to Hal Puthoff. "Swann said that if I were interested in investigating the boundary between the physics of the animate and inanimate, I should consider experiments of the parapsychological type," remembers Puthoff. Swann also referenced some apparently successful psychokinesis experiments he'd done in a laboratory at the City College of New York for Gertrude Schmeidler, the experimental psychologist and Harvard PhD who'd famously coined the parapsychological concepts of sheep and goats.

Puthoff wrote back, inviting Swann to come out to California and be tested in a lab at SRI. The experiments would take place inside a Faraday cage, under strict laboratory controls. For the first time in American history, Puthoff said, psychic functioning could be examined from a physicist's point of view, not from the perspective of a psychologist or parapsychologist. Swann said he'd think about it. Privately, he noted in his journal that he'd spoken way too soon. Puthoff's offer intimidated him.

The following month, on April 26, 1971, the American Society for Psychical Research held a large reception to honor "Ingo Swann, Dr. Karlis Osis, Ph.D., and Research on Out of the Body Experiences." The way the story was presented in the ASPR newsletter, an independent judge from the Psychology Board of America (allegedly blind to the fact that she was judging out-of-body experiments involving ESP), determined that Ingo Swann had correctly made and matched picture drawings of items hidden from view, and that this was a one hundred percent match, which was considered far above chance expectations. When a second judge asked for a retest, Swann allegedly again scored a one hundred percent match. The test results were going to be the lead story in the *Journal of the American Society for Psychical Research*, and the evening's grand reception was honoring this milestone.

"Reception for Ingo Swann: Expanded Awareness in Art," the sign outside the venue read. "Mr. Swann has been participating extensively in ASPR experimentation on out-of-body states." The gathering promised to provide guests with an opportunity to see Ingo Swann's artwork and meet the man with the X-ray eyes. Score of reporters were invited, and gossip columnists, too. Ingo Swann had mixed feelings about all this, he said. He was naturally shy and prone to feeling self-conscious in crowds. In his journals he lamented that he'd recently put on a lot of weight. "By now I was so fat, fat, fat, I couldn't fit into any nice United Nations suits, of which I had an even dozen," he wrote. "During the week before the reception I had drank only liquid protein in an effort to reduce. While dressing, I felt I was getting ready to volunteer for the guillotine." Then, "what the hell," he thought, "while slowly and reluctantly squeezing into my clothes, I smoked ten cigars and drank five vodka and sodas. And so I arrived at the dreaded reception a half-hour late."

It was 1972, and out-of-body experiments were in vogue. A huge crowd of people showed up for the event, and in local newspapers the following morning, Swann was hailed as New York City's "super psychic" and "the Superman of psi." But there are at least two sides to every story, as Ingo Swann soon found out. "I learned that I was, among other things, a drunkard; a debaucher; an alcoholic; a homosexual. I wasn't married, and so, it was said, I 'must be' [gay]." One gossip columnist noted that Swann was writing sex novels and speculated that maybe he was a pornographer. When it leaked that he and Cleve Backster were doing psi experiments with "biologicals," the rumors took a salacious turn. "The gossip line exploded regarding how and from whom [Backster] got his specimens, and under what circumstances," lamented Swann.

The disparaging press devastated Swann, but it also compelled him into action. He would go to Stanford Research Institute and be tested by a real physicist, he decided. Forget New York City with its double standards and its gossips. Either his extrasensory abilities were real or they were not. At SRI, he would be tested scientifically and the reality of psychic functioning would be vindicated, or he would fail and psychics would remain on the fringes of society where they'd always lived. If extrasensory perception was proven to be a figment of the imagination, chance, or a host of other disparaging things people had been saying for centuries, so be it. Swann decided he'd take a risk. What else, really, did he have to lose? He would accept Hal Puthoff's invitation after all. The only problem was, he lamented in his journal, he was fat and had no clothes. Why not shed that old idea, too? Swann decided to undergo a welcome shift in attitude and perception about his own physical body, about himself.

"After the reception at the ASPR, I began receiving invitations to dinners and parties by the score, often from people I didn't even know. I suppose everyone wanted to see what this odd mixture of gossip looked like. I became mildly amused by watching people try to fit me into their usually limited stereotype concepts—and took a small revenge by doing everything I could not to fit into any of them." Like a snake shedding its skin, a new Swann emerged. And since he could not fit into any of his conservative clothes, "I bought new ones at used clothing stores, and wore them boldly everywhere I went. But these tended to be religious, police or military clothes of one type or another. I mixed these with ordinary clothes, and went to the dinners and parties wearing them. I was expected to be abnormal, and so it was a pleasure to present myself as such."

It was liberating to Swann. He felt free of the bondage of this old idea that it mattered so much what people thought of him. "Prior to this," he explained, "I had tried very hard to not be considered an oddity. Now that changed. I said to myself, 'To hell with not trying to be an oddity, let me just experience being my true self for a while.' " And so he started appearing in public dressed in various new ways, adding what he called "discrete costume elements" to his daily attire.

In June 1972, Swann boarded a plane for California, ready and willing to be tested by a physicist at SRI. When he arrived at the San Francisco airport he was dressed all in white: white cowboy boots, white pants, and some kind of white religious frock. The ironic part was that Hal Puthoff barely noticed, and if he did, he did not bat an eye. The Stanford Research Institute was located thirty minutes south of San Francisco, which in 1972 was the hippie capital of the world.

Hal Puthoff's physicist colleagues at SRI warned him not to get involved with psychics. Anyone who claimed to have extrasensory powers was a charlatan or unstable or both, they said. Puthoff took note but remained undeterred. He decided to design a fail-safe psychokinesis experiment, he recalls, one in which there was no room for fraud. "I was able to gain access to one of the best-shielded devices on the planet, a superconducting-shielded magnetometer used for looking at subatomic particles known as quarks," he said. "In 1972, the quark was hypothesized to be a subnuclear constituent of nuclear particles such as protons but not yet isolated outside of a nucleus, and the search was on." The quark detector Puthoff borrowed for the Swann psychokinesis experiment was a highly sensitive machine designed to look at decay in a magnetic field. Puthoff's colleague Dr. Arthur Hebard, of the Stanford High Energy Physics Laboratory, had access to a magnetometer for quark experiments, and Puthoff made arrangements with Hebard to borrow it. In documents declassified by the CIA, the magnetometer had been developed under an Office of Naval Research contract and "is of the superconducting quantum interference device (SQUID) variety." It was now located "in a well [basement] under a building" called the Varian Physics Hall.

The SRI campus was located at the southernmost tip of San Francisco Bay, on the edge of a tree-filled park called Ravenswood. SRI was home to many government-funded programs at the cutting edge of the U.S. military and intelligence community's science and technology effort. One of the first nodes on the ARPANET, SRI had a cybernetics department and an artificial intelligence division. Its researchers had recently made history when they became the first in the world to wire a man's brain directly into a computer. For more than fifty years SRI had been part of nearby Stanford University, but in 1970 the school's trustees were forced to sever ties with SRI after student protesters exposed the fact that the institute's majority funding came from the Department of Defense, which rendered it a partner in weapons development during the Vietnam War. As Hal Puthoff and Ingo Swann walked across the Stanford campus, Swann noticed that many windows had been boarded up and others were covered with metal grates.

At Varian Physics Hall, Puthoff and Swann made their way into the basement where the magnetometer was located, down a set of stairs, through a long gray corridor, and into a room marked by bright-orange earthquake-engineering supports. The ceilings were traversed by pipes, vents, and conduits, and had an industrial, research lab feel, Swann recalled. Puthoff introduced him to Arthur Hebard, Martin Lee, and six doctoral candidates, all of whom had come to Varian Hall to bear witness to this test. The men shook hands. Swann felt conspicuous under the glare.

In one corner a chart recorder scribbled away, its pen moving methodically across a scroll of paper. Unperturbed, the magnetometer registered what is generally referred to as a straight line but what is technically called an oscillating wavy line. On the walk over to Varian Hall, Puthoff had told Swann what to expect. He was going to be asked to perturb the magnetometer in a psychokinesis experiment similar to those he'd done with Cleve Backster and Gertrude Schmeidler. Now, scanning the room, Swann realized the magnetometer was nowhere to be seen. He asked Puthoff if he could take a look at it before he tried to perturb it with his mind.

"You're standing on top of it," Puthoff said. The machine was five feet below where they were standing, someone volunteered, buried in concrete.

According to documents declassified by the CIA in 2000, one of the scientists explained how the quark detector worked and indicated that the function that looked for quarks was turned off. He pointed to the chart recorder and said the magnetometer had been running for an hour now with no noise, or perturbation, hence the recorder's uninterrupted oscillating wavy line. Swann asked what this machine looked like, so he could at least visualize it. Another scientist said that the design of the device had never been made public, which made it impossible for anyone to have preexisting knowledge of what it actually looked like. The only thing ever written about this magnetometer was that it contained what was called a Josephson junction—two layers of superconducting material sandwiching a thin layer of non-superconducting material. (The configuration was named for the British theoretical physicist Brian D. Josephson, who won the Nobel Prize in Physics in 1973 and became a vocal proponent of extrasensory perception.)

"The horrible implications of all this dawned on me without much difficulty," Swann later recalled. "I was being asked to 'poke around' with a 'target' I could not see, or even know exactly where it was in the ground beneath." Swann surveyed his surroundings. From his perspective, all nine witnesses were smirking at him. "He became angry," Hal Puthoff recalls, "his wrath focused on me." On the walk over, Puthoff and Swann discussed the desirability of a subject being completely informed regarding the experiment he or she was to undertake. Swann now feared he'd been set up to fail and to be ridiculed.

"How the fuck am I supposed to influence something I can't see?" Swann yelled a little too loudly for the staid environment.

Puthoff tried to assuage his fears. "You wanted an experiment with no loopholes in it," he reminded Swann. "Well, here it is." This was a test in which it would be impossible to cheat. If Swann were to affect the magnetic field in the magnetometer, it would register on the chart recorder. Since it was impossible for Swann or anyone else to touch or access the magnetometer, presumably the only way for Swann to affect it would be through what is generally referred to as psychokinesis.

"I was angry but not stupid," Swann recalled, taking stock of his options. If he walked out there would be nine witnesses to his retreat. He'd already been humiliated by the New York City press; he knew how that felt. And if he walked out he'd never know whether he would have succeeded or failed at this scientific test. "So, as in Cleve Backster's lab," Swann wrote, "I started probing—whatever that means."

For a few minutes he concentrated with all his mental might. Nothing registered on the chart recorder, Puthoff recalls. Zero. Nil. Swann looked up. Two of the doctoral candidates seemed to be smirking. Swann asked for a piece of paper. He said he wanted to sketch a drawing to help him focus on what he was being asked to perturb. No one had any paper, so Puthoff tore a piece of used chart recorder printout from a pile on the floor. Swann began to sketch the magnetometer as he saw it in his mind's eye. After a minute, he pointed to his drawing and asked, "Is this the Josephson junction? If so, I think I can see it quite well."

As he spoke, the pen on the chart recorder gave a small jerk. "All eyes went to the machine," Puthoff recalls. For a brief second, the recording pen stopped. Then it began "lifting up again," this time high above its previously uninterrupted oscillating wavy line. For roughly ten seconds the pen registered two wide wavy lines.

"Jesus Christ," Swann heard someone mumble.

"Is that an effect?" Swann asked, pointing to the wavy lines.

Puthoff and Dr. Lee began whispering. From Swann's perspective, Dr. Hebard looked pale.

"Can you do that again?" Puthoff asked.

Swann said he would try. He concentrated. The pen moved again. Puthoff shook his head. "I thought, *I'll be damned,*" Puthoff later recalled.

Puthoff walked over to the recorder and pulled off the paper. All the scientists had been standing near Swann. None had touched the chart recording equipment, and yet something in the magnetometer had been perturbed. This left Puthoff with only one conclusion, he would later write, and that was that Ingo Swann had perturbed the superconducting-shielded magnetometer by some means "outside the range of well-understood interactions [between] human subjects and the environment." Puthoff asked Drs. Lee and Hebard to sign the chart paper as witnesses to what they had observed. The two physicists signed. Swann remembered a commotion in the room and watched as one of the doctoral students suddenly ran out as if spooked, in such a hurry he hit his head against an orange structural support on the way out.

What had just occurred defied scientific principles as they were then understood. Not one but two mysterious phenomena had occurred, according to Puthoff: "the passive perception of information through some as yet unidentified communication channel" and "the active perturbation of the functioning of a laboratory device."

That night, Hal Puthoff, his fiancé Adrienne Kennedy, and Ingo Swann went out for ice cream to celebrate. Swann recalls having a chocolate milkshake, then a strawberry milkshake, and finally a sundae with five flavors of ice cream. After eating, they returned to the Varian Physics Hall basement lab. Dr. Hebard had left the quark detector running, to make sure it was not malfunctioning. Several hours had passed since the detector registered the effects of the psychokinesis experiment, and since its cessation there had been no perturbations in the chart recorder's signal—just a thin, uninterrupted oscillating wavy line.

It was time for Swann to return to New York City. Driving to the airport, Puthoff asked if he would consider returning for a second series of tests. "No way, José," Swann replied. He felt confident that the results of the magnetometer experiment would make their way through the American Society for Psychical Research community and he could at last feel a modicum of revenge. "I could rest on my laurels," wrote Swann. "I felt great." As for California, he had no intention of returning. He did not feel part of the SRI scene, he recalled, and the sunshine there was way too bright.

Puthoff wrote up his findings and sent his report to various colleagues at SRI and on the East Coast. Weeks passed. One afternoon he was sitting in his office when there was a knock on the door. "I wasn't expecting anyone," he recalls. When he opened the door, he was surprised to find two men standing in the threshold, "a copy of my magnetometer experiment report" in hand.

"Their credentials showed them to be from the CIA," he recalled. "They knew of my previous background as a Naval Intelligence officer and then civilian employee at the National Security Agency several years earlier, and they felt they could discuss their concerns with me openly." Puthoff invited them into his office and closed the door. "There was, they told me, increasing concern in the intelligence community about the level of effort in Soviet parapsychology being funded by the Soviet security services." They said that by the standards of most Western scientists, the field of parapsychology was considered nonsense, but the CIA wanted this subject investigated from a hard-science perspective.

"As a result," Puthoff explains, the CIA "had been on the lookout for a research laboratory outside of academia that could handle a quiet, low-profile classified investigation, and SRI appeared to fit the bill." The CIA men asked Puthoff if he could arrange to carry out a series of additional ESP experiments with Ingo Swann, simple ones, sometime in the next few months. "If the test proved satisfactory," they asked Puthoff, "would [he] consider a pilot program along these lines?" Puthoff said he was open to this idea.

In August, ignoring his previous vow, Ingo Swann returned to SRI. So did the two CIA intelligence analysts, identified to Swann as "scientific colleagues from the East Coast." With Swann in a shielded room, a Faraday cage, the team conducted a series of what's-in-the-box tests in which small office supplies were hidden inside a box, then set in front of Swann, who was asked to identify what was hidden inside. During a lunch break one of the CIA analysts decided to disrupt protocol. The objects concealed in boxes that had been secured with a seal had been chosen in advance of the test, meaning that if fraud was being perpetrated, here was an opportunity for Puthoff or someone else at SRI to help Swann cheat. One of the CIA officers decided to create a spontaneous, fraud-proof test. He walked outside into the SRI garden and located a small brown moth. He captured the moth alive, placed it inside a box, then closed and sealed the lid. He took the sealed box into the room where Swann had been waiting.

"Can you tell us what's inside?" the CIA officer asked.

Swann stared at the box. According to transcripts declassified by the CIA, Swann said, "I see something small, brown, and irregular, sort of like a leaf or something that resembles it." Swann paused, then said, "Except that it seems very much alive, like it's even moving." The analyst opened the box. Clinging to the lid was the small brown moth.

Two weeks later, on October 1, 1972, the CIA awarded SRI a contract for $49,909 for an eight-month research project. The program, classified secret, was given an obscure name to conceal its purpose. It was called the Biofield Measurements Program. Puthoff's colleague Russell Targ, a fellow laser physicist with a longtime interest in parapsychology, was brought on board to assist.

What Hal Puthoff did not yet know was that arrangements were being made to bring Uri Geller to SRI, too, and to have Geller tested on behalf of the CIA. The results, called the Swann–Geller phenomena, would set the stage for more than twenty years of classified government research into extrasensory perception, psychokinesis, and extraordinary human functioning.

CHAPTER NINE

Skeptics versus CIA

In anticipation of its program involving psychics at SRI, the Central Intelligence Agency sought to establish ground rules and decorum. The world of "purported paranormal phenomena" was incendiary territory, a declassified CIA memo makes clear—a strange domain that science could not explain and that most Agency personnel were loath to condone. "We are <u>not</u> in the business of pursuing paranormal phenomena <u>per se</u> but we try not to be arrogant about it—which is what a lack of objectivity about <u>any</u> issue usually amount [*sic*] to."

After the euphemistically titled Biofield Measurements Program was approved and funded, representatives from the CIA's Technical Services Division and its Office of Research and Development put together an "informal preliminary conference intended to establish the proper context for a proposed investigation into various purported paranormal phenomena." Those invited were told that "we wish to keep the conference low-key and limit the attendance as well as general awareness of the conference and the proposed investigations." The SRI tests were to be a closely held secret even within an agency of entirely classified operations.

"Ground rules for the conference" were laid down. "We do not feel that it makes any difference whether, at this stage, you are a 'believer' or 'non-believer,' or somewhere in between," the memo stated. "In the spirit of scientific detachment we merely seek your counsel in an approach to a problem which has eluded definitive resolution for eons—and of course may continue to do so." The CIA had no expectations that its psychic research program at SRI would solve the age-old mystery of ESP and PK overnight, but it was not afraid of trying. Decorum would be paramount for success. "There will be no rehashing of anecdotal accounts...there will be no idle, discursive speculation about the dynamics or meaning of the phenomena—that is what we hope, eventually, to establish. We merely ask that you come with an open mind and prepared to address yourself generally to [pertinent] questions." By establishing an impartial, value-free approach the CIA was trying to set a high bar for success. "If the phenomena are verified...what practical (offensive or defensive) applications might you envision for your component [at CIA]"? the conference organizers asked.

One of those in attendance was Christopher "Kit" Green, an analyst in the Life Sciences Division. Before joining the Agency, Green had considered becoming an Episcopal priest but decided against it after two weeks in seminary. Instead he earned a PhD in neurophysiology and later became a medical doctor. At CIA, Kit Green wore many hats. Some of his time was spent creating top-secret evaluations of the health and mental stability of foreign leaders. In another capacity he worked on biological and chemical threat analysis as part of an Agency effort to determine how weaponized toxins affect certain regions of the human brain. "My specialty was forensic medicine," says Green, "a rare area of scientific expertise used in determining what might have made a person ill, or caused their death, based on very little and often incomplete data." In other words, if a CIA agent died under suspicious circumstances, Green was called in to conduct forensic analysis of the body. For this work he was eventually awarded the National Intelligence Medal, the CIA's highest honor.

"I was interested in individuals who operate at the outer limits of human behavior," Green explains. He studied human performance in extraordinary circumstances, including the physiology of astronauts and submariners. It was also Green's job to understand the cutting-edge space- and submarine-based life support systems of foreign governments. He attended international conferences on religion, mysticism, and the paranormal in order to analyze emerging trends before they became full-fledged movements. "Some say I ran the weird desk," he says.

Green had been with the CIA since 1969, and in 1972 he was assigned to the psychic research program. One part of his job was to oversee the administration of medical tests on the psychics at SRI. This included everything from blood tests to brain scans to tests for personality disorders. With the invention of the CT (computerized tomography) scan in 1972, brain imaging offered exciting new opportunities in neuroscience. From the perspective of an analyst this was exciting territory, says Green. "We wanted to try and determine if individuals with extraordinary abilities had brain scans that were different from their fellow man."

With the imminent arrival of Uri Geller in November 1972, CIA anticipation was high and secrecy was paramount. Kit Green had been personally handling the Geller matter since he was assigned the job by CIA director Richard Helms. Declassified memos reveal two focused concerns during this time. One was Geller's celebrity, and the other was the presence of Andrija Puharich, who had by now taken on a Svengali-like role as Geller's official manager. Given Puharich's notorious background, the CIA needed to keep him at arm's length from any Agency affiliation. This issue was temporarily solved by using Edgar Mitchell's newly formed Mind Science Institute of Los Angeles (later the Institute of Noetic Sciences) as a conduit for payments to Puharich and Geller. But the problem of Geller's celebrity was not such an easy fix. In the months since Puharich first presented his research proposal to CIA, Geller had become an international phenomenon. Wherever he went, the press followed along. He was young, handsome, single, and spoke perfect English with a slight Israeli accent. From Barbara Walters to Brigitte Bardot, fans around the world could not seem to get enough of Uri Geller as he bent spoons, read minds, and performed simple telepathy acts.

In the months leading up to Geller's arrival in the United States he'd been traveling around Germany with journalists from *Bild-Zeitung.* As part of a six-part series on Geller, the newspaper printed fantastical stories about his alleged paranormal powers: Geller reportedly stopping a cable car on Mount Hochfelln in Bavaria; bending handcuffs at a Stuttgart police station; halting an escalator in a Munich shopping mall. In a matter of months, Geller amassed a legion of dedicated fans—but also an army of foes. The intense public interest followed him to America.

Puharich made matters difficult for the CIA by constantly involving the press. Geller's first meeting in America was with Wernher von Braun, former chief scientist of the Apollo Moon program, and Puharich made sure that a reporter was invited along. During the meeting, Geller asked von Braun to take off his gold wedding band and hold it inside his closed palm. "I put my hand over his, and in my mind said, 'Bend,'" Geller recalled in an interview in 2016. According to one news story, when von Braun opened his palm and examined his ring, he saw that it had been bent into an oval shape. "Uri Geller has bent my ring in the palm of my hand without ever touching it," von Braun told the reporter. "Personally, I have no scientific explanation for it."

There was a second incident with von Braun that commanded

the attention of the Pentagon. After Geller bent the ring, von Braun told Geller he had an electronic pocket calculator that wasn't working. The batteries had been charged but there was no power; the calculator simply wouldn't turn on. In von Braun's estimation something had gone wrong with the electronic circuitry, and he wondered whether Geller could influence the electrical system. Geller held the machine in his hands and concentrated. Several witnesses in von Braun's office confirmed the rocket scientist's declaration that the electronic panel inexplicably lit up. When analysts at the Pentagon learned of the incident, they ordered a briefing. Part of this briefing has been declassified and is quoted in a report entitled "Paranormal Phenomena— Briefing on a Net Assessment Study."

"It would not be conceptually difficult, for example, to imagine the utility of psychokinesis (if feasible) in disrupting the electrical systems associated with an ICBM's guidance program" as displayed by Uri Geller, they wrote. "There remains a serious need for detailed analytical studies of some of these phenomena by specialists in various scientific disciplines." There was a great challenge facing anyone working on this kind of study, the analysts warned. The subject matter "tends to be polarized into uncritical acceptance or total rejection" of fact. For as long as the research field was polarized into this kind of childish battle between "true believers" and "the incredulous [who] dismiss the matter out of hand," little progress was likely to be made.

At SRI, Hal Puthoff and Russell Targ hoped they would be the scientists to break this stalemate. By the time Geller arrived in Menlo Park with his entourage (which included Andrija Puharich, Edgar Mitchell, and Geller's assistant and friend Shipi Shtrang), "security had become an issue," remembers Kit Green. Geller was a foreign national, and in November 1972, Arab-Israeli tensions were escalating. Because of concerns that Geller's trip to America could be an Israeli intelligence operation, a security sweep of the SRI engineering laboratory was made in advance of Geller's arrival. "The ceiling panels, walls and furniture were all checked for electronic bugs," remembers Puthoff. Finally, with the distractions out of the way, the scientists began testing Geller in the lab.

Between December 1, 1972, and January 15, 1973, Puthoff and Targ completed nine days of official tests with Uri Geller. The experiments were recorded on film, videotape, and audiotape simultaneously. According to the scientists, Geller's tests with dice were among the most statistically significant. In these tests, he sat sequestered in a room with Puthoff and Targ while an SRI researcher in a separate room placed a single square die inside a closed metal box. The sealed box was brought into Geller's room, then shaken by a technician, and placed on the table in front of Geller. "Mr. Geller would then look at the box without touching it and call out which die face he believed was uppermost," states the declassified CIA Progress Report. "Geller gave the correct answer each of the 8 times the experiment was performed. The probability that this could have occurred by chance alone is approximately one in a million," the scientists informed the CIA.

A second experiment delivered even more extraordinary results, according to another declassified CIA report. This test was run by a CIA representative working inside an electronically shielded room. The representative lined up in a row ten identical aluminum film canisters with stainless-steel tops, then placed an object in some of the cans, leaving others empty. The objects were a steel ball bearing, a small magnet, and several droppers of water. Geller was brought into the room and scanned with a magnetometer. His hands, mouth, and ears were photographed and checked for electronic and magnetic devices. Once he was seated in front of a clear glass table, with cameras recording his hands from two different angles, each test began. "He would either pass his hand over the row of cans or simply look at them. He would then call out the cans he felt confident were empty," according to the report. When Geller identified what he sensed was an empty can, he would ask the CIA representative to remove it from the table. "When only two or three cans remained, Geller would announce which one he thought contained the [individual] target object[s]. He had no difficulty identifying the location of water, steel ball bearings or small magnets," according to the CIA report. "This task was performed twelve times, without error. The probability that this could have occurred by chance alone is about one in a trillion."

In another filmed test, the CIA had its first opportunity to witness Geller perform psychokinesis in a controlled laboratory environment. The test involved a delicate laboratory balance (i.e., a scale) designed to measure weights ranging from one milligram to fifty grams. A one-gram mass was placed on the pan, and the balance was then covered with a bell jar. A chart monitor continuously recorded the force applied to the balance, producing a paper record of the events. Geller was brought into the room, checked for magnets and electronic devices, and asked to try to perturb the balance. In archival film footage declassified by the CIA, Geller is seen waving his hands several inches above the balance, then clutching his hands into fists and raising them to his temples in what would become his signature theatrical style. "On several occasions the subject caused the balance to respond as though a force were applied to the pan," Puthoff and Targ wrote in the CIA report. "This was evidenced by a corresponding displacement shown by the chart recorder. These displacements increased from 50–1500 milligrams." The scientists' conclusion: "The experiment indicated an apparent ability of Geller to affect the apparatus by an as yet unidentified means."

The notion that Geller was being tested at SRI made its way into the upper echelons of the Pentagon. So did a declaration by Puthoff and Targ that they used only strict laboratory controls.

"Because of the history of charlatanism in this area," the scientists wrote in their CIA report, "our efforts to detect fraud were quite sophisticated, including the use of a consultant magician on our part." This claim caught the attention of Colonel Austin Kibler, director of the Human Resources Research Office at the Advanced Research Projects Agency (ARPA), the Pentagon's top military science division. "If [Geller] can do what he claims he can do, we should be involved," Kibler said, and requested to have Geller tested by his own people.

An ARPA project manager named George Lawrence, accompanied by two civilian psychologists, Robert Van de Castle and Ray Hyman, traveled to SRI to test Geller on their own. Their conclusion, later reported in *Time* magazine, was that anyone who believed in Geller's powers was falling for the "ridiculous."

The CIA asked to attend ARPA's briefing on its assessment of the SRI psychic research program. According to declassified documents, the ARPA group expressed "concern that Puthoff's and Targ's own experimental bias in favor of successful outcomes is undermining their objectivity in properly controlled experimental procedures." They opined that Puthoff and Targ were guilty of the same three claims Martin Gardner had leveled against J. B. Rhine's research decades before: 1) loose laboratory controls; 2) skewing of data; and 3) the premise that the attitude of the scientists conducting the experiment (i.e., Lawrence and Hyman) could negatively influence the subject or psychic (i.e., Geller). "Austin Kibler and George Lawrence [believe] there is serious doubt that Geller's accomplishment transcends the range of activities that a skillful magician can perform," they said.

The CIA's analyst came to an alternative conclusion as far as Geller was concerned. "It strikes me that what is of interest to CIA is not whether Geller's perceptions are sensory or extrasensory but rather whether his capabilities are exploitable by CIA." When the ARPA team learned that the CIA was continuing its work with Geller, they contacted a senior editor at *Time* magazine named Leon Jaroff.

ARPA's George Lawrence told Jaroff that "Geller was a charlatan," and encouraged the magazine to write an exposé of him. For Lawrence, a Defense Department employee, to speak with a reporter without authorization was a violation of his security clearance. At CIA, an investigation ensued. "Jareff [*sic*] says the source of the [information] was Dr. George Lawrence of ARPA. Lawrence, on the other hand, denies having talked to TIME. Jareff says this is nonsense, Lawrence has talked to TIME lots of times," declassified documents reveal. The prediction by the Pentagon was coming true: as long as the ESP research field remained polarized in a childish battle between "true believers" and "the incredulous [who] dismiss the matter out of hand"—Schmeidler's sheep versus goats—little progress was likely to be made.

But the battle was only beginning. Ray Hyman, the psychologist contracted by ARPA, and Martin Gardner, author of *Fads and Fallacies,* joined forces in an anti–Geller crusade. Gardner told *Time* that Geller's supporters reminded him of the supporters of Nazism. "Belief in occultism provides a climate for the rise of a demagogue," he said. "I think this is precisely what happened in Nazi Germany before the rise of Hitler." A reporter at *Time,* Stefan Kanfer, targeted SRI for blame. "SRI should be destroyed" for carrying out this kind of research, Kanfer said. "That's the way fascism began."

A popular magician and Houdini impersonator named James Randall Zwinge, who went by the name James Randi, made things personal. "Geller brings disgrace to the craft I practice," he declared. "Worse than that, he warps the thinking of a young generation of forming minds. And that is unforgivable." Randi spent the next two years writing his own 308-page exposé of Geller. One of the things he found most offensive about Geller, he wrote, was that he felt Geller had single-handedly ruined the careers of respectable scientists like Andrija Puharich. "Just how did a man of the learning and intelligence of Andrija Puharich ever get sucked into the Geller following?" Randi asked in all seriousness, insisting that Geller had "done more to destroy what authority Puharich once held in the scientific community" than Puharich would be able to recover from.

In the midst of this chaotic time, Kit Green received a telephone call at his CIA office. It was Hal Puthoff on the line. The men discussed the growing controversy around Uri Geller and SRI. Puthoff told Green he remained convinced Geller had ESP and PK capabilities. "He can see things at a distance," Puthoff said.

Green remembers saying something like, "No, he can't."

Puthoff asked Green to speak to Geller directly. "He's right here," Puthoff said. Geller and Green had never spoken before. Puthoff introduced Green to Geller as "a scientific colleague on the East Coast" and explained that his colleague was curious about Geller's ability to see things far away. Puthoff suggested they do a test.

Geller asked Green to select a book, any book in his office, and leave it open in front of him on his desk. Geller requested that the page exposed be something with a strong visual component. When this call came in, Green had been working on a classified study dealing with the neurological effects of a certain Soviet bioweapon on the human brain. Green opened a book that contained medical illustrations of the human nervous system, flipped through the pages, and landed on a picture of a cross-section of the human brain. "I'd written 'Architecture of a viral infection' in bold, black ink across the top of the page," he explains. As requested, Green stared at the image with intent. He told Geller when he had done so.

Inside the lab at SRI, with Hal Puthoff sitting beside him, Geller began making sketches on a sheet of paper. After a few moments, Green recalls Geller telling him that he'd made a drawing of a pan of scrambled eggs. "Then he said, 'I have the word "architecture" coming in strong,'" remembers Green. In 2015, Puthoff recalled his similar account.

"I was baffled," says Green. "How could Geller have 'seen' what I was working on?" It was implausible that SRI could have covert visual access to his CIA office, where he worked on highly classified intelligence programs. This was late 1972, decades before real-time video technologies like Skype and FaceTime were available to civilians. Still, it bothered Green that Puthoff had initiated the call. "When the time came," says Green, "I would initiate my own test, and make it fail-safe" against fraud.

In the meantime, Green supported Puthoff and Targ in their conclusion as physicists, in what the CIA called in memos the Swann-Geller phenomenon. "We have observed certain phenomena for which we have no scientific explanation," wrote Puthoff and Targ. Officers at headquarters had their say. "The paranormal field is so delicate, so suspect, so potentially explosive that only the most orderly of plebeian approaches seems likely to survive the bureaucratic atmosphere," one Agency representative wrote. "Let me state simply that I, at the present time, neither believe nor disbelieve in the phenomena—although I must frankly admit that, like many others, I find myself essentially disposed (philosophically/emotionally) in favor of the proposition that what we have so far learned about the nature of man and his environment compares poorly (qualitatively at least) with what we have yet to learn. Probabilistically, then, I find it easier to believe that there might be phenomena in this general area which we do not understand, than there are not."

Ultimately, the decision about the program's future was to be made by CIA director Richard Helms. After reviewing the reports and listening to briefings, Helms decided that there was value in the CIA's psychic research program. Not only would the SRI contract continue, Helms wrote, but it would expand. Officially, the program remained the Biofield Measurements Program, but in internal memos for Helms, analysts called it the Paranormal Perception Research Project. In a memo approved by Helms, the program was to be divided into four objectives. Fifty percent of the effort was to be directed toward determining "opportunities for operational use of 'gifted' individuals" like Geller and Swann; twenty percent was to be spent determining the characteristics that could help identify other people like those two; twenty percent was to be directed toward "investigation of the neurophysiological correlates of paranormal experiments" (i.e., Kit Green's job); and ten percent was to be directed toward validating the experiments themselves.

Acceptance of the notion that certain people were "gifted" with psychic powers was reiterated time and again in the declassified CIA memos from this period. As to the mysterious energy force powering these abilities, a parallel effort was also proposed. This proposition involved "elucidating the fundamental nature of the paranormal perception phenomena." Until then, Helms expressed the Agency's "established confidence" in the abilities of the principal investigators, Hal Puthoff and Russell Targ.

Shortly before Christmas 1972, Ingo Swann arrived at SRI to begin his eight-month contract, overlapping briefly with Uri Geller. Despite rumors of a rivalry between them, Geller and Swann liked each other tremendously. "Uri simply adored the ambrosia of the public stage," wrote Swann. And Swann, self-conscious as he was, appreciated the fact that Geller briefly stole the limelight. "His extraordinary luminosity attracted all of the negative attention that might have otherwise focused on me," he recalled. "He was a horse of strange color. No one knew what to do, or say, or think," around him.

To Swann, Geller had immeasurable talents, not just as a psychic but as what he called "the ultimate deconstructor of status quo." Geller defied stereotype, Swann said. Already he was mythic in stature, although Swann saw him as just like every other human: vulnerable and afraid. "On the exterior he appeared unfazed by the harassment. Almost bullet proof," wrote Swann, who watched from a distance as the skeptical community's contempt for Geller grew. "There was a collision between Geller and society, scientific and otherwise...and the collision was clearly won by Uri," Swann believed. "Psychic research was fully back on the map, not just in the U.S. but around the world."

Then a strange thing happened, one of those occurrences that in retrospect could be interpreted as a little too opportune to be written off as mere coincidence. One evening a few days before Christmas, Swann and Hal Puthoff took a drive over to the suburb of Mountain View, ten miles south of SRI. It was time to buy a Christmas tree for the SRI office. There, in a parking lot, they got into a conversation with a man in his late fifties who was selling evergreen trees.

"I'm Pat Price," the man said, extending his hand. He was short, midfifties, with a grizzled face and a spry smile. He told Puthoff that he recognized him from a convention in Los Angeles the year before. He also said he read the local papers, so he knew about the experiments going on at SRI. Puthoff and Swann smiled politely and did not say much more.

"If you ever need any help," Price said, "I can handle anything."

"It was a strange thing to say," Puthoff recalls. It would get even stranger. That Price met Puthoff and Swann at a Christmas tree lot sounds like something out of a folktale. But Pat Price would soon become a towering figure in the CIA's psychic research program, the central figure in a fascinating story about extraordinary anomalous abilities that has never been matched.

CHAPTER TEN

Remote Viewing

I n an effort to meet the CIA's objective and locate "opportunities for operational use," Puthoff and Targ worked to demonstrate a form of long-distance mental telepathy previously
known as traveling clairvoyance. Ingo Swann had already demonstrated success in this area, the scientists believed, during the
ceiling-tray tests with Karlis Osis at the American Society for
Psychical Research in New York. Swann called his process remote
viewing. Puthoff and Targ liked the term: it had a scientific feel
that they hoped would help distance it from occult associations.
In an attempt to establish an official procedure, they developed a
protocol called the outbounder-beacon experiment.

The way it worked was that two scientists or researchers,
called the outbounder team, would begin their day at SRI. They'd
randomly choose an envelope from a group of sealed envelopes
kept in a safe. The team would leave the office and, once inside
their vehicle, open the sealed envelope, which contained a photograph of a nearby landmark with an address written below.

Targets included the courtyard of the Stanford Museum, the exterior of Palo Alto City Hall, and the local public tennis courts. The outbounder team would then drive to the target site and wait there until a predetermined time, at which point one of them would survey the site with intent, mentally recording the target. At this same time Swann, who was back at SRI sitting inside a Faraday cage, would sketch what he perceived the out-bounder was seeing and sending to him telepathically. The theory was that the outbounder would act like a beacon for the psychic in the Faraday cage. In addition to Swann, SRI hired several other "gifted" people to participate in these tests—local individuals identified as being psychic who were read onto the classified program.

Puthoff and Targ were excited by the results, so much so that they made plans to publish their work in a national science journal (scrubbed of any CIA affiliation) and to perhaps even write a book about remote viewing. Swann was underwhelmed. "These ESP experiments are a trivialization of my abilities," he said, complaining that the experiments felt like grown-ups playing childish spy games. He was not supposed to know SRI's client was the CIA, but he later said he knew intuitively that this was most likely the case. And because of this, Swann accurately surmised that in the real world of espionage, the outbounder-beacon approach was implausible. If an intelligence agency could get a spy to a physical location, what would it need a remote viewer for? Real CIA targets, Swann figured, would involve classified military facilities deep inside the Soviet Union. The inaccessibility of these targets was the problem, he told Puthoff and Targ, and their team should be working on a way to address this real-world challenge.

One day in late April 1973, Swann was eating lunch in the SRI cafeteria with a colleague of Puthoff's, a computer scientist and astronomer named Jacques Vallée. French by birth, Vallée's first job in America was as a computer programmer at the University of Texas, where he had codeveloped the first computerized mapping system of Mars for NASA, using a combination of nineteenth-century telescopic observations and high-technology software. For his work at SRI, Vallée carried a top-secret security clearance, and he was assigned to the SRI psychic research program. "I was the de facto unpaid consultant," he remembers.

In early 1973, Vallée was working on a classified Defense Department contract for the Advanced Research Projects Agency (ARPA). The project involved a multiuser military computer network called ARPANET, later made public and renamed the Internet. Vallée was considered one of the most significant figures in the study of unidentified flying objects, along with J. Allen Hynek, with whom he worked on the Project Blue Book files for the U.S. Air Force. (Vallée would serve as the real-life model for the character played by François Truffaut in the film *Close Encounters of the Third Kind*.) With his expertise in information technology and computer programming, and his dedication to the study of UFOs, Vallée was someone Ingo Swann could relate to. "Ingo was frustrated" with the outbounder-beacon experiments, says Vallée. He wanted to be viewing locations more challenging than a hospital courtyard or a tennis court across town.

"I suggested he look at the problem from the perspective of information technology," recalls Vallée. "During lunch I asked him, What do you do [when remote viewing]? Do you move your consciousness around? Ingo said 'Yes, I can position it anywhere.'" As the two men discussed geolocation, recalls Vallée, he was struck with a thought about long-distance telepathy being analogous to some of the work he was doing for the Defense Department on the ARPANET. "You really need an addressing scheme," he said.

For centuries the word "address" generally meant a house or a building on a street, in a town, in a country. With the advent of computers, this concept had fundamentally changed. In multiuser computer systems there was direct addressing and indirect addressing, Vallée said, and virtual addressing: "searching out a piece of information that isn't there locally," he told Swann. Why not apply this kind of thinking to remote viewing? Vallée suggested. Accessing a virtual address on the ARPANET was "a means of accessing data which is clearly beyond the sensory grasp." This got Swann thinking. A few days later, he was sitting beside the pool at his apartment complex in Mountain View when he had an epiphany. "I was drinking a glass of scotch when a voice in my head said 'Try coordinates,'" he later recalled.

Geographic coordinates allow for every location on Earth to be precisely pinpointed by a set of numbers, letters, and symbols. The concept is more than two thousand years old. Credit for the invention of geolocation goes to the Greek mathematician and astronomer Eratosthenes, also credited as being the first person to estimate the circumference of Earth. He is said to have calculated this distance using a shadow-catching sundial called a gnomon, similar to the one Ed Mitchell carried on the Moon. Eratosthenes created the first map of the world that used latitudes and longitudes, or parallels and meridians, and he coined the term "geography," which translates as "writing about the Earth." Sitting poolside in Silicon Valley in the spring of 1973, Swann started thinking about how geographical addressing had evolved over history. He decided to create a new concept and a new term for long-distance telepathy, called coordinate remote viewing. He took the idea to Puthoff and Targ.

"Outrageous," Puthoff remembers himself saying. There were a number of reasons the concept was flawed, he said, starting with the idea that it could be relatively easy for a person to memorize the coordinates of the globe. "A person with an eidetic memory could read an atlas and reproduce the pictures from memory," Puthoff said. Swann insisted that he didn't have an eidetic memory. Well, the colleagues on the East Coast would never go for it, Puthoff predicted.

"But the idea stuck," says Puthoff, and he wondered whether coordinate remote viewing was worth a try. He called Kit Green at CIA.

Kit Green remembers sitting in his office at Langley when the call came. When Puthoff described Swann's idea for a new coordinate system for remote viewing, he thought the idea sounded absurd. Puthoff asked Green to at least give Swann's idea a chance. Perhaps Green could provide SRI with a set of coordinates known only to him; this would give Swann the opportunity to succeed or fail. Green agreed to give the idea a try.

Green hung up the phone. "I got an even better idea," he recalls. "Here was an opportunity to design an experiment that was essentially fraud proof." He would get map coordinates from a colleague so the location would be entirely unfamiliar to him. Green walked down the corridor and the first person he saw was a colleague he knew only as "Russ." Because Russ was with the clandestine service, "that wasn't even his real name," says Green.

"I told him I was testing a new geolocation imaging system," Green recalls. "I said, 'I want you to give me some coordinates.' I treated what was going on as if we were talking about photography or imagery, not human intelligence."

Green asked Russ to choose a place that meant something to him personally, so that if Green were later to show Russ a sketch of the place, Russ would immediately be able to discern whether the sketch resembled the physical location. A few hours later Russ handed Green a piece of paper with the following address written on it: 38° 23' 45-48" N, 79° 25' 00" W.

On May 29, 1973, Swann entered the Faraday cage at SRI at

4:03 p.m. He sat down in the orange imitation leather lounge chair used for remote viewing sessions, took a few puffs on a cigar, and relaxed. Hal Puthoff began recording the session, then showed Swann the geographic coordinates provided by Kit Green at CIA. Swann examined the coordinates and described what he saw: "There seems to be some sort of mounds and rolling hills," Swann said. "There is a city to the north. This seems to be a strange place, somewhere like the lawns one would find around a military base, but I get the impression that there are either some old bunkers around, or maybe this is a covered reservoir. There must be a flag-pole, some highways to the west, possibly a river over to the far east, to the south more city." Swann sketched a map of the target from an overhead point of view. He drew a circular area he labeled "Target," with one road leading to the south and another to the north. To the east, he drew a river. The session lasted six minutes. Puthoff collected the data and prepared a report. Blind to the target, he made no judgment about what Swann had said and drawn.

Swann went home to his apartment in Mountain View. The next morning he felt compelled to visit the target site again, so he sat down at his kitchen table, noted the time as 7:30 a.m., focused on the coordinates, and began sketching and writing. Working at home, unsupervised, was a clear departure from scientific method and would create problems and tensions down the road. Detractors and skeptics had good reason to argue that the SRI scientists included in their reports data that was not obtained in a laboratory setting under laboratory controls.

Swann's second narrative contained more details: "Cliffs to the east, fence to the north. There's a circular building (a tower?), buildings to the south. Is this a former Nike base or something like that?" he wrote. His impressions were vague, and he felt limited. "There is something strange about this area, but since I don't know particularly what to look for within the scope of this cloudy ability, it is extremely difficult to make decisions on what is there and what is not. Imagination seems to get in the way. For example I seem to get the impression of something underground but I'm not sure."

Ingo Swann's second map was more detailed than the first. It showed a facility inside a fenced-in area surrounded by forest on three sides. At the center of the map Swann sketched a circular driveway with a flagpole. He drew two rectangular buildings and a smaller square one. When he was finished, he packed up his notes and papers and headed over to SRI. He gave the papers to Puthoff, who marked the sketch "Map Number Two." Puthoff noted that Swann had done this second viewing at his own apartment, on his own initiative. Certainly Swann could have looked up the coordinates on a map and, using general region and geography as clues, guessed broadly what might be there. Puthoff indicated to the CIA that he knew Swann well and that he was not someone who would cheat. Puthoff typed up a report on Swann's second set of impressions and sent it to Kit Green at CIA.

The following day, Puthoff was sitting in his SRI office when the telephone rang. It was Pat Price, the Christmas tree salesman he and Swann had met six months before, in Mountain View. Price said he was calling from Lake Tahoe, where he lived, and that he could help.

"It was so odd and out of the blue that he called on that day that I decided to give him the coordinates," Puthoff recalls. "I asked him to describe what was located at those coordinates." This phone call was the second coincidence involving Price and the psychic research program. And the remote viewing session Price was about to perform would occur without any oversight or laboratory controls.

Three days later, on June 4, Puthoff received an envelope in the mail from Pat Price, postmarked June 2, from Lake Tahoe. Price had written a lengthy description of the impressions the geographic coordinates provided, which he said he had observed through extrasensory perception. "Looked at general area from altitude of about 1500' above highest terrain," he had written, as indicated in declassified CIA documents. "On my left forward quadrant is a peak in a chain of mountains, elevation approximately 4996' above sea level. Slopes are greyish slate covered with a variety of broad leaf trees, vines, shrubbery and undergrowth. I am facing about 3°–5° west of north." Details pertaining to terrain and geography went on for two paragraphs. Puthoff knew this was information a person could find in any good atlas. But Price also provided very specific details regarding the weather at 25,000 to 30,000 feet above the target site, including a colorful description of the "high cumulo-nimbus clouds" and "a cirrostratus air mass." While in 2017 this kind of weather information can be accessed on a smartphone in a matter of seconds, in 1973 it would have been challenging but not impossible to obtain, particularly if Price knew someone who worked at a weather station. Either way, thought Puthoff, it was a bold statement. Puthoff continued reading.

"Perceived that the peak area has large underground storage area," Price had written. "Road comes up back side of mountains (west slopes), fairly well concealed, deliberately so…Would be very hard to detect [this facility if] flying over area. Looks like a former missile site—bases for launchers still there." It was this missile site detail that caused Puthoff to pause. Swann, too, had described the base as a former missile site. Puthoff read on. "Area now houses record storage areas, microfilm, file cabinets; as you go into underground area through aluminum rolled up doors, first areas filled with records, etc. Rooms about 100' long, 4' wide, 20' ceilings with concrete supporting pilasters, flare-shaped."

Next, Price described the location as if he'd been able to get inside the underground facility. "Temperature cool—fluorescent lighted. Personnel, Army 5th Corps engineers. M/Sgt Long on desk placard on grey steel desk—file cabinets security locked—combination locks, steel rods though eye bolts," he wrote. "Beyond these rooms, heading east, are several bays with computers, communications equipment, large maps, display type overlays. Personnel, Army Signal Corps. Elevators."

Puthoff picked up the telephone and called Pat Price in Lake Tahoe. This information was more specific than what Ingo Swann had described. "I asked him if he could revisit the coordinates and pick up any additional information," remembers Puthoff, the more specific the better. Price said he'd work on it. Puthoff was uncertain how to interpret this scenario. Could the CIA be conducting some kind of psychological operation against SRI? Was this a test to see whether Puthoff could be deceived? Two days later, Pat Price called back. Puthoff wondered about the time frame. Why had it taken two days?

Price said he'd traveled back to the site in an out-of-body experience and gathered more words. Two code names seemed important, he said. They were "Flytrap" and "Minerva." Price also told Puthoff that he'd been able to view a set of documents that were sitting on top of a file cabinet against the north wall. The file was labeled "Operation Pool [something]," Price said; the second word was unreadable. Inside the file cabinet there were several folders, he added, and he could read the labels on four of them: "Cueball," "14 Ball," "8 Ball," "Rackup." Words resembling "Hayfork" or "Haystack" were also written down, Price said, and he'd been able to determine the names of three individuals: "Colonel R. J. Hamilton, Major General George R. Nash and Major John C. Calhoun." Finally, Price told Puthoff the classified code name of the site. It was "Sugar Grove," he said.

Puthoff had no idea what to make of any of this except that Price's description of the target site exterior was strikingly similar to the one provided by Ingo Swann. He thought about sending

Price's narrative to Kit Green but decided to wait and see what the Agency said about Swann's information. Pat Price was not part of the SRI program.

At CIA, Green received the information provided by Swann and shared it with his colleague whose cover name was Russ. "He said something along the lines of, 'What a stupid imagery system you're working on,'" remembers Green. "He said none of it was accurate, [not] the flagpole, the circular driveway, the multiple buildings. This was all nonsense, he said." Green asked Russ what was actually at the location. Russ kind of chuckled and said it was his summer cabin in Pendleton County, West Virginia, a simple cabin located in the forest at the end of a long dirt road. Green recalls taking a deep breath and resigning himself to the fact that this idea of remote viewing by geographical coordinates was a fool's errand. "Back to submarines and Biafra, I thought," recalls Green.

He called SRI and reached Targ. "We were about to get off the phone when Targ said, 'That's too bad. The other guy saw the same thing.'"

Green paused. "What other guy?" he asked. Targ told him about Pat Price.

Green was confused and frustrated. "Something about the situation bothered me," he explains. "I had to see for myself."

That weekend, Green piled his family into the car and set out with them on a drive. "I drove to the coordinates," Green recalled in 2015. "I found the cabin. I found the dirt road. Then I drove down the road a little further and I found a secure military facility. I saw the flagpole [described]. I saw the circular drive. I saw the building with the accordion door." Green was looking at a highly classified military facility called the Naval Radio Station, Sugar Grove, an ultrasecret facility run in part by NSA, designed to intercept international electronic intelligence from around the world. The site contained classified radar systems and deep-space telescopes. And it was right down the road from Russ's summer cabin. Apparently he had no idea it was there. On Monday morning Kit Green wrote up a report for his superior at CIA.

"On Tuesday, the [CIA's] security officers came," he recalls, security officers who were investigating a possibly treasonous violation of the Espionage Act of 1917. "The names on the folders were correct," says Green, referring to the names provided by Price. "The mensuration [measurements] of the details was correct. The location of the doors and the elevator, the number of floors, where the cabinets were located. The color of the cabinet was correct. It didn't take judging. It didn't take statistical processing. It was all correct."

The CIA's security investigation into the Sugar Grove remote viewing session remains classified. According to interviews with Kit Green and Hal Puthoff, each man was individually cleared by CIA of any wrongdoing. Neither had access to the classified material contained in Pat Price's report; they could not have cued him with information. So how was the information obtained? The government wanted answers. What was going on at SRI, and who was this Patrick Price?

"A significant investigation was launched," recalls Puthoff. He says it left "a trail of veteran security officers shaking their heads." As for Price, after answering questions that apparently satisfied the CIA and the Defense Department, he was hired to be part of the SRI remote viewing experiments. Now there were two test subjects, Pat Price and Ingo Swann.

Weeks later, when Kit Green met Price in person, Green asked Price if he'd seen his colleague's summer cabin in the woods. Green recalls Price saying, "Of course I saw the cabin. But you're in the intelligence business. You had to be looking at what was down the road."

Pat Price was born in 1918, in Salt Lake City, the ninth of ten children in a devout Mormon family. By the time he crossed paths with the CIA over the Sugar Grove remote viewing, he was fifty-five years old. His intent, said Price, was to make a nice sum of money and retire. He had been a wanderer for significant parts of his life, starting when he was a student pilot with the Army Air Corps during World War II. After that, he worked a series of jobs as a gold miner, a security guard, a construction worker, and the manager of an equipment packing plant. He married a nurse, had children, and for a time in the late 1940s and 1950s enjoyed a sub-urban lifestyle in Burbank, California. He became interested in local government and served as chairman of the Department of Parks and Recreation, on the Fire Commission, and as the City Council's representative to the Burbank Police Commission. In the late 1960s, when he was fifty, he joined the Church of Scientology, which was where his psychic powers were awakened, he said.

His apparent ability to remote-view the classified facility at Sugar Grove with such precision set off alarm bells across the intelligence community. "There was no one else like him," explains Kit Green. "His talents were immeasurable. His alphanumeric abilities were perfectly aligned with intelligence work." While no one at SRI claimed to understand how psychic functioning worked, the consensus before Pat Price came along was that it was a right-brain function, nonverbal and intuitive, generally associated with visuals rather than words. Whereas the right hemisphere of the brain is generally associated with creativity, imagination, and intuition, the left hemisphere is analytical. Left-brain people tend to be good in logic, sequencing, and math. Ingo Swann was visual and creative. But Pat Price used extrasensory perception to discern technical details such as let-ters, words, numbers, and dates. In the eyes of the CIA, says Green, this made Price an intelligence-collection gold mine.

"Everyone who met him liked him," remembers Puthoff. Except, perhaps, Ingo Swann.

Swann had created the concept of remote viewing. He was

committed to transforming psychic functioning from something that was laughed at to something respected in the intelligence world. Now Price was stealing the spotlight. In August 1973, when his Biofield Measurements contract was up, Swann told Puthoff he had decided California was not for him. "The permanent sun was unbearable to me," wrote Swann in his journal. Hal Puthoff recalls driving Swann to the San Francisco airport and saying good-bye.

The CIA now focused on Pat Price.

Kit Green was sent to California to run Price through a series of medical tests, including ones to determine his physiological, psychological, psychiatric, and intellectual health. Green also participated in a series of outbounder-beacon tests with Price. The Agency wanted to see whether Price could conduct a successful remote-viewing session against a moving target, ostensibly an aircraft or a submarine. The plan was for Green and Russell Targ as the outbounder-beacon team to go up in a glider. Hal Puthoff would wait with Price on the tarmac. Once Green and Targ were in the air, Green would write down three sets of three-digit numbers and put them in his breast pocket. At a prearranged time, Price would try to perceive the numbers.

"Price wrote down the correct numbers in the correct sequence," Green recalls. "He said that part was easy." The difficulty, Price said, was that there had been some kind of geometric shape or symbol interfering with the numbers as he was trying to see them. "He said the situation had made him queasy," remembers Green.

When Green asked Price to draw the symbol that was interfering, he drew a variation on a cross. Green reached inside his shirt and pulled out a necklace he was wearing. It was an Old Testament cross called a tau cross, shaped like the Greek letter *T*. Certainly Pat Price could have noticed Green's necklace at some point before the experiment; that wasn't what intrigued the CIA's neurophysiologist. "What interested me was the nausea," says Green. "Nausea has to do with how the cortex obtains but does not process visual data. There's a surge of serotonin in the area postrema. I began to think that remote viewing was as much neurology as it was psychology."

In a separate outbounder-beacon experiment with Price, a more dramatic physiological event occurred. Green was in the car with an experimenter from SRI. They had opened their sealed envelope and were headed to the target when, "ten minutes into our drive, I said stop the car," Green recalls. After his earlier experience with Uri Geller remotely viewing a page from one of the medical books in his CIA office, Green intended to devise a fail-safe remote-viewing test. This was it. The experimenter driving the car insisted that he wasn't allowed to deviate from protocol. Green told him, "I'm the contract monitor, and I say stop the car." So the experimenter stopped. "But I'm supposed to drive to the target," he said.

Green instructed the driver to back up. "I said, I want you to go to that church back there," pointing to a small Episcopal church beside the road. The driver did as Green asked and pulled into the church parking lot. Green checked his watch and waited until the prearranged time. Then he got out of the car. "I crunched across the gravel and into an arbor," Green recalls. "I caught my foot on something and nearly tripped. I walked down to the sacristy," the room where the vestments were kept. "I opened a window. I turned around, walked into the nave, walked down the right-hand aisle. Stopped and stared at a beautiful rose window over the altar." In this moment in the church, he says, he was reminded of his time in seminary school and the strange notion of how different his life might have been had he become a clergyman instead of joining the CIA. Green felt a wave of emotion and decided to pray. "I knelt down, said a prayer. There was this beautiful baptismal font in front of me. I leaned over and looked into it. Then I was done. I crunched across the gravel, went back to the car." The two experimenters headed back to SRI.

"Back at the lab, we went into the Faraday cage where the remote viewer [Price] had been [the entire time]. He was having a cardiac event," Green recalls. "At minimum he was having an angina attack, and possibly he was having an MI [myocardial infarction]," more commonly known as a heart attack. After Price's heart rate returned to normal, he turned to Green and said that that was the worst experiment he had ever done. Green recalls Price telling him, "It just made me so sick. You walked down an arbor. You almost tripped. You went into the most terrible building I've ever seen in my life. I saw you walk down an aisle and crumple to your knees. I began to worry about you. I saw you lean over and vomit into an octagonal basin. I began to feel nauseated. I got chest pains."

Over the next year Green began developing ideas about the physiology involved in remote viewing—"How the brain is involved for the sender [i.e., the outbounder] and the viewer, but in a very complex and precise way that connects emotionality," Green explains. But there was a bigger, far more daunting question he began asking, he says, and that was "*What* are we dealing with here?"

Like so many before him, Green was asking himself what force was powering anomalous mental phenomena. His search for the answer would continue for decades.

As word of Pat Price's talents spread through the intelligence community, SRI was flooded with requests. On February 5, 1974, the Berkeley police enlisted Price to use remote-viewing techniques to garner information about who might have kidnapped the heiress Patty Hearst. Hal Puthoff drove Price to the crime scene. In a memorandum for the record, one CIA analyst noted that Price's help was solicited "the night after the kidnapping and before any publicity occurred." According to CIA documents, Price provided law enforcement with a "significant amount of data, including identification of people later proven to be involved." The CIA wanted to learn more about the data provided. There were intelligence-capability opportunities to consider, including proof-of-life issues. But the Agency felt limited as to what they could ask the FBI. "Even the appearance of CIA involvement with domestic police operations is a political[ly] explosive association," an Agency analyst wrote.

Price's abilities were inexplicable. He was likened to an intelligence-gathering shaman. His talents were among those the CIA had been pursuing in its MKULTRA Subproject 58 quest, the search for the God's flesh mushroom. Price seemed able to travel across the globe, gather information, and come back. In the winter and spring of 1974, he conducted a series of operational tasks for multiple clients in the intelligence world. He provided NSA with valuable intelligence for a classified SIGINT operation in Africa. He helped CIA to "see" the interior of the Chinese embassy in Rome. He assisted the Navy in tracking Soviet submarines. As a result of his remote-viewing abilities, a concept called "the eight-martini results" was born. What Price seemed able to access through as yet unknown means was so unnerving that the CIA handler involved sometimes had to drink eight martinis in order to process the unfathomable nature of whatever "it" was.

On July 9, 1974, Price was given a highly classified target inside the Soviet Union. The facility was located in Kazakhstan, adjacent to the Semipalatinsk Test Site, Russia's primary nuclear testing facility, which meant that its existence was known to only a few members of the intelligence community. This facility had two code names: URDF-3, which stood for Unidentified Research and Development Facility-3, and PNUTS, for Possible Nuclear Underground Test Site. The CIA and the Pentagon were concerned that URDF-3 was home to a Soviet directed-energy weapons program to develop space-based laser weapons. Satellite photographs indicated there was machinery at this site that U.S. scientists were unfamiliar with, and that there was a lot of activity going on here, some aboveground, some below.

The geographic coordinates were sent to Hal Puthoff for Pat Price to remotely view. Inside the Faraday cage room at SRI, Price sat in an easy chair. With him was Russell Targ. Downplaying the classified nature of the site, Puthoff and Targ told Price they were giving him a geographical target from a world atlas published in London. Price took off his eyeglasses and polished the lenses, which, he said, helped him to see. Price closed his eyes. Puthoff turned on the tape recorder.

The first thing Price stated was that he was getting the impression that the Soviets "have done a lot of rocket launching and recovery out of that area." As had become customary, he first described the location through a lens of the weather, as if he were in a reconnaissance aircraft. "It's dark over there at the present time, quite a cloud cover, and a full moon," he said. He described a river and then told Puthoff he was "heading over to the facility now." Puthoff listened and took notes. "I am lying on my back on the roof of a two or three story brick building," Price said. "There's the most amazing thing. There's a giant gantry crane moving back and forth over my head. It seems to be riding on a track with one rail on each side of the building." He sketched a detailed drawing of a very large crane on rails. He said he saw "an assembly room with a sixty-foot metal sphere," something he described as "similar to a giant orange peel." He said he saw a cluster of tall gas canisters shaped like silos, with round spheres at the top.

The information was sent to the CIA where the lead analyst assigned to the operation, a physicist named Dr. Kenneth A.

Kress, compared Price's descriptions to classified satellite imagery. Reconnaissance photographs confirmed the presence of rails for railroad cars and a huge crane. The gas cylinders also matched what Price reported seeing. But the spheres were not locatable, and this agitated CIA. "From experience it was obvious that Price produced bad data as well as good," Kress wrote in a now declassified report. "I reviewed the photos of URDF-3 and chose two features which, if Price described them, would show the [information] channel at least partially working."

Kress flew out to SRI. He took Puthoff and Targ to a motel and briefed them on URDF-3. As cloak-and-dagger as it sounds, a randomly selected motel room is generally more secure than a laboratory where numerous people were working, according to the CIA. Kress told Puthoff and Targ that Price had been very accurate regarding his description of the crane but inaccurate in his descriptions of other buildings. Kress told the SRI scientists that the CIA wanted to read Price onto the top-secret program, and they should try to get additional information from him. Puthoff, Targ, and Kress headed over to SRI to talk to Price in an electronically shielded room.

"When the decision was made to make Price witting, I decided to test him," Kress wrote. "My branch chief and I sat in a conference room while Targ and Puthoff brought a smiling Pat Price into the room. I was introduced as the sponsor, and I immediately asked Price if he knew me."

"Yes," Price said.

"Name?" Kress asked.

"Ken Kress," Price said.

"Occupation?"

"Works for the CIA," Price said.

"Since I was a covert employee, the response was meaningful," wrote Kress. (The suggestion that Puthoff or Targ might have revealed the identity of what is termed a contracting officer's technical representative isn't plausible, says Puthoff. Release of that information would have been a violation of the Espionage Act.) After Price signed a CIA secrecy agreement, Kress asked him additional questions about the target site. He pulled out a map of URDF-3 and pointed to a specific spot. "Why didn't you see the four derricks?" Kress wanted to know.

Price sat back, put his glasses on, and closed his eyes. He concentrated for a few moments. "I didn't see them because they are not there anymore," Price told Kress, who made a note. Kress knew his satellite photographs were perhaps three or four months old.

Internal pressure was mounting at CIA. Scientists with the Office of Research and Development were becoming increasingly critical of Puthoff and Targ's experimentation controls. "The rigor of the research became a serious issue between the ORD project officers and SRI," noted Ken Kress. Given the highly classified nature of the URDF-3 operation, the ORD scientists reviewed the transcripts of Puthoff and Targ's sessions with Price and noted numerous occasions when experiments were not properly controlled. Seeking independent scrutiny, the CIA sent the information to an imagery analyst at Los Alamos National Laboratory for a second opinion.

The Los Alamos analyst focused on Price's knowledge of the rail-mounted gantry crane. "It seems inconceivable to imagine how he could have drawn such a likeness to the actual crane at URDF-3 unless: 1) he actually saw it though remote viewing, or 2) he was informed of what to draw by someone knowledgeable of the URDF-3." The analyst came to a troubling conclusion, one that echoed concerns at CIA. "I only mention this second possibility," he warned, "because the experiment was not controlled to discount the possibility that [Price] could talk to other people—such as the Disinformation Section of the KGB. This may sound ridiculous to the reader, but I have to consider all possibilities in the spectrum from his being capable to view remotely to his being supplied data for disinformation purposes by the KGB."

With this significant possibility broached, Ken Kress now questioned his own ability to be objective. In one of his CIA reports, he noted that the world of paranormal research was made up of "two types of reactions...positive and negative, with little in between," and he stressed the Agency-wide need for value-free assessment. Individuals who supported pro-paranormal data often "have had 'conversion' experiences," Kress wrote, something akin to a single "eight-martini result" that renders them "convinced that one unexplained success establishes a phenomenon." The Los Alamos report suggesting a KGB disinformation possibility that he had overlooked caused Kress to question his impartiality. "I began to doubt my own objectivity in evaluating the significance of paranormal abilities to intelligence collection," he wrote in a secret document marked "Personal Review."

At Kress's suggestion, CIA contracted with an outside scientist to evaluate the psychic research program. This scientist, described in declassified literature as "a disinterested consultant, a theoretical physicist with broad intellectual background," was given the CIA data to review. His conclusion was that "a large body of reliable experimental evidence points to the inescapable conclusion that extrasensory perception does exist as a real phenomenon, albeit characterized by rarity and lack of reliability."

Several weeks after Kress read Pat Price onto the classified program, the latest URDF-3 reconnaissance data was rechecked. "Two derricks were partially disassembled, but basically all four were visible," Kress wrote. "Because of the mixed results, the operational utility of the capability [i.e., remote viewing] was considered questionable but deserved further testing. Since I was judged to be a potentially biased advocate of paranormal functioning, the testing and evaluation of Pat Price would be transferred to a more pragmatic OTS [Office of Technical Services] operations psychologist."

The situation was baffling. "There are observations...that defy explanation," Kress wrote. The only thing easily understood was that the study of extrasensory perception was fraught with strong opinions and stronger reactions: "There is no fundamental understanding of the mechanisms of paranormal functioning and the reproducibility remains poor." Some of the most pragmatic, commonsense thinkers found themselves uncertain. Others would become unhinged.

CHAPTER ELEVEN

The Unconscious

In the early days of the Cold War, back in April 1953, CIA director Allen W. Dulles gave a now famous speech at the National Alumni Conference of the Graduate Council of Princeton University alerting America to the communists' most powerful secret weapon: brain warfare. "Its aim is to condition the mind so that it no longer reacts on a free will or rational basis, but responds to impulses implanted from outside," Dulles declared. To achieve this goal, Dulles said, the communists were running single-target programs such as the brainwashing of captured prisoners of war in Korea. The ability to influence key leaders or small groups of people through some kind of thought-influencing operation was also seen as a viable threat. One individual who continued to interest the CIA in this regard was Uri Geller.

Declassified documents show that CIA analysts were concerned by an ability of Uri Geller's they called "mind projection," a unique ability whereby "he 'forces' the researchers to name a city previously written down, by him, with apparently a high order of accuracy," wrote an analyst with the Office of Research and Development. Geller's posse of critics declared him a fake and a fraud, but declassified documents indicate that the CIA did not necessarily agree. "It may prove worth while to explore pursuing some carefully controlled experiments with Geller over and above the experiments TSD [Technical Services Division] is funding," suggested the ORD analyst, albeit with much tighter controls. After *New Scientist* ran a sixteen-page story on Geller, accusing him of possibly wearing "a radio receiver that can be concealed in a tooth," the CIA had Geller's mouth examined by a dentist who found no sign of an implant. When the magician James Randi speculated that Geller's assistant and friend Shipi Shtrang helped him cheat, the CIA denied Shtrang access to Geller during the experiments. According to "Special Management Guidelines for the SRI Paranormal Project," stricter controls would now include: "strip-down (removing rings, wristwatches, etc.) and put on a special lab garment (jumpsuit); X-Rays done on a spot basis during experimentation...limited to the chest, hands and skull; ultra-sound."

If Geller could plant a word in a person's mind through "mind projection," he could ostensibly influence that person's actions, and that idea was of national security concern to CIA. There was also mounting evidence that Geller's alleged powers produced secondary effects. A scientist with the Army Research Institute for the Behavioral and Social Sciences agreed. "Perhaps the most important consequence of the Geller craze [is] that a number of less celebrated individuals, particularly children and teenagers, reportedly [are] able to bend metal after watching Geller do it."

Which is what happened on November 23, 1973, after Geller walked into a London radio studio for a live on-air experiment with a veteran British broadcaster named Leslie Ronald "Jimmy"

Young. BBC Radio 2's *Jimmy Young Show* had an audience that extended throughout England and into Ireland and Scotland. After Geller arrived, Young welcomed him to the BBC and suggested they get started right away. A few minutes into the interview, Young took out a large key identified as an Automobile Association telephone-box key from his pocket and asked Geller to bend it. "I did what I usually do, laying my hand over the key and wishing it to bend," wrote Geller in a 1975 memoir. Geller was nervous, he said, having recently been unable to demonstrate psychokinesis on Johnny Carson's *Tonight Show,* but today there was excitement in the air. A group of radio engineers had left their booth and gathered around Geller to observe. With his hand over the key, Geller concentrated. He told people all over the United Kingdom that they should summon their own psychokinetic powers at this exact moment and bend metal in their homes—spoons, forks, keys, anything. "If there are any broken watches in your house, please concentrate on them and try to make them work," instructed Geller. After a few moments of concentrating on the audience, Geller took his hand away from Jimmy Young's key.

Live on national radio, Jimmy Young shouted out, "It's bending right in front of me, I can't believe it!" There was clapping and cheering throughout the studio. Young spoke of how crazy it was to be sitting in the BBC studio and watching metal bending right in front of him, as if it were alive. A producer rushed in and handed Young a note. Then an engineer ran in with a message, and after that another radio producer came forward with a handful of caller notes. Someone shouted, "The entire BBC switchboard is lit up like a Christmas tree!"

Calls came into the station from all over, Young announced on the air. Across the United Kingdom citizens were reporting metal objects in their homes inexplicably bending. A woman in Surrey said she'd concentrated and her gold bracelet bent. A woman in Harrow said she was stirring soup while she was concentrating and now her soup spoon was bent. A watchmaker called up to say the hands on one of his clocks, frozen for years, were moving again. People wanted to believe in psychokinesis, and now apparently many of them did. This was what the CIA called secondary consequences. All over Great Britain, people believed they had bent metal with their own minds.

Still in London the following night, Geller appeared live on BBC television. On the *Dimbleby Talk-In* show he bent and then broke a fork, started a broken watch, and reproduced a drawing hidden in a sealed envelope. Seated beside him were two scientists he did not know, King's College professor John Taylor and South African zoologist and anthropologist Lyall Watson. Both scientists expressed wonder. "I believe this process," declared Professor Taylor, "I believe that you actually broke the fork here and now." Variations on what the CIA's Ken Kress called "conversion moments" were now happening on live TV.

The following day, as part of a psychokinesis experiment for the British tabloid newspaper *Sunday People* (estimated circulation three million), Geller agreed to concentrate hard at 12:30 p.m. London time, and to shout out the word "Bend!"

"I was at Orly Airport in Paris at the time," Geller recalls. "I concentrated hard starting at 12:15, in an attempt to send thoughts and energies across the Channel...At exactly 12:30, I shouted, 'Bend!'" Reader reports flooded the newspaper's offices. The following day, the newspaper printed a tabulation of readers' results: "Clocks and watches restarted: a total of 1,031; forks and spoons bent or broken: a total of 293; other objects bent or broken: a total of fifty-one."

Overnight, Uri Geller became front-page news, across England and throughout Europe. The media referred to Gellermania as a force akin to Beatlemania. Cover stories about him appeared in *Paris Match, Der Spiegel, Norsk Ukeblad,* and *Apu.* Geller was invited to give demonstrations in Japan, Germany, Sweden, Switzerland,

Denmark, Holland, and Norway. From defense officials to religious leaders to celebrities, powerful individuals wanted to see for themselves whether Geller's abilities were real. In Oslo he was invited to the home of Alv Jakob Fostervoll, the Norwegian minister of defense; in Italy he met with the archbishop of Florence; in France he was a guest of Brigitte Bardot. In America, meanwhile, a group of prominent scientists formed a coalition to discredit him.

The cosmologist Carl Sagan was particularly offended by the public's acceptance of Uri Geller. Together with Martin Gardner, Ray Hyman, Paul Kurtz, and James Randi, the skeptics created the Committee for the Scientific Investigation of Claims of the Paranormal to make their position known. "The more serious-minded among us are starting to ask, what is going on?" wrote Sagan. "Why the sudden explosion of interest, even among some otherwise sensible people, in all sorts of paranormal 'happenings'? Are we in retreat from the scientific ideas of rationality, dispassionate examination of evidence and sober experimentation that have made modern civilization what it is?" Sagan and his colleagues expressed anger over the fact that any American scientist would waste time studying extrasensory perception and psychokinesis. It was the duty of their committee, he wrote, to force a confrontation between what he believed was a battle between "the rational and the irrational." Sagan lamented, "In the past, the raising and answering of such questions has been left to commentators and journalists. This time around, however, some scientists are beginning to fight back."

Fight back as their group would, it had no bearing on the decisions made at CIA. The Agency continued its research in paranormal phenomena in general, and Uri Geller in particular. Geller's actions and his purported abilities had real-world consequences, rational or irrational. Nowhere was this more evident than in a bizarre series of happenings in late 1974. They involved Geller and a small group of nuclear weapons engineers who worked at the

Lawrence Livermore National Laboratory, one of two nuclear weapons laboratories in the United States. The CIA closely followed the situation. It was, and remains, cause for alarm.

Lawrence Livermore National Laboratory is located in Livermore, California, roughly thirty miles east of the Stanford Research Institute. In keeping with its mission statement, "pushing the frontiers of nuclear weapons design and engineering," in the mid-1970s Livermore scientists were developing new nuclear warheads and designing emerging-weapons technologies that included classified laser systems and high-performance computers. Among these scientists and engineers was a small group closely following the Geller phenomenon. If Geller's psychokinetic abilities were genuine, this group wanted to know whether, and under what circumstances, these abilities might be a national security threat to their work.

Scientists and researchers working with Geller at SRI had reported that both inside and outside the lab, strange things sometimes occurred. Otherwise reliable equipment malfunctioned when Geller was around. Objects disappeared, then reappeared. Computers crashed. Magnetic tape became demagnetized. There was precedent for this kind of occurrence; scientists called it the Pauli effect, named after the theoretical physicist and Nobel Laureate Wolfgang Pauli. The Pauli effect had been coined after numerous instances were noted in which Pauli was present and technical equipment malfunctioned, fell, broke, or sustained unusual damage. On one occasion, in February 1950, during a visit to Princeton University, the cyclotron Pauli had come to observe inexplicably caught fire. Pauli wrote an article on the subject titled "Background Physics," in which he discussed the relationships between physics, the conscious, and the unconscious. In homage to the Pauli effect, the SRI scientists and researchers started calling the odd occurrences that were happening around them the Geller effect.

One theory behind this phenomenon is called associationism: the philosophical idea that like a chain reaction, each experience informs or influences the next experience. This concept has been given various names across the historical record. In 400 BC, Sophocles wrote about the self-fulfilling prophecy, a prediction that directly or indirectly causes that prediction to manifest, as in *Oedipus Rex*. The Tinkerbell effect is a more modern way of describing situations that exist because people insist they exist. For the CIA in the 1950s, the controversial anesthesiologist Henry K. Beecher studied the placebo effect, a remarkable phenomenon whereby a harmless pill or simulated treatment produces real-world physiological effects in humans. And the Thomas theorem states that "if men define situations as real, they are real in their consequences." Important to this story is the fact that perception of an event or a situation—real or imagined, rational or irrational, normal or allegedly paranormal—can cause consequential actions to occur.

In the winter of 1975, Uri Geller returned to Northern California at the behest of the Livermore scientists for a series of classified psychokinesis tests. The tests were recorded on videotape, audiotape, and film. Because everyone involved with the experiment except Geller carried a top-secret Q clearance (for nuclear secrets), the Atomic Energy Commission assigned a security officer named Ron Robertson to oversee national security issues between itself, Livermore, and CIA. Kit Green served as the contract monitor for the CIA.

"The program involved half a dozen nuclear physicists and engineers," Green confirms. Because of "ongoing security issues" (Geller was a foreign national whose potential role with the Mossad was yet unresolved), arrangements were made to test Geller off-site. The scientists set up their experiments in a laboratory adjacent to Lawrence Livermore, in an old wooden World War II barracks on University of California property.

Two sets of experiments were to take place. In the first, high-quality lasers were fired at a target. Could Geller interfere with the beam? For the second test, the scientists placed magnetic computer program cards in a lead container and sealed it. Could Geller affect what was inside? He did a series of these psychokinesis tests over several days, and the results of one of these tests was declassified. "The magnetic pattern stored in the iron oxide layer of a magnetic program card was erased," wrote Ron S. Hawke, one of the Livermore scientists. "Further experiments are warranted." In an interview in 2015, Kit Green summarized the Livermore group's conclusion: "The determination was that from a close distance, Geller *could* affect matter and materials. But he could not do it from far away." Yet it was not the results of the tests that were most troublesome, says Green, it was the strange effect Geller seemed to have on several of the nuclear physicists.

Each night, after finishing up their work with Geller, the Livermore scientists went home. Each morning, in keeping with nuclear clearance security protocols, the scientists were required to report anything unusual that had happened overnight. After the second day of tests, AEC security officer Ron Robertson called Kit Green at CIA headquarters. "He told me there was a serious problem," recalls Green. Several of the nuclear weapons engineers had reported seeing things they could not rationally explain. These included "items flying across the room. Lights flashing. A six-inch ball of light, rolling down the hallway. One scientist reported seeing a flying orb," remembers Green. "One of the scientists claimed to have seen a large raven, perched on a piece of furniture inside [his] home." Privately, Green thought these sounded "like poltergeist events" from folklore. The AEC was concerned, and so was the CIA. "I traveled to San Francisco," Green says, "to determine what could be causing these hallucinations. I was instructed to perform pathology tests on the Livermore scientists. Were these people going mad?"

Green flew to San Francisco and met with the scientists individually. "I examined them," he says. "Conducted extensive interviews and tests. My conclusion? There was no pathology here. These people were straight up. These were people who had more polygraph exams each year than I had. They were not psychologically impaired." So what was going on? One of the scientists confided in Green about a particular incident he could not get out of his mind. It happened in his bedroom, in the middle of the night. It made no rational sense, except he woke up his wife and she saw it too, Green recalls. "He told me that he saw a disincarnate arm, rotating like a hologram," meaning an arm that was free-floating, not attached to a body. "An arm wrapped in some kind of gray cloth...instead of a hand the arm had a hook. He talked about the [horror] of seeing this hook floating over the foot of his bed. How it rotated like it was on a spit."

Green was bedeviled. Perhaps what was going on was some kind of psychological operation, he thought, either by an enemy intelligence service or perhaps even the CIA. "Holograms were just coming on line," says Green, "although the technology was mostly classified at the time." He also knew there existed a long-standing rivalry between scientists at SRI and at Livermore and remembers wondering, "Was this some kind of confidence trick?"

He confronted Hal Puthoff and Russell Targ. "I asked Hal and Russ to meet me in [my] motel room," Green recalls. "I was furious." The scientists at Livermore were terribly upset, Green said. "The entire program was in jeopardy. I asked what in hell was going on. They swore to me they had nothing to do with any of it. My yelling was interrupted by a loud banging on the door." Green answered the knock. "Standing in front of me in the doorway of the motel was a man in a gray suit. He asked me something. I said, 'Wrong room,' and started to close the door.

The man turned and as he left I watched him go. I noticed there was something unusual about him." One of the arms of his suit jacket was pinned up. "The man had one arm," says Green. Hal Puthoff confirms that he saw it too.

Green concluded that what was going on had to have been "some kind of high-technology psychological operation," one that involved holograms, lasers, and small unmanned aerial vehicles, all advanced technologies that were just coming online as black programs at CIA in the mid-1970s. As an intelligence officer and a neurophysiologist (not an advanced technology weapons expert), Green remembers thinking that whatever classified technology was involved, it was above his level of security clearance. But as a medical professional, he was concerned about the real-world results that transpired.

"Rational or irrational," says Green, "two nuclear scientists who worked on U.S. nuclear weapons programs" at Livermore drew their own conclusion. "As far as I know, two of the Livermore scientists quit," he says. It was the Thomas theorem in action: if men define situations as real, they are real in their consequences. The scientists had apparently perceived the incidents to be some kind of omen or message "that they were not supposed to work on nuclear weapons development anymore," says Green.

The psychic research program at SRI was falling apart. Pat Price told Puthoff and Targ it was time to say good-bye. He had decided to make real-world use of his extrasensory talents, he said, and he'd been offered a stake in a West Virginia mining company searching for coal veins. His plan had always been to make a small fortune using his extrasensory abilities and then retire. What Price did not tell Puthoff and Targ, but what declassified documents reveal, was that he'd been hired away from SRI by the CIA. "To achieve better security," states one memo, "all the operations-oriented testing with the contractor [i.e., SRI] was stopped, and a personal service contract with Price was started." Price now worked directly for the Agency, with a personal handler in Washington, D.C. What Pat Price did for the CIA remains a mystery; these files have never been declassified despite multiple FOIA requests.

We do know that the partnership between the CIA and Price had a tragic ending. In early July 1975, Price was in Washington, meeting with his handler, when he reached out and made contact with old friends. According to both Hal Puthoff and Kit Green, Price told these friends he'd soon be spending a few days gambling in Las Vegas and suggested that they meet him there. They agreed. On July 14, Price checked into the Stardust Hotel. Later that evening, he had dinner with the two friends in the hotel restaurant. The meal was cut short when Price announced he didn't feel well and was heading up to his room for a rest. When he didn't return, his friends went to his room to check on him. They found him on the bed, in cardiac arrest.

Paramedics were called to the scene. EMTs tried to resuscitate him, but his heart did not respond to defibrillators. Pat Price was rushed to the emergency room, where he was pronounced dead on arrival. Kit Green says he traveled to Las Vegas to review the autopsy report.

"There was no report," remembers Green, "because no autopsy was performed." The coroner said a man had shown up with a briefcase full of Price's medical records and engaged hospital officials in a discussion, then waived the autopsy requirement on the grounds that Price had died of a heart attack.

At SRI, all kinds of rumors began to spread among the scientists and the psychics, including talk that Pat Price might have been killed. Possible assassins included the KGB, the CIA, even the Church of Scientology. In 1972, the Army's Medical Intelligence Office had warned that the KGB "was developing a way to use psychokinesis to stop the human heart." As for the CIA, recent Church Committee congressional hearings had revealed that Agency engineers had created a "heart attack gun" capable of shooting a poison pellet into a victim whose death would appear to have been a heart attack. According to Jacques Vallée, when the FBI learned that Price was a Scientologist, the church became a suspect. "After a raid against the offices of the Church of Scientology in Los Angeles, the FBI came to believe (falsely?) that Price was used by the Scientologists as a spy against the CIA," Vallée wrote in his journal.

In a move to disassociate itself from additional controversy, the CIA withdrew from its lead position in classified anomalous mental phenomena research. Pat Price was dead. Ingo Swann was in New York. Uri Geller was thought to be working for Mossad. The fate of the SRI program was up in the air. A Cold War chill set in. Was this the end of U.S. government phenomena programs, or a new beginning?

CHAPTER TWELVE

Submarines

The question that has bedeviled ESP practitioners and purveyors since time immemorial has always been, What is the source of anomalous mental phenomena? For thousands of years, from the ancient texts of the Assyrians circa 2400 BC, to the eighteenth-century writings of theologian and mystic Emanuel Swedenborg, one answer was God, a supernatural being. Then, roughly 150 years ago, with the development of a theory to explain electromagnetic waves (formed when an electric field couples with a magnetic field), the focus turned to the electromagnetic spectrum as the possible source of ESP. The idea was that telepathy was a kind of mental radio. This gave way to new research fields.

The radio analogy was a suitable metaphor and relatively easy to comprehend. With Heinrich Hertz proving the existence of radio waves, beginning in 1886, and the sending and receiving of the first radio signal, by Guglielmo Marconi nine years later, radio waves were understood to be a way in which information could be carried across space. When radio waves strike an electrical conductor, as in a mast at a broadcasting station or an antenna on a car, the information that originated at the distant place is transformed back into its original form and received locally. In 1930 the Pulitzer Prize–winning author Upton Sinclair, an enthusiast of psychic functioning, wrote a book about telepathy experiments he had conducted with his psychic wife and called it *Mental Radio*. The information contained in the book, as well as the subject of ESP in general, so fascinated Albert Einstein that he wrote a preface to *Mental Radio* for the German edition. Over the next three decades, and with the discovery and development of radar, microwave ovens, and space communications, the idea that the electromagnetic spectrum might explain anomalous mental phenomena widened in theoretical possibility.

The electromagnetic spectrum is broad in scope, with visible light waves the only electromagnetic waves the human eye can see. At one end there are the extremely high frequency (EHF) waves, as in ultraviolet rays, X-rays, and gamma rays. In the middle range are visible light waves, infrared waves, and microwaves. At the low end of the spectrum there are radio waves and extremely low frequency (ELF) waves. The quest to locate ESP's possible electromagnetic channel began with the process of elimination. Visible light is easily removed as a possible channel, since light waves can't pass through objects or barriers such as a wall or a door. X-rays can also be stopped by barriers, as evidenced in the lead aprons humans must wear around medical X-ray machines.

Back in the late 1940s, to block the middle-range electromagnetic frequencies, including radio and microwave, Andrija Puharich and Jack Hammond built a Faraday cage. They placed psychics inside it and did not find degradation of what they believed was psychic functioning, thereby ruling out lower-frequency elements of the spectrum as a carrier. The only electromagnetic fields a Faraday cage doesn't block are extremely low frequency waves, or ELF waves—waves that are literally thousands of miles long (10,000 to 100,000 kilometers). One of the only known ways to test ELF waves is in very deep water, and for that a scientist would need a submarine. Unless the scientist had access to a privately owned submarine, this meant that the U.S. Navy would have to be involved in such tests.

The submarine is one of the most technologically advanced machines in the U.S. military. Its computer technology, navigation systems, precision weapon systems, atmosphere regeneration capacity, and nuclear power systems make it a highly classified war machine. Ever on the move, submarines are the best defense against a nuclear first strike. They are the key to Mutual Assured Destruction, or MAD. But American submarines must stay deeply submerged so that Soviet satellites cannot detect the heat bloom from their nuclear propulsion systems. When it's far below the surface, a submarine is unable to receive ordinary radio signals. In the 1950s, ELF was the only known bandwidth on the electromagnetic spectrum capable of penetrating hundreds of meters of seawater. Because an ELF message is usually just one or two characters in length, the Navy can use ELF to signal a submarine to come closer to the surface, where it can receive a longer message broadcast by other means. These details remain highly classified.

As is the reality across all the military services, the overwhelming majority of Navy officials considered ESP to be quackery. But in the early 1970s, a minority group showed interest in ESP as a possible backup means of communication in a postnuclear strike environment. Among them was a young scientist named Stephan Schwartz, who served as a special assistant for research and analysis to Chief of Naval Operations Admiral Elmo Zumwalt. It was in this capacity, starting in 1971, that Schwartz was briefed on the Navy's telepathy studies. He also became familiar with Soviet efforts. One ESP experiment believed to have been conducted by the Russians around 1956 stood out.

According to a Defense Department analysis of the test, it involved a mother rabbit, her newborn litter, a submerged Soviet submarine, and a research station on shore. A military scientist named Pavel Naumov was in charge. "Soviet scientists placed the baby rabbits aboard the submarine. They kept the mother rabbit in a laboratory on shore where they implanted electrodes in her brain. When the submarine was submerged, assistants [in the submarine] killed the [baby] rabbits one by one. At each precise moment of death the mother rabbit's brain produced detectable and recordable reactions."

If the results of the experiment were to be believed, then ELF might be the ESP information carrier channel. In his capacity as special assistant to Admiral Zumwalt, Schwartz considered proposing an experiment. Mindful that most in the military establishment considered ESP pseudoscience, "I waited for an opportune moment," Schwartz explained in 2015. "While traveling in an aircraft to the Groton naval base, I found myself alone with Admiral Hyman Rickover." Admiral Rickover was Zumwalt's powerful colleague, a man referred to in history books as the father of the nuclear navy. "Rickover was an out-of-the-box thinker and an engineer," which meant he might be open to the idea of ESP, Schwartz surmised. "I asked him if he would let me put a distant viewer [i.e., a psychic] aboard one of the Boomers [submarines] on its sea trials," remembers Schwartz. "He thought about it for a while but ultimately said no, for fear the media would hear about it."

In 1975, Schwartz left the Navy for private enterprise. His enthusiasm for psychic research had eclipsed any desire for a naval career. He accepted a fellowship with the Philosophical Research Society in Los Angeles, where he would research and write books about extrasensory perception. He could not have foreseen that soon he would find himself in a submerged submarine with a psychic after all.

In Menlo Park, Hal Puthoff and Russell Targ struggled to

keep their psychic research program at SRI afloat. With their grant from the CIA terminated, they looked to the Navy as a potential client. By 1975, the Navy had spent roughly $125 million researching ELF. Puthoff and Targ proposed that they research the relationship, if any, between ELF and ESP. In 1976, the Naval Electronics Systems Command awarded them an $87,000 contract for "an investigation of the ability of certain individuals to perceive remote faint electromagnetic stimuli at a non-cognitive level of awareness." To avoid drawing attention to the controversial secret work, Puthoff and Targ discreetly titled their project "Sensing of Remote EM Sources (Physiological Correlates)." But during a briefing at the Pentagon, the Navy official in charge was not so tactful. He titled the SRI project "ELF and Mind Control." The sensational title was somehow leaked to the *Washington Post*.

The *Post* story was written by John L. Wilhelm, a skeptic and critic of all things having to do with extrasensory perception. One part of the exposé centered on the Navy's top scientist, Samuel Koslov. In an interview with Wilhelm, Koslov said he was outraged to learn about the SRI project. "As the briefer flashed his chart onto the screen and began to speak, Koslov stormily interrupted, 'What the hell is that about?'" wrote Wilhelm. "Among the glowing words on the projected chart, the section describing SRI's work was labeled, 'ELF AND MIND CONTROL.'"

Koslov insisted to Wilhelm that he had demanded that the SRI investigations stop at once, that he had canceled "$35,000 in Navy funds slated for more remote viewing work." He was "really upset," Koslov lamented. "*We* [Koslov's emphasis] do not fund programs in this area. If you ask me, 'Do you think it's a pile of crap?' I do, and you can quote me." He assured Wilhelm that the Navy "is simply out of this business. I don't believe it's the function of the military to support parapsychology research."

Koslov was using semantics to conceal the truth. In the Soviet Union, parapsychology researchers grouped ESP, PK, and electromagnetic weapons together, albeit under different names. (ESP, or mental telepathy, was called "long-distance biological signal transmission"; psychokinesis was "non-ionizing, in particular electromagnetic, emissions from humans"; electromagnetic weapons were called "the generation of high-penetrating emission of non-biological origin.") Following the unwritten rules of the Cold War arms race, which required each side to mirror the other side's weapons systems, these seemingly disparate "technologies" were part of the same programs, at least for now. As one of the lead scientists on Project Pandora, the classified, multiservice effort to duplicate the electromagnetic weapon called the Moscow Signal, Dr. Koslov was most certainly engaged in this research. As a countermeasure to the microwave-beam weapon being aimed at U.S. embassy personnel in Moscow, Samuel Koslov worked on the ARPA-led program. Initially, scientists beamed electromagnetic signals at monkeys in an anechoic chamber. Later they beamed these signals at unwitting sailors stationed in a submarine at the Philadelphia Naval Shipyard.

In 1977, when the *Post* article was published, Samuel Koslov had a public relations nightmare on his hands. The nefarious goings-on surrounding the Moscow Signal and Project Pandora had only recently become public. The government had succeeded in keeping the programs secret, from the discovery of the Moscow Signal in 1962 until February 1976, when the *Los Angeles Times* broke the story. The unraveling had begun in 1973, when a new and more powerful set of Soviet microwave beams were picked up by the CIA in Moscow. Like the original Moscow Signal, these new electromagnetic weapons were aimed at the upper floors of the embassy, where the ambassador and top intelligence officials had their offices.

Robert M. Gates, former director of Central Intelligence,

revealed the details in his 1997 memoir, *From the Shadows*. "Because of their duration and peculiar characteristics they were regarded as posing a greater health hazard. We knew that these signals were directional microwave beams—ultra- and super-high frequency radiowaves—coming from transmitters located in the vicinity of the embassy," Gates wrote. The CIA code-named this signal MUTS-2, the second Moscow Unidentified Technical Signal.

Two years passed. In July 1975, the CIA sent its specialist on biological and health effects of non-ionizing radiation, Donald A. Myers, to Moscow to work, in secret with State Department officials; employees were still in the dark. Only after the Soviets installed a second microwave transmitter on top of a building south of the embassy did the CIA decide to inform the U.S. ambassador and his staff. "I have been briefed on the implications that the MUTS and MUTS-2 signals are a possible cause of recent health problems of the embassy," then CIA director William Colby wrote to the ambassador. "The increased probability of health injuries to personnel at the U.S. Embassy in Moscow [redacted] warrant our immediate attention." The signal was getting more potent.

Finally, fourteen years after its discovery, in January 1976, U.S. ambassador Walter Stoessel was briefed on the Moscow Signal. Stoessel filed a formal protest with the Soviets and minimally informed embassy personnel about their exposure to high-powered microwave beam radiation. "Several members of the embassy staff display symptoms that are non-specific but have been reported frequently in patients chronically exposed to non-ionizing radiation," a State Department doctor reported. Symptoms included severe headaches, inability to concentrate, and fatigue. The story was leaked to the press. "Ambassador Walter J. Stoessel Jr. had told some of the 125 members of his staff that the Russians were using microwave beams to listen in on conversations inside the embassy, and that such radiation could be harmful to their health," reported the *Los Angeles Times*. Stoessel was reassigned to the U.S. embassy in Bonn, West Germany, and the State Department denied the press reports.

One hundred U.S. embassy employees previously stationed in Moscow filed $250 million worth of lawsuits against the government for exposure related to the Moscow Signal. In response, the State Department funded a $1 million study by the Johns Hopkins University School of Hygiene and Public Health, the same institution that had created the synthetic Moscow Signal tested against the monkeys. The study, released in November 1978, found "no convincing evidence" that any employees suffered "adverse health effects as of the time of this analysis." According to State Department medical consultant Dr. Herbert Pollack, who advocated on behalf of the victims in a Senate subcommittee investigation, every suit was eventually withdrawn, "without a penny being paid." In 1986, Walter Stoessel died of leukemia at the age of sixty-six. Two of the three ambassadors who had served before him and had also been subjected to the Moscow Signal also died of cancer: Charles Bohlen in 1974, age sixty-nine, and Llewellyn Thomas in 1972, age sixty-seven.

The reality of powerful electromagnetic weapons moved to the fore. Microwave and ELF weapons were now being debated in the public domain. Some scientists, like Samuel Koslov, downplayed the government's work in this area. By acting as a source for the *Washington Post* article, Koslov was able to cast himself as the stalwart man of reason pitted against pseudoscientists working on dubious programs involving ELF and mind control. But it is almost impossible to accept the idea that Koslov was unaware of the ESP program until the briefing; his official title was scientific assistant to the Secretary of the Navy.

A few government scientists broke ranks and discussed the government's shortcomings in the arena of electromagnetic weapons. They included the biologist Dr. Allan H. Frey. Since

1960, Frey had been working on classified and unclassified Defense Department contracts, including ones with the Office of Naval Research and the U.S. Army. He was one of the nation's most dedicated researchers working to understand the effects of microwave radiation on the human body. In 1961, Frey discovered a radical new technology, later called synthetic telepathy, in which a microwave input signal allowed the brain to receive a message that it perceived to be a voice transmission but that was really a microwave beam. To Frey, living organisms were "complex electrochemical systems that evolved over billions of years in a world with a relatively simple weak magnetic field." Much of his lifework was dedicated to figuring out the effects of electromagnetic energy on biological systems. "If one used electromagnetic energy sensors to view the world from space 100 years ago, the world would have looked quite dim. Now the world glows with electromagnetic (em)3 energy emissions," he wrote in 1969.

Most of the problems stemmed from fundamental lack of awareness and what Frey called "glib assumptions that government scientists had a complete understanding of the nervous system function." In a 1969 paper he asked, "Why is there so much misunderstanding and confusion and so little data collection in this area? I can recall being shown on a chalk board the calculations that 'proved' that nerves can not be affected by RF [radio frequency] energy." He added that "there was, however, one basic fault in this line of reasoning. The fault was the assumption that we have a good understanding of nervous system function. This assumption is wrong."

Frey worked hard to overcome the jurisdictional battles over who would control and be responsible for research. He had seen many Russian papers on this subject matter rejected as "uninterpretable." In fact, said Frey, atrocious translations were the problem. "In one [paper] the word for hypothalamus was translated as cerebellum," he wrote.

Frey's research and experiments added further resonance to the mysterious links between ESP and PK and electromagnetic weapons, links being actively studied by the Russians. In the late 1960s, Frey reported that he could speed up, slow down, or stop an excised frog heart by synchronizing the pulse rate of a microwave beam with the heart itself, an experiment that echoed what Nina Kulagina was reported to have done with her mind. "Similar results have been obtained using live frogs, indicating that it is technically feasible to produce heart attacks with a ray [electromagnetic] designed to penetrate the human chest," wrote Robert O. Becker, a colleague of Koslov and Frey. Becker, twice nominated for the Nobel Prize, worked on microwave weapons for the Defense Department until his resignation in the early 1970s, after working on a classified project that used microwaves to disorient people. "He quit because he considered such work immoral," wrote a reporter covering the subject for *New Scientist* magazine. Becker's government work convinced him that a microwave signal such as the Moscow Signal "could affect the central nervous system, put people to sleep, interfere with decision making capacity and induce chronic stress," he said, and noted that the Soviets had been "using embassy employees as test subjects for low-level EMR [electromagnetic radiation] experiments."

Was the Moscow Signal benign, as put forth by Koslov, or potentially lethal, as Becker and Frey believed? Did embassy employees really have elevated mutagenesis and carcinogenesis, or was this hype? And what were the Soviets trying to accomplish by linking EM weapons to ESP and PK? U.S. defense scientists wondered. The CIA hired a defense contracting company called AiResearch Manufacturing Group to conduct a classified study. AiResearch, located in Torrance, California, had an array of classified defense department contracts, including ones in avionics, hydraulics, and microprocessors. The company had also engineered the life support systems for the Mercury, Gemini, and Apollo astronauts, which gave it unique expertise in the area of human physiology in extreme circumstances and under duress.

AiResearch found much of the work in the Soviet Union to be "speculative, unscientific and sensationalistic." But in one area they found cause for alarm. The Soviets were developing ways to try to enhance psychic functioning by bombarding test subjects with very high frequency (VHF) sound and pulsing the brain with electromagnetic signals. Soviet researchers sought to bring humans to "the razor's edge between sleep and wakefulness," and to "facilitate hallucinations and altered states." The goal was "changing the psychological states of the subject." What Andrija Puharich set out to do with hallucinogenic field mushrooms more than twenty years before, the Soviets were now trying to accomplish with advanced technology.

Further details were elusive. The problem, wrote the authors, was that Soviet ESP, PK, and EM research was "cloaked in secrecy [and] camouflaged with false information." Access to more information was impossible because the Soviets likely conducted their experiments inside a "secret parapsychology laboratory inside a mental hospital." With such limited information available, the success of the research could not be determined. "Because the history of physics has been full of surprises, prudence dictates that one should consider [these concepts] until disproven. We therefore must suggest further research," the AiResearch study concluded.

The authors emphasized one critical difference between research that was going on in the East and in the West. In the West, the authors explained, ESP and PK researchers "cling to an undertone of a religious-like belief in transcendent mechanisms. The Russians reject this idea. As Marxists, or 'doctrinaire materialists,' everything has a scientific explanation." What made this more perplexing was that even without the mystical explanation, "The Russians assume the reality of thought transference."

The psychic research program at SRI was hanging on by a financial thread. Now that Puthoff and Targ's Navy contract had been unceremoniously canceled by Koslov, funds were running out. In the summer of 1977, the chances of Puthoff and Targ finding access to a submarine to test the ESP and ELF theory were close to nil—until Puthoff learned of a radical experiment being conducted by Stephan Schwartz, the former naval officer who had served as the special assistant to Admiral Zumwalt.

Six months earlier, in the fall of 1976, Schwartz had been sitting around a kitchen table in Los Angeles with two former Naval officers, Don Keach and Don Walsh. Keach and Walsh were two of the world's most famous deep-sea explorers. Keach was the submarine pilot who in 1966 had located a lost hydrogen bomb lying on the ocean floor off the coast of Palomares, Spain. The bomb, capable of destroying a major city if detonated, had been jettisoned from a B-52 bomber during a midair collision with its refueling aircraft. Walsh had performed an equally legendary feat, albeit with no weapons involved. In 1960, he and a crewmate made the deepest dive ever undertaken, to the bottom of the Challenger Deep in the Mariana Trench in the western Pacific Ocean. (Not for fifty-two years would anyone else make that dive, until James Cameron did, in 2012.) Keach and Walsh were now running the Institute for Marine and Coastal Studies at the University of Southern California. The conversation turned to Schwartz's earlier idea, back when he was in the Navy, about putting a psychic on a submarine. "I wanted to see if a remote viewer could locate a previously unknown shipwreck on the sea floor," Schwartz explained in 2016.

As circumstance would have it, Keach and Walsh happened

to be in a position to help. In a few months, and for a brief time, Keach and Walsh were going to have rare access to a submarine. "It was coming down from Canada for sea trials at their marine facility," Schwartz explained. "They said that I could have her for three days." For Schwartz, it was the opportunity of a lifetime. *Taurus I* was a state-of-the-art, five-man submersible capable of traveling to a depth of 1,000 feet. At thirty-one feet long, she cost $3 million to build. She had a large viewport and a claw to retrieve items on the ocean floor. With a submersible at his disposal, all Schwartz needed were the psychics. He wanted the most reliable psychics in the country for his project, so he reached out to Ingo Swann. Swann introduced Schwartz to the scientists at SRI; Hal Puthoff was particularly excited to collaborate.

The opportunity presented by Schwartz was fortuitous. Puthoff had recently been contacted by Dale Graff, a civilian scientist who worked for the U.S. Air Force. Graff, who worked in the Foreign Technology Division at Wright-Patterson Air Force Base in Ohio, wanted to keep a low profile, he said. He was interested in anomalous mental phenomena on a deeply personal level—something had happened to him, exactly what he was not yet willing to say. But Graff believed there might very well be an Air Force application or capability for ESP. If he and Puthoff could devise a modest but unique experiment, Graff believed he might be able to get the Air Force to supply funding. Schwartz's proposed submersible experiment was exactly the kind of opportunity both Puthoff and Graff had been looking for.

And so, in the summer of 1977, with a small contract from the Foreign Technology Division, Puthoff, Graff, the SRI team, and psychics Ingo Swann and Hella Hammid—a professional photographer and psychic who had replaced Pat Price—teamed up with Stephan Schwartz to conduct one of the most unique psychic functioning experiments of the 1970s, Project Deep

Quest. (Schwartz was unaware that Graff was working for the military.) To ensure an unbiased third-party observer, Schwartz hired a NASA satellite imagery specialist named Anne Khale, who accompanied the team and monitored all of the control elements for fraud. There were two elements to the program, an unclassified one in which Schwartz would hunt for a shipwreck, and a classified project for the Air Force to test long-distance remote viewing inside a submersible. The unclassified quest was later featured in an episode of *In Search of...*, hosted by Leonard Nimoy. The episode was called "Psychic Sea Hunt."

To begin with, Schwartz purchased a standard nautical chart that mapped an area around Catalina Island, off the coast of Los Angeles, that was roughly 1,500 square miles. He gave copies of the map to Swann and Hammid and asked each of them to locate by extrasensory perception any sea wreck on the ocean floor, to mark the location on the map, and to describe what would be found there. The method employed map dowsing, the same process used by Uri Geller to help Moshe Dayan locate lost archeological sites in Israel and the Sinai.

Using this technique, Swann and Hammid each marked multiple locations where they believed wrecks could be found. "I sort of look at the map not as much with my eyes as sort of get the feeling of it," Hammid explained in the film. "I tend to get a sort of feeling of a heaviness, I can't describe it any other way, and that's where I mark the map." Of map dowsing, Swann said, "You work up to it, you separate yourself from the environment, separate yourself and become psychic. That's how you do it."

Cartographer and career submariner Brad Veek created a composite from the two maps marked up by the psychics. Schwartz took this composite to the Bureau of Marine Sites of the U.S. Coast and Geodetic Survey for their official opinion, which was recorded live on film. The Geodetic Survey is the federally funded organization responsible for keeping track of maritime wrecks. In reviewing the map, an official confirmed numerous places marked by the psychics where shipwrecks were known to exist. These were eliminated as targets. In theory, the psychics could have cheated by secretly consulting government maps. What remained was a single target on the composite map that had been marked by both Hammid and Swann independently. What excited Schwartz was that these marks were just a few hundred yards apart. This was where the *Taurus I* submersible would go, Schwartz told the official, who gave his name as Thomas Cooke.

"Of all the existing known wrecks or suspected wrecks [including] fifty-three wrecks reported in the Catalina area, I am convinced there has been no known reported wreck in this area," Cooke told the film crew. He added how difficult it was to precisely locate a shipwreck on the sea floor, even when its location had already been identified by sonar or other technical means. "Finding a wreck, even when you know where it is, is an art in itself," Cooke warned, and compared the psychics' quest to a "wild goose chase."

For the classified Air Force project, Graff and Puthoff designed a simple remote-viewing experiment, a variation on the outbounder-beacon test designed by SRI for the CIA. Once the *Taurus* was deep underwater, at a predetermined time the psychics and the scientists were each given a set of six sealed envelopes. Inside each envelope was an image of a site in the San Francisco area. When the time came, Puthoff and Graff chose one of the six envelopes, opened it, then drove to the site and remained there as a beacon for the psychic in the submarine. At the same time, the psychic in the submersible was instructed to open all six envelopes, view the sites, and call out the location of the scientists. These experiments were also recorded, but not for the TV program.

Seated inside the submersible, 500 feet underwater and 375 miles away, Hammid quickly identified which photograph she believed was correct, which makes for a great story, but is also a one-in-six chance, not the worst odds. The scientists, Hammid said, were standing beside a giant oak tree on a hilltop, which in fact is where they were. The final step in the Air Force trial had been tailored for an emergency military scenario. On the back of each card was a message. Examples in this test included "Remain submerged for two days," and "Proceed to base one," and "Standby alert on priority targets." The submersible crew searching for the sunken treasure was not expected to act on the command. Rather, it was a dummy message designed to indicate to Graff's Air Force superiors at the Foreign Technology Division how ESP could be one part of a series of fail-safe protocols.

A second test with Ingo Swann delivered similar results, according to Graff's declassified report. Confident in the experiment's design, its protocols, and its strict controls, Graff took the results to his superior. "Two experiments of this type were carried out, one each with two subjects. For this first experiment the submersible was at a depth of 170 m in water 340 m deep; for the second the submersible rested on the bottom in 80 m of water...land-to-submarine communications by means other than the known five senses worked accurately," read Graff's report. From a counterintelligence point of view there were serious implications to consider, Graff wrote. Among them was the idea that there was no way to hide classified information from a talented remote-viewer like Hella Hammid or Ingo Swann. Air Force officials thanked Graff for his efforts and said they'd get back to him.

Stephan Schwartz's unclassified effort was also a success. A previously unidentified shipwreck was located on the seafloor in the vicinity where Swann and Hammid said it was. The claw on *Taurus I* pulled up several pieces of the wreck. How long it had been there no one knew. This was the first time in U.S. history that psychics had located an underwater archeological site from inside a submersible.

For Puthoff and Targ, a new funding opportunity was now at hand. The SRI scientists called on the ambassador of psychic research, Apollo 14 astronaut Edgar Mitchell, for help. Mitchell had created a nonprofit institute in Petaluma, California, called the Institute of Noetic Sciences, where he worked on metaphysical and consciousness studies full-time. On behalf of Puthoff and Targ, Ed Mitchell was able to secure a meeting with CIA director George H. W. Bush. Mitchell traveled to Agency headquarters, in Langley, Virginia, where the CIA director listened intently, Mitchell recalled in 2015. "He said his hands were tied because the Agency was in too much [trouble] with Congress." For the anomalous mental phenomena program to survive, Bush told Mitchell that it would need a military sponsor.

At Wright-Patterson Air Force Base, Dale Graff served as chief of the Advanced Missile Systems Forecast Section, the department assigned to keep the Air Force and Defense Department planners aware of the most classified, cutting-edge military research going on in the Soviet Union. Graff urged his superiors to fund a classified program with the SRI scientists that would focus on remote viewing research with special emphasis on locating lost airplanes. Several months later Graff got his answer: funding had been approved.

Graff could not have foreseen that his initial effort would turn into a colossal, twenty-year effort by the Defense Department to use psychic functioning in military operations. The program would involve numerous military and intelligence agencies, the National Security Council, the Joint Chiefs of Staff, even the president of the United States.

PART III

——

THE DEFENSE DEPARTMENT YEARS

Nature shows us only the tail of the lion. But there is no doubt in my mind that the lion belongs with it even if he cannot reveal himself to the eye all at once because of his huge dimension.

—Albert Einstein

CHAPTER THIRTEEN

Paraphysics

Through the U.S. Air Force, the Department of Defense was now officially running a psychic research program. When the CIA was running the program, DoD had been a client; now the Pentagon was in charge. One of the first actions taken by DoD was to assign the Defense Intelligence Agency—the Defense Department's top spy agency—to perform a classified study on parallel research programs going on in the Soviet Union and Warsaw Pact countries. The assignment went to civilian physicist Dale Graff, chief of the Advanced Missile Systems Forecast Section at Wright-Patterson Air Force Base.

"Nobody wanted the job," Graff recalls. The majority of individuals Graff worked with in his division did not take extrasensory perception and psychokinesis seriously, let alone perceive it to be a threat. So the first thing Graff did was pivot the existing nomenclature away from psychology toward physics, which was not unlike what the Soviets had done with their program a decade before. With an emphasis on hard, as opposed to soft, science,

Graff felt the report would get more traction at the Defense Department, which would disseminate it. For example, he titled his report *Paraphysics R&D— Warsaw Pact;* "paraphysics" a word he coined.

Graff's report highlighted Soviet research in electromagnetic fields, quantum physics, holography, and gravitation. He discussed biophysics and psychic healing, Kirlian photographs, auras, and map dowsing. He paid particular attention to psychokinesis. If PK was a genuine ability, it had the potential to disrupt or disable delicate electronics on Air Force weapons systems even on a micro level, so the research was critical even if it turned out to be a dead end.

A voluminous amount of military research material had been obtained from the Soviet Union, largely by the intelligence community, Graff found, but most of it had yet to be translated properly, if at all. "We had machine translators but they did a rough job," he recalls. "For more exact details, I had to find Russian linguists. This was not an easy task [seeing as] I had to have them assigned to translating ESP-related materials." Graff's report contained sections on Soviet and Warsaw Pact belief systems, political ramifications, and structure of government support. He profiled Soviet and Warsaw Pact paraphysics researchers, their laboratories, and how they were funded. He summarized the activities of individuals whose abilities were of concern to the U.S. intelligence and military communities, citing the "Geller effect" and the frog experiments of Ninel Kulagina, the Russian psychic who had allegedly stopped the beating heart of an animal, using only her mind.

The end result was a 125-page report. "It was a bump and grind job," remembers Graff, but well worth the effort as far as he was concerned because he had a vested interest in paraphysics research; it was deeply personal to him. Something had happened to him eight years before, in 1968, when he was stationed in Hawaii during the Vietnam War, and he attributed this mysterious event to phenomena that were real but that science could not yet explain. As a scientist, he vowed to find out.

It was August 1968 and Dale Graff, age thirty-four, had just returned from Vietnam, where he'd been sent by the Foreign Technology Division of the Wright–Patterson Air Force Base. Graff was an expert in Soviet weapons technology, including fighter aircraft, and he'd been sent overseas to teach U.S. pilots survivability tactics in air-to-air combat situations against the Soviet MiG.

Graff was a temperate man. Born in 1934 and raised just outside the Great Depression period, he spent much of his youth on a rented Pennsylvania farm. He loved maps, rivers, and watching birds. In 1958 he married Barbara Faust, his teenage sweetheart, and now they had two young children, ages seven and nine. He was thoughtful and soft-spoken, optimistic by nature. But war can push people to their limits, and the trip to Southeast Asia had left him feeling distressed. With so many of his colleagues getting shot down and killed or captured, it grated on him that as a civilian scientist he was not going to be sent into combat. He sometimes wondered if it was fair that scientists were spared the dangers of the battlefield. Intellectually he knew his work was as critical to the war effort as having his boots on the ground, but still, he felt bad. "I returned home in a foul mood," he remembers.

Graff had been with the Air Force for ten years, and was in Hawaii on a two-year transfer to Hickam Air Force Base. There were numerous beaches nearby, and on this day he made an early morning decision to go to one of them, swim hard, and disengage his mind from the feeling of powerlessness he couldn't seem to shake. Graff packed up Barbara and the two kids and made his way down Bellows Beach. Under one arm he carried a small surfboard. He was an excellent athlete and had recently taken up canoeing, but today he planned to surf and swim. His Achilles heel was his eyesight. "I have extremely poor vision, 20/2500 [uncorrected], and I'd forgotten my prescription goggles at home," Graff recalls. Using a trick called the pinhole effect that he'd perfected as a child, Graff squinted and was able to see.

There was a tempest brewing out at sea, the sky dark and foreboding. Even the lifeguard had gone home. Graff noted that the red flag was up, taut in a stiff wind. The waves were massive. Standing in his swim trunks at the water's edge he took stock of the situation and then made a decision. "The hell with it," he said to himself. "I'm going to go out and surf in these waves." Barbara and the kids would stay on the beach and build sand castles. Graff entered the rough ocean and paddled through the breakwater. Up and down he went, over large, powerful waves. He was of average build, five foot ten, thin but muscular and physically fit. The situation was challenging but not perilous, and for some time — it was hard to say how long — he rode the waves, squinting to see. Soon he was far from shore.

As the waves grew bigger and the sky darkened, Graff decided it was time to head in. "The wind was so loud I couldn't hear a thing," he says. The storm was moving fast. He realized that his arms were tired and the situation was rapidly changing. His scientist's mind assessed the situation. Things were getting treacherous. He needed to get in, now.

"Huge waves. Sore arms. Dark seas. Get to shore" — these were the thoughts running through his head. He paddled hard with intense focus. Get to shore, he told himself. Huge waves. Dark seas. Sore arms. Never mind, paddle. Get to shore. He told himself this again and again, the mantra of an athlete.

And then, over the deafening roar of wind and waves, Graff heard a distinct cry, "a sharp decisive human cry for help." It was clear. Undeniably clear. "Except this was impossible," he recalls. Was that his mind —? He stopped paddling. He looked around.

Could he have heard a seagull? he wondered. The wind howled. Out here in the vastness of the ocean the waves were immense. He was floating in an ominous, dangerous sea. Graff scanned the area around him. His heart beat intensely and the wind howled in his ears. He took stock of the situation and made a firm assessment: "There is nobody out here but me."

He resumed paddling. He knew his situation was extremely dangerous. His arms began to cramp. The sky above him was black and the storm was bearing down. He had a considerable distance to go. He had to get in, he thought. He paddled with all his might. Then, rather suddenly, something happened. Graff stopped paddling. He recalls: "With a few strokes I turned myself around and began paddling in the opposite direction, at a 45-degree angle, headed out to sea. 'You have to go out there,' my mind said. Dead ahead maybe fifty or a hundred yards...I spotted a coral reef."

Coral reef, huge waves. This was a suicide mission. He was now headed into a death trap, yet he was driven. "I paddled and paddled. I saw no one, heard no one. But I was compelled. It made no logical sense and yet I kept paddling," says Graff. "I got to the point where I was at the top of a huge wave. And as I began falling down [into the trough]...*Boom!* I crashed into a woman."

A drowning woman. "I saw it in her eyes," he recalls. "She was very close to death." The woman's mouth opened and she choked on seawater as she tried to grab a breath. She gasped. Then she went under. It was Barbara. She was out here in this dangerous ocean, too. Barbara couldn't swim, didn't know how to swim, yet she was here. Graff grabbed his wife and pulled her onto his board. His mind raced. She was barely breathing, going in and out of consciousness. Her life depended on him. He had to get to shore. Had to get Barbara to shore. "I realized we were caught in a rip current," he recalls. And now his scientist's mind kicked in. "I knew I had to swim at a right angle from the current, parallel to the beach," Graff explains. One wrong move and Barbara would slip into the ocean and drown. Where were their children? He could not think about such things now.

His mind attempted calculations. With every few inches of progress he made, the rip current seemed to gain a foot. Salt stung his eyes. Waves crashed around him as he tried to hold Barbara on the board. He was drifting closer and closer to the coral reef. The pinhole effect was no longer working and he was virtually blind. One arm had gone stiff from holding Barbara, the other was numb from paddling so hard.

Was this what it was like to face death? A terrible truth came over him. He had to make a decision. He could not save his wife and also save himself. He was a father. They had two young children. He asked himself a monstrous question: *Should I save myself and let Barbara drown?* He knew he had to make a choice. Then, just as he was about to decide, he heard a word loud and clear in his head. The word was No.

"And then the strangest thing happened," Graff reflects. "It was as if I went up over the situation. I was outside of my own body. I had a bird's-eye view of myself." From this impossible perspective, Graff could navigate the waves and the rip current. He could hold on to Barbara and he could see everything, including a pathway to shore. "There was a sense of timelessness. It didn't matter how long this would take. Time was meaningless. My arms were no longer sore. Paddling was effortless. Then suddenly, my knees hit sand." The children were standing in front of him on the shore.

Graff pulled Barbara onto the beach. "She had some water in her lungs. Using CPR, I made sure I got the water out. Made sure she was breathing. Then I walked back into a grove of pine trees, of Norfolk pines, and I collapsed. I had no idea what had just happened," he remembers. He wondered whether he ever would. It was 1968; the world was a different place, and husbands and wives often did not communicate so openly. "We did not discuss what happened," Graff recalls. "We would not discuss what happened that day for another thirty-one years. I myself could not say anything. I had to wait until Barbara brought it up. If I told her that I saved her life she would feel beholden to me, and our relationship would change. I couldn't do that." That's what he believed.

But the incident deeply changed his perspective and his own life. The next day he went to the public library in Honolulu and searched the card catalog for books that dealt with anomalous mental phenomena — aberrant occurrences in the mind that have no clear scientific explanation. Graff wanted to understand what might have happened to him at Bellows Beach. He was a sane individual. He carried a top-secret government clearance that required regular psychological tests. He did not take drugs. He had no neurosis or anxieties and had never experienced delusions of any kind. His had not been a religious experience; he was certain he'd not heard the voice of God. He also felt that what had happened to him was not a hallucination, it was real. He had perceived a human cry in an environment in which a human cry would have been impossible to hear: the waves were far too loud, and when he heard the cry, Barbara had been much too far away.

"It occurred to me the cry came from my own mind," Graff explains. "It had to happen in order for me to save my wife, the mother of my children. My mind made the sound. But how? And how did I travel outside my body in order to see myself and get to shore?" The answer to these mysteries had to be explicable by science, he believed.

He scoured the card catalog for books on consciousness, the state of being awake and aware. Consciousness equals sentience and perception, he learned; it is the executive control system of the mind. But there were as many questions as statements.

Does consciousness direct our actions and behaviors, or does it emerge from the operations of the brain? What is the function of consciousness? In the literature he learned there was no agreed upon or set idea. Reading about consciousness was like traveling down the proverbial rabbit hole. Scientists refer to "the hard problem of consciousness" because the nature of consciousness is a mystery that no one has been able to solve.

Graff searched for books that dealt with anomalous mental phenomena and arrived in a subcategory called parapsychology. Topics were broad and divergent, he found, and always excluded from orthodox psychology. Parapsychology included concepts as diverse as mental telepathy, psychokinesis, and out-of-body experiences, but also poltergeists and UFOs. The term "parapsychology" appeared to have been first used in 1889 by the German philosopher Max Dessoir, who defined the study as "a hitherto unknown fringe area between the average and the pathological states." Parapsychology was fringe science, he read, an area fraught with superstition and the occult. It was a domain most mainstream scientists labeled pseudoscience, a collection of beliefs or practices not based on the scientific method.

In the card catalog under "Consciousness" Graff came upon the works of the Swiss psychiatrist Carl Jung. In the stacks he located one of Jung's papers, "Concept of the Collective Unconscious," written in 1936, and began reading. In this paper Jung put forth the idea that in addition to each person's individual unconscious—meaning one's mind or psyche that is made up of experiences that happen only to the individual—there exists in all humans something Jung called the collective unconscious, a universal, impersonal, and inherited psyche that is common among all people. Jung described this collective unconscious as something akin to the reptilian brain, the oldest of the brain functions shared by all mammals, without which we could not have evolved.

Jung believed this collective unconscious was embedded deep

within every person, that it was a dynamic substratum common to all humanity. He rejected the idea that we are born as tabula rasae, blank slates. To Jung, the collective unconscious is populated by universal archetypes, or symbols—figures like the hero, the wise man, the trickster, and the savior; motifs like the apocalypse, the flood, the creation; events like birth, death, and the union of opposites. The collective unconscious is a force of nature and a product of evolution, Jung said, and it can sometimes cause men to act.

Graff was not sure what to make of Jung's idea or how it pertained to what had happened to him at Bellows Beach, but he knew it was a start of something powerful in his own mind. Jung's idea of the collective unconscious sowed a seed. Graff checked out a stack of books on consciousness, extrasensory perception, and the collective unconscious. At home in his spare time, he read.

The following year, he and his family returned to Wright-Patterson, in Ohio. The children were thriving, and Barbara began working at the hospital in Dayton as a nurse. Graff was promoted to chief of the Advanced Missile Systems Forecast Section of the Foreign Technology Division. He resumed PhD coursework at Ohio State University in aeronautical engineering. "I attended one course," he recalls, "but I could not focus. As interesting as it was, I just couldn't put my energy into this."

The mysterious world of anomalous mental phenomena had sparked something in him. He believed that there were pursuits beyond the confines of orthodox science that had greater significance and should be taken on. What had happened to him one summer day in Waimanalo, Hawaii, in 1968 was life altering. It had shaped him. He did not know how or why, exactly—only that his conviction was profound and that what he'd experienced was what the military called ground truth, a real situation.

Eight years passed. In 1976 he was now head of the Electro-Optic Threat Assessment Section of the Foreign Technology Group at Wright-Patterson. A scientist among scientists, he worked as division chief on numerous classified programs, many of which dealt with advanced sensor technology. As chairman of the Radar and Optical Intelligence Working Group, he oversaw research on electro-optics designed to detect military targets, including the Soviet ICBM, at very long range. "We would research Soviet technology in these areas, write papers, and estimate future capabilities," Graff recalls. United States–Soviet relations were in steep decline, and the need for foreign intelligence data on future threats never let up. Still, his interest in, and study of, extrasensory perception hadn't waned. He wanted to work on ESP research as a scientist. So he reached out to Hal Puthoff at SRI. After the submersible experiment, Graff received the go-ahead to proceed on a small Air Force program. The real work had just begun.

"Quietly, I began locating people at our facility who seemed interested in ESP. It was a classified effort," Graff recalls. "Rumors floated. Rumors that I was looking for 'sensitive people.' Remote viewers." He was put in touch with a young administrative assistant named Rosemary Smith who worked at the center for satellite photography. "She was interested," he remembers. "She came to me and said, 'I think I have this kind of ability.'" Graff ran some outbounder-beacon and picture-viewing experiments with Smith using SRI protocols. "Nice results," he says.

Five months had passed since Graff finished researching and writing *Paraphysics R&D— Warsaw Pact*. In the interim he'd been analyzing SRI data to learn how remote viewing might apply to the Foreign Technology Division in an operational capacity. "The Air Force has a repeating challenge, which is that aircraft go down. Because of this, the Air Force finds itself spending time searching for lost airplanes," says Graff, "ours and theirs." Figuring this was a good place to start, Graff wrote a proposal about how his division might locate a missing airplane with extrasensory perception. "I'd just finished writing out the protocols, the various steps involved, when there was quite literally a knock on my door. I was taken into an office in a classified setting and shown a photograph. 'This is a missing aircraft,' I was told. 'Can one of your people help find it?'"

By now an expert in foreign technology, Graff recognized the aircraft as a Soviet bomber, a Tu–22 Blinder. He said he'd see what he could do. He was told nothing about the location of the downed airplane. "I figured it had gone down somewhere in Europe," he recalls. He took the photograph to Rosemary Smith. Following the protocols he had recently designed in his proposal, he got to work with her. She had the correct clearances.

"It was informal," Graff recalls. "I showed her the photograph and asked if she could receive or achieve any impressions. After fifteen minutes she was drawing, scribbling, in a light altered state," he remembers. "She'd sketched a map, made little markings indicating north–south, noted a town and geological formations." Then she told Graff assertively that the aircraft had gone down "in mountainous terrain, not far from a lake." Graff asked if she could be more specific. "She was suddenly very focused and involved," he recalls. "She put her pen to the paper and drew a flight path. 'It went down here,' she said, and made a mark." On the map she wrote, "Plane possibly flew through pass or opening in mountains." Smith provided Graff with an intriguing detail. "She said she saw the pilot bailing out of the aircraft. At the time I didn't think it was important," Graff explains. This detail would later prove to be key.

Now Graff had a crude rendering of a map. He took that sketch to the search team working on the Tu–22 Blinder operation, along with a summary of Smith's remote-viewing session. The men thanked him for the work and he left. The following morning one of the team members came to his office and told him that his source had relayed something important. Graff was taken into a classified briefing room and read onto a classified joint CIA-USAF program.

"Laid out on a large table in this room was a large topographical map covering an area of two hundred by two hundred square miles," recalls Graff. "I was surprised when I realized I was looking at a map of Zaire, in Africa." He was told that the Tu-22 bomber was being flown by a member of the Libyan air force before it crashed. Wanting to defect, the pilot chose to bail out of the aircraft while it was in flight. The plane continued to fly on autopilot until it ran out of fuel and crashed in the jungle somewhere in Zaire. After the pilot made contact with U.S. officials, they realized that a gold mine of foreign technology had landed in their lap, if only they could locate the aircraft. Without fuel in the tanks it was likely that the plane had not exploded on impact, but U.S. officials had no leads as to where the bomber may have gone down. There had been no local reports about an airplane crash. Graff says the CIA dispatched a helicopter team to search for the missing Soviet aircraft but the remote jungle was dense. The search team quickly concluded that without an intelligence lead, they were unlikely to find the downed bomber.

With the topographical map laid out in front of him, Graff reviewed the terrain. He noted that Rosemary Smith's map was also being studied by the team. And he saw that what she'd drawn on her map lined up symmetrically with several of the lake-and-mountain patterns on the map before him. A decision was made to read Smith onto the program. She was brought to the briefing room and asked to look at the map. Could she home in on a spot where she perceived the aircraft might have gone down? Using an impromptu map dowsing technique, "She marked a spot," remembers Graff. "Map technicians converted her notation into a geographical coordinate, then sent that coordinate to the CIA station chief in Zaire."

Graff headed home feeling excited and apprehensive. He sensed that the future of an Air Force phenomena program hung in the balance. On earlier trips to SRI, and in his work with Puthoff and Targ, Graff had learned that combining information from two or more psychics working the same target often led to better results. Given the significance of the Zaire operation, Graff asked the Air Force to allow him to travel to SRI and work with another remote viewer. If he could have another day, he could likely deliver a second set of coordinates, Graff said. Air Force officials agreed.

In Menlo Park, Graff sat down at SRI with a remote viewer named Gary Langford, a former naval officer. "He came up with a sketch very close to Rosemary Smith's," says Graff. "As learned later, this sketch bore a resemblance to the general environment of the crash site. But Gary's data could not be sent to the field since the operatives in that remote area could only receive brief sentences or numbers due to the encrypted secure communication that had to be used." In the end, it was Rosemary Smith's coordinates that were used.

"These geographical coordinates were sent to the CIA station chief in Zaire, who turned them over to a search team made up of in-country clandestine officers and other people," Graff explains. He returned to Wright-Patterson, and with his participation in the search operation over, he wondered whether he would ever learn more about what had happened in Zaire.

Two and a half days later, there was a knock on Graff's door. "We found the airplane," he was told. The CIA's helicopter team landed in the village nearest to the coordinates provided by Rosemary Smith. The briefer told Graff that shortly after touching down, the team spotted a villager emerging from the jungle with an airplane part under her arm. This person led the search team back to the airplane. "The unit was able to extract valuable foreign technology" from the Tu-22 Blinder, says Graff, making the Zaire mission an unprecedented success.

On March 28, 1978, Graff was flown to the Pentagon to deliver a classified briefing to the acting chief of the Air Force and several other Defense Department officials. In a declassified Staff Meeting Minutes memo, officials learned of "a recent interesting case in which an Air Force 'sensitive' individual may have aided in the location of a plane which crashed in Africa after its crew members bailed out. Following intensive and unsuccessful efforts to locate the plane wreckage by other means, the sensitive [provided] coordinates." "Acting upon this information," the memo noted, "the Air Force has located an area corresponding to that described by the sensitive and is investigating what appears to be a crash site." The Zaire situation was now escalated to the commander in chief.

At the White House, President Carter was briefed by CIA director Stansfield Turner. Years later, in September 1995, Jimmy Carter publicly confirmed the incident as having taken place. He was impressed, Carter told a group of college students in Atlanta, that after spy satellites failed to locate the wreckage of a downed airplane, a psychic had pinpointed the location of the missing aircraft. "[She] gave some latitude and longitude figures. We focused our satellite camera on that point and the plane was there," the former president said.

Dale Graff experienced a moment in the limelight. As part of the intelligence community's Exceptional Analyst Program, he applied for a prestigious sabbatical that is awarded annually by the director of Central Intelligence. As a scientist, he was interested in locating evidence of the origins of anomalous mental phenomena. As a physicist he did not believe the answer lay in the supernatural but in the natural world. In his research proposal to the CIA, Graff laid out plans to study the electromagnetic effects that extrasensory perception might have on the brain, and whether the phenomenon had to do with electrical signals inside the human body.

While Graff waited to hear about the sabbatical, he was assigned to an Air Force program related to the MX missile basing system. In the late 1970s no issue was perceived to be more critical to national security than the threat of a Soviet preemptive nuclear attack, a first strike. America's land-based, nuclear-tipped ICBMs were stored in hardened underground missile silos across the country. Because of rapidly advancing satellite technology it was generally accepted in the intelligence community that the Americans and the Soviets knew the location of the other side's missile sites, and given that precision targeting technology had also advanced, strategists now feared the United States was vulnerable to a Soviet first nuclear strike. If this were true, then in a worst-case scenario the Soviets would be able to launch an attack that would cripple the American military and knock out its ability to respond.

As part of a program called Insuring Survivability, the Air Force devised the MX missile basing system (MX was an acronym for "Missile, Experimental"), and as bizarre as it may seem to modern readers, the proposed system worked like a shell game or confidence trick. Instead of keeping America's arsenal of nuclear missiles inside fixed storage facilities located underground, the new idea was to have actual nuclear-tipped ICBMs scattered among mock-ups of ICBMs, and to shuttle both the real and the fake missiles around a classified rail system built inside a 24,000-square-mile section of federal land in eastern Nevada and western Utah known as the Great Basin.

Those who were against this system said the idea was flawed, expensive, dangerous, and easy to defeat. But proponents of the MX program alleged that randomly shuttling an abundance of these missiles from shelter to shelter would "ensure location uncertainty," making it significantly harder for Soviet military planners to identify exact targets. Real missiles needed to be included in the mix because America had to be prepared to launch in a matter of minutes in the event that the president gave the order for a nuclear strike. One of the program's strongest supporters was General Lew Allen, the powerful Air Force chief of staff and a member of the Joint Chiefs of Staff. Allen was also the boss of Dale Graff's boss.

By 1979, plans for 200 road loops and 4,600 MX missile shelters were under way. With General Allen at the helm, the Pentagon was pushing the idea through Congress, with an estimated start-up cost of somewhere between $20 billion and $26 billion ($65 billion and $85 billion in 2017) and an annual operating cost of $440 million ($1.5 billion in 2017). Other divisions of the USAF were assigned to conduct operational security (OPSEC) diligence, in other words, to look for holes in the MX missile basing system. At Norton Air Force Base, in California, OPSEC teams developed theoretical schemes that might allow the Soviets to defeat the system. These teams then went out into the field to test viability. No idea was considered unworthy of investigation. After one team determined that cockroaches were attracted to materials in the ICBMs, another team studied desert insects. Dale Graff participated in satellite tests to determine whether their Soviet counterparts, using Soviet satellites flying over the Great Basin, could sense an abundance of cockroaches, thus indicating the real ICBM payloads.

As head of the Electro-Optic Threat Assessment Section, Graff was also involved in an array of brainstorming ideas designed to beat the MX missile basing system as part of an official Air Force vulnerability assessment team. He wondered whether remote viewers using ESP could determine which transport vehicles were carrying the real missiles and which were carrying dummy warheads. He contracted with Hal Puthoff to conduct a study. Using a computer-generated shell game, Puthoff's colleague Charles Tart, of the University of California, Davis, collected data from a group of psychics tasked to try to beat the shell game. Random guesses would produce a correct guess 10 percent of the time. On average, remote viewers trained in SRI protocols were correct 25 percent of the time. One "sensitive" individual in the group produced exceptional results, Graff learned. After fifty shell game trials times, she had guessed the location of a marble with an accuracy of 80 percent. Hal Puthoff's report for Graff indicated that remote viewers could significantly increase the odds in determining the location of the real ICBMs. This report was sent to the Pentagon.

"General Allen was furious," remembers Graff. The powerful general sent Graff a letter ordering him to immediately stop work on any programs that involved extrasensory perception, paraphysics, or parapsychology. Coming on the heels of the success of the Zaire operation, "it felt like a blow," Graff says.

A letter arrived in the mail. Its letterhead indicated it was from the Director of Central Intelligence (DCI). "Congratulations on your selection as one of the 1981 DCI Exceptional Intelligence Analysts," the letter began. "I can tell you that the competition this year was very keen. Your selection should be a source of pride both to you and to the Air Force." Not only had Graff won the prestigious yearlong CIA grant he'd applied for, but he and his family had been invited to CIA headquarters for a ceremony recognizing his selection. Graff collected his CIA-issued airline tickets and made preparations for the upcoming trip. He felt elated, he recalls.

The day before his departure Graff received another letter, this one informing him that General Lew Allen had, on Graff's behalf, stepped in and declined the CIA's Exceptional Intelligence Analyst award and its yearlong sabbatical program. "It was unheard of," recalls Graff. "But the decision could not be reversed." Allen was one of the most powerful figures in the U.S. military and at the Pentagon. "Here I was this little guy at the Foreign Technology Division getting squashed like a bug by the generals at the Pentagon," remembers Graff. He felt crushed and overwhelmed. A voice inside him told him to stay the course. That conviction paid off.

The following month he received an unexpected telephone

call from the Defense Intelligence Agency's Dr. Jack Vorona, who was assistant director for scientific and technical intelligence. Vorona was putting together a classified program called psychoenergetics, he told Graff, with the project's main goals "to evaluate the threat that foreign psychoenergetics achievements might pose to US national security, and to explore the potential of psychoenergetics for use in US intelligence collection." Vorona wanted Graff to come to Washington, D.C., and help him run this secret program.

Graff could hardly believe his good fortune. This was a real opportunity. There was a growing body of evidence demonstrating that extrasensory perception and psychokinesis were real phenomena, albeit rare and difficult to reproduce. With his access to classified information about the CIA program, Graff knew that part of the reason the Agency had canceled its remote-viewing contract was because its analysts had concluded that "there exists no satisfactory theoretical understanding of the phenomena," and that present theories were "speculative and unsubstantiated." Here, now, with the power and resources of the Defense Intelligence Agency's Directorate of Scientific and Technical Intelligence behind him, Graff believed there could be genuine progress toward a general theory. This was his quest.

CHAPTER FOURTEEN

Psychic Soldiers

At the Fort George G. Meade Army facility in Maryland, Second Lieutenant Fred Holmes Atwater read Dale Graff's *Paraphysics R&D—Warsaw Pact* report and felt a deep sense of foreboding and patriotic alarm. Atwater served in the 902nd Military Intelligence Group, a division of Army Intelligence called Operations Security, or OPSEC. As a member of the SAVE (Sensitive Activity Vulnerability Estimates) team, it was Atwater's job to visit Army facilities around the country in an effort to locate every possible security hole that the Soviets might try to exploit. Graff's monograph posited that the Soviets could be using extrasensory perception to conduct espionage against Army facilities and psychokinesis to potentially disrupt the delicate electronics on weapons systems. This was not something Atwater had ever seriously considered.

As an OPSEC officer, Atwater routinely conducted on-site surveys of Army facilities and attended security briefings with commanding officers. The procedures were routine. For example, if he was denied access to a classified area, he might come back later with a fake badge and try to get in. One of the nation's top targets for Soviet infiltration was the Army's Missile Research and Development Command Center at Redstone Arsenal, in Huntsville, Alabama. In the fall of 1977 the facility's commanding officer formally requested OPSEC support. The way Atwater remembers it, the missile command was concerned about security because so much of their testing involved ground-to-air missile telemetry, i.e., the radio signals that guide a land-fired missile to a target in the air. "Redstone wanted to know the actual hostile-intelligence threat posed and what OPSEC measures should be taken to counter this threat," recalls Atwater—in other words, how to plug holes.

Atwater went to Huntsville to examine the situation. After conducting the on-site survey, he sat down with a group of project managers to go over OPSEC suggestions, including counter-intelligence options and physical security measures that could be implemented by the team. The men sat around a conference table taking notes on Army-issue yellow legal pads. Just as Atwater was finishing his part of the exit briefing, one of the missile managers abruptly placed his briefcase on the table and dramatically opened it. He pulled out a book and slid it toward the center of the table for all to see. It was *Mind Reach: Scientists Look at Psychic Ability,* by Hal Puthoff and Russell Targ, which had been published the year before. The book discussed remote-viewing experiments at SRI, operations scrubbed of all CIA affiliation. Atwater was familiar with the book. After reading Dale Graff's classified *Paraphysics R&D—Warsaw Pact* report, Atwater had sought out and read all the unclassified material he could find on the subject.

"How are we supposed to protect ourselves from this?" the apparently alarmed Redstone missile manager asked Atwater.

The room fell silent. Atwater looked over at the commanding officer. "Based on the chief officer's reaction, I suspected the missile project manager had surprised him," Atwater says. He picked up Puthoff and Targ's book. The way he recalls it, he then said something to the effect of, "This subject is beyond the scope of this survey and today's briefing. I will have to get back to you later on this, sir." With that, Atwater and the SAVE team left Redstone.

Back at Fort Meade, Atwater met with his boss, Major Robert E. Keenan, and told him that, having reviewed the book and related subject material, he was concerned that the threat could be real. He'd looked through the outstanding Intelligence Collection Requirements (IRCs) to determine what, if anything, was being done to defend against possible Soviet parapsychology threats. Atwater cited Graff's report, which originated with the Defense Intelligence Agency. If the Soviets had research and development programs in this area, he told Keenan, OPSEC had an obligation to address countermeasures.

What was even more interesting, Atwater told Keenan, was that the DIA had been responding to an IRC on psychic phenomena, and that the original request had come from the CIA. Apparently the Soviets were heavily invested in paraphysics research, including ESP and PK, and had reportedly demonstrated experiments that showcased covert infiltration techniques against not only Redstone but numerous Army installations, operations, and facilities. The only way to establish the veracity of these reports, Atwater insisted, was to try to replicate them. He suggested the Army hire some of the so-called sensitives who were working with Puthoff and Targ at SRI to see whether they could access information about U.S. Army facilities using extrasensory perception. Places like Redstone Arsenal. This information could be helpful in future OPSEC vulnerability estimates, Atwater said.

Impossible, Keenan replied. These sensitives did not have security clearances, nor were they military trained. Atwater wondered whether the Army should create its own unit. From his personal investigation he had learned that one prevailing idea was that extrasensory perception was latent in all people but strong in certain individuals, and it could be learned if certain protocols were followed. The Army could ostensibly train its own people, Atwater said. It could teach intelligence professionals who already had security clearances and who were already trained in counterintelligence operations to become remote viewers. The plan was to create a small, low-profile unit, assemble it here at Fort Meade, and try and intercept signals from targets chosen by OPSEC. "Just as we use other intelligence-surveillance assets such as satellites, communications intercepts, and facility penetration agents to demonstrate OPSEC vulnerabilities to army commanders, we could use these trained remote viewers to demonstrate vulnerabilities to this unique form of surveillance," Atwater wrote.

Keenan sent Atwater's proposal up the chain of command. It landed on the desk of one of the most powerful people in Army intelligence, Major General Edmund R. Thompson. A pioneer in new technology systems, Thompson had played a major role in the formation of the U.S. Army Intelligence and Security Command (INSCOM). He was the general responsible for fielding the first Combat Electronic Warfare and Intelligence units. Now he was the assistant chief of staff for Army intelligence.

Strong opinions about extrasensory perception and parapsychology are almost always deeply personal beliefs. A few years earlier, Thompson later revealed, he'd read a book called *The Roots of Coincidence* by Arthur Koestler, which discussed Jung's concepts of synchronicity. Koestler's book put forth the idea that events with no causal relationship are meaningfully related, and that this underlying mechanism was also at work in extrasensory perception and psychokinesis. After reading Koestler's book, Thompson developed an interest in ESP and PK. When he read Atwater's proposal, he asked to be briefed on where the Soviets stood. He was startled by what he learned. "There was evidence that [the Russians] were particularly active in long distance, telepathic communication," Thompson said. "Also in PK, that they call telekinesis, and possibly in telepathic hypnosis, in order to disrupt individuals in key positions or handling sensitive equipment." This is similar to what the Army's Office of the Surgeon General, Medical Intelligence Office, had first warned about in its secret report in January 1972.

Atwater was sent to meet with Brigadier General John A. Smith, INSCOM's deputy commander and the man in charge of the unit's budget. Atwater's proposal was modest, with a budget of a couple of thousand dollars to cover travel expenses until the end of the year. Smith took out a budget request form, jotted down a few notes, signed it, and handed it to Atwater. "That was it," Atwater recalls. The project was given the temporary code name Gondola Wish, soon to be Grill Flame.

It was October 1978. Atwater and an Army major named Murray "Scotty" Watt were now in charge of this unusual new program. Their civilian partner in this endeavor was SRI, with Hal Puthoff and Russell Targ acting as lead scientists. Puthoff and Targ would teach Atwater and Watt protocols for running the program. And once a solid group of candidates had been preselected, they would help choose six or so psychics who would be part of Gondola Wish.

The first order of business for Atwater and Watt was to start looking for Army personnel. Using a personality profile created by Puthoff and Targ, the screening process began. Most of the interviewees were at the time working as imagery analysts at the National Photographic Interpretation Center, the CIA's photo interpretation unit, or at the Army Photographic Interpretation Center at INSCOM. Imagery analysts were people who had a special talent for detecting things in photographs that others couldn't see. Over the next few months Atwater and Watt screened 2,000 potential candidates. Finally they narrowed the pool down to 117. The interview process could begin.

Warrant Officer Joe McMoneagle worked at INSCOM headquarters at Arlington Hall Station in Virginia, building one-of-a-kind computer-driven black boxes for airplanes. A senior projects officer in Signals Intelligence and Electronic Warfare, he was thirty-two years old. His personal life was a mess, and he disliked the Army. From his perspective, he had given his employer everything, and it had given him back very little. He'd nearly died in a helicopter crash in Vietnam in 1967. Since then the military had moved him around incessantly, it seemed, from country to country, base to base. From 1971 to 1973 he was in Thailand, where he worked on classified missions that continued to give him nightmares. Now his second marriage was falling apart. He felt estranged from his only son. He had health issues. Pessimism was the dominant force in his life during this troubled time.

One day in October 1978, McMoneagle's senior adviser handed him a note. The instructions were cryptic, he recalls. He was to report to a sterile room on the third floor of the Arlington Hall Station headquarters building at a specific time, on a specific day. This was the Army, so he went. Inside the secure room were two men in civvies who introduced themselves as military intelligence officers and asked him to sit down. The men were Fred Atwater and Scotty Watt. Atwater opened his briefcase and spread a stack of papers across the conference table. Some were marked classified, others not. McMoneagle recalls that among the papers were many newspaper clippings, some from America but others from English-language papers published abroad. McMoneagle read the headlines, all seemingly referring to psychics, he recalls: "I thought, 'This is a setup.'" The two military intelligence officers asked what he thought of the subject matter in front of him. The way McMoneagle remembers it, he said something along the lines of, "I'm not sure I believe any of this, but if it's only half true it should be looked into."

The men gathered their papers and told McMoneagle not to discuss the meeting with anyone, not even his supervisor in Signals Intelligence and Electronic Warfare.

Back at his desk, McMoneagle's boss asked what the meeting had been about. "OPSEC people conducting a survey," McMoneagle replied.

Weeks passed. Then one afternoon McMoneagle received a telephone call from Scotty Watt. McMoneagle's presence was requested at another meeting, Watt said, details forthcoming. None of this could be discussed over the telephone. Watt told McMoneagle that if his supervisor asked any questions, he was to say he'd be attending a meeting at the behest of the Army chief of staff.

For the second meeting, McMoneagle traveled to Fort Meade. There, he reported to the 902nd Military Intelligence Group. The address was an old brick building, and McMoneagle was surprised at how many security doors he had to pass through before he arrived at the specified room number at the specified time. Inside this large room with oak-paneled walls he counted eighteen people sitting around a conference table: sixteen men and two women. Some wore uniforms and others civilian clothes. McMoneagle was asked to sit down. After a while two military intelligence officers McMoneagle recognized as Fred Atwater and Scotty Watt joined the group. As they'd done with him earlier, they spread a sheaf of papers across the table. Some were marked classified, others not, and as before, he spotted headlines about psychics from American and foreign newspapers. His intuition remained the same: Be careful here, he told himself. This could still be some kind of elaborate psychological operations experiment.

After the briefing finished, two men came into the room and introduced themselves as Hal Puthoff and Russell Targ, physicists from the Stanford Research Institute in Menlo Park, California. A movie was shown that featured something called an outbounder-beacon experiment, filmed at SRI a few years before. In the film, Puthoff and another researcher open a sealed envelope while sitting in the passenger seat of a car, then drive to the Stanford Medical Center courtyard as instructed on an index card. The film featured a simultaneous sequence of a man locked inside a sealed room, called a Faraday cage, at SRI's Radio Physics Lab. This man was a psychic named Pat Price, McMoneagle and the others were told. The film showed Price sketching what he "perceived" the outbounders (i.e., Puthoff and the researcher) were seeing in the Stanford Medical Center courtyard in real time.

McMoneagle remembers watching with fascination as Price "drew a very clear approximation of where Puthoff was in the hospital courtyard," and that "there was a clear accuracy to the size and relationships of objects." He recalls thinking that unless this was some kind of elaborate hoax or an INSCOM psychological operation, the film "was mind-boggling and frightening. It left me feeling that a new door to reality had just opened," McMoneagle says. There were situations in his past that he had never shared with anyone, things that remained inexplicable to him. When he saw the film, these strange occurrences made a faint kind of sense to him.

After the briefing ended, McMoneagle was taken into a room where he sat alone with Puthoff. For roughly fifteen minutes Puthoff asked relatively basic questions, to which McMoneagle gave relatively neutral responses, he recalls. Then came a question that tripped him up. "Have you ever experienced anything called a paranormal event?" Puthoff asked.

It was a direct question in a classified military environment. He decided to answer the question as accurately as he could, however unusual his response might seem. In Vietnam, when he was behind enemy lines in the jungle, he'd first experienced a hint of what might be called a sixth sense — "other forms of information transfer," he told Puthoff. His Army job title had been "emitter location and identification specialist," which meant it was up to him to locate where enemy transmissions might be coming from. "It was not an easy job," he recalls. "In wet jungle canopies you had to be nearly standing on top of a radio to know where it was." This meant that when you located what the Army wanted you to find you were very likely standing on a high-value enemy asset. The Viet Cong had the obvious advantage. Emitter location and identification specialists and their teams were regularly ambushed, individual members picked off by sniper fire. "My life was saved more than once by simply doing what my inner voice suggested," McMoneagle told Puthoff, "even if at the time it seemed foolish or stupid, or that I might embarrass myself." If McMoneagle felt compelled to clear out a certain bunker, he did. If he felt a violent urge to leave a site, he left. Others in his unit took notice and began to follow his moves.

Toward the end of his tour McMoneagle was flying back to the base at Pleiku when his helicopter was hit by enemy fire. One minute he was flying along listening to the rotor blades and the next minute, *wham,* his aircraft was going down. He woke up in an Army hospital with his leg in traction and pins in his skull. He recovered, was shipped out of Vietnam and sent to a small town in southern Germany called Bad Aibling. In 1970 he became detachment commander of a unit stationed at Pocking, Germany. That summer, he told Puthoff, he had a near-death experience at a restaurant on the Inn River, in Braunau.

He and his wife had met a colleague from the detachment for a drink. After a few sips McMoneagle began to feel queasy and excused himself. Had he been poisoned? he wondered. He'd just made it outside into the fresh air when he heard a weird sound, like a pop, inside his head. After that it was as if he were watching a film of himself, he said, standing on the cobblestone road, observing a surreal scene as it played out in front of him, outside the pub's front door. "Events then unfolded as though I were just outside the boundaries of reality," he recalled. He stuck out his arms and watched rain pass through his hands. Fears were replaced by fascination, he said. "I drifted over to see what the commotion by the door was all about and found myself staring down at my own body, lying half in and half out of the gutter." McMoneagle had swallowed his tongue and stopped breathing. He watched his wife and their friend load his body into a car. He watched the car drive to the hospital, in Passau, as if he were flying alongside it. He watched doctors and nurses try to revive him. He recalled falling into a long tunnel and observing the emergency room receding into the distance. For a while, he said, he remained there — wherever there was.

He reviewed his life. He felt sorrow and remorse. Growing up with two alcoholic parents in the Miami slums, he'd endured an unenviable childhood. Sometimes his father would hit him so hard his ears would ring and his face would bleed. Money went to booze, not meals. His twin sister was his best friend and his confidante — the one person who really understood him — but then she got pregnant in high school and the nuns took her baby away. She was sedated, became dependent on drugs, and was never "normal" after that. "And then I had an intense feeling of forgiveness flood over me," McMoneagle recalled. "At that point a voice in my mind said that I could not stay, that I had to go back. It was not time for me to die." McMoneagle argued with the voice, to no avail. "There was a second sudden popping noise and I sat up on the hospital bed and looked around." The room was empty.

When his wife came to visit, she explained that when McMoneagle had arrived at the hospital he was clinically dead. After he came to, the Army had moved him to this private clinic in Munich to convalesce. Here he began having out-of-body experiences, he said, a terrifying situation for him over which he had no control. He could read the minds of others, he believed: "I wasn't actually hearing them thinking, nor was I reading their thoughts verbatim but I was picking up on the general gist or subject matter contained within their thoughts." McMoneagle told the nurses what was happening to him, but then surmised that sharing these kinds of experiences in a hospital environment was not a good idea. He stopped discussing the situation with others, but he knew he had experienced some kind of change. "Once you have had a near-death experience it is almost impossible to act normal again. It alters the very color of the light in which you see things," McMoneagle says.

After several weeks he was released from the clinic and assigned a new job in Munich, in Army intelligence. Everything was different now. Fear of death abandoned him. He began reading voraciously: philosophy, theology, parapsychology, and ancient religious texts. He read everything he could get his hands on about these topics, from Carlos Castaneda to Madame Blavatsky to Aristotle. For a poor kid from the Florida projects this intellectual exploration felt exhilarating: "Parts of my character began to fade and be replaced with other elements that were totally strange to me." Life was about discovery now, with "the newfound clarity of my paranormal mind." He was twenty-five years old. But there were bills to pay, and he was an enlisted man in the U.S. Army. His next assignment was an operation in Thailand. Because this operation remains classified as of 2017, McMoneagle is not at liberty to share details. But this dark wartime experience further shifted his perceptions about the meaning of life, he says. Back in America after the war, he worked at a series of unsatisfying Army jobs. He divorced and remarried, and then his second marriage was heading toward divorce. That's when the two military intelligence officers named Fred Atwater and Scotty Watt showed up, asking questions about psychics and phenomenology.

After interviewing Joe McMoneagle, Hal Puthoff recommended him for the new unconventional Army program. McMoneagle was just the kind of person Puthoff believed could be trained in remote viewing for use in intelligence collection. Atwater and Watt asked McMoneagle if he was willing to join a prototype six-man unit at Fort Meade, a classified program called Grill Flame. This unit was experimental and part-time. McMoneagle would be sent out to SRI for training, and after that he would participate in a series of outbounder-beacon experiments at Fort Meade. McMoneagle signed on and was designated Remote Viewer 001.

Also chosen for the team were three civilian Army employees and two intelligence officers. They were Melvin Riley, a photo interpreter and former aerial observer; Hartleigh Trent, a National Photographic Interpretation Center officer and former Navy SEAL training instructor; Fernand Gauvin, a veteran counterintelligence officer who'd worked espionage operations in France since the early days of the Cold War; Captain Kenneth Bell, a counterintelligence expert; and Nancy S., an imagery analyst about whom little has been revealed. The unit's first office was located in Building 4554, in a secure room across the hallway from Colonel Keenan.

The group, called Detachment G, or Det G, was an oddity, a secret unit whose work was unprecedented in Army intelligence history. Because Grill Flame was a clandestine operation, its participants were allowed to dress like civilians and wear their hair long. After people began making inquiries, Colonel Keenan decided to move the viewers to a more discreet location down the road on Llewellyn Street. The unit's new home was inside a former World War II mess hall, across from a hospital in a grove of oak trees. Administrative work took place in Building 2560, a long skinny structure with desks and filing cabinets lined up front to back. Building 2561, across the street, was the remote-viewing facility. Here, inside an electronically shielded room, members of this unorthodox unit now found themselves lying in a dark room, eyes closed in a trancelike state, practicing how to perceive things that were not physically there. There was lots of downtime, and viewers were encouraged to cultivate habits that helped them relax. Fern Gauvin practiced yoga. Mel Riley did Indian bead-work. Joe McMoneagle painted a massive, multicolored mural of the cosmos on the office wall.

Early Army memos indicated that "preliminary results show high-level interest" in the unit's progress, not just from DIA but from superiors at the Pentagon as well. General Thompson approved a budget increase, and McMoneagle, Riley, and Bell were given full-time positions. Work progressed. Then, in September 1979, Det G garnered the attention of the National Security Council (NSC), the president's principal forum for considering national security matters. Members of the NSC were shown photographs, taken by a KH-9 spy satellite, revealing a beehive of activity inside a massive building at the Severodvinsk Naval Base in Russia. Located 650 miles north of Moscow near the Arctic Circle, Severodvinsk was strategically positioned at the edge of the White Sea and there was concern in the intelligence community that the Soviet Union was building its first aircraft carrier inside this mysterious building.

The National Security Council delivered an official request for information to the Office of the Assistant Chief of Staff of Intelligence, Department of the Army, which in turn relayed the request to Det G at Fort Meade. There, Fred Atwater assigned the intelligence collection effort to Joe McMoneagle. As revealed in declassified documents, what followed gave Det G its first, eight-martini results. In Remote Viewing Session C54, date unrecorded, Atwater placed a sealed envelope on the table in front of

McMoneagle and asked him to provide information about the photograph concealed inside. McMoneagle described a huge building "near some kind of a shoreline, either a big lake or some bay."

"It smells like a gas plant," McMoneagle said, "like there's a smelting or a melting or something [going on] inside the building." McMoneagle described "lots of people in funny hats... arc welding activity... standing on catwalks. They're cutting metal or bending metal, welding metal, shaping metal," he said. "Very unusual. Very, very large.... There's some kind of a ship. Some kind of a vessel. I'm getting a very, very strong impression of props," meaning propellers, he said. Atwater asked McMoneagle if he could be more specific.

"Jesus! This is really mind blowing," McMoneagle said next. "I'm seeing fins, but they're not rocket fins or [air]plane fins. They're... They look like shark fins."

"Alright, fine," Atwater said—a standard prompt.

"Very much like shark fins," McMoneagle clarified.

"Alright, fine," Atwater said again. He asked McMoneagle to try and describe what was inside the building but McMoneagle had trouble getting off the notion of the shark. He repeated the word "fin" nine times. "I wish I could tell what that God damn fin was too, because I think that's very significant," McMoneagle said.

"I'm seeing what looks like part of a submarine in this building," he said finally. "I'm getting a strong impression of a huge, coffin-type container. A giant coffin-type thing. It's like they created part of a submarine to... to... fasten this modification to."

Atwater asked how the coffin was connected to the submarine.

"I think this is like a prototype," McMoneagle responded. "Perhaps four, five stories or six stories tall.... I'm asking myself the question, what is this thing? This coffin-like thing? And the answer that I keep giving myself is that it's a weapon. And I don't know why. I don't see any weapon," he said. The transcript of the session was forty-seven pages long.

The Army's Office of the Assistant Chief of Staff of Intelligence sent Det G's intelligence collection report to the National Security Council for review. The report was interesting to some, including Commander Jake Stewart of the Office of Naval Intelligence, and dismissed by others including Robert Gates, an analyst on loan to the NSC from CIA. That the Soviets would build a submarine inside this building, and not in a dry dock located at the water's edge, seemed to defy logic. The building McMoneagle had been asked to view was located roughly one hundred yards inland from the shore at the naval yard. At one point in McMoneagle's session he had described "a concrete structure, like in Holland in a canal. For you know, controlling the flow of water." But the KH-9 spy satellite photographs from September 1979 showed no canal between the mysterious building and the navy docks—only flat, frozen earth.

Four months later, in January 1980, new images captured by a KH-9 spy satellite over Severodvinsk sent shock waves through the intelligence community. The January photographs revealed a massive submarine tethered alongside a navy dock at the Severodvinsk Naval Base, the likes of which had never been seen before. The photographs also revealed that a channel had been dynamited and dug—sometime in the past four months—between the building McMoneagle had remotely viewed and the dock. These new satellite images made clear to the CIA that the Soviets had covertly constructed a prototype for an entirely new generation of nuclear-powered, ballistic missile submarines. The Soviets called this clandestine effort Project 941, codename "Акула," or "Shark" in Russian. The Shark submarine would become known in the West by its NATO reporting name "Typhoon." Tom Clancy would make the Typhoon famous in his 1984 novel, *The Hunt for Red October.*

The Typhoon class submarine carries twenty submarine-launched ballistic missiles (SLBMs), each outfitted with ten multiple independent reentry vehicle (MIRV) warheads for a total of two hundred nuclear weapons on board a single submarine. Built for arctic patrols, the Typhoon was designed to quickly break through polar ice, surface, and launch enough nuclear weaponry to annihilate the United States in a single preemptive strike. It is the largest class of submarine ever built, its massive size owing to the fact that the prototype Typhoon was the product of two delta class submarine hulls welded together. It would become one of the most feared weapons of the Cold War. Joe McMoneagle had provided seminal information on the Typhoon submarine before any other intelligence asset in the United States. Fort Meade's Detachment G now had what is known in military and intelligence circles as an "intelligence first."

For the Army, it was imperative to determine whether regular military personnel could learn remote viewing as a discipline, or skill. As a general rule, psychics and the Army did not mix, so the plan was to spend year one establishing that the phenomena was real; year two would be for training; and year three for developing Army protocols. That was the plan. Instead, on November 4, 1979, one of the most dramatic national security crises of the twentieth century came to pass. In Tehran, revolutionaries stormed the U.S. embassy and the Iranian Foreign Ministry, taking sixty-six Americans hostage. It was a crisis of epic proportions, unprecedented in American history. Aware of the experimental unit at Fort Meade, the National Security Council authorized the Army's psychics-in-training to become an operational unit in support of the hostage crisis in Iran.

"I received a call at 4:00 a.m.," McMoneagle recalls, "asking me to report directly to the office." He was told not to listen to the radio, not to turn on the television, and not to look at any newspaper headlines. When he arrived at Fort Meade, his Det G team members were already assembled, seated around a large conference table covered with more than one hundred photographs. Atwater briefed the unit about the crisis in Tehran and gave the viewers a real-time operational task. They were asked to determine which individuals were hostages and which were not. Following SRI protocols, they worked to identify three Americans they believed were being held separately from the other hostages and whose whereabouts were not yet known to the Pentagon. When the National Security Council verified the accuracy of the information with the CIA, the Joint Chiefs of Staff became involved. The unit was then asked to provide information regarding people, places, and infrastructure in Tehran.

"What was targeted?" McMoneagle asks rhetorically. "Every building, every room, every person in each of those rooms... what they were wearing, what their health was like, what the furniture looked like, what kind of paint or pictures were on the wall." Weeks passed and the workload ballooned. NSA assigned the viewers to locate any underground infrastructure near where the hostages were being held. When they identified a pre-Roman sewer system running beneath Tehran with an entrance beneath the embassy, the Joint Chiefs determined the information to be "actionable intelligence." As hostages were shuffled between locations, the viewers worked to track movements between "Komiteh prison, Qom Prison, Evin Prison, Jahroum, Shiraz, Area J (Ambassador's Residence), Staff Quarters No. 7, The Chancery and the Mushroom Inn."

In mid-April, Grill Flame's work on the Iranian hostage situation was affected by a series of destabilizing twists. The remote viewers arrived at the office one morning to learn that they were being moved from their secure facility at Fort Meade to a suite of hotel rooms down the road in Laurel, Maryland. They were now part of a highly classified Special Access Program in support of the hostage crisis, they were told. Sequestered from the outside world, viewers worked around the clock. Then, during a session in the second week of April 1980, Hartleigh Trent went off-subject from his requested target in Tehran and described a dramatic scene in a stark desert environment. Trent told Atwater he saw American soldiers rappelling out of a helicopter, commando style. The session was abruptly ended. Several days later, viewer Fern Gauvin reported seeing a similar scene involving "fire and death," but not in a city.

Declassified documents indicate that on April 24, 1980, Nancy S. was conducting Remote Viewing (RV) Session CCC84 when she broke down. The tasker noted, "Admin note 0300 Hours in Iran," or at 3:00 a.m. local time, Nancy S. reported she was having trouble getting the target she'd been sent to, which was a building in Tehran code-named India. Instead, she said she saw "an attacking force of some kind." She apologized and stated that perhaps she was "hallucinating." What she saw was "weird and illogical" but "very vivid, horrible. Like a bad dream..." Her descripion was of "Big chest, big big gorillas. Great big chest beating gorilla leading these apes...they had tiny 9 inch long rockets, hundreds of them." She apologized again and said she'd "never lost control like this before." According to a report declassified by the CIA, she saw "a very boring sequence and all of a sudden you are aware something is amiss and something is very wrong, people are running...with great stealth....And all of a sudden you find you are in an attack....You, the audience in the middle of an attack." There was "Ground equipment...large caliber machine gun. Three or four of them, in a row."

The way McMoneagle recalls what happened, Nancy S. reported "a huge explosion...a huge fire she couldn't understand what for." And then she became overwhelmed with emotion and broke down in tears. The situation was intense: the viewers were exhausted from the stress of the situation, the hotel environment, and the hours involved. Then, late that same night, Scotty Watt declared the mission over. He turned on the TV. To a stunned nation, President Carter announced a failed hostage rescue attempt and helicopter crash in the Iranian desert, 200 miles southeast of Tehran. The desert location was code-named Desert One; the rescue operation was Operation Eagle Claw. The crash killed eight U.S. servicemen and one Iranian civilian. Scores more were injured. What would happen to the hostages now, as a result of the failed rescue operation, was unknown.

Had Hartleigh Trent and Nancy S. experienced precognition? What about Fern Gauvin? Had they traversed the barrier of time and obtained information about a future event? Were they seeing events in real time? Were the gorillas some kind of gestalt for, or a symbolic representation of, Special Forces operators? The Army remote viewers were not born psychics. They did not pretend to be like Ingo Swann, Uri Geller, or Pat Price. They were only recently trained in an experimental collection tool whose value had not yet been determined by the Army. Precognition was a nightmarish skill to possess. To see the future was to see death; who would want to cultivate this ability?

Nancy S. quit the unit, says Joe McMoneagle. So did Fern Gauvin. Reached in 2014 by telephone at his home in Maryland, Gauvin confirmed the events that took place at the Maryland hotel but refused to discuss further what had happened during the remote viewing of Operation Eagle Claw. "If you ask me, I will hang up," he said.

On April 25, 1980, Ayatollah Khomeini held a press conference. In a speech heard around the world, Khomeini condemned President Carter and credited Allah with throwing sand to protect Iran from the American invaders. "The big Satan has taken up his foolish mischief," Khomeini said. "God the omnipotent has defeated them."

At Fort Meade, the viewers continued to provide information for the National Security Council, the CIA, and the Joint Chiefs of Staff. Three months later, with the hostages still in captivity, President Carter took to the podium in the White House press room to provide facts about the ongoing Iran hostage crisis. In one hand he carried a folder. On the tab were two words, "Grill Flame." At the time, few people had any idea what those code words meant.

It is generally accepted that the failure of Operation Eagle Claw cost President Carter the election. On January 20, 1981, just minutes after Ronald Reagan was inaugurated as the new president of the United States, the government of Ayatollah Khomeini released all fifty-two remaining hostages.

An eerie chill descended on the Det G unit at Fort Meade. The unspoken question on everyone's mind was *What are we dealing with here?* The answer, also unspoken, was *We don't know, so don't ask.* Gone now was any sense of playing or practicing to be psychic. If the outbounder-beacon experiments carried the patina of a new age consciousness-expanding exercise, what happened during the Tehran crisis resulted in a paradigm shift. The U.S. Army's remote-viewing unit had been squeezed into an impossible position. On the one hand the message from the establishment was clear: We don't know what this is; we can't verify if it's real, but we're going to move forward anyway, scrapping the original three-year plan. But while such an open-ended situation might be accepted at an ashram in India, on a mountaintop in Tibet, or even at the Central Intelligence Agency, it was an unlikely undertaking for the U.S. Army. At Fort Meade the stage was now set for a state of utter confusion and chaos.

CHAPTER FIFTEEN

Qigong and the Mystery of H. S. Tsien

O n March 11, 1979, an article appeared a world away on the front page of one of China's top newspapers, *Sichuan Daily,* about a twelve-year-old boy named Tang Yu who was able to "read" with his ears. At CIA and DIA, analysts followed the story with acute interest, translating, interpreting, and analyzing what this might mean for U.S. national security. Before this article appeared, very little attention was paid to China as a possible threat in the realm of psychic warfare and military research into anomalous mental phenomena. This article changed all that, literally overnight. Intelligence analysts were startled by what they discovered about China and psychic functioning.

China has a long and rich tradition of spirit culture, extrasensory perception, and superstition. The *I Ching,* or *Book of Changes* (1000–750 BC), is one of the oldest and most widely read ancient divination texts in the world. It is said to have shaped Chinese philosophy, science, and statecraft for thousands of years. In the post–World War II era, after the 1949 Chinese Communist Revolution, activities such as ESP and divination were officially forbidden, much as the Soviets had sought to eliminate religion and mysticism in the wake of the Russian Revolution. But starting in the early 1960s, Russian government research into extrasensory perception was allowed to move out of the shadows and into the mainstream, justified, ironically, by international reports of American ESP experiments on the USS *Nautilus*. In Russia, ESP and PK research had been quietly gaining momentum ever since, but in China the revival was nonexistent or at least unknown to the U.S. intelligence community—until this front-page article appeared about a boy who could read with his ears. The CIA and the DIA had a mystery on its hands.

China's Politburo, or ruling party, controlled the nation's press. That a story about a boy apparently endowed with a bizarre form of extrasensory perception had been published in such a high-profile newspaper as the *Sichuan Daily* was unusual. That the article featured a photograph of Tang Yu standing beside a powerful Communist Party provincial secretary, both of them smiling, was unprecedented. For analysts at CIA, this signified a government seal of approval. Intelligence analysts sought to understand this phenomenon, referred to in classified documents as "skin-reading." But an equally important mystery was why the Communist Party had seemingly decided to endorse extrasensory perception.

The story had begun five months earlier, the CIA learned, in a remote mountain village in Dazu District. One day in October 1978, Tang Yu and his friend Chen Xiaoming were walking home from school when the two boys decided to stop on the footpath and have an impromptu wrestling match. "We were tussling together when my ear brushed against his coat pocket and immediately two Chinese characters sprang into my mind," Tang Yu told a reporter. The words he had seen with his ear were "flying" and "swan," he said.

The experience struck him as so powerful that he stopped

wrestling in order to describe his vision to his friend. Chen Xiaoming unbuttoned his coat, reached into the inside breast coat pocket, and pulled out a pack of cigarettes he'd secreted inside. The brand, Flying Wild Goose, featured the image of a long-necked bird in flight. So awestruck were the two schoolboys that they agreed not to tell their parents. Chen Xiaoming was far too young to be smoking cigarettes and would surely get in trouble. Instead, the boys began to test Tang Yu's skin-reading abilities on local townsfolk, the CIA learned.

Villagers were asked to jot a few Chinese characters onto a small slip of paper, roll the paper into a little ball, and place it inside one of Tang's ears. Time and again, the boy would "read" the words or phrase that had been written down. News of the boy's phenomenal abilities spread throughout the village and beyond. A local official with the People's Commune was summoned to conduct a test, then a top district authority with the county government, and finally a Sichuan Province Communist Party figurehead. In demonstration after demonstration, Tang Yu displayed his powers with astonishing regularity. "When the [paper] ball is placed into my ear, I feel a tingling and an image of the characters appears in my head like a film projected onto a screen," he told officials. Finally the governor of Sichuan Province—a powerful official named Zhao Ziyang—became personally involved.

Zhao was hardly a household name in the West, but to the CIA he was a formidable force, a rising star among Chinese Communist Party officials. Two years before, in 1977, he had been promoted to the position of alternate member of the Politburo by the Chinese Communist leader himself, Deng Xiaoping. By 1979 Zhao was made a full Party member, and in October 1980 he would succeed Deng as premier of the People's Republic of China. Why was Zhao involved? CIA analysts wondered. Who was behind this? U.S. intelligence analysts rushed to learn what exactly was going on, acquiring hoards of Chinese documents and scouring them in translation.

In China, the story about Tang Yu reached millions of Chinese citizens, and news of the boy's extraordinary powers spread. Officials of the Science Commission in Beijing were summoned to investigate. After laboratory tests, China's top party scientists determined that Tang possessed what they now officially called Extraordinary Human Body Function, or EHBF. Within weeks, what would soon become known as the first Extraordinary Powers Craze took hold. The CIA was puzzled by this remarkable turn of events. All across China people wanted to meet Tang Yu, the extraordinary boy who could read with his ears.

Party-sanctioned newspapers began reporting additional stories about children with EHBF. Each case, readers learned, was being authenticated by local science commissions at an official Party Commune branch. From Beijing to Heilongjiang to Jiangsu province, stories of anomalous mental phenomena began to unfold like falling dominoes, featuring children who could read with their fingers, hands, and feet. By September, China's top science periodical, *Nature Journal (Ziran Zazhi)*, published a lengthy article based on the observations of one of its in-house science writers. In controlled environments, the abilities were authenticated and new forms of eyeless sight were confirmed by Party officials. Interest grew.

Four months later, in February 1980, scientists from more than twenty colleges and research institutes gathered in Shanghai to test the extraordinary children as part of the government-sanctioned conference titled "First Science Symposium of the Extraordinary Function of the Human Body." Fourteen of the children were determined to possess EHBF, meaning that they displayed mental and physical powers that science could not explain. What was particularly interesting to CIA and DIA was how the Chinese framed their research. By calling the subject matter Extraordinary Human Body Function, the Chinese were assigning these remarkable powers to human biology. In the West, this notion fell under the rubric of human potential—the idea that untapped resources exist inside all people. This belief system had been growing in American counterculture since the early 1960s with programs like EST (Erhard Seminars Training) and had come to include countless other programs ranging from Neuro-Linguistic Programming (NLP) to information-coded biofeedback. In Communist China, all science programs were de facto government research programs; there was no science separate from the state. Now, motivated in part by this perceived threat from the Chinese, the U.S. military's interest in human potential as a means of gaining superiority over the enemy was stimulated. If China was advancing human potential, so must the United States.

"The discovery of this new power could shatter modern science," said Dong Taihue of the Department of Optical Engineering at Zhejiang University. EHBF could pave the way for a revolution in scientific thought. "We are facing a challenge to orthodox scientific theories," declared the professor. "Further research of this power could result in tremendous breakthroughs in physiology, physics and biological physics—a whole new branch of science could just be waiting to be discovered."

As more than a dozen new research institutes were set up across China, research into anomalous mental phenomena in the People's Republic was now an officially sanctioned, large-scale pursuit at the national laboratory level. EHBF was listed in the *Chinese Encyclopedic Almanac,* in the science and technology section. The craze gained further momentum as even more dramatic powers emerged, now including psychokinesis. A young girl could move an object across a desk using only her mind. Another could cause a flower bud inside a sealed jar to blossom in a matter of seconds. A boy could snap tree branches from a distance of several feet. Children with EHBF were tested in psychokinesis experiments. They could "turn the hands of watches, bend metal, break matches and cause spontaneous combustion of flammable materials at the wave of a hand," wrote an analyst with DIA. When it was reported that several of the children were endowed with a mysterious seventh sense whereby they could see through lead containers, the Chinese air force became involved. Yu Ruihua, a young girl from rural Cangxian County, was tested by a special physics research team with the Institute of High-Energy Physics of the Chinese Academy of Sciences, Beijing. The academicians reported that she was able to see through a lead container, the kind used by the military to store radioactive materials, and could read what was written on a sheet of paper inside.

Chinese air force scientist Luo Dongsu made a bold assertion: "Brain wave analysis of exceptional vision (eyeless sight) suggests that the children possessed a unique, still unknown radiation." Their minds could produce "rays similar to microwaves," he proposed, ones that were "a staggering ten million times stronger than the most powerful radar equipment in present use." As had transpired in the Soviet Union and America, when Chinese scientists began looking for the source of the mystery force powering EHBF, they looked first at electromagnetic waves.

But Chinese scientists also had an alternative idea about what could account for this mysterious power. Intelligence analysts found their first clue in the words of the keynote speaker from the First Science Symposium in Beijing, a martial arts master named Qu Hanrog. The source of his power, he said, was *qi*, which translates as "vital energy" or "life force." Qi was ancient, as old as the *I Ching*, or *Book of Changes*. For thousands of years the effects of qi had been studied, honed, and modified though an ancient martial arts practice called qigong, "mastery of vital energy." Qu Hanrog told the members of the First Science Symposium that through qigong he had cured himself of paraplegia and could now walk again. Through qigong, Hanrog said, he developed EHBF, including ESP.

To understand qigong, the CIA examined its history. The practice had been in existence in China, in various forms, for thousands of years. In ancient texts, qigong masters were said to possess supernatural, warrior-monk powers including invisibility and invincibility. Stories of qigong masters appeared across the historical record up to modern times. In 1948, shortly before the founding of the People's Republic of China, modern qigong was born. That year a small group of communists gathered in the mountains of Hebei province to perform breathing exercises under the direction of a qigong practitioner named Liu Guizhen. Their goal was to rid themselves of physical sickness and ill thoughts. When powerful Communist Party leaders learned of these gymnastic-like exercises and the health benefits they provided, they summoned Liu to their seaside enclave at Beidaihe to learn more. He explained that only two years previously he had been so riddled with sickness—including tuberculosis, gastric ulcers, and anxiety—he weighed less than eighty pounds and was on the brink of death. His doctor told him he had only a few months to live. So he took up qigong. Through a series of silent mantras and breathing exercises, and by focusing his mental awareness on his navel, his brain activity slowed and his inner organs regained strength. After 102 days of these exercises, Liu regained his health and returned to work.

Communist Party officials saw promise in this remarkable story and asked Liu Guizhen to teach them how to master qigong. Decades of war had decimated the early-twentieth-century Chinese health system. By 1949, when the Communist Party took power, "it was faced with the pitiful state of the nation's health system," explains David A. Palmer, the West's leading expert on qigong in China. "There were only 12,000 scientifically-trained doctors—one doctor for every 26,000 people—almost all of whom were concentrated in the cities." Communist Party officials saw qigong as a potential solution to the nation's health care crisis. Officials could use the benefits of ancient medicine in statecraft.

The leaders liked what they saw. Qigong was medicine for the masses. Through a series of simple gymnastics, breathing exercises, and mantras that required as little as thirty minutes a day, Party leaders found themselves cured of all kinds of personal ailments, including ulcers and insomnia. This idea of simple, nonscience-based medicine for the masses was in keeping with Marxist thought. Qigong could be performed anywhere, anytime, without medical equipment or drugs. What had been a long-standing, esoteric tradition passed down from master to student for millennia could now be propagated for the masses while being controlled by Communist Party directives.

A plan was put into action. With Liu Guizhen at the helm, the Party sought to remove all elements of superstition from the ancient practice to make it more Marxist and modern. For example, the ancient qigong exercise called the Claw of the Golden Dragon in Meditation was rewritten as "I practice sitting in meditation for better health." Qigong clinics sanctioned by the Party open up across China, based in state-run institutions and hospitals. From 1954 to 1959 the movement expanded rapidly. Chairman Mao Zedong personally named Liu Guizhen an Advanced Worker, an important title in Marxist nomenclature, and assigned him the role of qigong master to top Party officials. In 1957, Liu's *Qigong Therapy Practice* was published and would sell more than two million copies.

By 1958, Mao and the Chinese Communist Party had decided to transform the nation from an economy based on agriculture to an industrialized socialist model by initiating an engineering program called the Great Leap Forward. In an attempt to show that manpower, not machines, could foster industrialization, Mao announced a plan to increase steel production by 100 percent in one year. All across China, farmers, professors, factory workers, and just about everyone else was ordered to stop doing what they were doing and start forging steel in makeshift backyard fur-

Dr. Henry Karel "Andrija" Puharich (standing) in his laboratory at the Round Table Foundation in Maine, circa 1948. Puharich's quest to locate the unknown energy source he believed powered extrasensory perception caught the attention of the U.S. Defense Department. (Collection of Andrew Puharich)

In the 1950s, at the Army Chemical Center in Edgewood Maryland, Captain Puharich worked on a classified effort to locate drugs that could produce altered states and enhance psychic functioning. (U.S. Army)

In 1972, laser physicist Harold "Hal" Puthoff (left) was hired by the CIA to run a classified research program involving extrasensory perception (ESP) and psychokinesis (PK). One of Puthoff's first research subjects was a New York City artist named Ingo Swann (right). (Collection of Hal Puthoff)

Scientists Russell Targ and Hal Puthoff outside the Stanford Research Institute in Menlo Park, California, circa 1973. Officially, the program run by Puthoff and Targ was called The Biofield Measurements Program, but in internal memos for CIA Director Richard Helms, analysts called it the Paranormal Perception Research Project. (Collection of Russell Targ)

The CIA's second psychic research subject was a former Israeli solider named Uri Geller. The results, called the Swann-Geller Phenomena, would set the stage for more than twenty-years of classified government research and operations. (Collection of Uri Geller)

Fascinated by and the mystery of human consciousness and the idea of extremely long distance mental telepathy, Apollo 14 astronaut Edgar Mitchell decided to conduct secret ESP experiments on the way to the Moon. (NASA)

Walking on the Moon, Edgar Mitchell reads a map. Despite his heroics as an astronaut, Mitchell was ridiculed for his beliefs surrounding ESP and the paranormal. (NASA/Alan Shepard)

Edgar Mitchell's psychic research organization, Mind Science Institute of Los Angeles, was a conduit for CIA funds allotted for researching Uri Geller. (Collection of Uri Geller)

Uri Geller's first meeting in America, in 1972, was with Wernher von Braun, former chief scientist of the Apollo Moon program. The two men are seen here in von Braun's office at Fairchild Industries, in Germantown, Maryland. (Collection of Uri Geller)

Uri Geller outside the Stanford Research Institute in Menlo Park, California. (Collection of Uri Geller)

Patrick H. Price (in hat) was a towering figure in the CIA's psychic research program. He is seen here with Hal Puthoff, laser scientist Russell Targ (in glasses), and CIA analyst Dr. Christopher 'Kit' Green (in sunglasses) during an ESP experiment in California. Price died under mysterious circumstances in 1975. (Collection of Russell Targ)

Nuclear weapons engineers with the Lawrence Livermore National Laboratory tested Uri Geller's alleged psychic ability to disrupt the electronics on an Intercontinental Ballistic Missile (ICBM). The filmed experiment had a bizarre effect on the nuclear scientists and resulted in a CIA investigation. (Collection of Uri Geller)

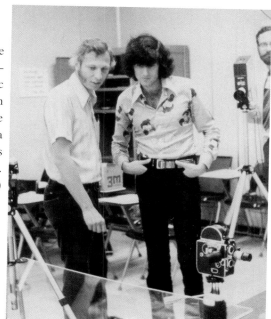

Decorated World War II hero Ninel "Nina" Kulagina was the Soviet's most famous psychic. In the 1970s, the U.S. intelligence community expressed alarm over allegations that Kulagina could stop an animal's beating heart using psychokinesis—the supposed ability to perturb matter with the mind. (Public domain)

The CIA and Defense Department were surprised to learn H. S. Tsien (Qian Xuesen), was behind China's psychic research program. Tsien, an early American rocket pioneer, switched loyalties, moved to China, and became science advisor to Chairman Mao. Seen here in this World War II–era photograph, Tsien (center) wears a cap displaying a U.S. Army rank of colonel. He believed qi, or vital energy, enhanced psychic functioning. (NARA, public domain)

Dale E. Graff, Chief of the Advanced Missile Systems Forecast Section at Wright Patterson Air Force Base, was responsible for the Defense Department's entrée into psychic research, circa 1978. Graff would remain a leader in DoD research and operational programs until his retirement in 1993. (Collection of Dale E. Graff)

Second Lieutenant Fred Holmes "Skip" Atwater served as the first operations manager of psychic research at the U.S. Army Intelligence and Security Command (INSCOM), Fort George Meade, Maryland. (Collection of Skip Atwater)

The Defense Intelligence Agency (DIA) ran operations out of this facility at Arlington Hall Station, located five miles southwest of Washington, DC, in Arlington, Virginia, until 1984. Arlington Hall served as headquarters of U.S. Army Intelligence activities from 1942 until 1989. (U.S. Department of Defense)

Warrant Officer Joe McMoneagle was singled out for the Army's psychic research program after his "sixth sense" became evident during the Vietnam War. He was given the classified title Remote Viewer 001, a term coined to remove the occult stigma associated with ESP. (Collection of Joe McMoneagle)

The remote-viewing operations building, T-2560, was located on the Fort George Meade Army facility in Fort Meade, Maryland. (Collection of Dale E. Graff)

Former electronic warfare operator Paul H. Smith had no knowledge of psychic functioning before the Army trained him in remote viewing, starting in 1983. (Collection of Paul Smith)

Major General Albert Stubblebine welcomed unconventional beliefs including ESP, PK, altered states, and out of body experiences. As Commanding General of Army INSCOM, Stubblebine oversaw Army's strategic intelligence forces around the world. (U.S. Army)

Lieutenant Colonel John B. Alexander, a former Green Beret and Special Forces commander in Vietnam with a PhD in the study of death, ran the Advanced Human Technology Office at INSCOM. (Collection of John Alexander)

Physicist Hal Puthoff has worked on psychic research programs for the U.S. military and intelligence communities since 1972. He is seen here (second from left) toasting with Chinese counterparts at a 1982 international psychic research symposium at Cambridge University, England. Also in attendance in Lt. Col John Alexander (third from right). (Collection of John Alexander)

John Alexander and Hal Puthoff discuss advanced physics concepts with Edward Teller, father of the hydrogen bomb, in Los Alamos, New Mexico. (Collection of John Alexander)

The Defense Intelligence Analysis Center, now known as DIA Headquarters, officially became operational on May 23, 1984. It is located on the premises of the Joint Base Anacostia-Bolling military installation in Washington, DC. (U.S. Department of Defense)

Former civilian intelligence analyst Angela Dellafiora became the most valuable psychic asset for the Defense Intelligence Agency (DIA). In this never-before-seen photograph, Dellafiora receives an award for her classified work from Dr. Jack Vorona, Chief Scientist for the Directorate of Science and Technology at DIA. (Collection of Angela Dellafiora).

Senator Claiborne Pell was a firm supporter of the DIA's Psychoenergetics Research Program, the primary component of which would become known as remote viewing. Pell is seen here at the Fort Meade office with Dale Graff, Director of the Advanced Concepts Office for DIA. (Collection of Dale E. Graff)

Psychic and remote viewer Angela Dellafiora poses for a photograph with Senator Claiborne Pell, Chairman of the Senate Select Committee on Foreign Relations. They are standing in front of the file cabinets, which housed classified documents for the remote viewing research and operations conducted at Fort Meade. (Collection of Angela Dellafiora)

In 1990, Paul Smith was transferred out of the remote viewing unit at Fort Meade and sent into the war theater during the Gulf War. He is seen here as part of a helicopter assault unit attached to the 101st Airborne Division, one of the first armored units into Iraq. (Collection of Paul Smith)

In 1992, DIA scientist and Fort Meade branch chief Dale Graff gathered a group of remote viewers for an onsite project at his house in Maryland. Seen here with Graff are (left to right) Nevin Lance, Kenneth Bell, and Joe McMoneagle. (Collection of Dale E. Graff)

As part of his official work for DIA, Dale Graff coordinated U.S. progress on psychic research with Israeli and British intelligence organizations. Seen here on a European Intelligence Exchange trip, Munich, Germany, are (left to right) unnamed German representative; DIA remote viewers Robin Dahlgren, Greg Stewart, and Angela Dellafiora Ford; unnamed DIA Executive Assistant; DIA Division Chief John Berbrich; Dale Graff. (Collection of Dale E. Graff)

Captain David Morehouse, a former Army Ranger commander, would play a significant role in the downfall of the U.S. government's psychic research programs. In his memoir Morehouse claimed remote viewing made him crazy, and that he believed evil demons possessed him. (U.S. Army)

To the end of his life, Dr. Andrija Puharich maintained a theory that extraterrestrials were trying to send messages to humans through psychic people. He is seen here on the estate of his last benefactor, tobacco heir R. J. Reynolds, where Puharich died in 1995, alone, impoverished and under threat of eviction. (Collection of Andrew Puharich)

When U.S. Army official and NATO Deputy Chief of Staff Brigadier General James L. Dozier was kidnapped by terrorists in Italy, in 1981, remote viewers were assigned to help locate him. Seen here in 2015, Dozier holds a photographs of the Italian paramilitary unit that rescued him. He calls psychic functioning "pure nonsense." (Author collection)

Chief Scientist Hal Puthoff inside a laboratory at the Institute for Advance Studies, in Austin, Texas, in 2015. Puthoff's present-day clients include the Department of Defense, NASA, Lockheed Skunk Works, and DARPA's 100-Year Starship project for interstellar travel capabilities. (Author collection)

Dale Graff continues to research psychic functioning, with a focus on quantum entanglement, or what Einstein famously called "spooky action at a distance." He is seen here in his home in Pennsylvania in 2015. (Author collection)

After his retirement from CIA, Dr. Christopher "Kit" Green continued to serve as a military and intelligence science advisor to the CIA and the Department of Defense. Since 1985, he has served on more than twenty Defense Department science advisory boards. In the past decade, he has returned to private medical practice where he conducts pro bono work on patients injured by anomalous events. (Collection of Dr. Kit Green, photo by Wayne State School of Medicine/Robert Stewart Photography, Ltd.)

On the streets of Jaffa, Israel, in 2016, Uri Geller bends a pair of hookah tongs for two adoring fans. (Author collection)

Outside the residence of Prime Minister Benjamin Netanyahu in Jerusalem, Israel, Uri Geller bends a spoon for the security team. (Author collection)

At his home in Florida in 2015, Apollo astronaut Edgar Mitchell displays the logs of the ESP tests that he conducted, in secret, on the way to and from the Moon. (Author collection)

naces. This was an impossible order, and where iron ore was unavailable, people melted down any objects they could get their hands on, including pots and bicycles. This effort failed, and China began its descent into what would be one of the worst recorded famines in history.

As people starved, and died, qigong rose in Party favor. Communist officials stated that qigong was the ideal Chinese medicine for the proletariat, as opposed to Western-style medical science that catered to the bourgeoisie. Qigong became an integral part of the nation's health policy and expanded exponentially. At the Great Leap Forward for the Cause of Health conference in Beijing in 1959, China's health minister singled out qigong for praise, citing its contributions to disease prevention. By 1960, a national qigong training course was organized. By the following year there were eighty-six qigong facilities in Shanghai alone.

By 1962, after the Great Leap Forward had proved to be disastrous and had been repealed, qigong began to be demonized. A new mantra was put in place. It was "unbecoming" for a Party official to promote qigong, communist officials said. Afraid of persecution, citizens stopped practicing it. In 1964 a Party edict called qigong "a rotten relic of feudalism" and "the rubbish of history." In 1965 the Party's *New Physical Education* magazine declared qigong quackery and a "poisonous weed." The nation's leading qigong master, Liu Guizhen, was labeled a class enemy and singled out for attack. He was fired from his hospital position, expelled from the Party, and sent to a reeducation camp at the notorious Shanhaiguan farm. His new job was cleaning the city's public toilets.

In May of 1966 Mao launched the Cultural Revolution, unleashing a new form of terror on China's citizenry. Weakened by the disastrous effects of the Great Leap Forward and in an effort to regain power, Mao called upon the youth of the nation to revive the revolutionary spirit by purging "impure" elements

of Chinese society. Schools were shut down, and student paramilitary groups known as the Red Guards were created to
harass the elderly and intellectuals. Gangs of children roamed the
streets in search of enemy offenders. Placards were placed around
offenders' necks, dunce caps put on their heads, and people were
paraded into public squares to be humiliated and beaten. Red
Guards destroyed libraries and museums. Communist leaders
who challenged Mao were removed from power and imprisoned.
Items associated with wealth—high-heeled shoes, furs, silk
gowns—were confiscated and burned in bonfires in the streets.
Hospitals and courts closed down. Chaos ensued, and the economy plummeted. By 1969 the country was in shambles. The Red
Guards fought among themselves and executions became wide-
spread. It was entropy manifest. Raw struggle.

What puzzled analysts at CIA was that the years from 1962 to
1978 were a dead zone for qigong in China. Not a word about
qigong appeared in print. Then came the single article about
Tang Yu, in 1979. It appeared as if emerging out of a vacuum.
That the article triggered such intense interest across China was
remarkable in the eyes of CIA and DIA. There had to be something else going on, someone responsible for the sudden adula-
tion of a practice that had been forbidden for fifteen years. When
CIA analysts dug deep, what they discovered was astonishing.
The man at the center of it all—from qigong to the concept of
Extraordinary Human Body Function—was Qian Xuesen, formerly one of the most valuable members of the U.S. military
science intelligentsia, now a sworn enemy of the United States.

Qian Xuesen (pronounced Chen Who-sen), or H. S. Tsien as
he was known in America, was an American rocket pioneer.
Born in China in 1911, he left for the United States in 1935, age
twenty-four, on a Boxer Rebellion Indemnity Scholarship. He
first attended college at the Massachusetts Institute of Technology, where he studied electrical engineering, then transferred to

the California Institute of Technology (Caltech) to study under Theodore von Kármán, the world-famous aerospace engineer. Starting in the late 1930s Tsien worked on early American rocket designs and in 1938 cofounded the Jet Propulsion Laboratory in California, America's first experimental rocket laboratory. So brilliant was Tsien that von Kármán declared him an "undisputed genius."

During World War II, Tsien was granted the U.S.'s highest security clearance in order to work on the Manhattan Project, where he helped build the world's first atomic bomb. Commissioned as a colonel in the U.S. Army Air Force, he applied to become an American citizen, but his paperwork languished during the war. After the Nazis surrendered, Tsien traveled to occupied Germany, where he interrogated Wernher von Braun, the world's first famous rocket scientist. In 1949, still waiting for his U.S. citizenship to be granted, Tsien was made the first director of what was officially called the Guggenheim Jet Propulsion Center at Caltech, which today is NASA's leading center for robotic exploration of the solar system. Then, on October 1, 1949, owing to faraway events entirely beyond his control, H. S. Tsien's life changed course forever.

When Mao Zedong officially proclaimed the existence of the People's Republic of China in the fall of 1949, China and the United States became enemies. The loss of China to communism was a severe blow to America, and H. S. Tsien's life would never be the same. Eight months later, on June 6, 1950, the FBI knocked on his door. It was the McCarthy era, and he was still a Chinese national, since his U.S. citizenship had not yet been granted. The Bureau's representatives demanded that he answer questions about possible communist ties. Tsien was insulted: how could these FBI bureaucrats not realize who he was in the context of U.S. national security and the kind of security clearances he held? The FBI's response was to revoke his coveted clearances and place him

under house arrest. After five humiliating years of quasi deten-
tion, Tsien was returned to China as part of a Korean prisoner-of-war
exchange. He spent the rest of his life avenging his treatment by
the United States.

The story of H. S. Tsien exemplifies the curious flexibility of
personal conviction. Tsien was betrayed by the United States, the
country whose ideals he believed in and which he'd served during the war. America was the land he called home. And yet by
the time he arrived in China, in October 1955, his belief system
and his loyalties had been transposed 180 degrees, as though
flipped by a switch. He remained a committed communist for
the rest of his life and would earn the rare distinction of becoming a science adviser to Chairman Mao.

Science was to be H. S. Tsien's weapon of revenge against the
United States. Almost single-handedly he revolutionized China's
technological capabilities from bare bones to cutting-edge. He
created and developed the Chinese rocket program, its satellite
program, and its manned space program. His work on China's
atomic bomb project allowed that nation to produce nuclear
weapons and their delivery systems. Further, he was deeply committed to the science behind anomalous mental phenomena, including extrasensory perception, psychokinesis, and teleportation. His
story has been remarkably underreported to date.

When Tsien returned to China in October 1955, China's
industrial development was primitive, with barely the technology
to build a decent automobile. The most common forms of travel
were bicycle and rickshaw. And so, even before Tsien arrived in
Beijing, he'd been cast as a hero. His return, brokered between
Communist Party officials and the U.S. State Department, was
seen as a victory for the Chinese. In Beijing, the scientific elite was
in awe of him, and it was firmly believed that Tsien would pull
China from the technological dark ages into the modern world.
Lavish banquets commemorating his homecoming were thrown at

the Chinese Academy of Sciences and Beijing University. Within a few months of his arrival, the government created the Institute of Mechanics in Beijing and installed him as director. At the time there was but one telephone. Technicians used hand-crank calculators. But Tsien was off and running, deeply invested in continuing his lifework, only now in service of Communist China.

In Tsien's first year back in China, as part of the Great Leap Forward, Chairman Mao instituted an unusual policy called "Let a Hundred Flowers Bloom." Intellectuals were encouraged to criticize the Communist Party, to "say whatever they want and say it in full," according to a statement by the Chairman. The policy actually was a plot to root out dissent, and as a result hundreds of thousands of critics were punished, tortured, or killed. Having witnessed McCarthyism, Tsien kept his head down, remained silent, and did not make waves. He traded in his Western clothes for the standard gray uniform of the Party. He denounced colleagues and promoted Communist Party doctrine.

There were benefits for steadfast loyalty, and Tsien earned such rewards. He was moved into a guarded compound in the Haidian District of Beijing and promoted to director of the Fifth Academy, where he led China's top-secret missile program. On November 5, 1960, the Chinese version of the Soviet R-2 rocket was launched, and a huge celebration was given in his honor. It was a turning point in China's history: a modern rocket had flown. Tsien was now put in charge of the Party's ambitious plan to build China's first generation of land-based ballistic missiles, the Dongfeng (East Wind). He developed China's satellite program, consulted on China's first nuclear program, and in February 1964 became Chairman Mao's private science tutor. On October 27, 1966, China became the first nation to deploy a missile with a live atomic warhead in its nose cone, an act internationally condemned as reckless. "The man believed responsible for the first test of its kind was trained, nurtured, encouraged, lionized, paid, and trusted for fifteen years in the United States," noted a *New York Times* reporter.

But science in China would come under attack during the Cultural Revolution. In an effort to sound pro-proletariat, the Fifth Academy changed its name to the Seventh Ministry of Machine Building, and Tsien was removed from the position of director. He remained one of what are believed to be only fifty scientists protected by the state during this time. He quietly worked on a classified program involving manned space flight, and in April 1968 spearheaded the formation of the 507th Research Institute also known as the Beijing Institute of Space Medical Engineering. In 1972 Mao suffered a stroke, and the moderate Deng Xiaoping took control of the government. In 1976 Mao died. With Deng Xiaoping now officially in power, China began steps toward reform. Science returned to the limelight, and H. S. Tsien once again became its mouthpiece, this time for the new government.

Here began a mysterious transition that the U.S. intelligence community sought to understand. With his reemergence into the spotlight, Tsien became a vocal advocate of Extraordinary Human Body Functioning, ESP, PK, and qigong. He was the man behind the emergence of phenomena research, and he did it almost single-handedly. After the publication of the article about Tang Yu and the Extraordinary Powers Craze, the Chinese opened a classified research institute dedicated to the study of anomalous mental phenomena. It was located inside the Beijing Institute of Space Medical Engineering, under the leadership of H. S. Tsien. It was here that China's leading scientists began developing military applications for Exceptional Functions of the Human Body, extrasensory perception, and psychokinesis.

Decades of rocket research had left Tsien with the deep conviction that there existed a symbiotic relationship between outer space and inner space, between the cosmos and man. The link, he said, was qi. What for "two thousand years [was] considered a mysterious ancient form of Chinese medicine" could now be understood in "the language of modern scientific technology," Tsien told a gathering of Communist Party leaders in June 1981. Citing "laboratory experiments with EHBF teenagers [who] demonstrated sight not by eyes" (i.e., ESP) and "influenced animate or inanimate objects" (i.e., PK), Tsien said that researching the "energy powered by the vital force of qi" would lead to the next "scientific revolution." There were military advantages to be had. "In time of war, the body in [a state of] EHBF is beneficial," declared the father of China's rocket program. "This enthusiastic atmosphere [in China] reminds us of the same atmosphere when Einstein's theory of relativity and quantum mechanics were introduced onto the stage of modern science," he said. "The only different is that the stage at that time was Western Europe and now the stage is the People's Republic of China."

In Washington, D.C., the Defense Intelligence Agency wanted a firsthand assessment of what was going on in China with these EHBF teenagers, H. S. Tsien, and the various labs involved. Arrangements were made to send Hal Puthoff to China in a clandestine capacity, as a contractor on the Special Access Program, Grill Flame. In October 1981, a delegation of eighteen American and Canadian researchers, scientists, and journalists traveled to China to meet EHBF scientists and researchers under the auspices of civilian interest in psychic research. Puthoff was a member of the delegation, working undercover for DIA. The twelve-day trip included visits to Beijing, Xian, and Shanghai. In Beijing, the group visited military science facilities at the Chinese Academy of Sciences and the Institute of High-Energy Physics.

Upon his return, Puthoff prepared a sixty-page classified

report entitled "Psychoenergetics Research in the People's Republic of China (1982)," now declassified. He confirmed the experiments, met many of the scientists, and observed the modern equipment being used in China's laboratories. "H. S. Tsien has been the driving force behind establishing EHBF science," Puthoff wrote, cautioning DIA not to underestimate his power and influence. "He is thought to have had a major role in developing China's first nuclear bombs."

The report was sent to Dr. Jack Vorona at DIA for review. The goals of the psychic research program had always been "to evaluate the threat that foreign psychoenergetics achievements might pose to US national security, and to explore the potential of psychoenergetics for use in US intelligence collection." The threats from foreign governments had previously been limited to the Soviet Union and its Warsaw Pact nations. Now China was added to that list. "A potential threat to US national security exists from foreign achievements in psychoenergetics in the USSR and China," a declassified memo made clear. "This research is well funded and receives high-level government backing."

At the Pentagon, Puthoff's report was sent to Richard DeLauer, undersecretary of Defense for Research and Engineering. DeLauer had attended Caltech, H. S. Tsien's alma mater, and was aware of the power and influence wielded by the man he called the "elder statesman" of Chinese scientific technology and development. Three months after receiving the report and a back-up briefing, DeLauer signed a memo allocating additional resources, Program Six funds, for the psychic research program Grill Flame.

There was an interesting story unfolding in California around this same time. It appeared anecdotal at first, but would come to have significance. In 1983, not many Americans were familiar with the ancient Chinese concepts of qi and qigong, and far fewer knew anything about the Chinese rocket scientist H. S. Tsien. But in Manhattan Beach, a systems engineer for Boeing Aerospace named Jack Houck was familiar with both. He saw a connection between qi and psychokinesis that no one in America had really considered before.

Observing Uri Geller bend spoons on TV, and reading reports of children being inspired by Geller to bend spoons in their homes—allegedly using the power of their minds—got Jack Houck to thinking. "During the process, people often [said] they felt energy coming from their hands," Houck stated. He also noted that several local martial arts practitioners he knew also spoke of an internal energy they could summon with their minds and that was felt as heat in their hands. "They call it 'qi,'" said Houck.

As an aerospace engineer Jack Houck was interested in the concept of bending metal with the mind. He began having discussions with a colleague from McDonnell Douglas Aerospace Company, a metallurgist named Severin Dahlen. Houck and Dahlen wondered whether the ability to bend metal this way had something to do with one's belief system. Perhaps psychokinesis was not a so-called paranormal superpower but an ability to harness the energy force the Chinese called qi that was latent in all people.

As an experiment, Houck decided to host a spoon-bending party with twenty-one people at his Manhattan Beach home in January 1981. If any of the spoons were bent, Dahlen would analyze the results from a metallurgist's point of view. The two scientists created a three-step protocol for guests at the party: "1). Make a mental connection to what you want to affect [bend]. 2). Command what you want it to do by shouting 'Bend! Bend! Bend!' 3). Let go." The "let go" part, Houck explained, meant allowing your mind to let go of the idea that it is impossible to bend metal with the mind.

"In the first experiment, to test the conceptual model, we had regular, average folks. Half of the people were interested in psychic-type things, the other half were members of a tennis club I belonged to," Houck recalled. Unlike a martial arts setting in which the practitioner concentrates silently, Houck and Dahlen wanted to create a high-energy environment of excitement with everyone shouting "Bend!" "This one young boy, fourteen, had his fork fall over," Houck wrote. "Everyone in the room saw it because he jumped up out of his chair, screaming." Houck said that what happened next was particularly fascinating. "Most of the people in the room...had what I call an instant belief system change. Everyone's fork or spoon started to get soft for five to fifteen seconds." In that window of time, says Houck, "nineteen out of the twenty-one spoons [or forks] bent." Houck began hosting spoon-bending parties. The results were almost always the same. "Roughly eighty-five percent of the spoons bent."

Dahlen the metallurgist tested the bent spoons in the lab. His conclusion, "Stainless flatware seems to be the easiest metal to [bend] with PK. This is because of [the] metallurgical characteristics of stainless steel. Stainless flatware is usually stamped out in large quantities. The process of cold stamping creates a large number of 'dislocations' along the grain boundaries in the metal. The PK energy is somehow dumped into the metal and these dislocations act as beacons for that energy. Once the PK energy lands at a dislocation, there is nowhere for it to go and it turns into heat, much as when neutrons and X-rays penetrate solid objects."

At his spoon bending parties Houck watched hundreds, then thousands, of average Americans suspend their disbelief and bend metal without physical force. Yes, it's likely that some percentage of the guests cheated. But hundreds of them bent hacksaw blades, silver-plated serving spoons, and five-sixteenth-inch steel rods that are physically impossible to bend by hand. By the time Hal Puthoff's paper on psychoenergetics research in China was making its rounds at DIA, Jack Houck had hosted more than fifty PK parties, attended by approximately one thousand individuals. His conclusion was that "everyone seems to be able to do PK. Metal often continues to bend for up to three days. This seems to correlate well with the 'qi energy' discussed in various martial arts disciplines."

Naturally, there were military implications in what Jack Houck had unveiled, and soon he would be contacted by the U.S. Army Intelligence and Security Command.

CHAPTER SIXTEEN

Killers and Kidnappers

On March 30, 1981, just seventy days after becoming president, Ronald Reagan was shot and seriously injured in an assassination attempt in Washington, D.C. As the president was leaving a speaking engagement at the Hilton, the assassin, John Hinkley Jr., was able to fire six bullets in the direction of the presidential entourage, striking President Reagan with a single shot. It was a perilously close call. The president's left lung was punctured and he suffered heavy internal bleeding. The attempted assassination was the first time a bullet had hit a sitting U.S. president since John F. Kennedy had been killed in Dallas eighteen years before.

Two months later in Rome, in St. Peter's Square, Vatican City, an assassin opened fire on Pope John Paul II, the leader of 600 million Roman Catholics around the world. Four bullets hit the pontiff; two lodged in his abdomen, another hit his left index finger and another his right arm. The Pope underwent more than five hours of surgery and survived. That fall, on October 6,

1981, Egyptian president Anwar el-Sadat was assassinated by Islamic fundamentalists in Cairo, an event that stunned the world. Sadat had been watching a military victory parade when a group of men in uniform threw grenades and fired assault rifles at him. Mortally wounded, Sadat was airlifted to a military hospital and died two hours later. In a span of roughly seven months, there had been three assassination attempts against world leaders, with three direct hits and one death. The perceived vulnerability of international figures escalated to alarming proportions.

The day after Sadat was murdered, newspapers across America and around the world hinted at future assassination plots against President Reagan. The Secret Service tightened protocols and the FBI was placed on high alert. Across the intelligence community, analysts were assigned a variety of threat assessments both foreign and domestic. At CIA and DIA, intelligence officers learned of a plot by Colonel Muammar Gaddafi to send Libyan hit squads to kill President Reagan and members of his cabinet. The president began traveling in an unmarked limousine. Secret Service members were assigned to protect National Security Council staff. A pair of surface-to-air missiles was installed on the White House roof.

The CIA learned of a second presidential assassination plot, this one spearheaded by the international terrorist Carlos the Jackal, who was thought to have already entered the United States. All kinds of intelligence collection were called up to thwart assassination plots, including human intelligence, signals intelligence, imagery intelligence, open-source intelligence—and the Detachment G remote viewers at Fort Meade.

In Washington, Dale Graff had just begun his new job working for Jack Vorona, assistant vice director for scientific and technical intelligence at DIA. Graff moved to the nation's capital and rented an apartment not far from his office, on the far side of Arlington National Cemetery. Barbara stayed behind in Dayton, where she worked as the head nurse at St. Elizabeth Hospital; she and the children would join him the following year. Graff's role as Vorona's action officer was to oversee both the SRI research in Northern California, now being financed by DIA, and the Grill Flame operation at Fort Meade. With the assassination threat level heightened, Graff traveled back and forth between Arlington and Fort Meade, where he worked with the information provided by remote viewers and tried to develop protocols to separate signal from noise.

The information was voluminous, and much of it was noise. For example, Fort Meade psychics drew sketches of would-be assassins that were male and female, and ranged in age from eighteen to sixty-five. Some had black hair, others wore wigs. Some had brown eyes, others had altered their eye color with contact lenses, still others wore glasses. One remote viewer was certain of an assassin who "always dressed in natural tones and wore brown shoes." Almost all of the remote viewers perceived an assassin carrying a 9mm automatic pistol. Descriptions of getaway vehicles included a Chrysler, a Ford, a light-blue sedan, and a purple GMC van with gold trim, black interior, and carpeting on the seats. The remote viewers pinpointed dozens of locations on maps around Washington where they individually intuited that an assassination attempt might occur. The information was as overwhelming as it was nebulous. Where to begin? Day in and day out, deciphering the information and devising a plan of action was Dale Graff's greatest challenge.

Given the critical nature of the operation, Grill Flame's ancillary support team at SRI was brought in on the high-priority effort. Staff at SRI consisted of two senior scientists, a research analyst, a consultant, and several support personnel. Normally the remote viewers at SRI worked on research programs. Now they too were shifted to operational status. As data from the SRI viewers came in, Graff examined it. On the afternoon of December 12, 1981, Hal Puthoff was working with remote viewer Gary Langford, the former naval officer who'd provided information on the Zaire operation and the missing Soviet bomber. In this particular session, Puthoff asked Langford to "determine if an event of major importance to the United States [will] occur in the near future." Langford worked the question for several days with no clear impressions coming in, he said. Then, three days later, on December 15, at 8:37 a.m., during a session identified in declassified CIA documents as Task Identification 0049, one of the most spectacular apparent instances of extrasensory perception intelligence in the history of the program occurred.

Out of Langford's mouth came a prophecy: "A United States Pentagon official would be kidnapped by terrorists on the evening of 17 December 1981." The information was so specific in terms of date and time, and Langford was so assertive in relaying this information, that Puthoff ran several additional sessions with him to try to learn more. Langford said he saw the terrorists breaking into this Pentagon official's apartment, binding and gagging the man, and then kidnapping him. Even more specifically, Langford saw this high-ranking official being shoved inside a trunk and secreted in the back of a van. The kidnappers were Mediterranean-looking, Langford said, and the van was blue with some kind of strange markings on the side. He drew a sketch of the trunk and its dimensions.

Puthoff alerted Dale Graff. The DIA passed Puthoff's information to the FBI, which issued a threatened kidnapping alert against a federal official. The International Criminal Police Organization was alerted, and by the next morning, INTERPOL had issued a worldwide counterterrorism alert.

At 5:30 on the evening December 17, 1981, Brigadier General James L. Dozier, a senior Army official and deputy chief of staff in the NATO Southern Command, was sitting in his penthouse apartment on Strada Lungadige Catena in Verona, Italy, with his wife, Judy, when the doorbell rang. Dozier, age fifty, was a graduate of West Point, a Vietnam War veteran, and a recipient of the Silver Star. He had been reading a letter when the doorbell rang. He stood up and walked toward the door. Interviewed in 2015, Dozier recalled thinking the situation was odd. The bell was the one that rang when pushed from inside the building, here on the top floor, not down on the street. The Doziers weren't expecting visitors, but perhaps it was a neighbor, Dozier recalled.

"*Chi e?*" Dozier asked. Who's there?

A man on the other side of the door addressed him as *Generale* and identified himself as a plumber. There was a leak in the building, the voice said; could he come inside?

Dozier opened the door. In front of him were two young men in workmen's uniforms. Each had a full beard and mustache. One carried a leather bag.

"I told my wife, 'Don't worry,'" Dozier recalled, explaining that the plumbers were trying to determine the cause of a water leak in the building. Judy had used their washing machine earlier in the day, and Dozier led the men toward the appliance.

"*Il termosifone?*" the plumber asked.

Dozier did not have any idea what a *termosifone* was. He headed into the library to get a dictionary and was looking for the translation when he was attacked. The leader grabbed him from behind. Dozier swung around just in time to see that the man had backed up. "I was looking down the barrel of a pistol," he recalled. The man pushed Dozier; Dozier struck back, and the two began fighting. The second man joined in, punching Dozier until he almost lost consciousness. He lay on the floor, an eardrum ruptured and bleeding from open wounds on his forehead and cheek. "When I looked up, I saw they had my wife on her knees with a pistol to her head. That's when the fight was over," he said. The kidnappers tied up Judy, gagged her, and put heavy tape over her eyes. They bound the general's ankles with rubberized elastic bandages and heavy packing tape, and taped over his mouth. With guns drawn, they ordered him to his feet. Using walkie-talkies, they summoned two accomplices, who arrived with a large steamer trunk on a mover's dolly. With a gun to his head, Dozier climbed inside. He was rolled down the hallway and into the service elevator. Outside on the street, additional accomplices waited in a blue Fiat van. The general's trunk was loaded into the back. The door slammed shut and the van sped away.

General Dozier had been kidnapped by a Marxist-Leninist paramilitary group called the Red Brigades, a terrorist organization whose stated goal was to foster revolution in Italy and force its withdrawal from NATO. The Red Brigades had been conducting kidnappings and murders for a decade, the most notorious of which had occurred two years before. In March 1978 the group ambushed and kidnapped former prime minister Aldo Moro. They held Moro for fifty-five days, then murdered him. Now the group had Dozier. Word reached Washington roughly six hours after the abduction. The Pentagon went into action; every moment mattered. The FBI offered a $2 million reward for information that could lead authorities to the general. A Joint Special Operations Command team left for Italy.

In Washington, Dale Graff was deeply concerned about Dozier's abduction, as were many of the other individuals involved. Five days after the kidnapping, an Arabic speaker called the Italian wire service Agenzia Nazionale Stampa Associata to say that the Red Brigades "claim responsibility for the death sentence and execution of the American general, James Dozier, found guilty by the people's tribunal," and that his corpse would soon turn up in a country village. At Fort Meade, Graff worked remote-viewing sessions with Joe McMoneagle, Hartleigh Trent, and Ken Bell, all three of whom had strong perceptions that General Dozier was still alive, still in the same place, and not being moved around. Every remote viewer was enlisted to try to pinpoint where in Italy the general was being held, but the multiple sessions produced an overload of vague and disparate information: Dozier was being held "near a small, Gothic style church with a watchtower nearby"; he was "in a large house with a tile roof in the rolling countryside with a domed structure and a large river nearby"; he was "in an open space, near the water or a shoreline, with lots of buildings close together, towers, and yellow hills, like sand," or "in a dome-shaped building near a shoreline and water with machinery nearby."

Graff culled the information to narrow search parameters and home in on what might be significant and what was merely noise, or analytical overlay, according to protocols SRI had developed for the Army. As time ticked on, the possible locations grew more scattered and less clear, and Graff feared that with every passing day the noose grew tighter and time was running out. The Red Brigades were known killers. To make matters more complicated, a raft of unsolicited information from civil-sector psychics flooded into the Pentagon. Declassified logs indicate that a trio of psychics living in Kent, Washington, insisted they knew where Dozier was being kept. "He is dressed as a shepherd...on a mountain tending his sheep. Please contact us," they wrote.

The general had been in captivity for two weeks when a powerful snowstorm brought the city of Washington to a near standstill. With twenty-one inches of snow on the ground, all government employees who were not in security or facility maintenance were advised to stay home. This included Dale Graff. Not one to sit inside, Graff ventured outside to hike through Arlington National Cemetery. He put on his snow boots, grabbed his new 35mm camera, and swung by a 7-Eleven to get a coffee. "It was 8:30 in the morning, sunny and clear. I was taking photographs when suddenly I got this overwhelming feeling: *I've to go to the office,"* he recalls. The subways were closed, and it was a four-mile walk. Graff set out, trudging through the deep snow to the DIA office in Arlington, across the river from Georgetown.

At the front door, the guard asked him why he was there. "I wasn't about to say I wasn't exactly sure why, so instead I said I'd come in to catch up on some work," he responded. He was standing in the office looking around when he heard a phone ringing in Jack Vorona's office. "It rang and rang, ten, eleven times," recalls Graff. This was long before the days of answering machines. "I thought, *Someone is really trying to get through. It must be important, to let it ring that many times."* Graff walked into Vorona's office and picked up the telephone. "The voice on the line said something like 'We're calling from the Pentagon. We need to talk to someone who knows about remote viewing.' "

Graff said Vorona wasn't in, "but you've got one of the right guys. That's me."

The person told Graff the situation was urgent and asked, "Can you come to the Pentagon and explain this program to us?"

Graff called Vorona at his house to make sure he was authorized to conduct this briefing. Vorona told him to head over there at once. Public transit was finally running. Graff took the metro from the Rosslyn stop to the Pentagon.

The Pentagon parking lot was empty. He'd been instructed to go into a classified briefing room in the basement. When he arrived, "the room was full of Army brass," Graff recalls. "I learned later this was the first grouping of Delta Force. They'd just been mobilized for quick reaction response, [to go] anywhere in the world."

One of the Army officers asked Graff to explain what remote viewing was. Graff talked and the men listened, took a few notes, and thanked him. The way Graff recalls the meeting, the officers got up as a group and left him sitting alone at the table. A few minutes later, a colonel came in. "He began making insulting remarks about remote viewing," recalls Graff. " 'This is terrible stuff,' he said. 'Nobody believes in this crap.' It was very confrontational. I remained calm, showing no defensive responses, and I wondered if it was some kind of psychological test." After a while the colonel left.

The original group returned. "Can you travel to Italy starting tomorrow evening?" one of the officers asked. "For a few moments, I was speechless," remembers Graff. "Travel to Italy!" Regaining focus, he said sure, except he didn't have a passport. The officer told him not to worry, that the Pentagon could provide that, and a translator, too. He explained to Graff that the idea was to see whether the Army could use remote viewing operationally, in the field. Graff headed home and packed his bags. The following day at 6:00 p.m., with the approval of DIA director General Edmund R. Thompson, Graff and an Army translator headed to Washington National, where they caught a commercial flight to Italy. When they landed, they drove to the U.S. Army garrison in Stuttgart. There, Graff and his translator were told they were being recalled. Since they'd left Washington, the commander of the American forces in Europe had decided there were too many people in the field working on the Dozier case. The military staffer who met them at the airport suggested that Graff and his translater turn around and catch the next flight home. Graff responded that since he was already there, he should at least have a brief discussion with the commander in charge. The staffer went away and came back. The commander will give you five minutes, the staffer said. Make it to the point and fast.

Graff walked into the commander's office. "Big desk. Tough looking guy. In charge of the Dozier operation," Graff recalls. He made a pitch for the merits of using extrasensory perception in a search-and-rescue operation. He told the commander he was convinced that remote viewing could add value to the effort to locate Dozier. The commander interrupted, Graff recalls. "I'm not sending anybody down there," he said. Graff recalls asking the commander whether he could at least explain the phenomenology involved. The commander interrupted him. "He told me to stop right there. He said, 'I don't believe a word of what you are saying. I know all about [J. B.] Rhine and that it's a bunch of fraud.'" Then came the part Graff found illuminating. "He said to me, 'I know it's hard to believe, but my aunt lived in Durham,'" where Rhine had his parapsychology lab at Duke University. The commander's aunt was part of a carpool of locals who knew all about this J. B. Rhine fellow and his fraudulent claims of ESP.

In the early 1980s, J. B. Rhine was still considered the most famous parapsychologist in modern American history. Starting in the 1920s, at the Institute for Parapsychology in Durham, North Carolina, he'd performed tens of thousands of now famous ESP experiments with Zener cards. But in 1974, one of his assistants, Walter Levy, was caught cheating. The experiment involved testing rats in an apparatus designed to see if they could use extrasensory perception to increase the number of pleasurable brain stimulations the apparatus was rigged to deliver. When Levy's research assistants spotted him tampering with the lab equipment, they rigged up a recorder and caught him on videotape. When confronted with the evidence against him, Levy confessed and resigned. The scandal became fodder for anyone skeptical of Rhine or his parapsychology research—skeptics who included the commander's aunt. What fascinated Graff was how a person's strong opinion is often shaped by the strong opinion of someone else.

Quickly and to the point, Graff filled in details of the Rhine cheating scandal as well as details of some of the work Rhine had done for the Navy. Graff recalls the commander taking a moment to digest what he'd said. "He said, 'Tell me more,'" Graff recalls. The two men had a debate about ESP for roughly twenty-five minutes. Graff remembers the high-ranking senior officers in the room sitting patiently, but also eyeballing a clock on the wall and giving him puzzled looks.

"Here was a commander who knew his stuff," explains Graff. "Great men don't become great leaders by being narrow-minded. He wanted knowledge, and I had the information. He was genuinely interested in what I had to say." As the meeting ended, Graff recalls the commander's parting remark. "There's one thing I really need to understand," he said. "This precognition stuff. That's a tough one. I was with you until you got to that. That part is beyond belief. You lost me there."

Graff told the commander that there was no theoretical explanation as of yet, and that ESP research was still in the hypothesis, or conjecture, stage. One hypothesis, he recalls saying, "has to do with electromagnetic modeling of the phenomena." Another involves quantum entanglement, or what Einstein famously referred to as "spooky action at a distance." Then Graff presented in basic terms how the electromagnetic wave equation has two potential solutions involving the forward and backward movement of time, that "although the reverse or precognitive solution is actually ignored in practice, and that some emerging concepts in quantum physics permit precognitive phenomenon."

The commander interrupted, remembers Graff: "Go south!" he said.

On the commander's authority, Dale Graff was now an ancillary member of Delta Force. He and his translator headed south to Vincenza, where the 584th Military Intelligence Detachment was working with the Joint Special Operations Command to find and rescue General Dozier. Graff was given a working space in a secure annex to the main headquarters. The place was teeming with people coming and going—operators, analysts, officers, and staff. From his secure telephone, Graff worked on information from the remote-viewing unit at Fort Meade.

Halfway across the world, in Room 2654 at Fort Meade, Joe

McMoneagle worked session after session. He saw Dozier in an apartment inside a building in a town he identified as Padova, or Padua. He drew details of the inside of what he thought was the apartment and the exterior of the building. But as the DIA office would later learn, the time difference made direct communication difficult. The action officer at DIA was out sick, and McMoneagle's information never reached Graff in Vincenza. As the days wore on, the pressure ratcheted up as the general's abduction passed the thirty-day mark.

In Italy, when Graff tried to sleep he experienced strange, vivid dreams. "The Dozier operation was a life-or-death situation. In a dream state, I began to get impressions," says Graff. It was as if he were doing remote-viewing sessions himself. "I saw the general upstairs in a room above a grocery store. I said to my translator, he's in Padua." Graff wrote up his experiences and gave them to his superior in Vincenza. "I didn't identify myself as the remote viewer," he remembers.

The following day, a U.S. signals intelligence team provided Italian police with information that led to the capture of key informants with direct knowledge about the activities of the Red Brigades. The informants' data broke the case and led Italian Special Forces to the exact street address where the general was being held, above a grocery store in Padua. The largest manhunt in Italian history ended with ten men from Italy's Central Operative Security Nucleus storming the apartment. Inside, Red Brigades member Antonio Savasta was holding a gun to General Dozier's head, but before Savasta could pull the trigger, a commando hit him from behind with the butt of a machine gun, knocking him to the floor. The forty-two-day ordeal was over, and the general was alive and free. Dozier was flown home and given a hero's welcome. Ronald Reagan invited him to the White House for lunch.

When the elation over Dozier's release wore off, Graff grappled with fundamental questions. "It was distressing, really," he recalled in 2015. "I had to ask myself, What good did ESP dreaming or remote viewing do? Once in the field, I learned quickly that there was no way to actually pass on any remote viewing information to the Italian search team. We had to wait until the operation was over to understand what information was correct." Yes, the location of Padua proved to be correct, but that was one data point in the volume of information that was coming in. It was the same old question again: How does one discern what is signal and what is noise? Yes, Gary Langford's precognitive information was remarkable after it became a fact. But what good did it do? It neither stopped the kidnapping, nor did it help locate Dozier once he'd been taken hostage.

Back at DIA, Graff wrote up an after-action report in which he identified the positives and the negatives from the Fort Meade remote-viewing involvement in the Dozier search. A few weeks later, he was invited to attend a conference with General Dozier at Fort Meade. The emphasis was on Special Forces, Graff recalls. "I wanted to talk about remote viewing. I waited until the end of the Q&A, until after most of the audience thinned out." With just a few individuals remaining, Graff introduced himself to the general and asked whether he'd ever heard of the remote-viewing program at INSCOM, the Intelligence and Security Command. Graff recalls Dozier asking if he meant ESP.

"Some call it that," Graff said. Dozier stated that the way he finally figured out where he was being held involved listening to voices and realizing that groceries were being sold. He said that later he heard his captors building a box. He thought it might be a coffin and started focusing hard on his wife, Judy, and his love for her. Dozier said he thought that if he concentrated hard, she might pick up on his thoughts, like a lighthouse or a beacon sending out a signal.

"Not using any names, I told him that two remote viewers

had given us the name 'Padua.' He seemed genuinely interested," Graff recalls. "I did not say one of the remote viewers was me."

Graff returned from Italy to find himself in the middle of a heated battle over the military's involvement in remote viewing. The existence of the classified program had made its way into the upper echelons of the Defense Department, various congressional intelligence committees, and the White House National Security Council. The subject matter was so contentious—the U.S. Army using psychics in military operations—that individuals felt compelled to take sides. The undersecretary of Defense for Research and Engineering, William Perry, stated in a memo that it was "not appropriate for Army to fund technology programs aimed at scientific development of parapsychology." Congressman Charlie Rose, a democrat from North Carolina, disagreed. "It seems to me that it would be a hell of a cheap radar system," Rose said during a debate on psychic research in a House Select Committee on Intelligence meeting for which he served as chairman. "And if the Russians have it and we don't, we are in serious trouble."

Religious elements crept into the debate. A fundamentalist Christian group aligned with a powerful congressman declared remote viewing to be the Devil's work and lobbied to have the program canceled. CIA director Stansfield Turner, a Christian Scientist and former Navy admiral, did not allow theology to get in the way. In an interview in 2002, Turner said, "When I was first introduced to this idea of parapsychology I was very skeptical. Then I began to think about it, and we all know of people who seem to have some kind of psychic powers."

Leading the charge in support of the remote-viewing program was Senator Claiborne Pell, a powerful Democrat from

Rhode Island and a ranking member of the Senate Foreign Relations Committee. A former Foreign Service officer who had worked behind enemy lines in Nazi-occupied Hungary, Pell was a proponent of extrasensory perception and reached out personally to Graff offering his support. National Security Council member Lieutenant Commander Jake Stewart of the Office of Naval Intelligence had been impressed when he first learned about the remote-viewing program during the MX missile basing era and like Senator Pell offered his unwavering support. Stewart had direct access to the president and other leading White House officials.

Polemics aside, for the Army's INSCOM program to survive, it needed clients, meaning operational requests from the military and intelligence services. In the spring of 1982, two months after Graff's return from Italy, the program caught the break it needed after Lieutenant General Lincoln D. Faurer, director of the National Security Agency, was given a briefing. Faurer saw extrasensory perception as a form of signals intelligence and believed in its potential operational value. In April 1982, he assigned the remote-viewing unit at Fort Meade a dozen new tasks.

But the crux of the matter was that the program's longevity depended on the quality of intelligence the Army psychics could provide. If the results were authoritative, the program would thrive—that's the way the U.S. military operates. During the Vietnam War, for example, a majority of generals opposed cutting-edge technology—namely, electronic warfare—being developed for combat applications. In their nascent stages, the sensor systems, computers, and overhead satellite technologies being pushed onto battlefields left many generals asking how electronic systems could possibly benefit their soldiers on the ground. Despite intense criticism, these technology concepts were pursued by the Defense Advanced Research Projects Agency

(DARPA) and other military laboratories, and they eventually led to a revolution in military affairs.

Extrasensory perception was hardly a new technology—it was an ancient discipline linked to magical, mystical, supernatural, and occult ideas. But how to uncouple ESP and psychokinesis from their primitive, pre-science past? The Army had a plan. The U.S. military is built on principles and protocols. It loves manuals, directives, and codes. The Army decided it would develop a manual and train soldiers to become remote viewers. It would jettison the idea that people were born psychic; remote viewing would henceforth be regarded as classified Army tradecraft. The job of creating the manual was assigned to Hal Puthoff and Ingo Swann at SRI. The two began developing a system to train soldiers and civilians with the U.S. Army in a six-stage process called Coordinate Remote Viewing, or CRV.

While Puthoff and Swann wrote the CRV manual, Fred Atwater, now serving as branch chief, traveled to Fort Huachuca, in Arizona, to locate two military intelligence officers who would be trained personally by Swann in CRV techniques. The men he chose were Captain Rob Cowart and Captain Tom McNear. In 1982, both men were read onto the classified Grill Flame program. The plan was that after Cowart and McNear had been trained they would become the program's CRV trainers.

The timing was fortuitous. In 1982 there was a new commanding general at INSCOM, Major General Albert Stubblebine, a powerful figure who welcomed unconventional beliefs. His purview was vast. Stubblebine was in charge of all the Army's strategic intelligence forces around the world, including signals, photographic, and human intelligence, along with counterintelligence. "They all belonged to me," Stubblebine said in an interview in 2009. "I was supposed to find out what the enemy was doing before the enemy did it, so that we could take action against the enemy. That's intelligence. *Before* the fact," he said. General Stubblebine had a long-standing interest in anomalous mental phenomena. He had studied altered states, out-of-body experiences, extrasensory perception, and precognition. These, he said, were "not hocus pocus, not superstitious and not occult." They were mechanisms that consciously tapped into "human potential." This was human technology, Stubblebine insisted, and like all technology it needed to be researched, developed, and advanced.

Under a Psychoenergetic Phenomena program banner, with access highly restricted, a series of new programs related to extrasensory perception and psychokinesis emerged. Some of these efforts sought to use the mind to affect biological systems, including one's own. This new work at INSCOM would resemble programs going on in China under the leadership of H. S. Tsien in which the mastery of qigong was seen as a pathway to such Extraordinary Human Body Functions as skin reading, clairvoyance, and psychokinesis.

General Stubblebine set up an entity called the Advanced Human Technology Office. The man he chose to run it was Lieutenant Colonel John B. Alexander, a former Green Beret and Special Forces commander in Vietnam with a PhD in thanatology, the study of death.

CHAPTER SEVENTEEN

Consciousness

The first time extrasensory perception and psychokinesis were written about in an official U.S. Army publication was on December 12, 1980. The article, titled "The New Mental Battlefield: Beam Me Up, Spock," was published in *Military Review*, the bimonthly magazine of the U.S. Army Combined Arms Center at Fort Leavenworth, Kansas. The author was Lieutenant Colonel John B. Alexander.

"While the concepts may stretch the imagination of many readers," wrote Alexander, "the possibility for employment as weaponry has been explored. To be more specific, there are weapons systems that operate on the power of the mind whose lethal capacity has already been demonstrated." Alexander was not yet part of the Grill Flame program, nor did he have access to information about any of the CIA, DIA, or Army projects involving ESP and PK, now also being called remote action (RA) and remote perturbation (RP). Alexander's article was based on personal experience and open-source information, material found in books and articles in the public domain, which in 1980 meant in the library.

The military establishment's initial response to Alexander's article was relatively subdued. Then *Washington Post* columnist Jack Anderson read the article and wrote about it in his column under the heading "Voodoo Warriors of the Pentagon." Anderson surmised that the generals at the Pentagon were "dabbling in the dark arts," using Ouija boards and the evil eye, and studying programs "a Haitian witch doctor might try." The wire services picked up the story and it went national.

"That's when the shit hit the fan," John Alexander recalled in 2016.

Back in January 1981, Alexander recalls, he was sitting at his desk at the Pentagon, where he worked for the inspector general, when an Army officer came in unannounced and highly agitated, and began asking questions about the "New Mental Battlefield" article. This was one in a series of "synchronicitous events," he says.

Hardly prone to magical thinking, Alexander is a former Green Beret. From 1966 through 1969 he commanded Special Forces A-Teams in Vietnam and Thailand, earning the moniker Assassin Six. After the war he engaged in a variety of pursuits that kept his brain and body challenged. He climbed mountains in Nepal and swam with whales in Tonga. In an effort to understand human belief systems he studied superstition, sorcery, and witchcraft around the world, interviewing witch doctors in Zimbabwe, shamans in Siberia, and tribesmen in New Guinea who still practiced cannibalism. What interested him most was how people faced fear, and how people feared death. For his PhD in near-death studies, working under the celebrated physician Elisabeth Kübler-Ross, Alexander was a founding board member of the nation's first Children's Hospice International, where he facilitated the development of protocols to help terminally ill children face death without fear.

"No hospital wanted to touch this [concept] at the time," Alexander says, as if the idea of children dying of cancer was somehow taboo. Alexander embraced a topic that had been ignored by the mainstream, and for his pioneering work with terminally ill children he received the President's Volunteer Service Award from Ronald Reagan.

The angry fellow on the other side of Alexander's desk was from the Office of the Assistant Chief of Staff for Intelligence, U.S. Army. He wanted to confirm that Alexander was the author of the article Jack Anderson had recently written about in the *Washington Post,* and if he was, then surely he was aware of clearance procedures for military employees with regard to publishing. When Alexander showed him the appropriate paperwork, the officer reviewed the documents and left.

By January 1981, John Alexander's esoteric interests had caught the attention of a high-level Army organization called Task Force Delta (not to be confused with Delta Force), led by Lieutenant Colonel Frank Burns and supported by several generals. Delta was "an Army version of a think tank," Alexander explains, whose purpose was to address the myriad post–Vietnam War problems the Army was grappling with, including its own image. Task Force Delta believed that perception was a key component of everything, Alexander explains. With the right formula in place, the Army could change the way its soldiers thought.

One such case was the Army's new recruitment strategy campaign. This huge success arrived on the heels of a decade of abysmal failures. In 1971, the Army's recruiting slogan was "Today's Army Wants to Join You." Not only awkwardly phrased, it made little sense, and it turned out to be one of the least successful advertising campaigns in Army history. Two years later, at the end of the Vietnam War, the slogan changed. Now it was "Join the People Who've Joined the Army," which was almost as feeble.

General Maxwell R. Thurman, a Task Force Delta participant,

understood the power of messaging. In 1979 he helped create a new slogan: "Army. Be All You Can Be." This crafty and empowering message would become one of the most memorable Army recruiting mottoes of all times, and it remained in use until the War on Terror. Its success underscores the power of words to influence perception.

Language, perception, and communicating the message were key components of Task Force Delta, but so were other more extreme, out-of-the-box ideas. "Nothing was too unorthodox to consider," recalls Alexander. "Task Force Delta was an organization that thought so far outside the box that its members didn't know whether or not a box existed." In 1981, there were five people permanently assigned to Task Force Delta. Lieutenant Colonel John Alexander was a part-time participant. He'd been invited to join the group before he'd written the controversial article.

The day after the awkward meeting about publication clearances, Alexander received word that the deputy undersecretary of defense, a retired Army four-star general named Richard G. Stilwell, wanted to see him. A lieutenant colonel being asked to meet with a four-star general was an uncommon occurrence, since it bypassed the chain of command. Alexander was unsure what to expect. Stilwell was an Army legend. He'd participated in the Normandy invasion in World War II, served as head of the U.S. Military Assistance Command, Thailand, during the Vietnam War, served in the CIA and as commander in chief of the United Nations Command in Korea. What did Stilwell want to see John Alexander for? he wondered.

At 12:30 p.m., that same day, Alexander made his way to the general's office, located in the elite E-ring of the Pentagon, for the meeting. "It was oddly informal," he recalls. "The general wanted to discuss various forms of phenomenology I'd written about in my paper." The conference ended without a specific request, which also struck Alexander as unusual. Walking back to his desk in the Pentagon's C-ring, Alexander wondered what the real purpose of the meeting might have been.

That afternoon, at a little after 4:00 p.m., an executive officer approached Alexander and told him this was his last day in the Office of the Inspector General. General Stilwell had arranged for his transfer to INSCOM, at Arlington Hall, Virginia. His new commanding officer would be Major General Albert Stubblebine. "I'd been moved formally into the psychic realm," says Alexander.

In the early 1980s a panel of scientists working for the Army Science Board had identified "a major challenge" facing the military institution. Machines were getting smarter, but humans were not. "Sophisticated high technology systems [are] changing faster than the human beings required to operate and maintain them," the panel found. The Army needed new ways to improve human productivity in order to offset what had officially been identified as "the growing human technology gap." The operational definition of human technology, wrote the board, includes "strategies and actions which improve human capability and/or performance." The Army did not want soldiers to be all they could be, they wanted them to be better than that.

At INSCOM, General Bert Stubblebine was the man in charge of developing human technologies that would be useful to the Army. John Alexander had been transferred to help him realize this vision. As part of a program called INSCOM Beyond Excellence, Alexander was now in charge of the Advanced Human Technology Office, and would interact with Stubblebine's High Performance Task Force.

General Stubblebine was a commanding figure. He was six foot three, with a shock of white hair, enormous ears, and a broad forehead. Colleagues described him as a dead ringer for the actor Lee Marvin. A West Point graduate, Class of 1952, Stubblebine had a master's degree in engineering. He had spent the first decade of his military career in armored units and as an instructor at the U.S. Military Academy, where he taught chemistry. During the Vietnam War he worked as an imagery analyst and became the third military intelligence officer to serve as a primary staff officer in a combat division. After the war Stubblebine worked his way up through the leadership ranks, distinguishing himself with pioneering ideas in the new, so-called electronic, battlefield. By 1982, as head of INSCOM, he had 16,000 soldiers under his command. Protected by his broad authority, Stubblebine had no qualms about expressing his interest in all forms of anomalous mental phenomena, extrasensory perception and psychokinesis among them. He once told a group of officers that his goal in meditation was to learn how to levitate.

Members of the Advanced Human Technology Office traveled across the country on a quest to learn what factors motivated people to strive for greatness in performance, and why. The team visited organizations as diverse as the Dallas Cowboys, the Menninger Foundation, Ford Motor Company, and Frito-Lay. They examined courses centered on New Age Thinking, Structured Writing, the Larazov Learning Method, the Cortex Program, Cohesion Technology, and SALTT (Suggested Accelerated Learning Teaching Techniques). The team examined a multitude of new age and self-help programs across America, including sleep discipline, neurolinguistic programming, and Silva Mind Control—a self-help practice in which students are taught to "rewire" their subconscious using guided imagery. The goal was to sift through volumes of data, pare down the results, and identify the five best human technology programs that Army INSCOM could get behind. Five programs to narrow the human technology gap and create soldiers who were better than they thought they could be.

In the remote-viewing unit at Fort Meade, Joe McMoneagle was exhausted. Between 1981 and 1982, he'd worked on more than one hundred intelligence missions targeted directly on terrorism, including ones in Africa, Europe, South America, the Middle East, and the United States. Ken Bell had left the unit, and just about everyone else was away training at SRI. That left McMoneagle and Hartleigh Trent with a heavy caseload. Army personnel don't get overtime pay for longer hours or more work. Salaries are finite, set by rank and years of experience. There were requests coming in from NSA, CIA, FBI, even the Joint Chiefs of Staff. While this was good news for the longevity of the program, it also placed considerable strain on McMoneagle and Trent. Remote viewing was grueling, intense work, the strain of which was exacerbated by the fact that someone working in a classified, Special Access Program couldn't tell anyone what he or she did all day. Even if he could tell, McMoneagle was practical enough to know that most people doubted the legitimacy of psychic functioning and might even laugh at it. The pressure was taking its toll.

To reduce the stress, McMoneagle and Fred Atwater played racquetball at the Fort Meade gym during lunch hour. Normally a gentle game, it became what the two men called combat racquetball. Full-body blocking was allowed, and so were body checks against the walls. Sometimes an audience gathered in the gallery upstairs. On one particularly intense day the two men were on a roll, with one recovery after the next and the ball moving at what seemed like lightning speed. As one of Atwater's returns came at him hard, McMoneagle twisted around to put a downward spin on the ball when *wham!,* his racket caught Atwater in the face, just over the eye. There was blood everywhere. "Fred just sort of stood there a few seconds; his eyes looked very strange," recalls McMoneagle. Then he fell down. "I thought I had killed him."

He hadn't, though the cut was serious enough that the two decided to stop playing racquetball. Atwater was fine, but without this regular exercise, McMoneagle put on weight. Health problems kicked in, he says, then snowballed. The disc injury from the helicopter crash in Vietnam resurfaced, with cold or wet days feeling particularly hellish. In the office, he struggled to meet demands. Kidnappings. Weapons assessments. The Iran–Iraq War. Special Access Programs were lonely. At least Hartleigh Trent could relate to what he was going through.

But Trent was also feeling physically ill, from a sharp pain in his left hip. "We would sometimes sit and talk with each other about how bad it felt," McMoneagle recalls. The Army threatened McMoneagle with probation for his weight problem; the military does not tolerate soldiers who are physically unfit. McMoneagle started having steroid shots at Kimbrough Army Hospital across the street. The pain got so bad, he says, he took up meditation, then started seeing a Chinese doctor who performed acupuncture. "I started to get better," McMoneagle recalls, but Hartleigh Trent got worse. When tests revealed Trent had Hodgkin's disease, McMoneagle felt devastated. A black cloud descended. Trent endured radiation and chemotherapy treatments, but modern medicine could not stop the cancer from invading his body.

McMoneagle struggled with ominous feelings. His second marriage was moving toward separation and divorce. On the way to work one morning he was involved in a multicar pileup on I-95 and narrowly missed dying. The Army and the CIA believed—or at least wanted *him* to believe—that he had extraordinary human powers, a sixth sense, or ability to see things other people could not physically see, and that it was his job—his duty—to develop these abilities. But on the human front he was as frail as the guy in the next cubicle. He couldn't make a marriage work, believe he was a good father, or live free of physical pain. Now his friend was dying right in front of him, and there was nothing he or anyone else could do.

When Hartleigh Trent was taking his last breaths, McMoneagle was standing beside his bed along with Hartleigh's wife. "His end was near," McMoneagle recalls. "His eyes suddenly popped open and he smiled at us." Then, after a moment, he spoke. "It's really quite beautiful where I'm going," he said. He closed his eyes and died.

"No more pain," McMoneagle remembers. "For me there was a very large hole." McMoneagle could not stop thinking about the nature of grief, and how soldiers deal with sorrow. "What happens to all this grief?" he wondered. "You put it away somewhere in the back of your mind, bury it under layers of calloused scarring from years of accumulated experiences." Soldiers are told to be tough, not to be crushed by experience, however painful those experiences may be. "A soldier learns to use his or her grief as a motivator," he says. But from McMoneagle's perspective, there was one thing soldiers rarely do. "They never take the time to process the loss. They suck it up and move on, putting one foot in front of the other," he says. "Over time, the grief they've accumulated and buried becomes so great it can never be processed. Opening the door to those feelings would be like splitting the face of a dam. Once the water started to flow, there would be no way to stop it."

And so Joe McMoneagle put the deep feelings of sorrow and loss of his friend Hartleigh Trent in the same place he'd put similar feelings about friends he lost in Vietnam. One foot in front of the other. One remote viewing session after the next. He was the only one left to conduct operational sessions now, and his stress levels skyrocketed, he says. During this difficult time Fred Atwater came up with an idea, something to help him relax. "Fred suggested I accompany him to a place called the Monroe

Institute," McMoneagle recalls. It was a new age retreat in the Blue Ridge Mountains run by a sixty-seven-year-old guru named Robert Monroe.

Monroe was a peculiar figure, someone who for the first half of his adult life lived a conservative existence as a radio executive and then, in his midforties, abruptly retired and immersed himself in consciousness studies and the supernatural. Monroe's mentor in these pursuits was Andrija Puharich, who according to Monroe taught him how to alter his consciousness on demand. The result, Monroe said, was an out-of-body experience, or OBE.

The mystical idea of an out-of-body experience is rooted in religion and has many names. Hindu scripture describes yoga-nandas who perform astral projection. Ancient Egyptian texts refer to a second, nonphysical body, or subtle body, called *ka*. The Wai Wai people of Brazil called it soul flight. In *The Secret of the Golden Flower,* an eighth-century Chinese handbook on alchemy and meditation, out-of-body experiences are referred to as "travel to the celestial sphere." Bob Monroe's modern out-of-body experiences were of a much more plebeian kind. Monroe claimed to be able to leave his body and travel to very specific places here on Earth, including the kitchens and bedrooms of various friends and acquaintances. In his memoir, he wrote that Andrija Puharich was one of his early test targets.

Desiring to be "reportorial and objective," Monroe kept a record of his experiences, he said. In a journal entry dated May 5, 1961, he wrote: "Applied mental lift-off, and concentrated mental desire to visit Dr. Puharich [in California]. After a short trip, stopped in room. There was a long narrow table, with several chairs and bookshelves. There was a man sitting at the table, writing on paper. He resembled Dr. Puharich. I greeted him and he looked up and smiled." Later, Monroe checked in with Puharich. "The locale was right, and actions were correct, but he has no memory of the visit," Monroe wrote. But the more Monroe practiced leaving his physical body the better he became at it, he said. Everyone has a "second body," he wrote, one that can travel around at will. He planned to keep track of his OBEs and write a bestselling book.

It did not take long for Monroe's out-of-body experiences to take a salacious turn. During one experience he desired to have sex with his wife, he wrote, but she was sound asleep next to him in their bed, he said, so he branched out with his "second body," and began enjoying sex with numerous women on the astral plane. Monroe described each experience as "unbearable ecstasy," but also "as ordinary as shaking hands." When Monroe's wife, Mary, found out, she made copies of her husband's journal entries and gave them to Puharich, ostensibly for his opinion as a medical doctor. According to Monroe's biographer, Ronald Russell, Mary never heard back from Puharich, who wrote about Monroe's sexual escapades in his own book, *Beyond Telepathy,* published in 1962. In it, Puharich declared Monroe's out-of-body experiences were a fraud. Monroe had a drug habit, he wrote, which involved sniffing model-airplane glue. Puharich surmised that Monroe was merely simulating out-of-body escapades while high on drugs (an ironic instance of the pot calling the kettle black). When Monroe read about himself in *Beyond Telepathy* he became furious and told his lawyer he wanted to sue Puharich for libel. The attorney advised against this, on the ground that a jury might instead question Monroe's sanity. In the end, Monroe decided not to sue. "The woolly world of consciousness expansion does not necessarily include integrity, empathy or honesty," Monroe said.

Bob Monroe published his own book in 1971, *Journeys Out of the Body,* in which he described his experiences on the astral plane. The book became a hit, selling more than 100,000 copies. Now Monroe had an audience to which he could market and sell a product he'd patented, an audiotape of binaural beats he'd trademarked as Hemi-Sync, short for hemispheric synchronization. The concept was more than a century old, built on the work of Heinrich W. Dove, a Prussian physicist who proposed the concept of the binaural beat in 1839. The idea was that when two pure tones of slightly different frequencies are played one in each ear, the brain perceives the difference between the two signals as a third, phantom sound. According to Monroe, listening to his tapes produced a state of mind conducive to astral projection. Hemi-Sync, he said, was a gateway to another level of consciousness—not awake, but also not asleep.

Across America, people wanted to have the same kinds of experiences Bob Monroe enjoyed, so he opened the Monroe Institute and became a celebrity in parapsychology circles. Monroe's ideas were far-out and unorthodox. He promoted the idea that life after death was real, and that with enough Hemi-Sync training, clients would be able to visit with dead loved ones "on the other side." This was all very new age, and it was accepted in certain circles, but the U.S. Army was historically not one of them. It would be safe to say that the average taxpayer would not condone this kind of training for soldiers. In the fall of 1982, however, in his capacity as branch chief, Skip Atwater thought the Monroe Institute would be a good place for Joe McMoneagle to learn how to relax. McMoneagle agreed and became the institute's first official U.S. Army client. Soon hundreds of INSCOM personnel would follow.

A thirty-minute drive from Charlottesville, Virginia, in the foothills of the Blue Ridge Mountains, the Monroe Institute sits on eight hundred acres surrounded by dense forest and rolling hills. In the winter of 1983 Fred Atwater accompanied Joe McMoneagle there with the goal of helping Remote Viewer 001, as he was designated, learn to relax deeply. After a weeklong seminar, McMoneagle returned home feeling different, he says. He slept a little better, felt less stressed, and seemed better able to focus. After a second trip to Monroe, McMoneagle recalls experiencing a shift. There was "a noticeable difference in my remote viewing," he says.

Atwater suggested that McMoneagle write a report and request more time at the institute. Permission granted, he began a fourteen-week intensive course in pursuit of a new goal. With Bob Monroe, McMoneagle would develop a system to have and repeat the out-of-body experience. Things started to "really open up," says McMoneagle. Atwater was pleased and encouraged him to write another review. This time, McMoneagle produced a very positive, ten-page classified report encouraging his commanding officers at INSCOM to allow other soldiers to learn how to expand their consciousness and have out-of-body experiences at the Monroe Institute.

"Intellectual horizons would be broadened and new concepts of perception would be unavoidable," McMoneagle wrote. "Light and heavy emotion-packed responses will result from the intensive [Hemi-Sync] tape experience. This experience can be expected to alter the participant's personality with regard to interpersonal relationships." McMoneagle cautioned that Monroe's program was not ideal for the average "military-minded [individual] unless participants across the board are willing and urged to divest themselves of peer pressure, rank consciousness, [and] ego-based self protectiveness," he warned. "The experience is intended to expand man's consciousness and broaden his perception of reality." If a soldier couldn't accept this, "the experience of the whole would be seriously diluted."

In hindsight, this is where a red flag should have been raised. The Army was and remains, by its very nature, "military-minded." Coupling Army doctrine with expanding consciousness and shifting perceptions of reality was a potentially catastrophic mix. But Fred Atwater was not the only officer at INSCOM working with Bob Monroe. So was Lieutenant Colonel John Alexander, director of General Bert Stubblebine's Advanced Human Technology Office.

In the winter of 1983, in search of "human technologies" to enhance soldier performance and shrink the technology gap, the Army Science Board hosted a retreat at the Monroe Institute to discuss "strategies and actions which improve human capability, potential and performance." Bob Monroe was one of four speakers to address the attendees. In documents declassified by the CIA, Monroe told Army Science Board advisers that in the five years his institute had been in business he had personally conducted 4,823 experiments on 1,200 individuals. The results, he said, illustrated that "the electrical effect [of Hemi-Sync] stimulated the brain to induce certain changes [in the] biological sphere of influence," including the ability to "cause sleep, cause wakefulness, increase concentration, increase recall of information, reduce stress, decrease pain, [and] increase speed of healing following surgery or injury." Cognitive benefits included "enhanced reading skills, rapid vocabulary learning, improved decision making, improved problem solving and improved muscular control"—all the things General Stubblebine was looking for.

A second advisory team not affiliated with Stubblebine's High Performance Task Group was sent to the institute to assess the results of the Hemi-Sync tape seminar. This group rejected Monroe's claims. In findings presented to Pentagon officials on April 18, 1983, the team found that "Exposure to the sleep tape did not appear to aid sleep [and] wakefulness effects were not convincingly demonstrated." As for enhanced cognition and medical claims, "concentration benefits were not convincingly demonstrated [and] medical claims and effects were not supported by scientifically acceptable studies, only testimonial type comments."

The Defense Intelligence Agency asked Central Intelligence Agency to weigh in. The CIA assigned Kit Green the job. Green read the reports, examined the data, and made a general assessment. Altered states make the brain unstable, he said, and can have effects similar to hallucinogens. "Enhancing an altered state in pursuit of intelligence collection," he wrote, would likely produce more noise and less signal. The CIA recommended to DIA that the Army disengage from its partnership with the Monroe Institute. General Stubblebine read the CIA's recommendation. He disagreed and overruled it.

In an interview in 2016, Dr. Green stated that he believed what General Stubblebine was doing was dangerous. "And that is where I started diverting from Dale Graff and Hal Puthoff and others. I do not believe you can train a soldier to be a psychic spy," Green insists. "I had conducted enough experiments with a few people [i.e., Uri Geller, Ingo Swann, and Pat Price] that it [was] clear to me that the phenomenology that had to do with remote viewing was, from time to time, one hundred percent accurate"—meaning that in certain people it was phenomenal in the literal sense of the word. "I felt that what I had found was that the people who were [almost] always right, and were doing the things that were the most dramatic—the Sugar Grove experiments, the experiments with Uri Geller, Pat Price's experiments—those were not average human beings. They were much smarter than the average human being. I looked at their blood tests, their genetic tests…their IQ tests…their neurological tests and their cardiovascular tests, which has a lot to do with endocrinology. I concluded that these people are abnormal." In Green's assessment, that was an indicator of why they were so good at remote viewing.

Green recalls his confrontation with General Stubblebine over this issue. "I said, 'You cannot take young soldiers and ask them if they want to be psychic spies and then train them in remote viewing.'" Green suggested what he believed was a wiser approach: "Take these physiological, psychological, psychiatric and genetic characteristics we identified [at CIA] and go recruit more people like that." Stubblebine disagreed. He was convinced that ESP and PK and other forms of psychic functioning were latent in all people and could be brought out through training, and as commander of INSCOM he had the authority to overrule Kit Green. Green's dissent, however, brought up the issue of research ethics and principles for human experimentation established by the Nuremberg Military Tribunals (i.e., the Nuremberg Code), and INSCOM was now required to create a Human Use Review Board in order to continue its training.

For General Stubblebine, one hurdle remained. Monroe's patented Hemi-Sync tapes were part of a Monroe Institute seminar called Gateway, and these seminars involved daily group discussions among participants. Army intelligence personnel could not mix with the civilian population in such an open-discussion environment. The Army would need its own program, an INSCOM version of Gateway, so Stubblebine arranged to have Robert Monroe's stepdaughter, Nancy Honeycutt, redesign the Gateway seminar to meet Army intelligence needs. The new program was called RAPT, Rapid Acquisition Personnel Training.

At Fort Meade, word spread fast. There was a new training program being offered, one that could teach a soldier or an Army civilian how to expand their consciousness and have an out-of-body experience. Scores of Army intelligence workers signed up for RAPT. It did not take long for chaos to descend.

More trouble was brewing. In January 1983, the magician James Randi's battle with Uri Geller over the issue of psychokinesis took an extraordinary turn, one that devastated the civilian parapsychology community. Since 1973, Uri Geller and James Randi had continued to appear on national talk shows, with Geller asserting that his ESP and PK powers were genuine and Randi insisting that Geller was a magician. Unable to put Geller out of business with rhetoric or to get the public to dismiss ESP and PK as fraud, Randi decided to up his game and perpetrate a hoax against a well-known parapsychology lab in St. Louis, Missouri.

Randi sent two young magicians pretending to be psychics to a privately funded institution called the McDonnell Laboratory for Psychical Research at Washington University. Steven Shaw and Michael Edwards told scientists there that they could use psychokinesis to bend spoons and move objects without touching them. In reality, they employed a form of prestidigitation, or sleight of hand, taught to them by James Randi.

Over a three-year period the two teenagers spent a total of five weeks in the Washington University lab. In the meantime, Randi sent twenty-two letters to lab director Peter R. Phillips warning Phillips that spoon bending could easily be faked by skilled magicians and offering ways to share methods the lab could employ to catch people who were cheating. Phillips never took Randi up on his offer. At one point, in 1982, the two magicians were dismissed from the lab on the grounds that they could not perform under certain controls but were rehired a few months later by a different set of researchers working for the same lab.

In January 1983, Randi held a press conference to announce that he had masterminded a hoax against the McDonnell Laboratory. When a reporter asked one of the young men, "Can you tell us how you do that?" Steven Shaw walked up to the microphone and said, "I cheat." The room went wild, and the story generated much negative press against parapsychologists. The *Washington Post* called the event "the slyest scientific hoax in years." Laboratory director Peter Phillips said he had trusted the research subjects and that "there are ethical issues involved" in lying to scientists. Randi retorted that this was exactly his point.

Ray Hyman, the psychologist hired by ARPA in 1973 to evaluate Uri Geller at SRI, weighed in. "Randi was very upset by Geller's using trickery to deceive scientists. He thought it was very immoral. And he felt that it was a prostitution of his beloved magic." Martin Gardner, the father of the skeptical scientific movement, also spoke out. "Paranormal metal-bending is so fantastic a violation of natural laws that the first task of any competent experimenter is to determine whether a psychic who bends spoons is cheating or not." The Pentagon assigned an analyst to examine the hoax and see how it might affect its top-secret Grill Flame program.

"The magician James Randi claimed a lab was taken in by trickery and that most, if not all, parapsychology research is suspect," the analyst noted, but insisted that Randi's claims were "gross distortions" of the facts. The two magicians had been dismissed from the lab the year before, the Defense Department analyst wrote, "when it became clear they could not demonstrate psychic abilities under tighter controls or formal scientific experimentation. It is clear Mr. Randi is solely interested in promoting his image as a clever magician and in enhancing his career as a showman at the expense of reporting accuracy. The use of tactics involving plants raises ethical questions as well." As for any potential impact on Grill Flame, the analyst concluded that the bad publicity "should in fact have an overall beneficial effect on open parapsychological laboratories that are not as tight in experimental technique and subject selection as they could be," which sounded a bit like wishful thinking. But the hoax did affect the INSCOM program, explained Colonel John Alexander in an interview in 2016.

"We started using magicians as consultants. Among the people I was involved with was Doug Henning," Alexander says. In 1983 Henning was one of the most famous magicians in the world. The first episode of *Doug Henning's World of Magic,* in 1975, still holds the record as the most-watched magic show in television history, with a reported audience of over fifty million. Another individual Alexander was working with at this time, also involving psychokinesis research, was Jack Houck, the Boeing aerospace engineer and progenitor of the PK spoon-bending party. "Jack would host spoon-bending parties at my house," Alexander says. Doug Henning was invited to attend. Alexander wanted the magician's expert opinion about whether some or all of a group of roughly twenty guests could collectively cheat at one of Houck's PK parties.

"There were two things that blew Henning away at a PK event at my home in northern Virginia," Alexander recalls. "The first was the bending [of a spoon] by an eleven-year-old girl. The other was that Henning's manager had a spontaneous bending happen," meaning that the spoon bent in his hand while he was holding it out in front of him. "That meant *no* physical force was involved. Since it was Henning's guy, obviously we had not set him up."

The controversial and contentious world of psychics, magicians, and skeptics experienced another extraordinary moment in 1987. At the height of his popularity, Doug Henning quit stage magic. He left "illusion magic" for what he said was "real magic," the kind that science could not yet explain. Henning thereafter focused on transcendental meditation (TM) and began spending much of his time with the movement's founder, Maharishi Mahesh Yogi. "Magic is something that happens that appears to be impossible," Henning told the *Los Angeles Times* in 1988. "What I call illusion magic uses laws of science and nature that are already known. Real magic uses laws that haven't yet been discovered."

In 1999, Henning was diagnosed with liver cancer and died five months later. James Randi blamed his death on the Maharishi. "He and his multi-million-dollar kingdom of sycophants caused the death of my friend Doug Henning, who dedicated himself to the Transcendental Meditation notion so deeply that he abandoned regular medical treatment for liver cancer, continued to pursue his diet of nuts and berries, and died of the disease," Randi wrote.

CHAPTER EIGHTEEN

Psychic Training

D ale Graff stood on an upper floor of the partially built U.S. embassy in Moscow, a high-powered, experimental X-ray scanning machine designed by the Los Alamos National Laboratory at his feet. He stared out over the Moscow River and across the city that represented America's arch-nemesis. It was 1983. Fierce winds whipped through what amounted to the shell of a building, just steel framing, floor joists, and window frames. Winter here in the Soviet capital was brutal, and the snow and wind stung his face. Graff was dressed in a mountaineer's jacket and boots, and carried mountaineering ropes. Pausing for a moment, he asked himself the proverbial *What am I doing here?*

There were easy short answers, including one that had to do with his job at the Defense Intelligence Agency. Graff was in Moscow as team leader on a classified counterespionage effort called Project Spitfire. But it was finding an answer to the bigger question that most interested him. What mystery lies behind causality? he wondered. Is there a force responsible for cause and effect? Or is a man's life a series of random events strung together from which meaning is derived? Graff considered another reason for his presence here, events that had occurred a few months earlier when he had attended lectures in the cafeteria at the new DIA headquarters at Bolling Air Force Base in Washington, D.C.

"DIA had a recreation club that would meet at lunchtime," Graff recalls. "By 1983, I'd been taking Arctic canoe trips for almost ten years. During lunch I'd show Super 8 movies of me dragging my canoe over icy rivers in the Arctic tundra." Bureaucrats and analysts alike crammed into the lunchroom to hear Graff talk about his sojourns in the far north. "Word got around," he recalls. Right around that time DIA issued a solicitation for a team leader needed for a classified mission with an unusual set of qualifications. "The person had to have a background in physical sciences and have a proven ability to survive in harsh winter weather," says Graff. "Apparently there was only one guy at DIA who fit the bill. Me."

So here he was in Moscow, in charge of Project Spitfire, a highly classified foreign technology investigation. The CIA had received intelligence that this new embassy, being built at a cost of $200 million ($485 million in 2017), had been bugged at its core, that sensors had somehow been embedded deep inside the structural framing materials. Graff was charged with determining whether this assessment was accurate.

"Paranoia was high. We had to be sure," he recalls. So much was at stake. In 1983, in the middle of what seemed like an ever escalating crisis between the world's two nuclear superpowers, the United States could not afford to falsely accuse the Soviets of espionage. At the same time, it could not afford to fall prey to a massive Soviet eavesdropping and surveillance program.

The new U.S. embassy in Moscow was not just any embassy. It was going to be the most elaborate and expensive such edifice built by the United States to date. Eight stories tall and set on a ten-acre parcel overlooking the Moscow River, it would stand as a Cold War symbol of prosperity, power, and freedom. It was located right around the corner from many important Soviet Politburo buildings and a short walk from the ambassador's private residence. The negotiations on erecting the building had been going on for more than a decade. Now, finally, the United States and the Soviets had agreed on terms, and construction had commenced. The Soviets were in control of fabricating the embassy's structural system, with Russian supply companies providing precast concrete blocks for the building's exterior. The Americans would be responsible for the building's finish work, including walls, flooring, windows, and doors—the places where bugging devices were traditionally hidden.

When Graff arrived in Moscow, the building was still a shell. "There was no elevator nor was any stairwell complete," he recalls. "We used mountain climbing ropes to get ourselves around the building, which was also how we got the X-ray machine in." This machine was the centerpiece of the counterespionage operation, engineered by Los Alamos scientists with specifications that were classified. "It weighed four hundred pounds," Graff recalls, and getting it to Moscow was an arduous task. First it had been flown from New Mexico to Helsinki on an Air Force plane. Then it was secreted into Moscow by rail, disguised as U.S. embassy office equipment. Graff recalls that in exchange for several cases of vodka, local construction workers helped him and his team raise the heavy machine from the street to an upper floor of the building with climbing ropes. For weeks, the Spitfire team had been using the machine to scan each concrete block for bugging devices. Soviet officials became suspicious of the machine, which they were told was checking for cracks in the concrete construction work.

"Each block weighed seven thousand pounds," explains Graff. "The suspicion was that the Soviets had embedded sensors directly into these massive precast blocks." There were several thousand of them in total, and each had to be inspected. Back at Fort Meade, remote viewers from Det G conducted sessions to determine where Graff and his team should look for bugs. "We had viewers targeting certain areas, certain pillars on specific floors," Fred Atwater recalls. The viewers' information would prove futile, but it did not take long for the members of Project Spitfire to confirm the CIA and the State Department's worst fears. Not only had the Soviets embedded sensors into the precast blocks, they had also devised a scheme whereby they mixed garbage with the concrete, which made it impossible to see high-tech sensors among the Russian trash. Thus there was no way to identify and remove individual sensors. The embassy was, in essence, a giant antenna. First the Moscow Signal at the previous embassy, now this. There was nothing left for Graff and his team to do but pack up and head home. When the story finally broke as news three years later, in 1987, the Senate Committee on Intelligence described the Soviet effort as "the most massive, sophisticated and skillfully executed bugging operation in history."

Back in the States, as director of the Advanced Concepts Office at DIA, Graff had an abundance of work to catch up on. When he'd left for Moscow, the Grill Flame program was on track, with two remote viewers working on intelligence operations and four individuals undergoing training with Ingo Swann. Upon his return, Graff found himself in the middle of the drama unfolding at the Monroe Institute. One of the sideline participants in the saga was a young Army captain named Paul H. Smith, who recalled the story in 2015.

When Paul Smith arrived at Fort Meade in September 1983, he had been in the Army for seven years. He'd worked as an Arabic linguist, an electronic warfare operator, and a strategic intelligence officer. Recently recruited into the remote-viewing unit,

Smith had no background in anything psychic or paranormal. He was a practicing Mormon who wore thick glasses and listened to heavy metal. He also possessed an artistic talent that helped recruiters identify him as a good candidate for the remote-viewing program. In college at Brigham Young University, Smith had worked as a botanical illustrator and had mastered the art of stippling, creating complex images out of thousands of dots.

Smith's first assignment in the Army's psychic spy program was to learn Coordinate Remote Viewing from Ingo Swann. At first it went well, he says. But just a few months into his training, he felt stuck. "I was having trouble acquiring and decoding the signal line," Smith recalls. He'd completed several stages of the protocol, out at SRI in California and also at Swann's home in the Bowery, in New York City, but Swann had recently told Smith he needed to loosen up. Stage One of the CRV training involved learning how to draw ideograms, quick visual sketches of the target or symbols representing an idea. His ideograms were "too stiff and scripted," Swann said, and suggested that the young captain place a Coke bottle under his wrist to relax his hand and get into the flow of drawing without intellect. It was weird, Smith thought, but it helped.

When Smith heard that Bert Stubblebine, INSCOM's commanding general, was sending hundreds of Army intelligence personnel to the Monroe Institute for Hemi-Sync training, he signed up. Smith knew quite a bit about the secret program, because for several weeks now, he and a personnel specialist named Charlene Cavanaugh had processed the paperwork for those who wanted to attend the RAPT seminar. There was a waiting list, and when Paul Smith learned that he'd been picked, he was thrilled with the prospect.

On December 2, 1983, with a weekend bag in tow, Smith headed over to the parking lot outside Nathan Hale Hall and boarded a bus headed to Monroe. His seatmate and roommate for the weekend, a former Morse code intercept operator named

Edward Dames, had also recently been assigned to the remote-viewing program. "He was smart, dedicated and very enthusiastic about remote viewing," Smith recalls. "He had a reputation as an innovative, imaginative thinker," someone known for thinking outside the box to solve intelligence problems.

To Smith's eye, Ed Dames looked more like a California surfer than an intelligence officer. He had a mop of sandy brown hair, with a thick set of bangs across his forehead in a razor-straight line. "He was an odd combination of single-mindedness and sardonic humor," says Smith. "One moment he could be gravely assuring you that the Soviets were likely to unleash vile biological weapons any minute now, and the next moment he'd be making a rude or irreverent joke." Smith liked him immediately, he says.

Dames loved to pontificate. "Most of the four-hour trip Ed spent talking about space aliens and UFOs," remembers Smith. Growing up in Utah as a strict Mormon, Paul Smith had been taught that intelligent life existed on other planets. "Mormonism holds these extraterrestrial beings are creations of Deity," he says, "not the stuff of flying saucers or invaders from Mars." Still, he listened to Dames talk and decided to remain agnostic on the subject of UFOs and Dames's obsession with the subject. "He exuded confidence. Seemed knowledgeable, and hinted at insider access to some of the details," Smith recalls.

The Monroe Institute's main building, called the Center, was set on a sprawling, grassy lawn lined with trees. It was three stories tall and warm and friendly inside, with wall-to-wall carpeting, soft comfortable furniture, and wood paneling. Because it was built into a hill, participants entered on the middle floor, which gave newcomers a sweeping view of the Center's Great Hall. All three floors featured wraparound balconies and double-occupancy rooms. Each room contained a pair of sleep chambers known as controlled holistic environmental chambers, or CHEC units. Each unit contained two bunks with twin air mattresses and blackout curtains that could be drawn around each bunk for privacy. The CHEC units were wired for sound, with built-in speakers that played Monroe's suggestions, Hemi-Sync audio signals, white noise, and new age music.

RAPT participants were encouraged to lie naked (most remained clothed) in their berths while Bob Monroe's voice guided them through various Focus Levels, starting at Focus Level One, which was physical waking consciousness, and moving through higher levels. On Focus Level Twelve, a person could achieve expanded awareness; Focus Level Thirteen was where no time existed; Focus Level Eighteen was where unconditional love resided. Focus Level Twenty-Three and above were inhabited by people who were already dead. "The signals were mixed with music or white noise on tapes that lasted for an hour or ninety minutes at a stretch," Smith recalls. After each audio session, everyone gathered in the meeting area to talk over their experiences: "imagery we encountered, or new insights, or—and this is what everyone was most anxious to hear about—the occasional report of something that might have been an out-of-body event." The sessions were always led by a trained psychologist. Other activities included strolling around the property and listening to Monroe's lectures. By day five, participants were expected to be prepared to move from Focus Level Fifteen to Twenty-One, a place where participants were most likely to enter an ethereal dimension, Monroe said.

As the RAPT session drew to a close, General Stubblebine came down from INSCOM with more than a dozen staff members and delivered a motivational speech. Then it was on to a final exercise. All RAPT participants were asked to assemble in the Great Hall for a group remote-viewing session. Stubblebine wanted all the Army intelligence personnel present to collectively try to predict the future, a feat he believed was possible. "The general had a lot of really far-out ideas," recalls John Alexander, and group precognition was one of them. Participants were asked to lie on their backs, close their eyes, and hold hands. On the surround- sound system, Monroe guided everyone through a series of relaxation exercises. Then came the questions, starting with "Will there be a terrorist attack against a government facility in Washington, D.C., area in the next few months?"

"The effect was jarring," recalls Paul Smith. It sounded as if Monroe was reading from a script. "After seven days of drifting without clocks in a setting designed to approach serenity and bliss," he says, "this sudden talk of terrorism was a shock." The way Smith remembers it, he and his fellow Army intelligence personnel did the best they could in these circumstances. They'd been given pens and paper, and many people began jotting down notes and recording whatever came to mind.

"Where will the next terrorist attack take place?" asked Monroe's disembodied voice. And finally, "When will the next terrorist attack take place?"

Smith was new to the unit, hardly an expert on protocol, but the procedure struck him as not likely to be successful, he says. "It began to remind me more and more of a game I had played in high school," the game where everyone lies on the floor with their head on someone else's stomach. "Someone would giggle and the bouncing of the laugher's stomach would set off the next person, then the next person, until in a chain reaction the entire room would be laughing hilariously." The difference, Smith says, was that during the RAPT seminar, everyone was seriously trying to look into the future. "No one laughed."

While this and other RAPT seminars were taking place, one hundred miles to the north, at Arlington Hall Station, Virginia, a thirty-year-old intelligence analyst named Angela Dellafiora was one of the scores of INSCOM personnel on the classified waiting list hoping for an opportunity to attend. Dellafiora worked at the INSCOM Watch

Center as a civilian intelligence analyst. Her specialty was Central America, which meant that she wrote papers on current military crises in hot spots like El Salvador, Guatemala, Honduras, and Nicaragua. One week she might be writing on the activities of leftist guerrilla forces and counterrevolutionaries, another week she could be profiling a country's political leaders. Before working for Army intelligence, Dellafiora had been with the FBI, entering fingerprints of convicted criminals into the new FBI database. She dreamed of becoming a special agent, but her eyesight was poor and she failed the bureau's vision test. When she learned that the Defense Intelligence Agency was hiring young civilians with degrees in political science, she leapt at the chance.

The work at Arlington Hall Station was challenging, and she received high marks for her contribution. One day she found out about General Stubblebine's paranormal program. As a Special-Access Program it was a closely guarded secret, but her twin sister's astrologer knew about the Army's black program, and told her. From that moment forward, says Dellafiora, "I just had to get into the program. All these people were training to try and become psychic. Well, I am psychic. That's who I am."

Angela Dellafiora was born in Coral, Pennsylvania, a poor coal-mining town fifty miles east of Pittsburgh. It was a roadside community of a few hundred people, predominantly immigrant families from Italy, Czechoslovakia, and Poland, most of whom who worked in the mines and coal yards up the road in Lucerne. Coral's few roads were named for trees and lined with small clapboard houses and trailer homes. The streets were unpaved. There were no sidewalks and no stores. The one business establishment in town was a tavern owned by Dellafiora's aunt and uncle. Her father, prosperous by coal miner standards, owned a beer distributorship in the next town over, across Highway 119.

Bertha Dellafiora, a housewife, raised her twin daughters Angela and Louise in an environment filled with books and radio programs about mystical and supernatural subjects, including reincarnation, channeling, and ESP. She read books by Edgar Cayce, the so-called father of mystical healing, and Ruth Montgomery, a foreign affairs reporter turned past-life advocate, and she encouraged the psychic abilities that seemed evident in her twin daughters. Angela remembered being psychic as a young girl, but in high school her abilities waned. In college they returned, owing to the encouragement of her chemistry professor, Carl W. Bordas. During World War II, Bordas had worked as a surgical technician with the Army and was part of the group that liberated Ebensee concentration camp in Austria. The experience altered his perception, he said, and he began to think about the sixth sense. After the war, Bordas offered adult education classes in extrasensory perception that Angela, Louise, and their mother attended. Through these and other courses, Angela learned to access her "third eye." "The third eye helps you see. It's a very old idea," she says. "It's located in the middle of the forehead. When you are being psychic, you have to open it up. When you are not being psychic, it's important to have it closed down."

The third eye is an esoteric concept said to allow for perception beyond ordinary sight. In eastern religions, it is described as an invisible eye located in the center of the forehead. In ancient statuary it is often represented as a circle or an eye symbol carved on the forehead of the statue. In qigong, third-eye training involves focusing one's attention on the space between the eyebrows while moving through a series of physical exercises, postures, and poses. In literature, it is through the third eye that a soothsayer or seer commonly obtains supernatural insight, including prophecy. The concept of the third eye and the claim by a person that he or she has one is about as far from U.S. Army doctrine as a person can get—except for the brief period in the early 1980s when Albert Stubblebine, head of the Army's Intelligence and Security

Command, was embracing paranormal concepts as a possible means of intelligence collection and encouraging the organization's staff to "approach new technology with an open mind."

Angela Dellafiora defied Army protocol by asking around to see if anyone could help to arrange for her to meet with General Stubblebine. Word came back that this was impossible. Dellafiora was a civilian analyst and Stubblebine was INSCOM's commander. Dellafiora recalls, "I kept pursuing this. I really wanted to meet Stubblebine. My management did not know I was psychic. I was working this on my own. Finally word got to Stubblebine and back to me. The general wanted to see my abilities. So I went in and channeled for him."

Channeling was what Dellafiora did. She opened her third eye, and the words came, she says. "He wanted to know about his future. I can't remember exactly what I told him. I wish I could," says Dellafiora. "I was nervous. He was the commanding general at INSCOM. My focus was to show him I am psychic and to get myself into the program."

Stubblebine thanked Dellafiora for coming and said he would see what he could do. In the meantime, Dellafiora applied to take the RAPT seminar at the Monroe Institute, and was put on the waiting list. After months of waiting, she was thrilled to learn she had finally been chosen to attend. Then a sudden change of plans: "I was told by my supervisor and his colleague, a fellow INSCOM employee, that they were going instead. So I'd lost my place for the [RAPT] seminar and was put back on the list." Dellafiora was disappointed, until she learned what had happened during the seminar, what a disaster it had been. During one of the Hemi-Sync sessions the fellow INSCOM employee reportedly had some kind of breakdown. "Agitated and threatening [he] approached the Institute director Nancy Honeycutt, Bob Monroe's daughter, who was running the office that day," remembers Paul Smith. "Sweating profusely, [he] removed his shirt and began toying with a ball point pen suggesting that his martial arts training made it possible for him to kill her with it. Then he accused her of working for an enemy intelligence service." Nancy Honeycutt called for a staff member and the two of them were able to defuse the bizarre situation. "I saw him when he was brought back to Arlington Hall," John Alexander confirms. "He was raving. He did not make any sense." Court documents indicate the man was sent to Walter Reed Army Medical Center in Washington for psychiatric evaluation.

A classified investigation ensued. Army command was livid, recalls Dale Graff. "They wanted to know how did this happen?" General Stubblebine quietly retired. Dale Graff returned from Moscow in the middle of the fallout. "I was the person who had to write up the report," he says. "It was a genuine mess. I had to make clear these were not our people from the remote-viewing unit; they were under General Stubblebine's command. He had a lot of strange ideas." An unforgiving light was shined on the program. Dellafiora says, "It made everybody paranoid at INSCOM."

Dellafiora was called into her boss's offices at Arlington Hall Station. How and why had she broken rank and gone to see General Stubblebine? she was asked. "Only then did I realize I'd made a terrible, terrible mistake," says Dellafiora. "Here I was, a young civilian. A female. I had gone way over my chain of command to get myself in to see the general. When my management found out that I went to Stubblebine, and *why* I went to Stubblebine, real problems began to materialize." She had not considered the consequences. "I was so focused on getting into the psychic program I had not seen the bigger picture," she says. "I am a quiet person. All my bosses knew was, here's this quiet person who gets up out of nowhere and goes to see the commanding general and tells him she has a third eye. My bosses decided, Well, she must crazy. I was told that they thought that the same thing that happened to [the INSCOM colleague] happened to me."

Dellafiora received word that she'd been scheduled for a psychiatric evaluation at Walter Reed hospital. "I was worried I'd lose my job. What if I was locked up? I asked to see the staff psychologist, who made a few things clear. He said, 'Angela, these people follow protocol. You skipped the chain of command. And you held a séance with General Stubblebine.'" The staff psychologist wrote a letter on Dellafiora's behalf, she recalls. "He said [something like], 'This is who Angela is. She has these abilities. This is a part of her. This is her belief system.'" Official documents reveal the psychologist to have been Colonel Dennis Kowal. Of Dellafiora he stated, "I find nothing psychiatrically wrong with her. She was referred to the command because she had been participating in behavior that was actually encouraged by the commander [Stubblebine] and they thought it was crazy. She was an automatic writer." But orders were orders, and Dellafiora's commanding officer insisted that she be evaluated at Walter Reed, so she went. "I met with a doctor and told them my version of events. The doctor said I wasn't crazy and discharged me."

Back at Arlington Hall, Dellafiora was effectively demoted—not officially, but it was obvious. "I used to do a briefing once a week. Now I did briefing maybe once every six weeks," she recalls. She was moved to an office in the attic. She did her job. She analyzed military crises in hot spots across Central America, wrote reports, and wondered what the future might bring.

More than a year passed. Then one day the phone rang. It was an Army captain named Paul Smith calling from the 902nd Military Intelligence Group at Fort Meade. Smith said he wanted to interview Dellafiora about a Special Access Program. He couldn't say much more over the phone. How soon could she come down? Dellafiora could barely contain her excitement. She knew enough about the program and the participants to know that Captain Smith was calling about the psychic program. After a year in the attic at Arlington Hall Station, she could hardly believe the good news.

CHAPTER NINETEEN

The Woman with the Third Eye

It had taken two years for the fallout from the fiasco at the Monroe Institute to clear. The battle had been a contentious one, full of hostility, bureaucratic maneuvering, and strife. In July 1984, just weeks after General Stubblebine was forced into early retirement, INSCOM's new commander, Brigadier General Harry Soyster, canceled the remote-viewing program. Then it came to light that Soyster lacked the authority to cancel the program, because it had been authorized by the secretary of the Army, which meant that only the secretary of the Army could cancel it. In effect, the Army's psychoenergetics program was now up for grabs. The CIA considered taking the reins, then passed. According to declassified documents, so did NSA. For several months the assistant surgeon general of the Army, Major General Garrison Rapmund, engaged in discussions to move the program under his command, within the Army Medical Research and Development Command at Fort Detrick, Maryland, where the emphasis would be on testing the physiology of the viewers.

But after several rounds of negotiations the Office of the Surgeon General also declined.

During this time Dale Graff and Jack Vorona had been lobbying for the DIA to absorb the psychoenergetics program in its entirety. "RV has potential for U.S. intelligence application," they wrote, and the "implications are revolutionary." Finally, on August 24, 1984, Secretary of the Army John Marsh authorized negotiations for transfer to the DIA. But this was the Pentagon, and so the bureaucratic entanglements continued for another seventeen months.

On January 31, 1986, the Special Access Program was finally given a new code name, Sun Streak. Jack Vorona, chief scientist for the Directorate of Science and Technology, was still officially in charge. The chairman of the oversight panel was Donald C. Latham, assistant secretary of defense. The unit's offices remained at Fort Meade. Sun Streak's new science panel included three of the nation's top physicists, Donald M. Kerr, director of Los Alamos National Laboratory in New Mexico; Fred Zachariasen, professor of physics at Caltech (also a ranking member of the Defense Department's elite JASON Committee); and W. Ross Adey, chief of staff of the Research Division at Veterans Hospital in Loma Linda, California. Three heavy hitters. And the official definition of Psychoenergetic Phenomena had been further refined: "Remote Viewing (RV): The ability to describe remote areas or concealed data via unknown mental processes," and "Remote Action (RA): The ability to influence physical or biological systems via undefined physical means."

During the first year and a half after the RAPT debacle, while the battle raged on, Joe McMoneagle, Remote Viewer 001, was the only person actually assigned to remote-viewing operations at Fort Meade, which were still functioning with funds left over from the Stubblebine era. Records indicate that he conducted thirty-three sessions on seven different operations for clients that included CIA, NSA, and SED, the Army's Systems Exploitation Division. When McMoneagle retired in the fall of 1984, the assistant deputy chief of staff for human intelligence at INSCOM awarded him the Legion of Merit for exceptionally meritorious service. After a short respite, he went to work at SRI, where he participated in research studies. Multiple sources indicate that he was almost certainly working for the CIA. If these files exist they are still classified, unlike a majority of the Army INSCOM and DIA files, which have since been declassified. The same mystery attends the files on Pat Price, also still classified as of 2017.

By the time DIA took over the program, five viewers from INSCOM remained. They were Bill Ray, Paul H. Smith, Ed Dames, Tom McNear, and Charlene Cavanaugh Shufelt. They were all sent to New York City to be trained in the six stages of Coordinate Remote Viewing with Ingo Swann. When General Stubblebine was forced to resign, the Advanced Human Technology Office had been shut down and the High Performance Task Force was disbanded, but one concept had not disappeared with Stubblebine, and that was the idea that Army soldiers and civilians could be trained to be psychic.

The DIA had its reasons for insisting that this was the case. If remote viewing was a skill that could be taught, then ostensibly it could be unlinked from its magical, mystical, supernatural, and occult past. The expectation at DIA, says Dale Graff, was that "charges of pseudoscience" by defense officials, members of Congress, and eventually the public "would be put to rest." But this logic was flawed, and it flew in the face of thousands of years of human history. The fact remains that until science can account for anomalous mental phenomena, prevailing opinion will keep it elemental to the belief system from which it sprung: the unknown.

A declassified six-page summary entitled "Coordinate Remote Viewing Theory and Dynamics" makes clear the uphill battle DIA was now facing. "Coordinate Remote Viewing (CRV) is a psychic technique which permits a 'viewer' to transcend time and space to 'view' or 'perceive' people, places or objects—without the 'viewer' being physically present," reads the summary. But even a layman knows that transcending time and space defies the known laws of physics. How could remote-viewers-in-training believe that they could view or perceive information from a distant place unless they accepted that divination was in play? And divination by its very definition involves seeking knowledge of the unknown through supernatural means. So to declare that psychic functioning was science and not the supernatural (or at least scientifically unexplainable) was to ask remote viewers to live in a catch-22—a paradoxical situation from which they could not escape because the rules contradicted the rules.

The DIA issued memos of doublespeak. "DIA [has] refined the process of teaching CRV to the degree that individuals possessing no known 'natural psychic abilities' can be taught to remote view with extreme accuracy in a relatively short period of time," one declassified memo read. Another predicted that training would take approximately six months to complete, depending on the individual. CRV was divided into six stages, with each stage promising, "to increase the scope and ability of the viewer." And as per the training protocols, "the stages must be completed in sequence [because] movement to the next stage of training is entirely dependent upon successful completion of the preceding stage." None of this proved to be accurate.

Some of the most intractable problems came from the remote-viewers-in-training. Invariably, students have questions, and questions require answers. Ultimately, the DIA would have to explain where the remotely viewed information came from. For this, DIA provided a cryptic, quasi-theoretical explanation for ESP, as hypothesized by Ingo Swann. "Somewhere, perhaps in the unconscious mind, there exists what we will label 'The Matrix,'" Swann's declassified summary states. "The Matrix knows no boundaries and has no limitations," he wrote. "It contains all information about all things. It could be thought of as omnipotent or you could think of it as a data base, etc." Here was Ingo Swann, a committed believer in the magical, the mystical, and the supernatural, attempting to give generally skeptical military personnel a metaphor to work with. The Matrix concept was to be interpreted as a figure of speech akin to Carl Jung's archetypes of the unconscious. But some took it literally.

Paul Smith recalls what happened when viewer-in-training Ed Dames first heard about the Matrix and how excited he became. The viewers-in-training were sitting around the kitchen table at Ingo Swann's home in New York City when Dames exclaimed, "Why, that sounds just like the Akashic Records," a concept introduced by the famous spirit medium and occultist Madame Helena Blavatsky. Smith said he wasn't familiar with the concept, so Dames took the opportunity to lecture to the group. The Akashic Records were located on the astral plane, where all of human history and its memories are stored, Dames said. And according to the Edgar Cayce Association for Research and Enlightenment, "the Akashic Records contain every deed, word, feeling, thought, and intent that has ever occurred at any time in the history of the world."

The seeds of calamity were being sown. The original Army screening protocols were meant to identify individuals whose minds were not closed to the possibility of psychic functioning. Dames exemplified an individual who appears to have been at the other end of the spectrum. His belief system was such that he was already fully invested in UFOs, extraterrestrial visitations, and the so-called Akashic Records. To suggest to someone with this set of preexisting beliefs that he could become a psychic spy for a top-secret military program was in hindsight a recipe for fiasco.

After finishing their training with Ingo Swann, the viewers returned to Fort Meade, where Joe McMoneagle was preparing to retire. McMoneagle did not have a good feeling about the direction the program was headed, he says. Earlier in the year, when he'd been asked to help locate nonpsychic people who could be trained to become psychic, he declined. "There is no indication that training enhances remote viewing," McMoneagle says. Perhaps "bright and intelligent officers" who were already prone to psychic functioning "could become proficient," he wrote, but in the majority of cases, people with extrasensory perception are born, not made. Tom McNear was an exception. McNear, an intelligence officer, was one of the two original Swann trainees, starting in 1981. He immediately showed considerable talent, but his training moved slowly.

It took him two-and-a-half years to get to Stage Six, the level where viewers learn how to remote view a target, then create a three-dimensional model of that target out of clay. McNear's clay models were so accurate in both concept and scale that photographs of them, alongside pictures of the target, were used in National Security Council briefings.

By the end of his training, which included all seven stages, Tom McNear had become so good at identifying training targets that Ingo Swann confided in colleagues, "he is better than me." But McNear didn't want to be part of the viewer unit at Fort Meade anymore. "The program was a series of ups and downs. We had funding; we didn't have funding. Two members of the unit died of cancer and Rob Cowart, my fellow trainee and friend, was medically retired due to cancer. My wife said I had become very withdrawn and introverted...I felt the time was right to move on. I requested a transfer," McNear explained in 2015. The Army granted his request, and he went on to build a successful career in Army intelligence, where he still works as of 2017. In 1985 the Defense Department published a forty-one-page how-to manual, "Coordinate Remote Viewing, Stages I–VI and Beyond." Declassified in 2000, the manual's project officer, or author, remains redacted. The author was Tom McNear.

Why did Swann insist that military personnel with no predisposition to psychic functioning could be trained to acquire extrasensory perception? The answer remains a mystery, though Joe McMoneagle believes he knows why. In the late 1970s and early 1980s, says McMoneagle, "Ingo was forced into an impossible situation. The higher-ups wanted training methods, and they wanted it right then and there." This flawed idea "eventually set the stage for tearing the unit apart." The irony was that as soon as DIA took over the psychoenergetics program, it parted ways with Ingo Swann.

On January 31, 1986, what had once been Stubblebine's remote-viewing program (by then codenamed Center Lane) was officially transferred from Army INSCOM to DIA. Jack Vorona made administrative changes he felt were long overdue. He converted the job of branch chief and operations officer from a military to a civilian position. He allowed for the rotation of military officers who'd served previously to come back into the program. He reduced training time from two years to one. Viewers who had been trained by Ingo Swann would now train new recruits. Assisting Fred Atwater was Ed Dames, assigned the role of operations officer, which meant it was his job to supervise viewers and handle administrative affairs. In 1986 there were six viewers and three taskers (individuals assigned to monitor viewing sessions).

In July 1986 Angela Dellafiora joined the Special Access Program Sun Streak. Unlike the other members of the DIA's psychic spy unit, she identified herself as psychic. Everyone else insisted they were not psychic; they were remote viewers. This immediately caused friction, Fred Atwater explained in 2015. "To begin with, she'd gone around the chain of command to get into the program. Went straight to General Stubblebine himself, and that is not allowed." Fred Atwater believed "that is a violation of Army code of conduct. There are rules; people are expected to follow them." When asked to elaborate, he said, "she ignored what is sacred to soldiers: chain of command." In the military, if a soldier has a query, he or she is allowed to report only to a direct superior, who in turn decides whether that query moves higher up the chain. Angela Dellafiora did what is common practice almost everywhere in America except in the military: she went to the person she believed was in the strongest position to help her achieve her goal.

Paul Smith says what incensed him most was that Dellafiora called herself a psychic, which made him and every other soldier wince. "At Fort Meade we'd worked hard to establish ourselves as remote viewers," says Smith, "to separate the process from the terrible stigma of the occult." Dellafiora's insistence she was psychic flew in the face of all that, he says. "She read tarot cards and did automatic writing," he says, and "this was unacceptable" to a unit of military men and women. "I told her she had to lose the bad habits if she wanted to stick around," Atwater recalled. Her worst offense? The concept that none of the soldiers could accept was that Angela Dellafiora still insisted she had a third eye.

In order to follow Sun Streak program protocols, Angela Dellafiora needed to be trained in the six stages of Coordinate Remote Viewing. Declassified documents demonstrate this training to be something of a farce: she apparently didn't need to learn how to draw ideograms or identify gestalts or make clay models of things she perceived. When given a long-distance target to remotely view, Dellafiora closed her two eyes, opened her self-described third eye, and in a matter of minutes arrived at DIA's target site. This made operations managers and taskers uncomfortable.

Starting in November 1986, operations officers Eugene Lessman and Fred Atwater took turns monitoring Dellafiora. Lessman went first. A former Special Forces soldier with two tours of duty in Vietnam, his disdain for the occult was as palpable as his hard-charging personality. Large and burly, with a signature handlebar mustache, he liked to talk about Vietnam. On his last mission in the war theater, he was ferrying a Viet Cong intelligence asset back to Da Nang when the man revealed himself to be a double agent and opened fire inside the helicopter. With the pilot dead and Lessman seriously wounded, the aircraft was crashing. Putting his quick-reaction training to use, Lessman killed the Viet Cong fighter and crash-landed the helicopter at the air base. "Lessman was happy to show his torso-full of bullet scars to anyone who asked about Vietnam," Paul Smith recalls. Now he was tasking Angela Dellafiora on a remote-viewing session. He and the other soldiers had devised a plan to mold her into a good remote viewer. Privately, they called her a witch.

The remote-viewing room had been designed as a monotone environment, free of distraction. The walls were gray, the carpet was gray, and so were the desk and chairs. The room was wired for sound. The viewer sat in a relaxation chair, which was part chaise longue and part dental chair. Wires connected the viewer to equipment that tracked physiological data including respiration, temperature, and pulse. Across the hall in the monitoring room, the tasker sat in front of a rack of television monitors, microphones, and audio and video recording equipment. In this case, Dellafiora sat in the viewing room wearing headphones through which Lessman communicated from the monitoring room. As he worked this Global Beacon Target session, Lessman took notes that are now declassified.

"Start time, 10:00 a.m.," wrote Lessman in the log. He spoke into the microphone. "This is a manmade object at 37°24' 31" N / 122°10' 41". Begin your relaxation now. When you arrive at your sanctuary, you must tell me," he instructed. "Sanctuary" was a Fort Meade term for a metaphorical place of safety, somewhere in the Matrix where a viewer was to travel first, not at Fort Meade and not at the actual target site. Lessman continued, "I will provide you the coordinates again from your sanctuary," he said. "This will be your cue to go to the target and begin describing your impressions. Remember to relax your body completely from foot to head and prepare that thing you call a 'third eye' for the task at hand." Lessman and the others had such disdain for Dellafiora's third eye that they could only refer to it as "that thing you call a 'third eye.'"

In the monitoring room Lessman opened a sealed envelope and looked at the target for the first time, a photograph that only he could see. He gave Dellafiora the coordinates again. The target was the Stanford Dish, located in the foothills near Stanford University. It was a massive, 150-foot-diameter radio telescope built by the Air Force to communicate with satellites. From the logs, Lessman learned that the dish was "built on top of a large, rounded hill with grass in wide abundance" and that it was "an antenna consisting of concentric circles in a vast array of metallic framework." These kinds of descriptions were provided so that the tasker knew what to look for in the viewer's details.

In 2017, if a person were to type the above coordinates into Google Maps (which did not exist in 1986), an image of the Stanford Dish would almost instantly appear. It took Dellafiora twelve minutes to arrive at her so-called sanctuary location, then another three minutes to arrive at the target site. By November 1986, Gene Lessman had been overseeing remote-viewing operations for seven months. Most viewers spent at least twenty minutes listening to music or meditating in the relaxation chair before they were ready to begin a viewing session. Getting to the sanctuary often took a viewer twenty or so minutes, then another fifteen or twenty to get to the target. Not only was Angela Dellafiora fast, she was really fast. She spent the next twenty-five minutes describing to Lessman what she saw at the Stanford Dish coordinates.

His notes read: "Source described a large open area, windy with green and brown colors associated with the land mass (true!!).

There was a feeling of isolation at this site but it was at least visible by many people (true!!). The object consisted of a wide array of shapes with triangles and circles being the predominant shape (true!!). A general feeling of roundness, curving and pointed curves were also described (true!!). An opening or center portion of the structure appears to be of importance (true!!) with the concepts of transference of 'things' back and forth as prime purpose (true!!) and a concept of seeing without using eyes (true!!). There was an impression of heat but non-specific heat in that it did not burn or even give off warmth—radio waves? but rather tickled the body (probably true!!)."

In the official, declassified operations log, Lessman could not hide his awe. He'd been doing tasking operations for long enough to know that it generally took a viewer several noisy sessions to get close to receiving a good signal line. For example, in a recent session in which the target was the Great Pyramid at Giza, Remote Viewer 017 saw "liquid, fluid...a man-made structure, a thin gray bridge." In another, in which the target was Madison Square Garden, Remote Viewer 023 saw "hospital corridor," "stone columns," and "an altar inside an Egyptian temple." Most viewers training in Coordinate Remote Viewing protocols were way off-target. In hundreds of pages of declassified documents, there are a fair share of target descriptions that read like a drowning man grasping at straws.

Yet in her very first tasking session, Angela Dellafiora was getting majority signal and almost no noise. Lessman asked her to "get in closer to the object" and to describe the structure in more detail. Dellafiora began laughing—"loud giggling," as Lessman noted in the log.

"You are happy," he said.

"Grass, hay!" she cheered.

"Tell me about your happiness."

"I moved away from the structure. I'm sorry," she said.

"OK," Lessman said.

"Round things make me crazy," Dellafiora explained.

"Tell me its purpose," Lessman directed.

"Its purpose is the opening. It's the opening," she said, and began giggling again.

"You are laughing," he scolded.

"I feel something tickling me."

"Tell me about that," he said.

"I don't know. The heat is under the roundness. Causing movement [at] me."

Lessman noted in the log that Dellafiora's voice began to "quiver" and her body began to shake. This was the kind of occult behavior, too reminiscent of witchcraft, that the military men in the group decided must be terminated.

"Return now to your sanctuary," Lessman demanded, and ended the session. Still, he noted in the log that she'd done an excellent job. He graded the session as a 5 on a scale from 1 to 6.

Lessman reported the results to his superior, Fred Atwater. According to the operations log, in an effort to curtail Dellafiora's occult habits—the quivering voice and shaking body—a new protocol was installed for her next session, as indicated in the operations log. For this one, the target site was the Eiffel Tower.

"Today we will be working on another Global Beacon target," Lessman said through the microphone. "One difference today needs to be discussed. Very often you begin to shake and your voice begins to quiver." For the integrity of Coordinate Remote Viewing protocols, said Lessman, "it needs to be controlled. If it occurs again you will hear me state 'refocus.' That will be a signal to stop reporting, reacquire the site and to fix the images in your mind. You will then hear me state 'continue' at which point you can continue to report." Lessman repeated, "refocus." This time it took Dellafiora three minutes to get to the sanctuary, then four minutes to get to the target site.

"OK, structure, structure, triangle, I see another triangle," she said.

"Describe the structure," he said.

The log indicates that Dellafiora's voice started to quiver and her body began to shake.

"Refocus!" commanded Lessman.

Dellafiora went silent.

"Continue!" he said.

But the connection was lost. Dellafiora's signal line went dead. "Nothing..." she said.

When shown these declassified documents in 2016, Dellafiora recalled the sessions and remembered that time in her professional life when the unit's managers and taskers worked hard to gather extrasensory information according to the military's rules. "My process is my process," she says. "Trying to change it isn't going to help. But still, I should have gotten the Eiffel Tower. How can you miss the Eiffel Tower? It's huge."

Dellafiora's third Global Beacon session took place on November 24, 1986. She sat in the relaxation chair, and Gene Lessman read the coordinates to her from the monitoring room. "I have read you the coordinates," he said. "I will read them again when you reach the sanctuary. Begin your relaxation now in preparation for your tasking. This is a manmade object."

The logbook indicates that Dellafiora's target was the Great Pyramid at Giza, a huge four-sided edifice containing numerous chambers and passageways. "This ancient tomb was built as the final resting place for the Fourth Dynasty Pharaoh, Khu'fu (2800 B.C.)," read the description in the log. "At one time the tomb contained fabulous treasures, most of which were stolen by grave robbers over the centuries. In recent history archeologists have uncovered several heretofore unknown chambers containing colorful hieroglyphics and a large amount of ancient artifacts including gold and jewel encrusted jewelry."

It took Angela Dellafiora five minutes to get to the sanctuary, then another three minutes to get to the target site. And while some might argue that she simply had an amazing memory for coordinates and therefore knew this location was near Cairo, others might think she was divining information through unknown means. From the notes, we know that Lessman did not hide his surprise over the ease with which she reported what she saw and the specificity of details: "Source reported a rolling, breezy, soft warm area which closely correlates to the general geographic description of the site. Source further stated that at this site there are at least two structures (true!!) one of which is 'huge' in its dimensions (true!!). Inside the structure there are 'pictures of animals, designs and faces on the wall of long hallways,'" a clear reference to the hieroglyphics on the walls inside the chamber. "Source reported that one of the overwhelming impressions of the site is the 'preservation of history and culture' and that the people on the walls of the site wore unusual clothing and were noted for their 'culture and refinement as well as their life of luxury and ease,' (true!!). The area, according to the source, has witnessed many wars and invasions in the area around the site." For this session, Lessman gave Dellafiora a grade of 6.

It did not take long for Dellafiora to begin delivering eight-martini results. On average, she could get to the sanctuary in three minutes, then the target site three minutes after that. The taskers stopped trying to correct her "hypnagogic voice," and instead let her report what she saw.

The following month branch chief Fred Atwater ran Dellafiora on what was called a dual target—two locations near one another, to be viewed in one session. This was a skill that was supposed to take more than a year of CRV training to acquire. The first target was a coordinate. In the monitoring room, Atwater looked at a photograph of the rustic home of Ulysses S. Grant, eighteenth president of the United States. Now restored, the home is a national historic monument located inside a tourist park near St. Louis, Missouri. The second target, 14.8 miles to the northeast, was the 630-foot stainless-steel monument called the Gateway Arch.

In the operations log Atwater wrote that at Grant's house, "source began by describing a structure in a breezy, hilly area with a generally open feeling about it. This structure was correctly reported as being 'square, sloping, monumental, fenced in by a short, low fence, divided room or perhaps the effect of stacked logs.' The source correctly reported that the place 'was associated with a man,' and its purpose was to 'look, to wander about and [to view] awards, medals and displays.' Source correctly associated this structure with 'an important person who wore a blue uniform and was associated with a terrible war.'"

Next, Atwater noted in the log, "Source was asked to switch locations and to move to the second target that was of interest to the tasker." He reported that "Source correctly identified this as being 'high, overwhelming, modern, two halves exactly like making a whole, a mirrored image,' which very accurately describes the actual symmetry of the arch." Atwater was impressed. He gave Dellafiora a score of 6 and wrote, "Based on the very concise description there can be no doubt that she was able to successfully acquire the proper sites and accurately describe the major components of the targets in such a manner that an analyst would have no difficulty in correlating these perceptions to the actual target."

In an intelligence collection operation, the ability to access a site next to a site is key. For example, a viewer might be sent to a known military facility like Semipalatinsk in the Soviet Union, then asked if there was anything of interest nearby. This concept was the result of Kit Green's first experiment that used coordinates to remotely view a target, in that case the summer cabin of Green's colleague, a CIA clandestine officer. When Pat Price described the NSA's top-secret Sugar Grove Station facility nearby, it was because this was the far more interesting target, Price said. Which is similar to what happened in Dellafiora's next Global Beacon session, when she was given coordinates for the Devil's Tower in Wyoming.

The Devil's Tower is a natural stone outcropping, tall, monolithic, and conical in shape. It has a flat top and striations running down the side. After arriving at this site and describing the Devil's Tower accurately, "Source asked to move to something more sinister [nearby] and began describing some kind of underground facility," wrote Atwater in the declassified log notes. At the time, Atwater was unaware of any underground facility nearby, but he was curious about what Dellafiora might be referring to, so he encouraged her to provide further details. She described what she saw: "special areas, railings, circular, things go in there to make things occur, domed shaped rooms, cold, testing, controlling, innovative, shiny, new with people working around." The primary object in this facility, she said, was "man-made, hard, modern, flying, tossing, turning, fenced off with a sign I can't read. Special area...Power." After the session ended, Atwater did an internal Special Access Program search that showed him the locations of highly classified nuclear weapons facilities in Wyoming. "A subsequent check found that in the area there are several US Defense [underground] missile silos" classified top-secret, that are not far from the Devil's Tower. Grade: 6.

In her final consecutive Global Beacon Target session, Dellafiora delivered what is considered the holy grail of remote viewing: the ability to access alphanumeric data. On February 4, 1987, she was given a coordinate and told that "this is a new target. You have not seen this before." It took her two minutes to get to the sanctuary, then another five minutes to get to the target site. The target was the Thoroughbred racetrack Churchill Downs, home to the Kentucky Derby. As noted in the logs, it is a place "characterized by the wearing of antebellum costumes, toasting with champagne and eating of strawberries and cream."

Once Dellafiora arrived at the target site, she described the location as a "nice place where people play games." They are "pretending," she said, "wearing costumes... toasting with champagne." She saw food vendors and smells. "People walking, people talking, animals," she said. "Tall, wild, animal. Exotic. People get dressed up to have fun, the animals walk around. They are controlled by the people. The animals are used for the fun, to show how smart they are."

Atwater asked her to describe the animals.

"A riding feeling, up and down, fast, when I get this riding feeling I can feel wind and I feel I can move fast," she said.

Asked for more specifics, Dellafiora said the place was called "Church. Church." Then, "town. Town. Town." Not a far stretch from Churchill Downs.

When Dale Graff and Jack Vorona read the report, they knew they had a rare and unique viewer in Angela Dellafiora. They also knew they had a potential problem as far as operations were concerned. In point of fact, their best remote viewer could access reliable information because she was psychic, not because she had learned how to be psychic from a military manual. The Coordinate Remote Viewing manual was created to teach soldiers and civilians to be psychic because the Defense Department believed such a guide would solve some of its problems with antagonistic forces within the military and the Congress who had declared the program to be voodoo warfare, hocus pocus, and occult.

Government programs are designed to be egalitarian and training based. Battlefield skills are to be taught, learned, and honed. Too much reliance on one person was not good for protocol. So a new protocol was implemented to try to smooth over these interconnected problems. It was called large-scale remote viewing, and involved several individuals viewing the same target. The information was collected by the operations manager and delivered to Dale Graff. It was Graff's job to cull the information and pass it on to his boss, Jack Vorona. Finally, Vorona would run the information by analysts at DIA who would help him decide what information to pass on to the client, be it the NSA, the Air Force, the CIA, or a host of other military and intelligence agencies.

The year 1986 marked a significant buildup in advanced technology weapons facilities, both in the United States and in the Soviet Union. "The Soviets were pursuing advanced technologies applicable to strategic defense, including laser, particle beam, kinetic energy and microwave technologies applicable to strategic weapons," recalls Robert Gates, deputy director of Central Intelligence at the time. "The scale of the effort was impressive, with more than half a dozen major research and development facilities and test ranges." Inside the Pentagon, Gates was known to be a vocal adversary of the psychoenergetic phenomena programs, but not everyone at CIA shared his views. Between 1986 and 1988, says Graff, "We did many facilities targets for the intelligence community. And with acknowledged, ground truth success."

Many of these facilities targets involved large-scale remote viewing efforts. At Fort Meade, several people would view the same target, with coordinates provided by the client. The branch chief and operations monitor would sort through the data looking for common threads in a signal line. Viewers who delivered the most promising results would return to the target site for more information.

For Project 8701, viewers were sent to coordinates located outside Dushanbe, Tajikistan, in what was then south central USSR. Viewers consistently reported "large metal structures near a large building in a barren area," with confirmed accuracy. For Project 8704, viewers were sent to coordinates where they described workers in protective clothing, containment areas, and livestock pens filled with chickens and pigs. Satellite photographs confirmed the location as a Soviet chemical and biological test site. For Project 8609, viewers were asked to gather information about a top-secret Soviet research and development facility in Kazakhstan. They "described infrastructure consistent with anti-ballistic missile testing," according to declassified memos. The site was later revealed to have been Sary Shagan, an antiballistic missile, antisatellite systems testing range. Projects 8715, 8716, and 8717 were all facilities targets for the CIA. The detailed results of these three projects remain classified as of 2016.

In Washington, Graff and Vorona chaired the Remote Viewing Tasking Group for Sun Streak. Declassified memos reveal that representatives from CIA, NSA, and the National Geospatial-Intelligence Agency regularly attended, as did intelligence officers with the Army, Navy, Air Force, Coast Guard, and the Drug Enforcement Administration. Also present was a congressional staffer from the House and Senate intelligence committees. Targets included underground tunnels near the DMZ in Korea, Silkworm missile launch facilities in Iran, and an errant nuclear-powered Soviet satellite called Cosmos 1900. The CIA requested information on a possible mole working deep inside the Agency. Declassified documents reveal that their target was Aldrich Ames, an American CIA analyst turned KGB mole.

For Dale Graff, the challenge remained what it had always been: how to pare down volumes of information in order to determine what might matter. With ten years of experience examining data, Graff believed he'd developed a sense of what was signal and what was noise. "I did not want to appear impartial," Graff recalled in 2015, "but Angela's results were consistently the best results." This meant that Graff now gave many of the high-priority targets to Dellafiora. For some of the most sensitive projects, he took trips down to Fort Meade to run Angela Dellafiora's remote-viewing sessions himself. And as the number of her sessions increased, so did tensions in the unit.

The remaining viewers were kept active doing remote-viewing training sessions with operations manager Ed Dames. But instead of cultivating and refining tradecraft on DIA-sanctioned targets, which included over one hundred landmarks, bridges, and monuments around the world, Dames began sending viewers to what would become known as anomaly or chimera targets— nonstandard destinations not in the DIA protocols. These targets did not exist or could not be verified—places like "alien bases" beneath the desert in Phoenix or on Mars. Dames's personal interest in supernatural concepts like the Akashic Records, extraterrestrial visitations, and an impending apocalypse began working their way into his professional life and, by default, into the unit at Fort Meade.

Joe McMoneagle says of this time, "One difficulty in the study of psi [psychic functioning] is that it is not only *possible* to delude oneself into thinking something that isn't true, in some cases it is highly likely. It can happen to anyone." In time these actions would have grave consequences for the program. It was thoroughly ironic. In trying to divorce itself from the mystical and the supernatural, and by insisting remote viewing was a skill that any soldier could learn, DIA had opened the door to the irrational. For reasons that have never been explained, Dames was allowed to run wild with his anomaly targets. In an interview in 2016, Fred Atwater says he was getting ready to retire and had already been assigned to standard, outgoing administrative duties, and that he was not made aware of Dames's anomaly targets until after he left Fort Meade. Dale Graff says he was not privy to the anomaly targets until the records were reviewed at a later date. But Graff's deputy, a man by the name of Jim Salyer, raised a larger issue, one Salyer believed allowed problems such as Ed Dames's anomaly targeting to exist.

In his "Secret Working Papers," Salyer outlined what he called "existing problems" at Fort Meade. "Whereas the SRI group is managed by scientists with extensive experience in understanding and researching psi [psychic] phenomena, the Army group has no one associated with it who has any understanding of psi phenomena or experience in researching or utilizing remote viewing," Salyer opined. The experienced scientists were at DIA, located an hour south of Fort Meade at the new headquarters, in Washington, D.C. "The unit at Ft. Meade consists of Army personnel who were selected and trained to do remote viewing. Their problems are that no selection criteria were available when they submitted to an unevaluated training program, which was completed by only one member who has now left the unit," Salyer wrote, referring to Tom McNear. "Essentially what you have is a group of amateurs, led by another amateur, and being trained by yet another amateur. Success in any science is rarely achieved by an amateur, hence it is not surprising that the results produced by their group have not been astounding."

The damning assessment led to a critical review of the program, says Graff. "This document helped DIA establish a psi/RV intelligence community working group with representatives from CIA, NSA, State Department, and several of the military operational commands." And eventually resulted, Graff remarks, "in DIA being given control of the Fort Meade personnel." But before that occurred, the craziness would escalate.

CHAPTER TWENTY

The End of an Era

The mid-1980s marked the end of an era for the scientists who originally worked on anomalous mental phenomena programs for the CIA at Stanford Research Institute. Kit Green retired from CIA to work for General Motors' Asia–Pacific division in China, where he became a member of the Chinese Academy of Sciences. Hal Puthoff left SRI to lead a private research foundation in Texas, the Institute for Advanced Studies at Austin. Jacques Vallée resigned from his contract position on the SRI team and became a venture capitalist specializing in high technology in Silicon Valley. As general partner of Euro-America Ventures, he spearheaded the early-stage investments of what would eventually total sixty start-up companies, more than a dozen of which would go public through IPOs or acquisitions.

At the end of this era, while some of the pioneers of U.S. government psychic research thrived, others struggled. Apollo 14 astronaut Ed Mitchell was not faring so well. He remained deeply interested in ESP and consciousness studies, and this made him endless fodder for journalists. He began speaking out against the Reagan administration's Strategic Defense Initiative, or Star Wars, which he said could lead to the weaponization of space. The former astronaut's outspoken opposition to the president's ambitious space weapons program made him a pariah in military and defense science circles. Almost every news article about Mitchell made disparaging reference to the ESP tests he'd conducted in space.

In 1985 news broke that Mitchell was involved in a paternity suit and that the child's mother was a former Playboy Playmate with whom he'd been having an affair. When Mitchell denied being the father and dismissed the suit as "extortion disguised as paternity," the press descended upon him. When blood tests confirmed he was the child's father, the press chastised him. In turn, he tried blaming the press for his hardship. "Publicity about the case had a devastating effect on my credibility, my reputation, and most of all my income," he said, opening the door for further criticism. "If Edgar Mitchell left his footprints on the moon as an American hero, he has since become the man who fell to earth," wrote a reporter for South Florida's *Sun Sentinel*. "While Mitchell has been pursuing his goals for a higher understanding, he has also led a life of turmoil." He was enmeshed in five separate lawsuits; he was under threat of eviction; he was getting another divorce—this and more was reported in the press. "I was suicidal," he told a reporter. Life had become "a disaster," he lamented.

The anti-ESP and -PK crusader James Randi had also fallen on difficult times. In 1986 he won a MacArthur Foundation grant worth $272,000, but according to the *New York Times Magazine* he "burned through almost all of [it]" in legal costs fighting libel cases brought on by Uri Geller. The organization James Randi helped found, the Committee for the Scientific Investigation of Claims of the Paranormal, told him to lay off making false statements, but Randi wouldn't stop. His campaign against Uri Geller ultimately cost him his position on CSICOP. "When CSICOP board members demanded he stop discussing Geller in public, Randi resigned in fury," wrote reporter Adam Higginbotham.

For Uri Geller, life was good. He had spent most of the 1970s and early 1980s in the spotlight, but by 1985 he'd become more private and family oriented. For a while he'd lived in a compound in Stamford, Connecticut, with his wife, Hanna, and their two young children, but had recently moved to England. He'd made a fortune divining information for petroleum and mining companies. The technique he used was map dowsing, what he'd done for Moshe Dayan in 1970. Geller's clients included Petróleos Mexicanos, or Pemex, in Mexico; Rio Tinto-Zinc, in England; and Zanex Ltd., in Australia. According to the *Financial Times,* Geller's map dowsing fee was £1 million, and he'd been involved in at least eleven known dowsing projects—for an income total of roughly $35.75 million in 2017 U.S. dollars. He maintained contact with numerous government sources, Geller says, and on occasion assisted with FBI searches for missing persons. Then, one day in January 1987, he received a call from the State Department. The caller identified himself as being from Ambassador Max Kampelman's office, in Washington, D.C., Geller says. Since 1985, Kampelman had served as head of the United States Delegation to the Negotiations with the Soviet Union on Nuclear and Space Arms in Geneva. His office was calling with an unusual request, Geller remembers, and he was asked to meet with Kampelman in London for a private discussion. There is no way to independently verify the call, but photographs taken by Shipi Shtrang show Geller and Kampelman shaking hands outside an office building in what appears to be London. "He wanted to know if I thought that a human mind could influence others at a distance in a positive way," says Geller.

The following month, Geller was invited to attend a reception at the U.S. embassy in Geneva. Also in attendance would be Soviet and U.S. arms negotiators and their wives. Negotiations between the two nuclear-armed superpowers had been going on for years, and now it seemed as if closure might finally be at hand. The goal of the talks was to eliminate the Soviets' ground-launched ballistic and cruise missiles, called Intermediate-Range Nuclear Forces, or INF missiles, stationed in eastern Europe. Presidents Ronald Reagan and Mikhail Gorbachev had met three months before in Reykjavík, Iceland, but the talks had recently stalled. Much was riding on these Geneva disarmament talks, in which Ambassador Kampelman played a primary role.

Geller was flown to Geneva and driven to the U.S. embassy. Already present at the reception were five senators, including Al Gore, Arlen Specter, and Claiborne Pell, as well as Ambassador Kampelman and Anthony Lake, the U.S. national security advisor. "If the press spotted me, I was told to be described as an entertainer," Geller recalls, "although whoever heard of entertainers at disarmament talks?" Geller had been given a secret mission that involved Yuli M. Vorontsov, Russia's first deputy foreign minister and the lead Soviet arms negotiator in the Geneva talks, he says. Geller's instructions were to stand near Vorontsov and try to influence his thoughts in a way that would get him to sign the INF treaty. As preposterous as it may sound, in 2009, British journalist Jonathan Margolis traveled to Claiborne Pell's home in Rhode Island and verified the story.

At the reception, Geller located Vorontsov, who was engaged in a conversation with Senator Pell's wife, Nuala. Geller joined the discussion. "I liked Vorontsov at once," he recalls. "I felt no trace of hostility from him, and we soon began a pleasant and informal conversation ranging over world affairs in general and the abilities of individuals to alter the course of events by no more than the state of their minds and their real desire for peace. Vorontsov knew who I was, and since I had been brought along as an entertainer, I thought I had better do some entertaining." Geller asked Vorontsov whether he could have his watch so that he could make the hands stop with his mind. Vorontsov refused. "So I decided to demonstrate how I could make a seed sprout in the palm of my hand by closing my palm and concentrating very hard," Geller remembers.

Nuala Pell later said, "What I remember was Uri putting the grass seeds in the palm of his hand and they grew. He did it in front of us all. We just couldn't believe it. Everybody was floored. The Russians just looked stunned. They didn't know whether to believe it or not to believe." Finally, Geller did what he'd been asked to do by Ambassador Kampelman, he says. "I went and stood behind Vorontsov. I stared at the back of his head. I repeated in my mind, 'sign, sign, sign!'"

Seven days later, on March 6, 1987, Ronald Reagan made a statement to the world. "I have just met with Ambassadors Kampelman, Glitman and Lehman to hear their report on the nuclear and space talks in Geneva," the president said, and added that "the Soviet Union has recently offered to move ahead with an agreement to cut longer range INF missiles. This is something the United States and our allies have long urged." Now it had finally happened. "They signed," remembers Geller. "Of course I would never take full credit for such a significant thing. But it worked. Whatever 'it' may be."

Two months later Claiborne Pell asked Geller to come to Washington for a classified meeting on Capitol Hill. The meeting took place in the Capitol building's Sensitive Compartmented Information Facility, which is located in the top of the rotunda. "They wanted to know about my ability to place a single thought in someone's mind. They wanted to know about what happened with Vorontsov. I showed them my abilities. I did a telepathy test with a senator. I bent a spoon." Colonel John Alexander was sitting in the front row, watching. "By now I'd been trained by magicians on how to bend a spoon and I'd watched James Randi's spoon bending video frame by frame," he says. "Uri bent the spoon using no physical force. Then he laid it down on a chair a few feet in front of me and went back to talking. As he talked, the spoon continued to bend and fell on the floor," says Alexander, who picked up the spoon and took it home with him. The meeting was supposed to remain a secret but appeared in the May 4, 1987, issue of *U.S. News and World Report*. "In a vault in an attic of the Capitol... government officials gathered to hear Israeli psychic Uri Geller reveal what he has divined of Soviet strategic intentions," quipped a "Washington Whispers" columnist.

Geller says that several officials asked privately whether he would meet with them discreetly, in their homes. He recalls being surprised at how similar these meetings were. "They wanted to know about themselves. About their own personal careers. What the future would bring for them." Many people are superstitious. Some will admit this publicly, but most will not. It is human nature to grapple with the powerful ideas of destiny, providence, and fate. Geller recalls going to Al Gore's house and telling him that one day, Gore would be elected president. Reached for confirmation, the former vice president declined to comment.

The following year, the association of divination with national security was once again in the news, this time involving the president of the United States. In May 1988, Donald T. Regan, former White House chief of staff, revealed in his memoir that President Reagan had sought the advice of a private astrologer during his tenure at the White House. "Virtually every major move and decision the Reagans made during my time as White House chief of staff was cleared by a woman in San Francisco who drew up horoscopes to make certain that the planets were in favorable alignment for the enterprise." The revelation was stunning to some, perhaps even more so when the White House press secretary, Marlin Fitzwater, went before the cameras and confirmed the statement.

"President Reagan and his wife, Nancy, are both deeply

interested in astrology," Fitzwater said. Others, like *Washington Post* reporter Sally Quinn, said it was simply a well-kept secret. "I have known since before Reagan was elected [president] that they went to astrologers, and that's why I'm surprised at all of the surprise and shock."

The astrologer was a San Francisco socialite named Joan Quigley. After it was revealed that Quigley allegedly cast star charts for the president, she became the subject of considerable public interest. In her memoir, *What Does Joan Say?*, Quigley wrote, "Not since the days of the Roman emperors—and never in the history of the United States Presidency—has an astrologer played such a significant role in the nation's affairs of State." When a reporter with United Press International asked the president whether he believed that psychics could see the future, he said, "I've found it difficult to write them off entirely. The Scriptures say there will be such people."

The potential of prophecy as a military intelligence tool was also being investigated by the Defense Intelligence Agency under the Sun Streak banner. The classified project was identifiable inside the Special Access Program by its code name, Project P—as in prophecy. Graff and Vorona were examining the possibility that remote viewing could be used as a tool to foresee future events. As per declassified documents, Project P was "a utility assessment initiated to determine a remote viewer's ability to function effectively in a purely predictive mode."

In 1987 the Persian Gulf was a particularly dangerous place, and America's military presence there represented the largest massed naval strength since the Vietnam War. "Based on the premise that near-time exposure to future events might enhance remote viewer access to significant occurrences (e.g., the President Kennedy assassination) four remote viewers conducted 'free-flight' sessions against events of foreign intelligence significance in the Persian Gulf," reads a declassified Sun Streak report covering the winter of 1987 ("free-flight" meant that viewers functioned without the assistance of a monitor). When analysts at DIA reported that sessions were yielding "weak correlations" to actual events, "remote viewer enthusiasm of Project P waned considerably." Upon review, it was "Suggested this project be held in abeyance pending completion of an in-depth review of this effort," according to DIA.

There was more than enough work to keep the remote viewers at Fort Meade busy. In addition to sessions against foreign facilities targets, a new methodology was being developed for Project N-1. This new utility assessment tested a viewer's ability to read a document remotely "and substantially determine the nature of its contents." The broader military intelligence goal was "To access and report against foreign documents with a reasonably acceptable rate of success." Declassified documents indicate that during training sessions, only two viewers "successfully described the substantial content of the [test] document and provided conceptual drawings in support of their findings." Dale Graff confirmed that one of the successful viewers was Angela Dellafiora (the other's viewer number is not specified and could not be confirmed), which meant that she was assigned to many Project N-1 operations while other viewers were asked to continue training sessions with Ed Dames. This led to many of the same problems that had arisen the year before, namely that Dames was directing viewers to anomaly targets.

Declassified documents reveal that in the winter of 1987, Dames tasked remote viewers to dozens of sites of celebrated UFO encounters and alien abductions. Paul Smith reports that many in the unit were "fed up with Ed Dames's shenanigans and chafed at his parade of extraterrestrial targets," but official documents indicate that his folly seems to have had a Pied Piper effect on others in the unit, with many viewers following his lead. This is evident in hundreds of pages of declassified operations logs.

One example of this kind of target assignment involved a visit to the J. M. Davis Arms and Historical Museum in Claremore, Oklahoma, with instructions that the viewer learn about an alien "visitation" alleged to have occurred there. In the log, Dames noted that aliens likely visited this museum to learn about human weapons technology; the gallery of guns included "firearms from the 1300s" as well as ones "used by Pancho Villa and Pretty Boy Floyd." In another example, on June 23, 1987, Dames sent viewer "LB" back in time to inquire about "a possible UFO encounter [and] abduction," at a Methodist parsonage in Midway, Texas, "between hours of midnight and dawn." The viewer spent two hours and six minutes on the task. His report included contact with "a long rounded object," covered with "red and black raspy, sharp" points. For a while during the experience the remote viewer reporting feeling paralyzed: "a liquid (semi-solid) has me stuck in place." Dames's goal, he wrote, was to support his hypothesis that a group of extraterrestrials called the Supreme Galactic Council of Aliens was working to control Earth. With the help of other remote viewers in the unit, Dames sought to identify various alien bases already established on Earth, he said, including ones on Mount Hayes, in Alaska, in South America, and in Africa.

Dames's anomalous targets were not limited to UFOs. He asked viewers to examine crop circles, to search for the lost city of Atlantis, and to try to locate the Ark of the Covenant. He asked viewer 032 to go back in time to learn the truth about who shot President Kennedy and to watch gladiator games at the Colosseum, in Rome, circa 79 AD. When an unidentified commander examined the data on these rogue targets he wrote, "Not Verifiable, Cannot Evaluate, No Ground Truth" (militaryspeak for the reality of a tactical situation) and had the reports filed away.

Smith says a new Detachment G commander, Lieutenant Colonel William Xenakis, ordered Dames to lay off the bogus targets. While not excusing Dames's frivolous actions, which were performed at the taxpayer's expense, Atwater says he had witnessed enough strange behavior in his decade running the remote-viewing unit at Fort Meade that Dames's targeting was not uniquely aberrant. Fred Atwater, just months from retirement, was also expanding his own supernatural ideas, he says, but insists they did not interfere with his professional life. Atwater had recently purchased a parcel of land at the Monroe Institute, where he would eventually serve as president. There, he would lead instruction in the Human Plus seminars, teaching clients how to communicate with nonphysical entities who, according to conference-approved Monroe literature, were "inhabitants of the distant future." Given Atwater's personal belief system, Dames's ideas were not so far afield. Whether they were appropriate for U.S. military projects was a separate issue.

On November 26, 1986, Ed Dames had asked Paul Smith to remote-view Titan, one of Saturn's moons, keeping the extraterrestrial nature of the target secret. Dames's goal, he wrote in the Sun Streak operations log, was to locate evidence that aliens lived and worked there. During this training session Smith reported seeing "land, water and some structures" at the target area, which Dames took as confirmation that this was "part of an observation post" on Saturn. When Smith found out that he'd been sent to an anomaly target, he was furious. "You have to remember, as viewers we were like mushrooms," he recalled in 2016. "Kept in the dark. We were blind to the target. We did not know if Dames was sending us to a real place or an anomaly. He was the operations manager. We went where we were told."

Eventually the information about the anomaly targets reached Jack Vorona, DIA's head scientist at the Directorate of Science and Technology. Repercussions followed. Dames had originally been slated to replace Atwater after he'd retired. Vorona denied the position to Dames and redesigned the branch chief position as a civilian job. The position went to Fernand Gauvin, a former viewer from the Tehran hostage days. He had been working in human intelligence as a civilian at INSCOM.

The unit's morale took another hit, while viewer accusations about Angela Dellafiora continued to swirl. Some posited that she might have an eidetic memory and had memorized Earth's coordinates, which might account for her uncanny accuracy. A new protocol was put in place, one that had originally been designed by scientists at SRI back in 1985. Viewers would now be given what were called encrypted coordinates: "For example, 20 degrees, 34 minutes west, 48 degrees, 13 minutes, would be put into a programmable calculator and come out as 7308 2159," explains Smith. Because real coordinates are synonymous with real places, some of which were familiar to operations managers, the idea was that the encrypted coordinates would remove any level of cuing, either subconscious or intentional, and clear up suggestions about the system being gamed.

Then, in late 1987 or early 1988, all members of the unit were summoned for a meeting. For the first time in Sun Streak history, a new training technique was going to be added to the Coordinate Remote Viewing (CRV) protocol. This new technique was called Written Remote Viewing, or WRV. Paul Smith was horrified. "WRV means automatic writing," he observes, as in "a tool of the occult." In an interview in 2015, Smith explained why this was intolerable to him. "What this new approach amounted to," he says, "was channeling." He'd been training in Coordinate Remote Viewing for years. There were six stages to follow, each with its own specific set of techniques, Smith explained. Automatic writing was not one of them. Now, as if with the wave of a magic wand, a new protocol was being introduced by management, and he was certain Angela Dellafiora was behind it.

Of the numerous occult practices, channeling is among the most maligned. It is generally defined as a process whereby an individual, the so-called channeler, speaks through an entity, or a force, outside themselves. A channeler is similar to a medium or a seer. Ancient history's most famous seer, the Oracle of Delphi, was a woman who would go into a trance and channel information for kings and generals. This figure was so important to national security that in 585 BC, Greek tribes fought the First Sacred War to determine who would control it. The historian Herodotus indicates that Croesus, king of Lydia, visited the Oracle of Delphi in 560 BC to learn what his next conquest should be.

Mediums, oracles, and seers have been around for millennia, but in the mid-1970s the activity took on a contemporary twist when a young poet named Jane Roberts wrote a bestselling book, *Seth Speaks,* about her channeling. Now, a decade later, channeling was again part of the public discourse. While the WRV drama was unfolding at Fort Meade, ABC television was airing the five-hour miniseries *Out on a Limb,* based on Shirley MacLaine's autobiography, which included her work with mediums and channelers. The magician James Randi became so incensed with the channeling craze that he embarked on another hoax. This time he created a fake channeler he called Carlos, and took the young man on a tour around Australia to prove how gullible people are. Publicity material claimed Carlos was a young American artist named Jose Alvarez, who was able to channel a 2,000-year-old entity who had last appeared in the body of a twelve-year-old boy in Venezuela in 1900. Audiences across Australia fell for the Carlos hoax. When the deception was revealed on *60 Minutes,* Australian news outlets felt duped. Randi's point, he said, was that audiences were gullible and journalists were not doing their jobs. No one bothered to fact-check the story of Jose Alvarez, Randi said, and he had a valid point. People were easy to deceive.

At Fort Meade, Paul Smith became angry during the meeting about Written Remote Viewing. Automatic writing was channeling, and channeling was occult, he said. As Defense Department employees with secret clearances, it was their duty to know who their intelligence sources were, Smith argued. "How do we know [the entities] aren't liars, pranksters, or evildoers?" he asked. Who vetted them as intelligence assets? "My misgivings were shared by nearly everyone else at the table," Smith later wrote. In his opinion Angela Dellafiora was getting undue praise and attention. Now, it seemed, she was essentially being allowed to rewrite the rules. He was frustrated. He wanted to be useful to the Army. And he was tired of working rogue targets with Ed Dames.

On May 15, 1987, Ed Dames tapped Smith on the shoulder and told him to get ready to head over to the viewer room for a session. "Protocol forbade me from asking what the session would be about," Smith recalls. He figured he was in for another anomaly target, something or someplace that did not really exist.

Smith headed over to Building 2560 and into the viewing room. He put on his Sony Walkman and hit Play on a mixtape of hard rock. AC/DC came on, his favorite band, followed by Guns N' Roses, his second favorite. The lights went down in the room, and with music pounding in his ears he began to relax. After the twenty-minute cool-down period, Dames came into the room and sat down at one end of the long table, Smith recalls. Smith got out of his chair and sat across from Dames. What some viewers did before a session, Smith among them, was to make a list of anything that was bothering them before a viewing session began. This was a way to clear the mind of worries that could distract them from the task at hand. On this day, Smith's list was long, he recalls. His car kept breaking down, and bills were due. His wife had moved out two weeks earlier, and his three children were understandably upset and confused. Smith was over the proverbial barrel at this moment in his life. It felt good to get all this off his chest. When he finished the list, Dames recorded the date and time in the operations log and the session began. It was May 15, 1987, 10:23 a.m. The coordinates came first.

Smith saw "land, water, then structure," he said and wrote this down. He heard a clanging sound and sniffed a faint odor, he said, something "like sautéed celery." After a few moments, he wrote down the words "forbidding" and "taken aback." His hand began moving, and he sketched out a tall structure like a tower, with steep stairs. He wrote "tall" and "weapons." There was water. This was a vessel. The U.S. Navy was involved. In declassified logs, Smith made three similar drawings. Each unmistakably resembles a radar tower attached to a frigate, or warship.

"Weaponry, water, stanchions, extrusions, braces, appurtenances, radar," Smith wrote in quick succession. He recalls looking up at Dames and seeing what appeared to him to be a lack of research protocols and laboratory controls. "He was clearly bored, his chin resting on his hand, his eyes staring at the tasking sheet in front of him. Whatever I was reporting didn't seem to be what he wanted," Smith later wrote. This wasn't a UFO site, and Dames often appeared uninterested during sessions that had nothing to do with UFOs, aliens, or unsolved mysteries.

Smith continued reporting what he saw at the target site. The vessel was a "moving structure," he said. It had something to do with "waiting and watching," and a "magnetic envelope," whatever that meant. He saw "people" and got the word "tasking." He wrote, "reminds me of PSP [pierced steel planking] runway or flight deck of a ship." Then the session took a radical turn. "Loud sound," he reported. "Zzzzt sounds," he wrote. "Sense of unexpected. Degree of occurrence greater than anticipated. Effects pronounced. A dome of light. Misidentification. Accidentally on purpose. Like a game of chicken," he said aloud and wrote down "Troubling." Something had happened. The target was an event, some kind of an incident. He wrote, "Aircraft involved. US Ship...blinding crew and electronics."

He finished the task, returned to the headquarters building, signed out, and went home. On Monday morning, as he was getting his children ready for school, the phone rang. It was Fred Atwater. He sounded agitated and wanted to know where Smith's notes were from the session on Friday morning. Smith said they were where they were supposed to be, locked in the office safe. Atwater told Smith to get over to the office fast.

When Smith arrived, there was a newspaper on his desk. The headline read "28 Killed on U.S. Frigate USS *Stark*—Didn't Use Defenses—'Don't Know Why,' Navy Says." The *Stark* had been patrolling within the general vicinity of the coordinates Paul Smith had been given by Ed Dames, off the coast of Saudi Arabia near the Iran-Iraq war exclusion boundary, when it was struck by two missiles fired from an Iraqi aircraft. Thirty-seven U.S. sailors were dead, twenty-one wounded. For reasons unknown, the ship's electronic warfare support systems had not detected the incoming missiles. Iranian prime minister Mir Hossein Mousavi called the incident a "divine blessing," and said the Persian Gulf was "not a safe place for the superpowers."

Smith reviewed his notes. He was stunned, he recalls. He had perceived the USS *Stark* incident fifty hours before it happened. He'd dedicated much of his recent life to the remote-viewing unit. His marriage had suffered. It had reordered his sense of what was real. But precognition? Seeing an event before it happened? That astounded him. "My impression had seemed real," he says. "I was vicariously living an event that it turned out had not happened yet."

Fred Atwater sent the details of Paul Smith's precognitive remote-viewing session up the chain of command, where it was analyzed at DIA. But nothing came of it, says Smith. No positive feedback, no accolades, nothing, despite the fact that DIA was examining prophecy as a potential military intelligence tool and that remote viewers were specifically asked to "foresee future events...of foreign intelligence significance in the Persian Gulf." When asked about this in 2016, Dale Graff said that "it was hard to evaluate." When questioned further, he revealed that there were "some religious issues" involved, including with "some members of Congress and their associates." For some in this group, says Graff, to hear about information received through extrasensory means was one thing, but to hear about remote viewers divining information about the future was considered heretical.

As summarized in the 1987 Sun Streak Report on Project P, "Except for a few, isolated, eye-catching successes, there was no evidence of consistency or reliability in the results obtained from remote viewing efforts conducted in a predictive mode. Remote viewing the future does not appear to be a feasible or marketable aspect of this program at this time."

Paul Smith's remarkably accurate prophetic viewing of the USS *Stark* incident would be filed away among the facilities targets, the Global Beacon tasks, and the imaginary research facilities on Saturn and on Mars.

CHAPTER TWENTY-ONE

Hostages and Drugs

In the mid–1980s Americans and western Europeans were being taken hostage by radical Islamic terrorist groups in the Middle East at an alarming rate. The remote viewers were detailed to help determine whether these hostages were dead or alive, and if they were alive to help find them. The effort was called Project 8808.

Over a ten-year period, from 1982 to 1992, a total of 104 foreign hostages were seized, including CIA bureau chief William F. Buckley in 1984, Associated Press reporter Terry A. Anderson in 1985, and Church of England envoy Terry Waite in 1987. The kidnappers called themselves Islamic Jihad, the Organization of the Oppressed on Earth, and Islamic Jihad for the Liberation of Palestine; hostage testimony later revealed that almost all the kidnappers were part of the same Shiite terrorist organization, Hezbollah.

On February 17, 1988, Marine Lieutenant Colonel William Richard Higgins was abducted in Lebanon after meeting with the Amal Militia, a local paramilitary group, in the coastal city of Tyre. Higgins, who served as chief of the United Nations Military Observer Group Lebanon, was returning from a meeting to discuss procedures between local militia and the UN in the event of a kidnapping when he was pulled from his vehicle and kidnapped. His abduction was an international incident. At the Pentagon it generated a crisis of some magnitude. Before joining the UN team, Higgins had served as a military aide to Secretary of Defense Caspar W. Weinberger from June 1985 until he went to Lebanon, in June 1987. His in-depth knowledge of classified military matters made him a high-value hostage. Unlike a captured journalist or church envoy kept alive for leverage purposes, there was reason to believe that Higgins would be tortured to death by the Hezbollah terrorists in their effort to extract classified information. Time was precious.

Four days after the kidnapping, on a Sunday, Angela Dellafiora, Paul Smith, and Ed Dames were brought to the Defense Intelligence Analysis Center (DIAC) at Bolling Air Force Base, in southeast Washington, D.C., to help in the effort. Inside a Sensitive Compartmented Information Facility the trio of viewers were shown satellite images and video footage, some of which was from an Israeli drone (uncommon in 1988), of locations in Lebanon, including a small village. Was Colonel Higgins anywhere locatable in these images? DIAC officials asked the viewers.

Working the case was a DIA analyst named Louis Andre. He had never spoken to a reporter before. "The nature of this operation was so sensitive," Andre said in 2016, "there are many aspects that are still classified." What he could say was that before the operation began, "I was highly skeptical" of remote viewing. But this was a critical mission, and there was no room for pause, doubt, or distrust. There was strong reason to believe that Higgins's abduction had been carefully orchestrated by Imad Mughniyah, the leader of Hezbollah's terrorist operations. Mughniyah had overseen the 1983 suicide bombing of the U.S. embassy in Beirut in which sixty-three people, most of them CIA and embassy staff, were killed. And he had overseen the Beirut Marine barracks suicide bombing six months later, a terrorist attack in which 241 U.S. service personnel were killed, including 220 Marines. In the 1980s, Imad Mughniyah was considered one of the leading terrorist masterminds in the world. The DIA feared he was holding Higgins captive.

Dellafiora was shown a map of a Lebanese village. She identified where she thought Higgins was being held, and she perceived him to be alive. She said Higgins was being kept inside a "small structure." Imagery analysts told Dr. Vorona that the area Dellafiora had pinpointed was a large, barren patch of land and that there were no structures there. Dellafiora said she was confident about the location, which was on a hill not far from a major road. Dale Graff had the analysts check the dates on the satellite images and learned that they were outdated, but newer photographs were not available. Smith and Dames also viewed targets, with different results. After a long day of intense work, the viewers went home.

Louis Andre suspected that working with remote viewers was a waste of time. But in another session, Angela Dellafiora produced phonetically the name of one of the Amal Militia commanders involved in the Higgins case, providing details about his role in the region that were accurate. This included his role in the militia and information about his family members. "It was astonishing," Andre recalls. "These were incredibly sensitive components." He could not comprehend how Dellafiora could have accessed this information, only that she had. The work continued. Seven months later, in September 1988, West German hostage Rudolf Cordes was released by the terrorists. Cordes had seen Colonel Higgins alive shortly after his capture and confirmed in a debriefing with a U.S. official that he had been held captive in a specially constructed shed. Cordes also confirmed the small structure as being "very likely near" the barren location Dellafiora had identified that first Sunday after Higgins's capture.

Andre came to accept that Dellafiora's information was valuable to the overall mission. "Her talents continued to be applied," he says. The search for Higgins gained momentum over 113 sessions. Declassified memos indicate that Dellafiora perceived that Higgins was being moved from location to location and that he was "on water." In March, Dellafiora continued to report that Higgins was alive and that he would eventually be released. Something about his "feet would be a clue to investigators," she said. Dellafiora was wrong. Colonel Higgins was already dead. Intelligence agencies later confirmed that he had likely been killed between four and six weeks after his capture. Then it was learned that the terrorists had kept Higgins's body on ice to preserve it, for reasons that would later be revealed. "Higgins *had* been on water," says Dale Graff.

It would be eighteen months before the world learned the fate of Colonel Rich Higgins. In the summer of 1989, Israel Defense Forces captured Hezbollah leader Sheik Obeid. Forty-eight hours later, Hezbollah issued a statement demanding the return of the sheik or they would hang Higgins. When the sheik was not returned, Hezbollah released a video of Higgins's dead body with a noose around his neck. An FBI forensics team examined the tape and determined that Higgins had died before he'd been hanged. "When a human body is suspended from the neck by rope, the feet naturally hang with toes pointed straight down at the ground," former DIA analyst Scott Carmichael explained in an interview for this book. Carmichael had also worked with Dellafiora. "The FBI's examination of the videotape established, by contrast, that the Colonel's feet projected [out] with the ankles at right angles, not with toes pointed straight down," Carmichael clarifies. The terrorists put a rope around Higgins's neck and videotaped him that way because they wanted to project power. Higgins's body was not recovered for another two and a half years, when his mummified remains were found in a bag left in a school parking lot in southern Beirut.

Dellafiora's signal about the feet had played into the investigation. "Higgins's feet were the clue investigators used to prove he'd already been killed," says Carmichael. When Higgins was confirmed dead, Dale Graff was again forced to confront a distressing reality. What good did remote viewing really do? None of the information divined had saved Colonel Higgins's life. Yes, small details had proved correct after the fact, but the information was never of operational use. Remote viewing promised to be useful in intelligence collection; Dale Graff was convinced this was fact. But at times like this, he felt despondent. Higgins was dead, and the remote viewers had in essence failed.

As 1988 drew to a close, Captain Ed Dames was nearing the end of his assignment at Fort Meade. Declassified logs indicate his anomaly targeting had continued full bore to the end of his tenure, culminating in an anthology of reports entitled "Galactic Federation HQs," full of colorful descriptions of "three types of entities associated with ET bases at various locations within the solar system." When Dames was transferred out of Sun Streak at the end of the year, he received no recommendations or awards.

Shortly before Dames was set to retire, a new recruit arrived at the unit. He was Captain David Morehouse, a former Army Ranger commander. Paul Smith remembers getting along with him right away. "He was outgoing and friendly. He had been a successful combat-arms officer. He exuded charm." Like Smith, Morehouse was a Mormon; he and Smith attended the same church. "He won people's confidence, cultivating them as friends and allies," recalls Smith. Morehouse's commendations immediately placed him in the good graces of his superiors. In his first review, on May 24, 1989, branch chief Fern Gauvin wrote, "[his] eagerness to learn is equaled only by his ability and desire to be as highly proficient as possible in the pursuit of operational success." In Morehouse's second review, Gauvin had more praise: "Exercises strong leadership, demands high standards of performance while insuring genuine concern as a compassionate leader. A person of high moral fiber whose word is unquestionable. Maintains the highest level of physical fitness."

Morehouse had been participating in remote-viewing training for roughly a year when several members of the unit noticed odd behavior on his part. "We began to realize Dave was around less and less frequently," says Smith. Viewers Mel Riley, Lyn Buchanan, and Angela Dellafiora reported seeing the office phone number emblazoned on a sign attached to Morehouse's van advertising a construction company called House-Tech. "I fielded at least one phone call from one of Morehouse's prospective customers," says Smith, who remembers telling the caller that the number was not for the House-Tech office but was a government telephone.

This kind of problem had been predicted by Jim Salyer, in his "Secret Working Papers," written several years earlier. Regarding the operational structure of the Fort Meade unit, Salyer observed that "some potential disadvantages are that it is composed of mostly military personnel who have time limited assignments and that there is little to do during periods where there are no operational assignments." The problem of too much free time was endemic to the unit.

It does not appear, in hundreds of declassified documents dating from this time, that Morehouse was ever reprimanded.

The unit was rife with contention among personnel, making it difficult to discern how much was merely office politics. While moonlighting was not exemplary behavior, it did not appear to violate the Standards of Conduct for Department of the Army personnel, which focused more on the prohibition of unauthorized relationships, misuse of government equipment, and gambling. In Morehouse's official performance evaluations he continued to earn high praise from his superiors and was promoted to Major. "Truly outstanding in every respect," wrote Lieutenant Colonel Douglas B. Hudson, a commander at INSCOM, Headquarters, in Major Morehouse's exit review. "A rare, talented officer with unbelievable abilities. A true work horse that you want on your team." No one in the unit foresaw that David Morehouse would eventually play a significant role in the downfall of the entire program.

In 1989, precipitated by an act of Congress, the DIA acquired a roster of new clients for its remote-viewing unit. America had been fighting a so-called war on drugs since the Reagan administration's initiative. Then, in 1989, with the Defense Authorization Act, the military was formally enlisted in the national drug control program. This placed the Department of Defense at the helm of the war on drugs. Almost overnight a profusion of military assets were part of this protracted effort, including Navy radar frigates and airborne radar pickets, Air Force Airborne Warning and Control Systems, and U.S. Customs aviation units, as well as the full force of the Coast Guard. The operation escalated from state to federal, and from local to global. In addition to the Drug Enforcement Administration, the DIA's new clients included the Coast Guard, Customs, and the Joint Interagency Task Forces in Florida and California. Key to narcotics work is knowing where to look for the drugs. Remote viewers were brought on board to help interdict cocaine coming into the United States from South America, to see into the cargo holds of huge vessels and to pinpoint exactly where drugs were being stored.

Declassified memos reveal that a new protocol was implemented in this effort, the pre-science invention known as dowsing. The DIA termed its protocol Remote Map Sensing, or RMS. "Remote Map Sensing is an intellectual process in which a person is able to identify the location of an object/person which is remote to him by simultaneously focusing his attention on the object/person and concentrating on a map," one memo states. In this case, the objects being sought were cargo vessels. Viewers were encouraged to use a variety of tools historically associated with dowsing. Among them a pendulum—a weight hung from a string—described in an official memo as "a hand held tool [that] responds by gyrating when the proper location has been found." Each member of the unit was given a thick file folder of articles to read on dowsing, including newspaper stories on how the Marines used dowsing rods to locate tunnel systems built by the Viet Cong during the Vietnam War. Each viewer was given a book of instructions titled, "The Study Guide for Use of the Pendulum as a Focusing Tool." Paul Smith went the extra mile to learn the procedure by attending meetings of the Chesapeake Chapter of the American Society of Dowsers, which assembled at a Quaker meeting hall roughly twenty miles north of Fort Meade. Angela Dellafiora developed her own technique, she says. "I used my finger to pinpoint a location on a map."

For the viewers involved in the DIA's drug interdiction efforts, the top priority task was to locate the "big loads" of cocaine being trafficked into the States by the Medellín Cartel, in Colombia. The paranormal components of these drug operations were so classified that they had their own subcompartment within Sun

Streak, code-named Switch Plate. Sun Streak was a black program to begin with, and yet deep within the Sun Streak/Switch Plate classified system, there were additional levels of compartmentalization, identifiable only by a single classified code word, one of which is indicated in declassified logs to have been "Stippled." Even deeper within the Sun Streak/Switch Plate/Stippled black program was a compartmented, three-tiered level of access: administrative access, normal access, and highest-level access. "Program material is only transmitted or communicated point-to-point between named, cleared individuals," notes one declassified cover sheet. Most of the Sun Streak/Switch Plate/Stippled counternarcotics programs were "eyes only," meaning that information could only be viewed, never copied or written down. The primary client controlling the information was the Army's deputy chief of staff for intelligence. Because this information was so highly classified—compartmentalized within a black program that did not officially exist—the DIA's clients wanted to protect their identities. To this end, they often used their own taskers, not the operations managers at Fort Meade. For this work, DIA wrote a briefing manual, some of which has been declassified.

"The information provided by SWITCH PLATE sources is obtained through a unique and highly sensitive collection technique," the DIA manual states. "Your care in evaluating this information will insure that we are better able to assess or modify the technology to provide you, the customer, with a better product." The anonymous author of the monograph gave a metaphorical example that unintentionally but brilliantly sums up the conundrum of the anomalous mental phenomena research that had been going on in the postwar era.

"Sources, like all humans, tend to be attracted to aspects of the target that attract them, personally. They also tend to ignore or gloss over aspects which do not attract them." For example, wrote DIA, consider the story of four blind men asked to report the shape of an elephant. "One stood in front, felt the trunk, and said that an elephant is actually a huge variety of snake. Another felt the ear and described the elephant as being like a living leaf; another felt the tail and reported that it is like a long, hairy rope. The fourth man felt one leg and reported that the elephant is a tall, vertical animal, shaped like a tree trunk." The point was—and remains—that one's perspective is everything. Each viewer sees only a small part of the whole. How to differentiate between a tail and a rope, an ear and a living leaf? An elephant's leg and a tree trunk? This was the puzzle: how to interpret and manage what people perceive.

The DIA advised its clandestine clients to understand that "sources using this technology tend to answer questions very literally," and that the customer must understand that the more precisely he or she words a question, the more exact the source's answer will be. "Time spans should be as exact as possible: Where will Mr. X be next Thursday at 3PM?" And when dealing with targets, "locations should be as exact as possible: Describe the den of X's home." Still, the problem remained. In military operations, events happen fast. The time spent learning to separate signal from noise, and then deciphering that the rope is really a tail, always seemed to get in the way of using remote-viewing information. For this reason, the holy grail of remote viewing was and remains the ability to access alphanumeric information. Numbers, letters, and words were actionable intelligence. But this kind of intelligence was extremely rare. In the history of the government's ESP programs, only a few people had produced alphanumeric information. Now, after years of struggling to keep the program funded, one thing was becoming obvious to Dale Graff and Jack Vorona. Providing clients with alphanumeric information that they could act upon was likely going to be the only way the remote-viewing program could stay alive.

In December 1988 press reports indicated that Libyan leader Colonel Muammar Qaddafi was producing chemical weapons at a facility called Rabta, sixty miles south of Tripoli. The weapons included blister agents and sarin nerve gas, a weapon of mass destruction (WMD). Further reports indicated that President Reagan was considering using force to destroy the Libyan chemical weapons complex. Declassified documents indicate that DIA learned that Qaddafi was set to move a large stockpile of WMDs out of Rabta in anticipation of a possible U.S. airstrike. Angela Dellafiora was assigned to the operation. Because of the sensitivity of the case, Jack Vorona sat with her in the viewing room at Fort Meade, an action that incensed many of the other viewers, who had experienced no such high-level handling. The only time any of the viewers had sat with Vorona was the day after Higgins's kidnapping, when Dames, Smith, and Dellafiora traveled to DIA. Dale Graff was also actively involved. Because of the urgency of the situation, and given that it involved a WMD, Dellafiora was given a prompt to help her focus on a specific geographical location. Graff recalls the single question as being "Where will a stockpile of weapons outside Tripoli be moved to?"

"It was one of those sessions where the signal line was very clear," Dellafiora recalls. "I concentrated for a moment. A word came to me and I wrote it down." She handed the paper to Dr. Vorona. "On the paper, Dellafiora had written 'Potato' or 'Patuta,'" Graff recalls. When Vorona asked for clarification, Dellafiora said, "a ship by the name of Potato would arrive in Tripoli to transport chemicals to an eastern Libyan port."

Graff explains what happened next. "Vorona walked into the

DIAC with the piece of paper and the word 'Potato' or 'Patuta' on it and asked the analysts, 'Does anyone know what this means?'" One analyst spoke up. "The analyst said Libya had a vessel in their inventory named Batato," says Graff.

Two days later, *New York Times* reporter Stephen Engelberg broke a story headlined "U.S. Says Libya Moves Chemicals for Poison Gas away from Plant." Engelberg reported that "The officials declined to specify the source of their information." The source was Angela Dellafiora, confirms Graff.

"I was told that the U.S. Navy sent a submarine to hunt for Qaddafi's" vessel, Dellafiora says. Graff is not at liberty to confirm this.

Positive reinforcement of people's work generally affects their abilities. The reverse is also true. There was no question that Angela Dellafiora's work was favored above that of the other viewers. Her results were being shared in congressional meetings, in intelligence committee meetings, and in briefings across the military and intelligence communities. This created its own chicken-and-egg scenario. Her intelligence information was more likely to be considered by analysts, and she continued to get more tasks and produce actionable results. In the summer of 1989, the results of a particular Dellafiora search-and-locate effort would become one of the most celebrated cases in the program's twenty-five-year history. It involved a customs agent turned drug smuggler named Charles Frank Jordan.

Charles Jordan had worked for the U.S. Customs Service in South Florida as a special agent. In 1986 he was accused of taking bribes from drug traffickers smuggling big loads of cocaine into the United States. When Jordan realized that law enforcement was on to him, he became a fugitive. For more than two years he remained at large, earning a place on the FBI's Most Wanted

Fugitives list. In federal law enforcement circles, a rogue agent on the run is a highly sought-after target. Jordan had been a fugitive for three years when in 1989 the Customs Service requested that the DIA's viewers target him. Jordan was believed to be hiding in the Caribbean or South America, customs officials said.

All six viewers on the Fort Meade team were asked to locate the fugitive. After multiple sessions, the operations manager wrote a report stating that four viewers had put Jordan in four different locations. Viewer 003 said he was in Mexico, in the coastal area due west of Mexico City, where he lived in a large, multistory building with a red roof as a guest of the owner. Viewer 011 said Jordan was in south-central Minnesota, between the two small towns of Madelia and Lake Crystal, living in a farmhouse with an adjacent smokehouse. Viewer 025 said Jordan was in Florida, in the western coastal area near the southern tip of the state, living in an apartment in a one- or two-story clapboard house. Viewer 095 said he was in central Mexico, near the town of Ciudad de Rio Grande, living in a large, three-story white building with a brown roof. Mexico, Minnesota, Florida? Where to start? "My instinct was to go with Angela's information," says Graff.

According to declassified memoranda, operations manager Fern Gauvin supervised Angela Dellafiora while unit secretary Jeannie Betters took notes.

"Where's the fugitive Charles Jordan?" Gauvin asked.

"He's in Lowell, Wyoming," Dellafiora said. In 2016, she clarified, "It just came to me as two words. Fern wanted more information, and I said something like, Well, you don't need any more information because that's where he is."

"There's a Lowell, Massachusetts," said Gauvin. "Is that what you mean?

Jeannie Betters said, "She said Wyoming, Fern."

Gauvin asked for more information, but Dellafiora said she'd better end the session immediately. "We'd been doing a lot of drug interdiction," Dellafiora recalls. "I told Fern I was getting flooded with information, and if I didn't get out of the session right then and there, I was going to put the fugitive Jordan in Florida or the Caribbean." That is, somewhere where the drugs were and where Jordan wasn't, she explains.

Gauvin went to the office bookshelves and pulled down a world atlas. He flipped through the index. "There's a Lovell, Wyoming, not Lowell," he said.

"Well, that's probably it," Dellafiora confirmed.

Automatic writing is not science, Dellafiora explained in 2016, and it is definitely not an exact science in the literal or metaphorical sense. "When you do automatic writing, you get things phonetically. Lowell sounds like Lovell." At least it did as Dellafiora heard it.

Gauvin sent the information to Dale Graff at DIA. After the success of the Qaddafi chemical weapons assignment, Dellafiora's clear signal information was generally passed along to superiors, according to Graff. A few days later, Fern Gauvin asked Dellafiora if she could work another session on the fugitive Jordan.

"Absolutely not," she recalls saying. "It was the same problem," she clarified in 2016. "Too much overlay on the counternarcotics operations," which involved scores of customs agents in a myriad of places "like South America, the Caribbean, and South Florida."

Graff and Vorona agreed that Dellafiora's lead was solid and worth following up. Lovell, Wyoming, "was not a heavily populated area," says Graff. "We arranged to have FBI send the fugitive's photograph around to federal employees at post offices and national parks" in the surrounding area. Several weeks passed. Gauvin approached Dellafiora again. Could she work the fugitive Jordan case one more time? Dellafiora said fine. The signal line came to her right away, she recalled in 2016.

"Angela said, 'If you don't go get him now, you'll lose him.

He's moving from Lowell,'" Graff remembers. She sensed that Jordan was living "at or near a campground that had a large boulder at its entrance." And she said that she "sensed an old Indian burial ground is located nearby."

Customs agent William Green increased the local law enforcement effort regarding the fugitive alert. A ranger at Yellowstone National Park spotted Jordan and notified the FBI. Agents were sent into the field. Graff recalls being on the telephone with the Customs Service when the news broke: "They found the fugitive Charles Jordan at a campground located on the border of an old Indian burial ground. He was roughly fifty miles from Lovell, Wyoming." When the FBI retraced Jordan's movements, it determined he'd been in Lovell, Wyoming, a few weeks earlier.

Between March 1989 and March 1990 remote viewers conducted 982 counternarcotics sessions; 565 were training sessions and 417 were operational. Declassified documents reveal the number of "search projects of intelligence value" to have been 52 percent, while 47 percent were listed as being "of no value." Because there is no narrative description of other factors involved in the operations, it is impossible to determine exactly what these numbers meant. But a new conflict loomed on the horizon. In the spring of 1990, the Defense Department began pulling resources from the war on drugs and directing them toward the coming Persian Gulf War. Paul Smith was transferred out of the Fort Meade unit and sent to the war theater in Iraq on an assignment that had nothing to do with remote viewing. He served as part of a helicopter assault unit attached to the 101st Airborne Division, and was one of the first U.S. Army units into Iraq. There, he was involved in the capture of Iraqi infantry troops. He missed the remote-viewing unit immensely, he says, and that his efforts at Fort Meade were, by far, the most interesting assignments in his twenty-year Army career.

In October 1990 Dale Graff was notified by DIA security personnel that the Sun Streak code name needed to change. Given the classified nature of the program, a name change helped throw off foreign spies seeking information about military intelligence. Graff was allowed to pick the new name from a list of computer-generated words; he settled on Star Gate. The wheels of bureaucracy churned, creating a new Project Review Board, a new Project Oversight Panel, and a new Scientific Oversight Committee. Jack Vorona was no longer head of the Directorate of Science and Technology; now he was chief scientist, thereby severing his ties with the Psychoenergetic Phenomena program. Shortly thereafter Jack Vorona retired after twenty-five years of service at DIA. (In 2011, he was inducted into the DIA's Torch Bearers Hall.) The new DIA division chief, John Berberich, gave Dale Graff the position of branch chief at Fort Meade, replacing Fern Gauvin. Graff would be in charge of the remote viewers now, with close proximity and a hands-on role.

Graff saw the creation of this so-called new program, Star Gate, as a perfect opportunity to redesign a program to be as operationally effective as possible. This meant "draw[ing] heavily from lessons learned," he wrote in an early Star Gate briefing. His first order of business was to allow the program to return to its scientific roots. "Star Gate is a new, dynamic approach for pursuing this largely unexplored area of human consciousness/subconscious interaction," his program overview declared, a document that was distributed to the intelligence community working group. Star Gate planned to undertake research programs that would foster "discoveries into how this phenomena work." After sixteen years immersed in anomalous mental phenomena programs, Graff knew that until a general theory about the sources and origins of paranormal phenomena was developed, programs like the remote-viewing unit would be relegated to the fringe.

Thus Graff wanted to widen the program so it was not limited to remote viewing. Star Gate would research a wide range of anomalous mental phenomena, including "psychological, physiological/neurophysiological, advanced physics (new wave concepts) and other leading-edge scientific areas." All of the programs would have a "strong focus on applications research and an eye toward U.S. national security," Graff wrote. Blue-sky thinking would be encouraged. Scientists and researchers would be asked to develop better scientific methodology and evaluation procedures in order to provide DIA with better documentation of activities and plans. The program would also develop a database to track foreign efforts in psychic research, particularly efforts by the Soviets and the Chinese." This database would be available to military and intelligence officers alike. The concept of training also needed to change, wrote Graff, because the attempt to train nonpsychic people during Grill Flame and Sun Streak had proved problematic. Star Gate would identify individuals with "talent," people like Rosemary Smith, Gary Langford, Joe McMoneagle, and Angela Dellafiora. The concept of Extraordinary Human Functioning developed by Albert Stubblebine and John Alexander in the early 1980s would be reintroduced. Locating the sources of anomalous mental phenomena such as extraordinary human body functions, extrasensory perception, and psychokinesis "could lead to break-through achievements in human potential," he wrote. This is what the Chinese were doing.

Graff sought to rid the program of its Special Access designation. That classification added unnecessary concealment to an already esoteric program, he said, and the draconian rules that came with a black program fostered not just secrecy but furtiveness. Keeping the Psychoenergetic Phenomena program so tightly under wraps "did more harm than good," he says. As the new branch chief, he hoped that by giving the program Limited Distribution Status, they could dismantle the program's distorted image. He hoped to stimulate other branches of the federal government to engage in similar research. Limited Distribution Status would help cast a wider net and attract like-minded individuals—at least that was Graff's hope.

By the end of the Persian Gulf War only three remote viewers were left at Fort Meade. In May 1991, a little over a month after war's end, DIA branch chief John Berberich, Dale Graff, and the three viewers, one of whom was Angela Dellafiora, traveled to England, Germany, and Israel as part of an annual intelligence exchange. The trip to Israel was particularly notable, an exchange between DIA and its Israeli counterparts, remembers Graff. After giving his Star Gate briefing to Israeli intelligence in Tel Aviv, British intelligence, in London, and German intelligence representatives in the Munich area, Graff felt the future of the Star Gate program was on the upswing.

But the aspirations, optimism, and confidence about where Star Gate was headed couldn't prevent the program from beginning to unravel after a single newspaper story was released by the Associated Press in November of 1991.

Downfall

The beginning of the end of the government's twenty-three-year history in extrasensory perception and psychokinesis began on November 19, 1991, when the Associated Press ran a three-column story under the headline "U.N. Enlists Psychic Firm to Find Iraqi's Weapon Sites." According to the AP, the "Psychic Firm," identified as a private business called PSI Tech, was run by a retired major in military intelligence named Edward Dames.

"A United Nations team is turning to extrasensory powers to help it find Saddam Hussein's weapon sites," wrote Washington correspondent Ruth Sinai. The story focused on the work of a UN inspector and Army major named Karen Jansen, who was said to have carried with her to Baghdad "sketches of two sites where the Iraqi leader has supposedly stashed biological weapons." The sketches had been provided to Jansen by PSI Tech president Ed Dames, according to the AP. Dames told the news agency that he and five PSI Tech associates, "mostly retired military officers...drew the sketches through 'remote viewing,' the ability to locate and accurately describe unknown things and events from afar." Remote viewing was a U.S. government weapon, said Dames, but "remote viewing doesn't require psychic powers. It's more a matter of suppressing one's imagination and concentrating on a target with rigorous discipline," he said.

Dames told Ruth Sinai that Jansen had contacted him about Iraq's biological weapons sites after she saw him discuss remote viewing on a Seattle television show. Asked to provide a copy of the invoice for the weapons of mass destruction (WMD) assignment, Dames said he'd provided the information to the UN team for free, but that normally he charged between $6,000 and $8,000 a week. PSI Tech's mission statement, he explained, was "solving the unsolvable," and added that PSI Tech also trained people to become remote viewers, because the talent was a learned technique.

According to legal documents filed in California, PSI Tech had been in business since 1989. The three individuals who signed PSI Tech's official documents were Ed Dames, David Morehouse, and Mel Riley. The trio, along with Paul Smith—all government employees with secret or top-secret clearances—had been moonlighting their services to private clients.

"Yes," says Smith, "I agreed that as long as no classified information was compromised and I was not put into any conflict of interest with my military duties, I would be willing to moonlight as a viewer...And I did." He also says he was not violating any military code in doing so: he did not personally work on any PSI Tech assignments from the UN during the Gulf War, only ones from wealthy individuals interested in solving such mysteries as whether crop circles and the Tunguska explosion (over Siberia, in 1908) could be attributed to aliens. In 1990, Colonel John Alexander and General Bert Stubblebine, both of whom had retired from the military, joined PSI Tech's corporate board. "It was a mistake," John Alexander said in 2016.

Not much attention was paid by the public to what seemed like an anecdotal article by the AP. Major Karen Jansen could not be reached for comment. But at the Pentagon, the fallout was tremendous. "General Clapper could not go anywhere without being hounded about the psychic spying program," remembers Alexander. Lieutenant General James Clapper was director of the Defense Intelligence Agency at the time.

In June 1993, after sixteen consecutive years leading much of the research and operations in government ESP and PK programs, Dale Graff retired. His efforts made him the longest-serving civilian scientist in the program's history. He left a sinking ship. With Graff gone, the speed of the unraveling was swift. News surfaced that Ed Dames and David Morehouse were collaborating with a former Texas newspaper reporter named Jim Marrs to write an exposé about the still-classified remote-viewing program. But before a draft of the book was completed, Dames and Morehouse were preparing to sue each other.

"Without Dale Graff, the program really took a downward turn," recalls Angela Dellafiora. Graff's replacement, Al Girard, "thought the unit was totally out of control," she says. "He was the kind of government official who wore a three-piece suit to work," and it seemed as if "he had inherited something that was way beyond his comfort level."

Then, one day in the winter of 1994, a phone call came in from the Pentagon. David Morehouse was being court-martialed by the Army. The military charges against him were serious, and included adultery, sodomy, assault, theft of Army property, and conduct unbecoming an officer. Morehouse was being investigated by the Intelligence and Security Command as well as by the Army Criminal Investigation Division and the Defense Investigative Services. He was facing jail time. Dellafiora was asked to accompany Al Girard to the Pentagon to meet with Morehouse's lawyer. "The situation came out of left field," Dellafiora recalls.

"Morehouse was with the psychic program for a short time. He came and went. Why we were getting dragged into this, nobody knew at the time. Al Girard didn't know Morehouse from the man on the moon. I went along as a character witness because I'd worked alongside him."

After his two-year service with the remote-viewing unit at Fort Meade, Morehouse had returned to school at the Command and General Staff College at Fort Leavenworth, Kansas. As part of a master's program, he wrote a thesis on nonlethal weapons, including the use of remote viewing as an intelligence collection tool. Upon graduation, Morehouse received high praise from the Deputy Commandant. "Major Morehouse is the smartest and most dynamic of the three Executive Officers I have had in the last twenty-four months," wrote Brigadier General William M. Steele, in June 1992. "None has worked harder and pushed for excellence with his zeal. He is truly one of a kind. Everyone Dave Morehouse comes into contact with is a better soldier because of his intense professionalism." Morehouse was assigned to the 82nd Airborne Division at Fort Bragg, North Carolina, and it was there that the troubles arose. He was accused of having had an affair with the wife of his driver, an enlisted man, and having stolen government computer equipment and given it to his married paramour. When Angela Dellafiora was summoned to the Pentagon for a matter related to David Morehouse it was unclear to her what Morehouse's legal troubles had to do with remote viewing. The crimes he was being accused of occurred more than three years *after* he'd left the program.

Angela Dellafiora recalls the meeting at the Pentagon. "The lawyer told us that what it boiled down to was the defense was going to take the position that remote viewing had made David Morehouse crazy," she says. Some months later, Dellafiora accompanied Girard to a preliminary court-martial hearing at Fort Bragg. She had been called as an expert witness on the DIA's remote-viewing program.

"The entire situation was absurd," she recalls. "Here I was, testifying on the DIA's [behalf]. Here I was, psychic, [remembering back] to when people accused me of being crazy because I *said* I was psychic and that I had a third eye. Here was Morehouse, saying he'd gone crazy because the Army *made* him a psychic. This was his defense [as to] why he'd slept with another man's wife and stolen government computer equipment. It felt like some kind of comedy" of errors, she says. An extravagant, improbable farce.

The Army did not accept Morehouse's contention that remote viewing had made him crazy, and the judge ordered the court-martial proceedings to commence. In early April 1994, Morehouse checked into Walter Reed Army Medical Center in Washington. He told doctors there that evil demons possessed him, a result of working in the remote-viewing unit at the Intelligence and Security Command, he said. He was assigned to Ward 54, the inpatient psychiatric facility. In June, Paul Smith received a call from Debbie Morehouse, David's wife, whom he knew from the Mormon church they both attended.

"She asked me to visit Dave at Walter Reed," Smith recalls. "Since I was now a bishop's counselor in my local Mormon congregation, she was hoping I could offer advice about how the church might be able to help her and her family in their time of crisis." Smith traveled to Walter Reed. On June 6, he met Debbie in the hospital waiting room, and together they walked down the corridor to David Morehouse's hospital room. Debbie told Smith that her husband was preparing to do an interview with *60 Minutes* in which he would say that the DIA's remote-viewing program at Fort Meade had made him crazy. "Howard Rosenberg, one of the *60 Minutes* staff had already been to Walter Reed to interview Dave," Smith recalls. "Dave was arranging to be released from the hospital for a day of leave so *60 Minutes* reporters could interview him in depth."

Smith recalls thinking this was a "very bad idea." The remote-viewing unit was a Special Access Program that was highly classified, and revealing anything about it could be a violation of the Espionage Act of 1917. The entire situation struck Smith as tragic and he recalls being unnerved by how terrible his old friend looked: "wearing a hospital gown...unshaven and with a caged look in his eyes. He admitted to the affair, calling it a stupid mistake. He said he was being unfairly persecuted.... He described 'evil spirits' that beset him 'all the time.'" But the crux of the matter, says Smith, was that "he wanted me to testify that remote viewing had caused the mental problems he was manifesting. He hoped that if he were diagnosed as mentally ill, traceable to a military-related cause, he would be granted a medical retirement rather than being sent to the military prison at Fort Leavenworth." Smith told Morehouse he could not do that. "Since no one else from the unit had ever gone crazy," Smith explained in 2015, "it seemed unlikely that if Dave really was having mental problems, that remote viewing caused it."

In late June, David Morehouse was transferred from the psychiatric facility at Walter Reed to the psychiatric ward at Womack Army Hospital at Fort Bragg, where the court-martial was to proceed elsewhere on base. Prior to transfer, the Walter Reed Army Medical Center Sanity Board concluded, "it is the opinion of the sanity board that Maj. Morehouse did not have a severe mental disease of defect," and that his "clinical psychiatric diagnoses are: major depression," and "alcohol abuse, episodic, in remission."

60 Minutes decided not to air the show it was working on. Because the DIA remote-viewing program was still classified, America's oldest and most-watched TV newsmagazine could find no other sources to corroborate that the program even existed. "No one would talk about it on the record," *60 Minutes* producer Howard Rosenberg later recalled, "and the principal promoter of the story [i.e., David Morehouse], and of the program, was of questionable credibility and seemed to me to have multiple agendas."

The Morehouse saga ended in January 1995, when he proposed resigning his commission in lieu of being tried before the court-martial. His proposal was accepted "in the best interests of the Army," and he was discharged from the service "Under Other than Honorable Conditions."

Congress ordered an evaluation of the Star Gate program by an outside research firm, and the CIA was put in charge as custodian. The Agency hired the American Institutes for Research to conduct a review of Star Gate and an investigation into government's decades-long research into ESP and its potential for intelligence use. Most of the work in psychokinesis was left out of the report. The results were presented in two documents totaling 232 pages. "Studies of paranormal phenomena have nearly always been associated with controversy," the researchers warned, and described how the U.S. government's efforts were no different. "Conceptually, remote viewing would seem to have tremendous potential utility for the intelligence community," it was noted, but after comprehensive review, the analysts found only "a compelling argument against continuation of the research program within the intelligence community." The reason was a restatement of what had been said all along. Although laboratory studies demonstrated "the existence of a paranormal phenomenon, remote viewing," in the absence of evidence regarding "the sources or origins of the phenomenon," there was no rationale for continuance. "The remote viewing phenomenon has no real value for intelligence operations," the researchers wrote. "One must question whether any further applications can be justified."

It was a curious situation. The researchers were given less than two months to review nearly a quarter of a century's worth of work. One of the team leaders on the report was the psychologist Ray Hyman, a founding member of the Committee for the Scientific Investigation of Claims of the Paranormal and a critic of the government's psychic research ever since he had investigated Uri Geller on behalf of the Advanced Research Projects Agency back in 1972. Because the time was so limited, the researchers did not examine any of the research or reports done at SRI in the 1970s. It was later revealed that the American Institutes for Research based its evaluation on roughly forty sessions conducted in 1994 and 1995 by three randomly chosen remote viewers.

On June 31, 1995, the CIA ordered DIA to cease all Star Gate operations. Angela Dellafiora's last task for the Psychoenergetic Phenomena program was to travel to CIA headquarters in Langley, Virginia, to box up the documents for the National Archives. In October, CIA declassified 262 documents related to the psychic research programs, some dating back to 1972. Starting in the year 2000, the CIA began to declassify and release tens of thousands of additional documents; an untold number remain inaccessible.

Five months after the original CIA order, on November 28, 1995, a *Nightline* exposé made the Star Gate program public. Ted Koppel interviewed the DIA's Dale Graff and the CIA's Robert Gates on national television. Graff defended the integrity of the programs. Gates downplayed the significance of it all. Koppel also interviewed customs agent William Green, who confirmed the amazing story of how one DIA psychic, an unnamed woman, had located one of the FBI's Most Wanted Fugitives, Charles Frank Jordan, thereby bringing closure to what had been an otherwise futile two-year manhunt.

The story generated additional press in local and international news reports. The general tenor was skeptical and satirical. Former DIA director General James Clapper told reporters that he and his three predecessors had all tried to kill the program. "It just didn't feel appropriate for DIA to be doing anything like that," he said. "It was just too far out at the leading edge of technology to maintain very well as an ongoing intelligence activity. But we got directions [from Congress] every year in our appropriation and specific language to sustain the operation." After a few months in the spotlight, the public's interest in what was generally referred to as the government's psychic spy program seemed to wane. But it was interesting that General Clapper categorized the Defense Department's ESP and PK research as "leading edge technology," not leading edge parapsychology.

The year 1995 marked the end of another era when Andrija Puharich died tragically—alone, impoverished, and under threat of eviction from the North Carolina estate of his last benefactor, R. J. Reynolds. Reynolds, heir to the tobacco fortune, had died seven months before, and Puharich refused to leave the 1,000-acre estate, Devotion, where he'd been living—as a scientist in residence. The once-brilliant medical doctor and research pioneer whose Puharich Theory had set the CIA and the Defense Department's psychic research programs in motion in the early 1950s had somehow lost his way. To the end, Puharich wrote papers in service of his theory that extraterrestrials were trying to send messages to humans through psychic people, and that extremely low frequency, or ELF, waves were responsible for the sicknesses of the age.

Surrounded by filth and feral cats, early one evening in the winter of 1995 Puharich fell down a set of stairs to his death. He was seventy-six. According to the *Winston-Salem Journal,* he had been suffering from dementia, kidney failure, and the onset of gangrene in one leg.

And so, the twentieth-century chapter on secret U.S. government research into extrasensory perception and psychokinesis came to a close. The scientists and psychics went their separate ways. For some, the quest to understand the phenomena continued to be an epic pursuit. For others it remained an affliction, like a curse.

Members of the scientific skeptics community saw victory in the program's exposure, cancellation, and subsequent ridicule. But for a growing number of Americans, the revelation that the government was keenly interested in anomalous mental phenomena renewed its appeal. With the increasing popularity of late night talk radio shows like Art Bell's *Area 2000,* and the growth of the Internet, paranormal topics gained new traction and evolved.

But what of the military and intelligence communities? Efforts to use prophecy, prediction, and extrasensory perception for military gain is as old as civilization itself. To see the future, to know the unknowable, has been an ageless obsession. It is as controversial in the modern era as it was in 585 BC, when Greek tribes fought the First Sacred War over who would control the Oracle at Delphi. Regular people and world leaders alike have coveted esoteric knowledge since time immemorial. Would the U.S. government begin the twenty-first century any differently?

Will modern technology unravel the mystery of anomalous mental phenomena once and for all, or will the search be forever unresolved, like Nietzsche's eternal return?

PART IV

———

THE MODERN ERA

What is past is prologue.
——William Shakespeare

CHAPTER TWENTY-THREE

Intuition, Premonition, and Synthetic Telepathy

Are ESP and PK real? Back in the early 1950s, when the U.S. government's postwar research into them was just beginning to take off, the Nobel Laureate Wolfgang Pauli and the psychiatrist Carl Jung had a lively conversation about the phenomena. The two men were discussing a paper that had recently been written by physicist Robert A. McConnell called "ESP—Fact or Fancy?" Jung remarked to Pauli how some age-old mysteries never change. "As is only to be expected," Jung said, "every conceivable kind of attempt has been made to explain away these results, which seem to border on the miraculous and frankly impossible. But all such attempts come to grief on the facts, and the facts refuse so far to be argued out of existence." The physicist and the psychiatrist could have been having this conversation in 2017.

For seven decades, the CIA and the Department of Defense have been actively conducting research on anomalous mental phenomena. "A large body of reliable experimental evidence points to the inescapable conclusion that extrasensory perception does exist as a real phenomenon," the CIA concluded in 1975, "albeit characterized by rarity and lack of reliability." The Agency ultimately canceled its program: "There exists no satisfactory theoretical understanding of these phenomena. Present theories, of which there are many, are both speculative and unsubstantiated." Without a theory, the CIA was left with hypothesis, or conjecture.

A decade later, in 1986, the Army concluded similarly that its ESP and PK researchers and program managers had "succeeded in documenting general anomalies worthy of scientific interest," but that "in the absence of confirmed paranormal theory...paranormality could be rejected a priori." Still, laboratory research operations continued. But in 1995, a joint CIA/Defense Department–sponsored review of the government's ESP and PK programs resulted in the programs' cancellation based on this same paradox. Although "a statistically significant effect [of the phenomena] has been observed in the laboratory...the laboratory studies do not provide evidence regarding the sources or origins of the phenomenon." "Remote viewing is vague and ambiguous," the scientific reviewers of the CIA/Defense Department programs wrote, "making it difficult, if not impossible, for the technique to yield information of sufficient quality and accuracy." No source, no origins, no general theory.

Carl Jung had something important to say about this notion of possibility versus impossibility. "The so-called possibility of such events is of no importance whatever, for the criterion of what is possible in any age is derived from that age's rational assumptions." What was possible in the early 1950s, when the CIA and the Defense Department began its ESP and PK research, is light-years from what is possible today. Today's Defense Department programs in anomalous mental phenomena research leverage modern technology. They exist in research domains involving cognition, perception, and the human brain and have been retooled and rebranded as distinctly twenty-first-century pursuits. They fall under the rubric of anomalous human cognition, and the research is being conducted not by parapsychologists but by neurophysiologists, neurobiologists, information technologists, computer engineers, and other scientists whose areas of research did not exist as such in the 1950s. These professions have been made possible by the advent of certain technologies and the astonishing speed of technology's advance.

In the late 1940s, when Dr. Andrija Puharich first began researching ESP for the Department of Defense, home radio technology was just twenty years old. Thirty years later, in 1976, NASA landed a spacecraft on Mars. Ten years after that, high-temperature superconductivity was discovered, opening the way for order-of-magnitude increases in faster, more efficient computer technology that could record, produce, and analyze information. In 1998 automated DNA sequencing was patented. In 2009, NASA launched the Kepler space observatory to survey the Milky Way galaxy and discover Earth-sized planets orbiting other stars. All this technology is the product of the human brain. We live in an age totally transformed by the human brain, and yet humans and their brains are still relatively the same. Outer space is now known to humans in ways unimaginable in the 1950s. Inner space is still lodged in the dark ages. What consciousness is, and how it works in the brain, remain as puzzling to scientists today as chemistry was to early man.

There presently exists a huge gap between where researchers are on a hypothesis for anomalous mental phenomena and where the science needs to be for them to move toward general theory. But it took more than a thousand years for man to move from the hypothesis that the Sun, not Earth, was the center of our solar system to the general theory of Copernican heliocentrism. Will modern technology allow for more interest in scientific research into the paranormal, or will the stigma prevail? If the stigma regarding ESP and PK research were removed from the world of science, what might be uncovered?

In 2014, the Office of Naval Research embarked on a four-year, $3.85 million research program to explore the phenomena it calls premonition and intuition, or "Spidey sense," for sailors and Marines. "We have to understand what gives rise to this so-called 'sixth sense,' says Peter Squire, a program officer in ONR's Expeditionary Maneuver Warfare and Combating Terrorism department. Today's Navy scientists place less emphasis on trying to understand the phenomena theoretically and more on using technology to examine the mysterious process, which Navy scientists assure the public is not based on superstition. "If the researchers understand the process, there may be ways to accelerate it—and possibly spread the powers of intuition throughout military units," says Dr. Squire. The Pentagon's focus is to maximize the power of the sixth sense for operational use. "If we can characterize this intuitive decision-making process and model it, then the hope is to accelerate the acquisition of these skills," says Lieutenant Commander Brent Olde of ONR's Warfighter Performance Department for Human and Bio-engineered Systems. "[Are] there ways to improve premonition through training?" he asks.

According to the Pentagon, the program was born of field reports from the war theater, including a 2006 incident in Iraq, when Staff Sergeant Martin Richburg, using intuition, prevented carnage in an IED, or improvised explosive device, incident. Commander Joseph Cohn, a program manager at the naval office, told the *New York Times,* "These reports from the field often detailed a 'sixth sense' or 'Spidey sense' that alerted them to an impending attack or I.E.D., or that allowed them to respond to a novel situation without consciously analyzing the situation." More than a decade later, today's Defense Department has accelerated practical applications of this concept. Active-duty Marines are being taught to hone precognitive skills in order to "preempt snipers, IED emplacers and other irregular assaults [using] advanced perceptual competences that have not been well studied." Because of the stigma of ESP and PK, the nomenclature has changed, allowing the Defense Department to distance itself from its remote-viewing past. Under the Perceptual Training Systems and Tools banner, extrasensory perception has a new name in the modern era: "sensemaking." In official Defense Department literature sensemaking is defined as "a motivated continuous effort to understand connections (which can be among people, places, and events) in order to anticipate their trajectories and act effectively."

Over decades, wars change location and weapons design evolves, while man's perceptual capacities remain relatively close to what they have been for thousands of years. Fifty years ago in Vietnam, Joe McMoneagle used his sixth sense to avoid stepping on booby traps, falling into punji pits, and walking into Viet Cong ambushes. His ability to sense danger was not lost on his fellow soldiers, and the power of his intuitive capabilities spread throughout his military unit. Other soldiers had confidence in this subconscious ability and followed McMoneagle's lead. In a life-or-death environment there was no room for skepticism or ignominy. If it saved lives, it was real. Since 1972, CIA and DoD research indicates that premonition, or precognition, appears to be weak in some, strong in others, and extraordinary in a rare few. Will the Navy's contemporary work on "sensemaking," the continuous effort to understand the connections among people, places, and events, finally unlock the mystery of ESP? Might technology available to today's defense scientists reveal hypotheses not available to scientists in an earlier age?

At Naval Hospital Bremerton, in Washington State, defense scientists and military researchers are exploring cognition and perception in soldiers' virtual dream states. Starting in 2011, as part of a research program called Power Dreaming, soldiers plagued by PTSD-related nightmares have used biofeedback techniques similar to those studied by Colonel John Alexander in the Intelligence and Security Command's Beyond Excellence program, under General Albert Stubblebine. For today's Navy, biofeedback has been updated with twenty-first-century virtual reality technology that did not exist thirty years ago. Sponsored by the Naval Medical Research Center, the Power Dreaming program involves a process called Cognitive Behavioral Treatment for Warrior Trainees. Participants are active-duty soldiers suffering from PTSD-related nightmares who are eligible to be sent back to the battlefield. The method, called redreaming, is alleged to be a learned technique that produces changes in the way one's brain processes information. Its goal is to teach trainees to transform their debilitating nightmares into empowering dreams using biofeedback techniques and computer technology.

Biofeedback, born in 1962, draws on the idea that the human brain (millions of years in the making) can benefit from seeing itself work in real time. Some of the life processes the trainee can see in real time are his brain waves, heart rate, muscle tension, skin conductance, and pain perception. The process goes like this: when the soldier wakes up from a nightmare, he gets out of bed and goes to a nearby government-issued computer. He puts on 3-D goggles and straps a Heart Rate Variability biofeedback device onto his forearm so that biofeedback can be integrated into the redreaming process. Hooked up to these two devices, the soldier opens a software program called the Book of Dreams. With a few clicks on the keyboard, he enters the virtual world Second Life.

A soldier's first Power Dreaming session will begin with a virtual scenario crafted to simulate the event that likely caused the PTSD nightmares. It features an avatar of the warrior trainee—a 3-D human cartoon of the self. In one of the Book of Dreams training videos, a soldier's avatar is seen driving a Humvee behind another Humvee along a narrow mountain pass in a place that looks like Afghanistan. The first Humvee is hit by an IED, and the avatar soldier in the second Humvee watches the explosion happen. All around him people die and bodies fly. The soldier's avatar tries to help a dying colleague (who appears to be missing his legs) but fails. The trainee is instructed to look at his biofeedback information, which appears on graphs on the computer screen, and to begin creating, or redreaming, a new narrative.

Using the Book of Dreams software, the trainee can make his avatar run, walk, or fly away from the carnage to any pleasant environment imaginable. New geographical scenarios can be set at the beach, in the jungle, on a mountain, even in an underwater dream world filled with fish. The Book of Dreams allows the avatar to share his utopic virtual world with human or animal companions, including real pets (like a dog) or imagined ones (like a dragon). The warrior trainee can customize the weather, the time of day, and the background music (in the Navy training video available to journalists, the music is distinctly Chinese). While moving through this pleasant virtual world, the trainee is instructed to observe the real-time biofeedback data on his computer as the redream continues. This information is also monitored and tracked by naval medical research doctors. Can humans alter their consciousness and change their dreams? The Navy thinks so. Using one's mind to change the chemistry of one's brain is psychokinesis dressed up in a new name for a new age: Power Dreaming.

Government programs that claim to harness the power of the mind to influence matter exist across the Defense Department today. The Pentagon currently supports more than fifty qigong-based programs for soldiers and veterans, the majority of whom suffer from PTSD. But the National Institutes of Health and the U.S. Department of Health and Human Services still consider qigong "unproven as medicine," and the NIH cautions that so-called energy medicine "can improve outcomes, have no effect on outcomes, and worsen outcomes with respect to healing effects." Scientific skeptics insist that qigong and all forms of traditional Chinese medicine are "chicanery," including acupuncture and acupressure. The belief in "the mind's ability to affect the health of the body" is pseudoscience, according to the Committee for Skeptical Inquiry, successor to the Committee for the Scientific Investigation of Claims of the Paranormal.

The Army and the Marines appear to disagree. The Operation Warrior Wellness program, offered at Army and Marine bases and Veterans Administration medical centers across the country, teaches Transcendental Meditation to PTSD sufferers. The TM-based Resilient Warrior Program has been the subject of 340 peer-reviewed studies and has received more than $26 million in grants from the National Institutes of Health. Key findings of the program—with its NIH caveat, "unproven as medicine"—include a 40 percent to 55 percent reduction in symptoms of PTSD and depression, a 42 percent decrease in insomnia, 30 percent reported improvement in satisfaction with quality of life, and a 25 percent reduction in plasma cortisol levels. The man behind Operation Warrior Wellness is the film director David Lynch, who has been meditating since 1973 "twice a day, every day. It has given me effortless access to unlimited reserves of energy, creativity and happiness deep within. This level of life is sometimes called 'pure consciousness'—it is a treasury. And this level of life is deep within us all," says Lynch.

This drives skeptics wild. *The Skeptic's Dictionary* describes Lynch's efforts to help traumatized soldiers recover from PTSD through meditation as being as effective as "sharing ice cream cones. At least one study has found negative health effects from meditation," the *Dictionary*'s author, Robert Todd Carroll, writes, including "feeling addicted to meditation; uncomfortable kinaesthetic sensations; mild dissociation; feelings of guilt; psychosis-like symptoms; grandiosity; elation; destructive behavior; suicidal feelings; defenselessness; fear; anger; apprehension; and despair."

At the Defense Advanced Research Projects Agency (DARPA) and the U.S. Army, scientists are building technology-based mental telepathy systems, called "synthetic telepathy," for the modern era. Under the rubric of brain–computer interface technology, the goal, says the Defense Department, is to enable future "soldiers [to] communicate by thought alone." Present-day brain measuring and recording technologies like electroencephalography (EEG) have advanced to the extent that the brain's alpha rhythms (electrical oscillations that predominantly originate from the occipital lobe) can be detected, translated into a computer-based speech recognition system, and transmitted to another person at a remote location. With a four-million-dollar grant from the Army Research Office, scientists at the University of California, Irvine, are at work on synthetic telepathy helmets for the Defense Department to allow soldiers to "tell machines to do what [they] want by telepathically thinking about it," as reported in *Digital Journal* in May, 2013. "Initially, communication would be based on a limited set of words or phrases that are recognized by the system," says program director Michael D'Zmura, chairman of the Department of Cognitive Sciences at the university. "It would involve more complex language and speech as the technology is developed further."

This synthetic telepathy technology builds off of work pioneered in the early 1960s by physicist Edmond M. Dewan of the Air Force Cambridge Research Laboratories in Bedford, Massachusetts. Motivated by a desire to gain philosophical insight into the nature of consciousness, Dewan trained himself and members of his research staff to modulate the brain's alpha rhythms. They practiced until they were able to control their own brain waves at will, and—hooked up to 1960s state-of-the-art machinery—filmed the results of their experiments (which can presently be viewed on YouTube using the keywords "brainwave control device by Edmond Dewan"). After advanced training, Dewan was able to imagine individual letters of the alphabet in Morse code and then send these coded signals to machinery—first letters, then words, and finally phrases. Dewan's first Morse code message took twenty-five seconds per letter to transmit and record. The phrase was, "I can talk." Upon authentication of this seminal laboratory experiment in 1964, the *Washington Post* carried a page one above-the-fold article titled, "Man's Brain Waves Can 'Talk' Overcoming Speech Barriers."

At the Institute for Learning and Brain Sciences (I-LABS) at the University of Washington in Seattle, similar studies are under way. If the first milestone toward synthetic telepathy was to compose messaging using thought alone, the next step was to be able to send those messages to a designated recipient (human or machine) using thought alone. Dr. Andrea Stocco, a co-director at the laboratory, explains. "Evolution has spent a colossal amount of time to find ways for us and other animals to take information out of our brains and communicate it to other animals in the forms of behavior, speech, and so on," Stocco says. "But it requires a translation. We can only communicate part of whatever our brain processes. What we are doing [with this new technology] is kind of reversing the process a step at a time...taking signals from the brain and with minimal translation, putting them back in another person's brain." Experiments filmed in Stocco's laboratory on August 12, 2013, performed in collaboration with computational neuroscientist Rajesh Rao, demonstrated synthetic telepathy between two human test subjects for the first time in human history.

In 2014, direct brain–to–brain communication was achieved on an international scale, this time by a team of scientists led by Dr. Alvaro Pascual-Leone, professor of neurology at the Harvard Medical School, in Cambridge, Massachusetts, using the Internet as a pathway. The work was partially financed by the European

Commission's Future and Emerging Technology program, often referred to as the EU's DARPA. "The telepathy experiment involved technology, not ESP," Dr. Pascual-Leone assured me in a telephone interview in 2015. The sender, or "emitter," sat in a laboratory in Thiruvananthapuram, India, wearing an EEG cap that detected and captured his brain's electromagnetic activity. Using the same system of messaging developed by Edmond Dewan in the 1960s, this sender transmitted the mental message, "hola," ("hello" in Spanish) to three test subjects sitting in a laboratory in Strasbourg, France. Each recipient in France wore on his head a magnetic field generating device called a transcranial magnetic stimulation (TMS) cap. The test subjects in France received the sender's information as a sequence of tiny jolts to their occipital lobes, which caused sensations and showed up as flashes of light in the corner of their vision. As a result of this experiment, a coded message was successfully transferred between human brains separated by a distance of approximately five thousand miles. "By using advanced precision neuro-technologies, including wireless EEG and robotized TMS, we were able to directly and non-invasively transmit a thought from one person to another without the person having to use language, to speak, or to write," Dr. Pascual-Leone said. "It is a remarkable step in human communication."

These direct brain-to-brain communication technologies would have been impossible to fathom in an earlier age. In the modern era, they have become reality. With technology-based synthetic telepathy research far outpacing traditional forms of mental telepathy research, what might become of psychic research?

CHAPTER TWENTY-FOUR

The Scientists and the Skeptics

Three pioneers involved in the government's anomalous mental phenomena programs—ones that began in the 1970s—remain active in the work, still searching for the sources of the phenomena. Since 1985, Hal Puthoff has been chief scientist at the Institute for Advanced Studies at Austin, in Texas. Located in the suburbs, the facility is a two-story brick-and-glass building surrounded by oak and elm trees in a research park. Inside the lab, some of the most exotic propulsion physics research in the nation takes place. The institute's research arm, EarthTech International, manages thirty-two subcontracts, mostly military and intelligence related. As chief scientist, Puthoff oversees the work of three physicists and two experimenters. "We pursue novel ideas in gravity, cosmology, and new sources of energy," he tells me when I visit the institute in 2015. The client list includes the Department of Defense, NASA, Lockheed's Skunk Works, and the Defense Advanced Research Projects Agency's 100-Year Starship project for interstellar travel capabilities.

Puthoff confirmed that he continues to act as a consultant on government black programs. "Yes, I presently work on classified programs in the aerospace sector," he says. "Given my past activities I fall into the class of consultants that, when an enigma arises, [I get] the call."

Puthoff shows me around the lab, which takes up the ground floor. It's filled with measuring systems, gauges, and analytical instruments. Sources at the Defense Intelligence Agency confirmed to me that EarthTech International has for years maintained a Defense Department contract to investigate what are known as "excess energy" claims, devices that allege to be powered by things like magnetic motors and cold fusion (also known as low-energy nuclear reactions). It is ironic that a scientist who has spent decades of his professional life fighting claims by skeptics that he is a fringe scientist is in fact one of the go-to people when the Defense Department needs a credible laboratory to disprove an extraordinary excess energy claim. "These claims are a primary focus of our investigations here," Puthoff says. "So far we have disproven all of them." The findings are made public on the EarthTech website.

At the institute, Puthoff works in yet another domain of contemporary physics fraught with contention. This work involves quantum vacuum energy, or zero-point energy *(Nullpunktsenergie)*, a concept originally developed by Max Planck in 1911 (Planck's work on quantum theory won him a Nobel Prize in 1918). The contentious aspect is not whether zero-point energy exists, but whether it can be harnessed for useful purposes. If proven, says Puthoff, zero-point energy could be a radical breakthrough in deep-space propulsion technologies. "The possibility of extracting useful energy from vacuum fluctuations [would be] the 'Holy Grail' of energy research," he says. For example, a manned space probe powered by zero-point energy could, theoretically, make a trip to Mars in seven to forty days, depending on the separation distance between Earth and Mars, as opposed to NASA's current figure (using more traditional advanced propulsion techniques) of seven or eight months.

Critics deride Puthoff's efforts. In my interview with Lawrence M. Krauss, the astrophysicist known for popularizing the term "dark energy," Krauss stated that harnessing quantum vacuum energy was impossible: "Zero-point energy is the lowest point in the universe. If you could extract energy out of it, there would have to be a lower point. There isn't a lower step on the staircase. So by definition, if it exists it can't be used." Krauss called Puthoff a "crackpot," and added, "besides, he has a history of backing crazy schemes." Then Krauss said something interesting. "Views of reality must conform to reality, not the way you want the world to be. If zero-point energy were feasible or available, the universe would have used it," Krauss observed. But Einstein taught us that two contradictory pictures of reality can and do exist when he spoke of the wave-particle duality that is quantum mechanics. Scientists who have witnessed ESP and PK phenomena, Puthoff among them, seem to have a different view of reality than scientific skeptics, including Krauss.

To harness zero-point energy could, Puthoff posits, lead to a general theory about ESP and PK phenomena. In our interview he summarizes this hypothesis. "Throughout mankind's cultural history there has existed the metaphysical concept that man and cosmos are interconnected by a ubiquitous, all-pervasive sea of energy that undergirds, and is manifest in, all phenomena. This pre-scientific concept of a cosmic energy goes by many names in many traditions," he says, citing the Chinese concept of qi and the Hindu concept of prana as examples. He wonders whether this metaphysical concept of cosmic energy is analogous to zero-point energy. In pursuit of this theory, Puthoff and his team conduct quantum optic experiments using lasers, beam splitters, lenses, and diffraction gratings. It's a challenging, long-term quest, he says. At age eighty, he has no intention of slowing down.

Puthoff's search echoes what China's H. S. Tsien proposed in a discipline he called somatic science, "where man [humanity] is considered to be a giant system embedded in the supergiant system of a cosmic world." Research experiments in this field, wrote Tsien, would likely lead to "an increased understanding that all of us are immersed, both as living and physical beings, in an overall interpenetrating and interdependent field in ecological balance with the cosmos as a whole." Tsien believed that this vital force known as qi was the key to the next scientific revolution—this from the man who codeveloped the original U.S. rocket program, cofounded the Jet Propulsion Lab, and built China's rocket, satellite, and manned space programs.

In 2007, *Aviation Week & Space Technology* named Tsien the Person of the Year and put him on the magazine's cover. "China is now at the forefront of space exploration, with two key developments in 2007: a successful anti-satellite (ASAT) weapons test and a planetary mission," wrote the magazine's editor in chief. The article highlighted Tsien's primary role in China's early aerospace programs and his enduring legacy in the modern era. That same year, *New Scientist* named Tsien one of the Top Ten Influential Space Thinkers of all time. Because of the stigma associated with anomalous mental phenomena research, including Extraordinary Human Body Function (EHBF), ESP, and PK, Tsien's work in this area has remained almost entirely unreported in the West. He died in October 2009 in Beijing at the age of ninety-eight.

To interview Dale Graff, I traveled in 2015 to Pennsylvania, where he and his wife, Barbara, live in the country not far from where they both grew up. I confirmed with Barbara the near-drowning story that happened in the strong surf off Hawaii in 1968 and that the couple did not speak of this mysterious, existential event for roughly thirty years. It was Graff's conversion moment, he agrees. In service of a general theory about ESP and PK, he continues his research and experiments today at age eighty-two. "In the seventies and eighties, we were looking at the electromagnetic spectrum," he says. "Now it's quantum physics, nonlocality and quantum entanglement," or what Einstein famously called "spooky action at a distance."

The concept of quantum entanglement is difficult to comprehend yet has been elegantly simplified by the theoretical physicist Michio Kaku. Kaku explains quantum entanglement this way: "According to the quantum theory, everything vibrates. When two electrons are placed close together, they vibrate in unison. When you separate them, that's when all the fireworks start," where quantum entanglement begins. "An invisible umbilical cord emerges connecting these two electrons. And you can separate them by as much as a galaxy if you want. Then, if you vibrate one of them, somehow on the other end of the galaxy the other electron knows that its partner is being jiggled," he says. While entanglement has puzzled physicists ever since Einstein spoke of it (most scientists originally disputed it), quantum entanglement is now an accepted theory. "Today, physicists create entangled particles in huge numbers in labs all over the world," the *MIT Technology Review* reported in February 2016. "They routinely use entanglement to send perfectly encrypted messages, to study quantum computation, and to better understand the nature of this profound phenomenon."

Where this profound phenomenon gets spookier still is the question of how quantum entanglement might affect the forward one-directionality of time—time's arrow—that governs the universe as a whole. Some physicists suspect that causality (the relationship between cause and effect) itself may be different when it comes to the phenomenon of quantum entanglement. The PBS *Nova* reporter Allison Eck explains it this way: "Entangled particles start off close together, and when separated, they're able to communicate with each other and share information at a rate that's seemingly instantaneous—faster than the speed of light. Whatever one particle does, the other follows suit in a consistent way. But according to the theory of relativity, nothing can travel that quickly," i.e., faster than the speed of light. Here is where some physicists and philosophers of science, including Dale Graff, propose the impossible. They say the solution could lie in a contentious concept called retrocausation, or backward causation—"the idea that the future might influence the past," says Graff.

In a *Nova ScienceNow* article titled "Retrocausality Could Send Particles' Information Back to the Future," Eck interviews physicists at the University of Cambridge who are conducting experiments to this end. "In our non-quantum lives, we can't see these things happening. We're locked into our perception of time and causality. Time is still a forward arrow, and action comes before reaction," she writes. "At the particle level, though, some physicists believe this logic could be sound, and they're beginning to use it [i.e., retrocausation] to explain existing results."

Dale Graff is one of those physicists. In 2016 I met up with him at the Quantum Retrocausation III symposium at the University of California, San Diego. There, Graff delivered a lecture entitled "Perceiving the Future News: Evidence for Retrocausation." He discussed the data he'd obtained from a recent series of remote-viewing experiments with a viewer in Florida who allegedly used precognition to "view" photographs in Graff's local paper days in advance of when the AP photographs were taken. Graff displayed his data as a series of slides and gave his analysis as he presented them. The majority of those in the audience were PhDs and doctoral students interested in and accepting of retrocausation as a thought experiment (Schmeidler's sheep). For a skeptic, the lack of scientific controls would be self-evident. One had to take Graff at his word that the experiment unfolded as he said it did. After Graff finished there was a question-and-answer period. A man in the audience raised his hand. "What you're talking about has already been discredited," he declared in an angry tone. "The U.S. Army ran a remote-viewing program in the 1980s, and it turned out to be total garbage." A lively discussion ensued.

"There is an underlying reality," Graff insists. "Remote viewing illustrates that this underlying reality exists, although it is the tip of the iceberg. It bubbles up in places like precognition."

To interview Kit Green, I travel to Detroit, where Green has returned to private medical practice and also serves at the Wayne State University School of Medicine, in Michigan. Over the past thirteen years, Dr. Green has been a professor in the Departments of Psychiatry and Radiology at the Harper University Hospital, and the Detroit Medical Center, and served as the medical school's executive director for Emergent Technologies (i.e., forensic brain scanning applications). Green's career path is unusual for a former intelligence officer. He returned to medical practice after a long, meritorious government career. "These new positions afford access to state-of-the-art technology in high-field brain MRIs, neuroradiology, and software," Green says. And he exploits this technology, he explains, in order to pursue an area of research that he had not shared publicly until our interviews for this book.

Green's identity as a CIA officer remained secret until 2007, when he appeared in an episode of the PBS series *Secrets of the Dead*. The episode, called "Umbrella Assassin," was a Cold War case file involving the murder of Bulgarian dissident Georgi Markov, killed at a bus stop in England in 1978. "If we hadn't suspected Markov had been murdered by the KGB," says Green, "his death would have likely been written off as 'cause unknown,' or 'death from natural causes.'" But because Green and his CIA colleagues had a strong hypothesis to work from, they went the extra mile in the laboratory. "Our Intelligence services found a tiny platinum–iridium pellet in Markov's leg and removed it. We prescribed specialized blood tests and identified ricin, which we looked for because of the victim's signs and symptoms. An assassin used a weapon disguised as an umbrella," says Green. For his work breaking this and other forensic medical cases over the next five years, Green was awarded the National Intelligence Medal.

After Green officially left the CIA in 1985, he worked for General Motors' Research Labs, and was eventually promoted to chief technology officer for Asia-Pacific. He has remained an active military and intelligence science adviser to the CIA and the Department of Defense, serving on more than twenty Defense science and advisory boards. His positions have included chairman of numerous National Academy of Sciences Boards and Studies; Fellow, American Academy of Forensic Sciences; founding member, Defense Intelligence Agency Technology Insight–Gauge, Evaluate, and Review Committee; chairman of the Independent Science Panel for the Undersecretary of the Army for Operations Research and later for the Assistant Secretary of Defense for Chemical, Biological, and Nuclear Matters. He also recently served as chairperson of a nineteen-member National Research Council effort to examine the future of military-intelligence science and brain research over the next twenty years. Green's bona fides are clearly not lacking. In 2016, he was asked to join a classified science advisory board for James R. Clapper, director of National Intelligence (to whom the directors of all seventeen U.S. intelligence agencies and organizations report) and the man who, in the 1990s as director of DIA, criticized the anomalous mental phenomena programs calling them "just too far out at the leading edge of technology."

Kit Green finds advising the Defense Department and intelligence community stimulating and challenging, he says, but what interests him most is his work for eleven years now in his private medical practice. "I'm interested in the notion of people injured physically by anomalous events," Green tells me. "Often these events are perceived as [involving] unidentified aerial phenomena, or UAPs, drones, high energy radio frequencies that confront people face-to-face and cannot be explained." In an earlier age, some UAPs were known as UFOs. Green does not agree with the use of that term "because it is imprecise," he says. But the nomenclature change helps to destigmatize the research. (Hillary Clinton spoke of UAPs while on the 2016 campaign trail.) The impetus of Green's work, he says, can be traced back to an unresolved component of the CIA's psychic research program in late 1974. The notion of people touched by anomalous events was a concept that Green was first confronted with when working with Uri Geller and the nuclear scientists at the Lawrence Livermore National Laboratory.

"These individuals carried top-secret clearances that were as high as mine," says Green, including Q clearances for nuclear secrets. "And yet they told me they saw things that could not be easily explained. They reported seeing raven-like birds on their bedposts... orbs floating down the hallways in their homes. A disembodied arm hovering in the air. These individuals were not crazy," he says. To paranormalists, these close-contact sightings are known as close encounters. "The idea of close encounters touches upon a lot of pathologies," says Green, "but not all encounters involve pathologies." This mystery plagued him for decades, he says. In 2005, he began working on a research project to address this enigma. He began creating "a structured database of individuals that were suffering enigmatic injuries, burns, skin lesions, cancers, diseases—and who also had face-to-face encounters with UAPs," says Green.

"We would comb through each narrative," remembers Green.

"Compare statistics. Pare the information down. Pull out people with pathologies. What was left? Many *very* interesting cases. Cases that could not be easily explained." After two years of data analysis, in 2007, Green took this research project from academic to operational. "I began performing much pro bono work," he says, "forensic investigation and diagnosis of patients injured by multiply witnessed physical anomalous events with UAPs, drones, and other visible physical devices."

Green accepted his patients carefully. "They are all high-functioning individuals, many prodigious savants, most of whom carry a high security clearance," he says. "They are members of Special Forces, members of the intelligence community, employees of aerospace companies, officers in the military, guards of military bases, policemen. Often injuries take place on a military bivouac, [which is] an overnight mission at a secure location for the purpose of guarding, reconnaissance, or some kind of exploration....Common injuries are from something that is airborne. [Something] that emits some kind of a light or a beam. Some orbs."

Green takes on patients who already have a thick physician case file, and whose doctors have been unable to determine what injured them. "My patients were physically injured by something. They have signs on their body. Markings. Illness," he says. They agree to give Green access to their medical history and permission for him to speak with their other doctors. None have mental illness. "They and their physicians have exhausted many avenues and find themselves at the end of their rope," says Green. "These patients are by majority not prone to conspiracy or PTSD. This kind of thinking would interfere with their career path. They and usually their superiors come to me because my specialty is forensic medicine. I try to determine diagnosis from very little and often highly incomplete data." Like the assassinations he investigated while in the CIA.

Using the technology available to him, Green orders brain scans, specialized blood, DNA and endocrine tests, and compiles the results. At present he has more than one hundred active patients. His original hypothesis was that a majority of his patients had "been exposed to technology from black programs," he says, that is, advanced state-of-the-art, high-energy technologies developed in Special Access Programs. "Nonlethal weapons programs. Holograms. Cloaking devices. Drones. Twenty-five percent of my patients die within five to seven years of my diagnosis, and I have no idea of how any programs I knew about years ago can do these things," Green says.

To advance his hypothesis, based on the demographics and high-functioning of his patients, Dr. Green teamed up with the Nolan Lab at Stanford University, run by Garry Nolan, one of the world's leading research scientists specializing in genetics, immunology, and bioinformatics. Nolan trained under the Nobel Prize– winning biologist David Baltimore, has published over 200 research papers, and holds twenty biotechnology patents. Age fifty-five, he has been honored as one of the top twenty inventors at Stanford University. His research is funded by grants from the National Institutes of Health, the Food and Drug Administration, the National Cancer Institute, and others. In 2012, Nolan was awarded the Teal Innovator Award from the Defense Department, a $3.3 million grant for advanced cancer studies. The Nolan Lab is perhaps best known for pioneering advances in large-scale mapping of cellular features and human cells at an unprecedented level of detail. "We are building on technologies that are just coming into existence," Nolan told me in 2016. Dr. Kit Green and his colleagues sought out Garry Nolan for help.

"I have met and worked with many of Kit's patients," Nolan confirms, "and I have looked deeply at the relevant medical data. These people were injured. I have seen the physiological consequences of the harm they've endured. He agrees with Kit Green that in many cases it looks as if it is an electromagnetic field of some sort. "It has led to inflammation and other biomarkers in their bodies that can be seen in MRIs, tissue, blood. We are now working on both the genetic and epigenetic components," Nolan says. "I am relatively certain we are the only individuals in the field doing this." Using mapping technology the Nolan Lab is renowned for, technicians are mapping Green's patients' DNA and their immune systems. They are looking for patterns among the patients, using biological data to create an integrated theory.

"All kinds of trauma can be picked up by the immune system," Nolan says. "Every event that happens to you is recorded by your immune system," which in turn creates a biological database of the self. "Every surgery or bee sting," he says, every incident of H1N1 flu, head cold, allergy, or chicken pox "is all sensed and recorded by the immune system." With the technology that is emerging from the Nolan Lab, doctors will likely soon be able to take a snapshot of a person's blood and read the historical record of that person's physiological life. Access to this kind of high-technology, nonsubjective biological data would have been impossible to imagine in any other age.

But what, I ask Garry Nolan, does this have to do with anomalous mental phenomena research? With ESP and PK? With Uri Geller and hallucinations experienced by scientists at the Lawrence Livermore Nuclear Laboratory? "We are also mapping [DNA and immune systems of] people and their families who claim to be remote viewers or have anomalous perception," Nolan confirms. For example, Joe McMoneagle is part of their research program; he provided them with a sample of his DNA, and the team is considering how to access the DNA of his deceased twin sister, who was also allegedly a remote viewer, says Nolan. "Whether real, perceived, or illusion, there appears to be a genetic determinant." And while Dr. Green maintains that his patients' injuries may have come from high energy devices or their components, both Green and Nolan think there is more to it than that. "Some people [seem to] repeatedly attract the phenomena or the experiences," Nolan says. "They act like an antenna or are like lighthouses in the dark."

For some it might be a blessing, Nolan speculates. They are comfortable with these ocurrences and make it work in their lives (think Uri Geller, Joe McMoneagle, Angela Dellafiora, and Paul Smith). For others it's a curse (for example, Green's injured patients and the Livermore nuclear scientists who quit their jobs). Nolan makes clear that his ideas are only hypotheses, but he explains that the raw data from which his hypotheses have been drawn are clear. "It's important to remember DNA does not invent stories," he says. Gene mapping and advanced single-cell analysis techniques reveal biological truths. "Imagine if you could understand how this all connects to mentation [i.e., mental activity]," Nolan says of claimed UAP encounters and ESP or PK abilities. "You could make a drug to block [the genetic aspect] for those who don't want it—or even enhance it for others."

In effect, Kit Green and Garry Nolan are searching for a gene for paranormality. Or, as Green prefers to say, "The genomics of supernormality."

The skeptics, led by Martin Gardner, Ray Hyman, and Paul Kurtz— the founders of the Committee for the Scientific Investigation of Claims of the Paranormal (CSICOP)—have maintained an almost united front around their message for more than forty years. In the middle 1970s they asked, "Why the sudden explosion of interest, even among some otherwise sensible people, in all sorts of paranormal 'happenings'?" Surely skeptics are asking that same question today. In 2006, the group removed the word "paranormal" from its name and shortened it to the Committee for Skeptical Inquiry. They continue to promote science and reason and, they say, work to resist the spread of pseudoscience, superstition, and irrational beliefs, which members believe includes any concept of God.

There have been a few notable cracks in the unity. *Fads and Fallacies* author Martin Gardner, generally accepted as the father of the modern scientific skepticism movement, experienced a religious epiphany that he discussed openly before his death in 2010. He told the people around him that he believed in a supernatural being, a higher power, or God, asserting that this belief was not pseudoscience because it could neither be confirmed nor disproved by science or reason. "I believe in a personal God," he stated in an interview in 2008, "and I believe in an afterlife, and I believe in prayer, but I don't believe in any established religion.... This is called philosophical theism.... Philosophical theism is entirely emotional."

"God is the Great Magician," he wrote.

In 2011, Martin Gardner's magician friend, James Randi, was exposed as being involved in a decades-long double deception and criminal fraud. It was revealed that Randi's Carlos-the-channeler hoax involved a federal crime. This created a public relations problem for the Committee for Skeptical Inquiry, because the group vows to "disseminate factual information about such [hoax] claims to the scientific community, the media and the public." Here was one of their highest-profile members perpetrating a fraud. The crime took more than twenty-five years to uncover, according to the *New York Times*. In 2011, federal agents knocked on Randi's front door in Florida and asked to speak with a man who went by the name of José Alvarez—the same José Alvarez who, according to publicity material given to *60 Minutes* and other news outlets, had played Carlos the channeler in the hoax decades earlier.

A man thirty-three years Randi's junior emerged from elsewhere in the house. José was Randi's long-term boyfriend; the two men came out of the closet together in 2008. Federal agents cuffed Alvarez, read him his Miranda rights, "took him out to the car, took him to Broward County Jail and registered him as FNU, LNU: first name unknown, last name unknown," the *New York Times* reported. At the county jail, the man told federal agents that his real name was

Deyvi Orangel Peña Arteaga, that he'd come to this country in the mid-1980s, met James Randi, in a Florida public library, and fallen in love. He didn't want to go back to Venezuela, he said, where it was dangerous to be gay. He illegally assumed another man's identity and with it applied for a passport in order to travel to Australia for the Carlos hoax. "I felt like a phony but I had to go along with it," Alvarez said. He was charged with aggravated identity theft and making a false statement in the application and use of a passport.

Alvarez/Arteaga faced a $250,000 fine, up to ten years in prison, and deportation. He was eventually released, pending trial. After numerous high-profile magicians and skeptics wrote to the judge on his behalf, including the magician Penn Jillette and the biologist Richard Dawkins, Alvarez was given a lenient sentence. In defense of Randi's participation in the deception and fraud, Alvarez said, "The reason he does what he does is to help people who are being taken advantage of. He will go to any lengths to keep somebody safe from harm. And that's what he did for me." James Randi and José Alvarez were married the following year.

When I interviewed Randi in June 2016, he was eighty-seven years old. In a brief moment of vulnerability after his partner's arrest and incarceration, Randi told the *Los Angeles Times* that he'd felt despair. "I didn't know which way to turn. It was the hardest moment of my life. I've been dangled over Niagara Falls [as part of a magic act], but nothing compares to this—nothing," he said. When I interviewed him, I asked whether this experience had softened him in his crusade against Uri Geller. "Never!" he shouted. "When I die, I want to be cremated and have my ashes blown into Uri Geller's eyes."

I asked Randi what he thought of his friend Martin Gardner's conversion to religion at the end of his life. "I was surprised," he said, and quickly changed the subject back to Uri Geller. "There is no such thing as the paranormal. Uri Geller is a magician...his life is a lie!"

CHAPTER TWENTY-FIVE

The Psychic and the Astronaut

Uri Geller insists that his powers are real. So does the prime minister of Israel, Benjamin Netanyahu. "I think he has these special powers," Netanyahu said in a television interview in 2015, and he told this story. "My wife, Sara, and I were at a restaurant in Caesarea. We were having lunch with Uri. Everyone came in and they wanted to see Uri...to have him bend their spoon. He said, 'I can't do it right now, I can't bend all these spoons.' He is very gracious, you know, but they kept [asking]....Finally he said, 'Oh, all right.' So he stood at one corner of the restaurant and he simultaneously bent the spoons of all the people who were there." The television reporter conducting the interview then asked the prime minister whether Geller could have performed this feat as a magic trick. "If you give me a convincing explanation how he could have worked that as a trick, I'll say, 'Wow, he's a great magician.' But he did it. And I saw it, and I've seen it time and time again. The fact that you can't explain it doesn't mean it didn't happen."

The secret history of the U.S. government's investigation into extrasensory perception and psychokinesis owes much to Uri Geller. He set in motion the CIA's psychic research program. And because he captivated so many people's attention around the world, starting in the early 1970s, Geller put psychic research on the map. The first time I interviewed Geller, in 2015, I traveled to his home in England. There, despite my efforts to remain a detached and objective journalist, he captivated my attention as I watched him bend spoons and appear to read my mind in a telepathy test. Before I arrived, I'd watched scores of magicians' spoon-bending videos on YouTube in order to understand how prestidigitation works — magic tricks performed by nimble fingers. My intention with Geller, and with everyone else interviewed for this book, was not to prove or disprove anyone or any concept, but to report objectively on the government's long-standing interest in ESP and PK phenomena. Of all the things I saw, and all the people I interviewed regarding Geller (including the Nobel Laureate Brian Josephson), the most telling revelation about Geller's abilities came from the legendary former curator of mammals at the Zoological Society of London, Desmond Morris. Morris wrote *The Naked Ape: A Zoologist's Study of the Human Animal,* which was chosen by *Time* magazine in 2011 as one of the Best 100 Nonfiction Books of All Time.

"Uri Geller came to see me in 2005 to talk about art, but when he was leaving he asked if I would like him to bend a spoon for me," Morris recalls. "I fetched a heavy teaspoon, and he rubbed it between his forefinger and thumb and it did, indeed, start to bend. I watched the process very closely but I could not see how he did this. He asked me if, as a biologist, I could explain to him how this strange ability of his could have evolved. I pointed out that iron was only discovered about three thousand two hundred years ago, so his special ability would have been useless before that date." Morris was well aware of the controversies surrounding Geller, the legions of magicians who "claimed that he uses clever hand pressures to make the spoon bend," Morris said, so he asked Geller to do something unusual for him, as a test. "I asked him if he could do it [bend metal] using only his big toe."

Morris says he fetched from his kitchen the heaviest teaspoon he could find and set it on top of his library table. Geller "took off his shoe and sock and lifted his foot up," Morris recalls. "He found it awkward to rub [the teaspoon] with his big toe but managed to do so, and again the spoon started bending. During this second bending his hands were nowhere near the spoon, and he did not have enough leverage in his toes to use them to apply force to the spoon. So I was completely mystified by his ability," Morris said. I asked the zoologist what he made of this.

"As a scientist I would like to make it clear that, because I cannot explain how he bends the metal, [this] does not mean that I accept any supernatural or psychic explanation for the ability. I have studied firewalking in Fiji, and I cannot understand that ability either. If I cannot explain a phenomenon I keep an open mind, but this does not mean that I resort to a paranormal explanation. It simply means that I have not yet found a satisfactory scientific explanation."

Geller's 12,000 square foot home in Sonning-on-Thames is a sight to behold. Set beside the great river, it features broad lawns, several dwellings, a greenhouse, a pool house, statues by Salvador Dalí, a koi pond, and a helipad. This home, which Geller shares with his wife, Hanna, is one of many properties the Gellers own around the world. Geller says the real estate represents some of the fruits of his map dowsing labors by means of which he is said to have located oil and precious minerals for mining corporations. His friend and assistant of forty-eight years, Shipi Shtrang (Hanna's brother), also lives on the compound. After our interview in England, Geller agrees to let me interview him again at a later date.

In 2016 I traveled to Israel to see him; he and Hanna had abruptly moved to the outskirts of Tel Aviv in the fall of 2015. I found it noteworthy that a contemporary BBC television documentary, aired in the United Kingdom in 2013 and called "The Secret Life of Uri Geller," suggested as its central thesis that Geller worked for the present-day Mossad, the Israeli equivalent of the CIA. Mossad is responsible for covert operations, intelligence collection, and counterterrorism, and its director reports to the Israeli prime minister, who in 2016 was Benjamin Netanyahu. Given Netanyahu's public statements about Geller, I found this line of inquiry worthy of investigation. Numerous U.S. government scientists interviewed for this book confirm that Geller likely worked for Mossad in the 1970s. But is Geller working for Mossad now, in the modern era? And what of his famous abilities? I went to Israel to learn more.

The Geller home I visited in Israel is located in the ancient port city of Jaffa and is set high on a hill. Jaffa has had strategic military importance since prehistory, when superstition and magic influenced national security the way science and technology do now. Its harbor has been in use since the Bronze Age (circa the second millennium BC), when durable weapons and proto-writing emerged. To reach Geller's place, I walk through town, past the Jaffa Clock Tower and the Al-Bahr Mosque, up over Jaffa Hill, and into the Old City. From there, I find my way through the labyrinth of ancient stone alleyways, through a maze of shops and homes three and four stories high, until I arrive at Geller's front door.

It's spring in Jaffa. The weather is nice, and Geller likes to walk. So do Hanna and Shipi. For three consecutive days, we walk while I record interviews and take notes. We walk through old Jaffa, through the port, up along the coast to Tel Aviv and back. Geller is tall and thin and full of energy. He is now seventy years old. Everywhere we go, people recognize him. Back in 2007 he created and starred in a television show titled "The Next Uri Geller," which aired in Israel, Germany, Sweden, Holland, Hungary, Greece, Turkey, Russia, and in the United States, under the title "Phenomenon." The show's talent show format presented a live audience with young mentalists and illusionists who demonstrated magic tricks, with Geller acting as the judge. The show was a hit and accounts for much of Geller's current success.

As we walk around Tel Aviv we are stopped by tourists from Germany, Ukraine, Russia, and Hungary. In the majority of encounters Geller is asked to bend a spoon, which he does, to each stranger's delight. In the afternoon, at an outdoor ice cream shop, a young couple asks Geller to bend a spoon. At dinner, at a restaurant along the Tel Aviv seashore, our waiter asks Geller to bend a spoon. Geller goes into the back kitchen and, for an audience of roughly twenty of the staff, bends a large soup spoon and does a telepathy reading, which I videotape. When he finishes, the workers spontaneously cheer.

"I get energy from people," Geller says as the four of us walk home along the beach.

Late at night, we stop in a convenience store in Jaffa. Two Ethiopian Israelis recognize Geller and ask him to please bend a spoon. When no one can locate a metal spoon in the shop, one of the young men hands Uri a pair of hookah tongs, charred from handling hot coals, and asks him to bend it. Hookah tongs are made of two parallel pieces of metal separated by roughly half an inch. Since their purpose is to handle burning coals, these tongs are generally forged to withstand high heat. Given the awkward shape, they appear difficult to bend by deception (prestidigitation), at least according to the magicians' videos I watched. Standing outside under a street lamp, Geller touches the arm of the tong with his fingertip and commands, "Bend!" When the tong bends, the young men go wild with enthusiasm.

The next day I interview Geller while he exercises on a stationary bicycle in his house. "Why did you come back to Israel?"

I ask. "Was it to work for Mossad?" We both know it's a rhetorical question. If he does work for them, he won't say.

"Let's focus on the powers," Geller suggests. "Have you and I done a telepathy test?" Still peddling his bike, he picks up a black ink marker and a sheet of paper. When I remind him about the telepathy tests we did in England, he suggests we do another one.

"Clear your mind," he says. "I'm going to place a thought in it."

"I don't want to do a telepathy experiment," I tell him.

"Why not?" he asks.

"It's awkward. It puts me on the spot. Besides, no one wants to read about it. It's like hearing someone's dream secondhand," I say.

Ignoring my request, Geller gives me instructions about how this telepathy test is going to work. He says he's going to write down a capital city on a piece of paper, out of my view. Then he's going to hide the paper and send me a word telepathically. "The transmission will come from my mind to your mind," he says. "You're going to write down the word that you receive from me." This is the test Geller is most famous for, planting a thought in someone's mind. In declassified documents, the CIA calls this phenomenal ability of Geller's "mind projection." The only person who would be able to cheat in this scenario is the receiver, me. Geller writes a word on a piece of paper. Folds it in half. Tells me to clear my mind.

I say, "I really don't want to do this."

"It's done," he says. "Tell me the city."

"Paris or Scotland," I say. "I know Scotland isn't a city, but that was the second thing that came to mind."

Geller unfolds the paper. It reads "Paris." Paris is generally considered one of the ten most popular cities in the world. But still.

He says, "Let's do an image now," and quickly begins drawing. He folds this paper in half and puts it out of view.

"Draw," he commands.

A snowman comes to mind. So I draw three different-sized circles.

"Stop!"

Geller turns over his paper. "Look!" he says. "Mine's a cat." He has drawn two different-sized circles, one above the other, with ears on top.

"What's important here," he says, "is this." He takes my paper and holds it up to his. The circle in the middle of my snowman is identical in size to the center circle in his cat. "It's like a mimeograph or a Xerox copy," Geller says, measuring it to the millimeter. He is correct. "You see, there is something going on here neither of us understands," Geller says. "My brain sent the image to your brain." Modern computers can do this instantly, over the Internet. Geller does it with his mind, somehow engaging or entwining my mind with his. Or did he? Maybe it's common to draw a circle, one of the oldest shapes in the human psyche. Maybe it was just a lucky guess.

"I still want to know about the Mossad."

In addition to interviewing Geller, I'm in Israel to fact-check stories from his early days, in the 1970s. I interview a former officer with the Israel Defense Forces who confirms that Geller used to map-dowse for Moshe Dayan. I interview Amnon Rubinstein, the founding father of Israeli constitutional law and the Israeli equivalent of a long-serving U.S. congressman. Rubinstein served as minister of communications; minister of Science and Technology and Space; and minster of Energy and Infrastructure, and has been an outspoken proponent of Geller's ESP and PK abilities since 1969. I ask Rubinstein about Geller's work for Israeli intelligence. "Oh, I wouldn't know anything about that," he says politely and switches topics.

One day Uri, Hanna, Shipi, and I drive to Abu Ghosh, an Arab village located nine miles west of Jerusalem. March 2016 is a violent time in Israel known as the Intifada of the Individuals, or the Knife Intifada, marked by lone-wolf stabbing attacks by Palestinians. Since September 2015, a total of 225 casualties have been attributed to the Knife Intifada. Forty-eight hours before I arrived, a Palestinian went on a stabbing rampage in Jaffa, wounding ten people, including a pregnant woman, and killing an American graduate student named Taylor Force. In what seems like a cruel twist of fate, Force, a graduate of the U.S. Military Academy at West Point, had recently served two tours of duty as an Army officer in Iraq and Afghanistan. The stabbing occurred three blocks from the hotel where I'm staying. Whenever I pass by, I regard the dark bloodstain on the sidewalk.

Inside the Arab restaurant in Abu Ghosh, we appear to be the only non-Arabs: three Israeli Jews and an American. Lunch is served. Falafel, hummus, olives, salad, bread. We eat. In comes a man carrying a briefcase. A young blond woman is with him.

"I don't have to be psychic to tell you that man is a lawyer," says Geller. He stands. The two men shake hands and exchange a few words in Hebrew. The man introduces the young woman as his daughter.

During lunch, we discuss anonymity. This is the only place we've been during my trip where Geller hasn't been approached by fans. It's the first time we've sat down for more than a few minutes and no one has come up and asked him to bend a spoon.

Geller says he enjoys the attention. "Maybe there's some egotism on my part," he says. "A streak of narcissism. But everyone has this. Maybe it is dormant in them."

After lunch we have coffee with cardamom and dessert. Geller disappears into the back of the restaurant. To bend spoons, I think. We regroup in the parking lot. I ask about Mossad from a different angle. "If, hypothetically, the Mossad needed someone with a psychic ability, what ability would be useful" to an intelligence agency? Geller tells me that he will never confirm or deny that he works for Mossad. I tell him that unless I learn otherwise, this part of his story seems more like fiction than fact, a carryover from his childhood experience with the grain trader

Yoav Shacham, who challenged him to be a good soldier and someday work for the legendary Mossad. Perhaps it's egotism on his part, but this slips out: "You don't get it," he says, an edge to his voice. "The Arab restaurant. The lawyer. The daughter. I can go anywhere. No one suspects me. It's the perfect cover. I'm just the guy who bends spoons." Like Frank Sinatra, Moe Berg, Harry Houdini, or Louis de Wohl—all of whom worked for intelligence services and none of whom were suspect because each was so famous in his professional field.

Maybe, I think. Maybe not. And if true, what would this mean with regard to his alleged powers? Would that mean the powers are deceptive? Or would that mean he really has powers, and that he uses them as a spy? It's a rabbit hole of possibilities, a puzzle that cannot easily be solved. But then something very unusual happens.

We drive to Jerusalem. In the Old City we park the car and walk a little, until we come up to a barricade. In Hebrew the placard on the barricade reads "The office of the Head of State, the Prime Minister." Heavily armed guards wave us through. We enter the residence of Benjamin and Sara Netanyahu, passing through intense security. My handbag goes through an X-ray machine. This is an informal meeting, not a reporting trip, I am told.

We sit in the garden courtyard with Sara Netanyahu and the family dog, a white Siberian named Kaya. The dog is old and has a terrible limp, which we discuss for a few moments. Kaya sits down at Uri's feet. Sara works full-time as an educational psychologist for children in Jerusalem, and she has just finished a long day of work. We discuss many interesting topics, but all of them are off the record. When a bird flies into the courtyard, Kaya gets up and runs after it. "The dog is running," I say. We all watch the dog chase the bird around the garden. No limp. Sara is equally surprised. "Uri, you healed Kaya," she says.

"I'm not a healer," Geller clarifies. "But she does look better."

Geller stands up and excuses himself. He will be gone for a little while and then he will be back, he says. He and Sara disappear into the kitchen.

Is this how it works? Is this the real world of espionage unfolding in front of me? Does Geller really gather information and bring it here, to the prime minister's house, himself? Maybe yes, maybe no. Maybe Uri Geller and Benjamin Netanyahu are just old friends. The story Netanyahu told a television reporter, of Geller bending spoons en masse, comes to mind. Why would the prime minister of Israel say such a thing unless he believed it? Unless it was part of a disinformation campaign, another rabbit hole. Either could be true. Either Uri Geller works for the Mossad or he doesn't. Either he has extraordinary powers that no one in the world has been able to explain or he's performed a singular magic act for forty-eight years.

Perhaps the true energy source powering the phenomena is conviction—conviction of belief. The belief that there is something more out there, that all things are connected in ways science simply cannot yet explain. Perhaps reality really is what one perceives it to be.

Whether ESP and PK are fact or fancy, as Carl Jung once remarked they just don't seem to go away. What is known for certain is that over a span of decades, hundreds of people led by a small cast of about a dozen scientists have worked at the request of the U.S. military and intelligence community (spending untold millions of dollars) to use the human mind to do what many believe is impossible.

Hanna, Shipi, and I sit in the Netanyahu garden and drink coffee. It's just the three of us enjoying an evening in Jerusalem, one of the most storied cities in the world. Or so it seems. Shipi tells me that whatever I say can be heard, whatever I do can be seen. There's a security team behind the black glass wall to my right;

all kinds of people are watching and listening, he says. This is the home of the prime minister of Israel. We are in the Middle East, one of the most volatile and violent regions in the world. Nothing here in Jerusalem is simple, and nothing is only what it seems.

Soon it is time to go. Uri Geller emerges from the back of the residence, and we are escorted through a long hallway, through the security office, and then outside. Night has fallen. The heavily armed security guards continue to patrol the streets. One by one, the prime minister's security detail outside recognize Geller. One of them asks him to bend a spoon.

The month after I returned home, an article entitled "Israelis Find New Tunnel from Gaza into Israel" appeared in the *New York Times*. Benjamin Netanyahu was quoted as saying that "the state of Israel has achieved a global breakthrough in the ability to locate tunnels," and that the breakthrough was "unique," but he could not provide any details of the technology involved. The tunnel did not have an exit at the surface, said Lieutenant Colonel Peter Lerner, a spokesman for the Israeli military, which means that it was detected deep underground.

I asked Geller whether map dowsing was involved. "I can't comment," he wrote in an e-mail. I asked Dan Williams, the Thomson Reuters senior correspondent for Israel and the Palestinian Territories, what he thought. "I have not heard about map dowsing being involved in Israel's tunnel-detection technology," Williams said. "My gut tells me it's unlikely, given the skepticism such a method would meet from Israeli planners [and] the big expense and human stakes of this project. From the little I've been told, the technology combines half a dozen methods including seismic mapping and aboveground radar."

In March 2015, I travel to Florida to see Edgar Mitchell, the sixth man on the Moon. His Lake Worth home is situated in a middle-class neighborhood ten miles from the sea. I drive along a single-lane paved road through a forest of palm trees, struggling to identify which house is his. Then I spot an American flag raised high on a flagpole, rippling in the morning wind. I park in the circular driveway and walk to the front door. Accompanied by his dog, Mitchell greets me at the threshold.

He wears a tan shirt with a pen tucked in a buttonhole, and brown slacks with suspenders. The house has a 1970s feel. The walls are adorned with Apollo 14 memorabilia and artifacts. There are many NASA photographs of the Moon, Cone Crater, the Frau Mauro Highlands. In numerous images, a much younger Ed Mitchell stands smiling beside presidents and kings. In another, the Apollo 14 astronauts are greeted by U.S. Navy personnel after splashdown.

In the living room Ed Mitchell and I sit on reclining chairs. I set up my tape recorder and begin taking notes. We discuss Mitchell's background, his work, the Moon, consciousness, anomalous mental phenomena, and Uri Geller. The relationship between the two men was unique; they were like two sides of the 1970s psychic research coin. In Israel, Geller told me that Ed Mitchell's support of him had a profound impact on his life, and that without him he would not have become the person he is today. "I idolized him," said Geller. "He walked on the Moon. That he supported me made me feel extraordinary. Like I could do anything."

Upon returning from the Moon, Mitchell had experienced a paradigm shift. Forever after, he saw the world through a different lens. Uri Geller represented everything Ed Mitchell wanted the world to embrace, Mitchell says. They became each other's foils. Both men were lionized and criticized in equal measure, Geller for his powers, Mitchell for his belief in Geller's powers and alleged psychic abilities like them. Uri Geller rose above the controversy. Ed Mitchell was crushed by it.

"I want to show you [something] that demonstrates what Uri Geller is capable of making happen," Mitchell tells me during our interview. I follow him through the house to a room in the back and into a walk-in closet where he kept a safe. Mitchell enters the combination and swings open the heavy door. Inside, he says, are several items that mean the world to him. The first is a set of laminated papers. I can see columns of numbers and symbols neatly written in black ink.

"Star, cross, wavy line, circle, and square," Mitchell says, pointing. Five of the most archetypal symbols on Earth, symbols that have appeared on cave walls and potsherds and graves since man has been making his mark on history. "These are the Zener cards logs I recorded in flight," Mitchell explains, the physical evidence of the ESP tests Mitchell conducted in secret on the way to and from the Moon. They're meaningful relics, Moon voyage artifacts. For all of our history, man was Earthbound. Then, starting in 1969, owing to the minds and abilities of American scientists and engineers, man left Earth to make six trips to the surface of the Moon. Mitchell hands the laminated papers to me. There is a golden seal in the upper right corner, folded across the seam. The papers look old and worn. In two places there are water stains. At the bottom, a blue tape label reads "ESP note card used in flight by Edgar Mitchell on Kittyhawk." I recognize the labeling technology: the handheld Dymo Label Maker from the 1970s.

Next Mitchell takes out a bent spoon, twisted at the neck. The spoon was not bent by Uri Geller. "This was bent by a child, after Geller appeared on a television show," Mitchell says. "I'd gone on the Jack Paar television show with Uri," he explains, "and Uri encouraged children at home watching to try psychokinesis for themselves. To command their spoons to bend. And all over the world [they did]. A mother sent this to me. She said it had been bent by her son."

The bent spoon inspires him, Mitchell tells me. Children

who grow up believing they can do anything generally do great things. Children like him. He was a Depression-era kid, impoverished, he says, but people around him helped him have dreams, and despite the odds, he learned how to fly at age thirteen. The rest of his life story is well known. The question people should ask themselves, he says, is, "What are we really capable of? Space travel . . . psychokinesis . . . what else can we do [that] we think we can't? These are the questions I've wondered all my life."

Everyone has heroes. Ed Mitchell is one of mine. In researching and writing this book, awash in anomalous mental phenomena, Ed Mitchell's professional work on Apollo 14 was for me a beacon of ground truth. To read the 1,019-page Apollo 14 transcript—a chronicle of the 216 hours Ed Mitchell, Alan Shepard, and Stuart Roosa spent in outer space—is to read a testament of what extraordinary human functioning really is. Because of the near-catastrophic failure of the Apollo 13 mission, the Apollo 14 astronauts were under intense pressure to make the mission appear as if everything were rosy. NASA could not afford any negative publicity, the astronauts were told; the entire Apollo program was at risk of cancellation if anything went wrong on Apollo 14. When Mitchell and Shepard faced an extraordinary problem having to do with the guidance system on the spacecraft, they had to forfeit communication as they traveled around the dark side of the moon while the problem was being solved. How many people could function under pressure like that? The astronauts persevered and succeeded. That, to this reporter, is truly phenomenal.

"I think forever, humans have asked the question, Who are we?" Mitchell observes. "Why did we get here? What is this really all about? And all of our science, all of our religions, all of our studies have presumably been adding something to the answer to that question. And we frankly still don't understand. We still don't have the answer. We still don't know . . . One answer we have..." He launches into a brief summary of his theory about extraterrestrial visitors to our planet when he's interrupted by a knock at the door. Believers (those sheep) would call this a deus ex machina moment; unbelievers (goats) would say this was interesting timing. One of Mitchell's assistants presents the visitor. It's a technician from AT&T.

"I'm here to fix the Internet connection," the man says.

Mitchell stands up, and I do, too.

"Yes, yes, come in," Mitchell welcomes him.

The technician looks about twenty-five years old. He has thick red hair, a long beard, is tall and overweight. He wears an AT&T-logo shirt, jean shorts, sneakers, and tall white socks.

"Where's the box?" he asks.

There is an awkward moment of silence. Mitchell is from my grandmother's era, a time when manners dictated that when a guest arrives, expected or not, you take a moment to make introductions so everyone present knows who everyone else is.

"I'm not sure if you know who I am—" Mitchell says politely.

The man looks around. The Moon artifacts and iconic photographs that adorn every wall don't seem to register on the technician.

"—If you're familiar with who I am," Mitchell restates.

"Nope," the technician says, uninterested.

Silence.

"This is Edgar Mitchell," I say brightly, pointing. "He was the sixth man to walk on the Moon."

"I was an astronaut on Apollo 14," Mitchell clarifies, with the good kind of pride.

The technician shrugs. "Yeah, well, I'd like to get the fuck off this planet, too," he says. "So where's the box for the Internet?"

And that's that. The tragedy of being an Apollo astronaut becomes real. For many, the power of the Moon voyages has faded over time. Mitchell points, and the man disappears into the back part of the house. Like a gentleman, Ed Mitchell motions for me to sit back down.

I reach into my bag to retrieve an item I've brought for the interview. It's a copy of the map Mitchell carried on the Moon, downloaded from NASA's website. I hand it to him. We discuss the Moon map. There's a NASA photograph of Mitchell holding this map on the Moon, and when I saw it, it made me want to write this book, I say. All work requires effort. All goals require conviction. All conviction is entwined with doubt. Belief gets us where we are going, but what saves a man when he gets lost? This, I tell Ed Mitchell, is the question I came to ask.

Mitchell reviews the map, then apologizes. "I'm not so good at map reading these days," he says.

We sit quietly. In the background, in another room, the AT&T technician can be heard banging around.

Mitchell sighs and says, "I'm not so good at traveling any-more. I fatigue."

"You, the adventurer, the great explorer. Is that difficult to accept?" I ask.

"Yes—well, no," he says. "I travel by Skype now." And then he says, "I'm in the final stages of my life. I'm content."

The dog barks. It's time for me to go.

Eleven months later, Edgar Mitchell died. His passing coin-cided by a matter of hours with the fortieth anniversary of the Apollo 14 Moon landing, the moment Mitchell set the *Antares* down on the lunar surface just eighty-seven feet from its target. So Ed Mitchell is stardust again, as he had always been.

We are all made of stardust, of elements created in explosions in the depths of space. In the most elemental way, we are all con-nected. Deep questions go to the root of that connection. The Cold War spawned more scientific inquiry than anyone on Earth could have dreamed of at the time. Carl Jung was right. What is possible, what becomes reality, emerges from the rational assumptions of the age. As new documents become declassified and sources talk about their roles in secret ESP and PK programs past and present, clarity will improve. With advances in new technologies, scientists will begin to see under the surface, learn to ask new questions, and move from hypothesis to general theory.

There is no question that man is extraordinary, each of us a phenomenon.

ACKNOWLEDGMENTS

In the winter of 2014 I was driving in my car in Los Angeles when I heard a radio interview that I found remarkable for a number of reasons. On the show, a journalist was interviewing a British professor of mathematics who told the following story.

In the summer of 1972 the actor Anthony Hopkins was in London to purchase a copy of the novel *The Girl from Petrovka,* by author George Feifer. Hopkins was preparing to shoot an American film based on the novel and he wanted to read the book first. None of the London bookstores he went to had a copy in stock, so Hopkins headed home empty-handed. As he waited for a train at the underground station at Leicester Square, Hopkins happened to see a discarded book lying on a bench. When he picked it up, he saw it was a copy of *The Girl from Petrovka*—the very book he'd been trying to buy. Things got stranger still. Flipping through the novel, Hopkins noticed that someone had made notes in the margins, including how to change certain British spellings to American spellings (i.e., "labour" to "labor"). Months later, during filming, Hopkins met George Feifer and recounted to him the story of finding a unique copy of *The Girl from Petrovka* on a bench in the subway. Feifer asked to see Hopkins's copy. Lo and behold, it had belonged to George Feifer. The markings in the margins had been made by Feifer's own hand. Feifer explained to Hopkins that several years prior, he'd been annotating the book for the forthcoming American publication when a friend borrowed this exact copy, then lost it somewhere around Bayswater, in central London.

So there I was in my car in Los Angeles, listening to the British professor tell this remarkable story. By this time, I had already arrived at my destination, but I found the tale so compelling I'd remained in my car. What unknown force had brought a copy of this book around full circle: away from the author, into the possession of Anthony Hopkins, and back to the author again? I instinctively knew there was no answer, but I wanted to hear what the professor had to say.

The professor, a former president of the Royal Statistical Society of the UK, claimed to have the answer. It was mathematics, he declared. This kind of thing happens all the time. I listened to the professor argue the case that there was *absolutely nothing extraordinary* about the story he had just told. The events could be explained scientifically by the mathematical law of truly large numbers, as well as the law of combinations, he said, and that people who assign words like miraculous or mysterious to such events were simply wrong—and perhaps intellectually flawed. I turned off the radio, and in the silence of the car, I got the idea for this book.

I wondered: If all improbable, rare, or seemingly miraculous phenomena that occur in this world can and must be explained by science, why did the U.S. government research anomalous mental phenomena for so long; what were the results of these programs and operations; does the work continue today? An initial search of the open-source literature on the government's work revealed that most nonfiction books written on the subject catered to one side only—they seemed to be either *for* the so-called paranormal (ESP, PK, etc.) or *against* it. In researching and reporting this book, I hoped to write about the subject from the perspective of advocates and critics alike.

I'd like to thank all the scientists, psychics, government officials (present and former), academics, soldiers, sailors, mystics, and magicians who spoke to me on the record, and all of those who spoke to me on background and asked not to be named. A particular debt of gratitude goes out to Robert Knight, a photographer and documentary filmmaker who generously made introductions to individuals who might not otherwise have agreed to speak to me.

The assistance of record keepers and librarians continues to remain invaluable to my research and reporting. Thank you Michele Meeks and John Giuffrida, Information and Privacy Coordinators, Central Intelligence Agency; Michael Bigelow, historian, U.S. Army, INSCOM; Jeffrey Flannery, Manuscript Division, Library of Congress; Kathryn Hodson, Special Collections and University Libraries, University of Iowa Libraries; Tamra Temple, archivist; Mallika Yedla, research assistant; and all of the anonymous Freedom of Information Act researchers who scoured databases on my behalf.

I am most grateful to John Parsley, Jim Hornfischer, Steve Younger, Tiffany Ward, Matthew Snyder, Liz Garriga, Nicole Dewey, Michael Noon, Chris Jerome, Allison Warner and Gabriella Mongelli. Thank you to Alice and Tom Soininen for being my unconditionally loving parents, and to Kathleen and Geoffrey Silver, Rio and Frank Morse, Keith Rogers, and Marion Wroldsen. And to my fellow writers from our intrepid group: Kirston Mann, Sabrina Weill, Michelle Fiordaliso, Nicole Lucas Haimes, and Annette Murphy.

The only thing that makes me happier than finishing a book is the daily joy I get from Kevin, Finley, and Jett. You guys are my best friends and demonstrate what I believe to be the ultimate, indisputable supernatural force: love.

Abbreviations used in Notes

ARCHIVES

Apollo 14 Transcript	Apollo 14 Air/Ground Transcript (216 hours, 1,019 pages): Lyndon B. Johnson Space Center, National Aeronautics and Space Administration, Manned Spacecraft Center, Houston, TX
APS	American Philosophical Society, Philadelphia, PA
Author FOIA, Army	author's Freedom of Information Act request granted by U.S. Army
Author FOIA, CIA	author's Freedom of Information Act request granted by CIA
Author FOIA, DARPA:	author's Freedom of Information Act request granted by U.S. Department of Defense
Author FOIA, FBI	author's Freedom of Information Act request granted by FBI
CIA	Central Intelligence Agency, digital collection
LOC	Library of Congress, Washington, DC
NARA	National Archives and Records Administration, College Park, MD

OSTI	U.S. Department of Energy, Office of Scientific and Technical Information, digital collection
Star Gate Collection, CIA	Pursuant to a 1995 congressional mandate, the CIA has since released more than 89,900 pages of declassified documents covering anomalous mental phenomena, presently available though the FOIA on DVD as .tif files or at the National Archives and Records Administration, College Park, MD
TNA, Kew	The National Archives (United Kingdom), Kew, UK

U.S. GOVERNMENT AGENCIES & AFFILIATES

CIA	Central Intelligence Agency
DIA	Defense Intelligence Agency
DoD	Department of Defense
FBI	Federal Bureau of Investigation
INSCOM	Intelligence and Security Command
LLNL	Lawrence Livermore National Laboratory
NASA	National Aeronautics and Space Administration
NATO	North Atlantic Treaty Organization
SRI	Stanford Research Institute (renamed SRI International in 1977)

Prologue

6   "extrasensory perception does exist": Author FOIA, CIA: "An Overview of Extrasensory Perception," January 27, 1975.

Chapter One: The Supernatural

12   he bailed out: "Hess Drama," British Paramount News; 1941 official newsreel features an interview with the man who captured him.

12   Hess later said: Albert Speer, *Spandau: The Secret Diaries,* 176. According to Speer, Hess intended to tell the Duke of Hamilton,

"We will guarantee England her empire; in return she will give us a free hand in Europe." The full details of Hess's subsequent interrogation by British intelligence remains classified until 2041.

12 "provide phony horoscopes": "Sybil Leek, The South's White Witch," BBC Home, October 28, 2002.

12 "Mum stayed silent": Interview with Julian Leek, Sybil's son, who maintains her archive. In 1972, Sybil Leek was quoted in a classified DoD monograph on ESP that gives credence to the rumor that she became an American intelligence asset after the war; she moved to America in 1962.

13 Hitler declared Hess legally insane: Manvell and Fraenkel: *Hess: A Biography*, 142, 212.

13 "predict future events": Wilhelm Wulff, *Zodiac and Swastika*, 112.

13 Führer told Albert Speer: Speer, *Inside the Third Reich*, 94. The rest of the quote is, "At least it had tradition. To think that I may some day be turned into an SS saint! Can you imagine it? I would turn over in my grave..."

13 *"privilegium singulorum"*: Wulff, *Zodiac and Swastika*, 110–111. Himmler had Wulff released from Fuhlsbüttel concentration camp and placed in his personal custody.

14 Schellenberg said: Ibid., 94.

14 same kind of manipulation: William Stephenson, *A Man Called Intrepid*, 363–365.

14 highest-profile astrologers: TNA, Kew, "Louis de Wohl File," Minute Sheets, August 1, 1940–March 15, 1945, n.p.

14 "Seer Sees plot to Kill Hitler": Ibid; "Press cutting from 'New York Sun,' 22.6.41."

15 fabricated by MI6: Stephenson, *A Man Called Intrepid*, 364–365.

15 British spy agency first fed information to de Wohl: TNA, Kew, "Louis de Wohl File," Minute Sheets, August 1, 1940–March 15, 1945, n.p. Stephenson ran the operational arm of UK intelligence inside the U.S., innocuously called the British Security Coordination Office, which was disguised as part of the British Passport Control Office in Rockefeller Center, New York.

16 "oversee U.S. intelligence collection": "The Intrepid Life of Sir William Stephenson," *CIA Studies in Intelligence, News and Information*, February 5, 2015.

16 "convinced of his supernatural powers": Author FOIA, TNA, Kew, De Wohl File, Minute Sheets, National Archives, KV2/2821.

16 seized by the Gestapo: Wulff, *Zodiac and Swastika*, 95.

17 committed to a mental institution: Stephen E. Flowers, *The Secret King: Karl Maria Wiligut, Himmler's Lord of the Runes*, Appendix E: "An Interview with Frau Gabriele Winckler-Dechend, 1997."

17 mission of Ahnenerbe: Samuel Goudsmit, *Alsos*, 203. Literal translation is "something inherited from the forefathers."

18 Survey of the So-called Occult Sciences: Fritz T. Epstein, *War-Time Activities of the SS-Ahnenerbe*, 79–81.

19 human experiments: Goudsmit, *Alsos*, 207.

19 "a thorough investigation": Ibid., 207. In 1943, after the Royal Air Force bombed Hamburg, Himmler began the evacuation of the Ahnenerbe's collections into secret places across the occupied territories. Until these collections were located, Alsos hoped that what was left behind in the Ahnenerbe's former headquarters might offer clues.

19 "weird Teutonic symbols and rites": Ibid., 124.

20 Ahnenerbe science first appeared outside Nazi Germany: Interview with Serge Kernbach. Also see Kernbach, "Unconventional Research in USSR and Russia," *International Journal of Unconventional Science*, Cornell University (Fall 2013): n.p.

20 truth serum: Annie Jacobsen, *Operation Paperclip*, "Chapter Nineteen, Truth Serum," 364–372. The Maryland Facilities were Fort Detrick in Frederick, and the Army Chemical Center, in Edgewood.

20 CIA hired magicians, hypnotists: John Marks, *The Search for the "Manchurian Candidate,"* 87, 194-198; interview with Julian Leek.

21 Nazi scientists to measure and monitor results: *International Military Trials, Nurnberg: Nazi Conspiracy and Aggression, Supplement A*, Office of the United States, Chief of Counsel for Prosecution of Axis Criminality, United States Government Printing Office, Washington, 1947; Translation of Document 087, "Ahnenerbe Society: Institute for Military Scientific Research, June 21, 1943,"

"Excerpts from 1944 diary, 'Das Ahnenerbe,' regarding medical experiments in concentration camps, GB 551."

21 programs required countermeasures: Kernbach, "Unconventional Research in USSR and Russia," n.p.

21 "Very early accounts": Memorandum for the Record, Subject Project ARTICHOKE, November 21, 1952, signed by Sheffield Edwards (National Security Archives). See also Boxes 3 and 10, MKUTLRA 58: J.P. Morgan and Co. Agency Policy and Conferences; Wasson File.

Chapter Two: The Puharich Theory

23 worked as a milk delivery boy: Transcript, "Talk Given By Dr. Andrija Puharich at the Understanding Convention at Astara, Upland, California, Nov. 6, 1982."

24 the natural world: Library of Congress (LOC), Marcella du Pont Papers (1861–1976); also discussed in H. G. M. Hermans, *Memories of a Maverick*, "Early Life and Adolescent [sic]." Much of the information in this chapter comes from Puharich's papers and letters located inside the Marcella du Pont Papers. These rare original documents provide information about the Round Table Foundation previously unreported.

24 "few people really know their own mind": Andrija Puharich, "An Intellectual Autobiography of Henry Puharich," quoted in Hermans, *Memories of a Maverick*, "College and Medical School," 37. (Hermans uses several pseudonyms in her book.)

25 "untangle the jungle": LOC, Marcella du Pont Papers, Letter to Dr. Garfield, director of Kaiser Permanente Hospital, from Henry Karel Puharich, 1947. Also in Hermans, *Memories of a Maverick*, 39.

25 mentor, Dr. Andrew C. Ivy: Author FOIA, CIA, "Henry (Andrija) Karl Puharich, Career Résumé," n.p., n.d. (15 pages). By the late 1950s and early '60s, Dr. Ivy had become associated with a bogus cancer treatment called krebiozen. The drug, developed from the blood serum of horses in Argentina, promised to reduce the size of tumors in cancer patients. The American Medical Association led a campaign that eventually denounced the drug as a fraud; Ivy never recovered his once stellar reputation.

26 elemental to his character: I discussed Puharich with Andy Puharich, Uri Geller, Edgar Mitchell, Charles Tart, John Alexander, Jacques Vallée, Hal Puthoff, Stephanie Hurkos, and others.

26 "Watch long trails of birds": LOC, Marcella du Pont Papers, Puharich, "Introduction to the Round Table Laboratory of Experimental Electrobiology," Camden, Maine, 1949, n.p. "This force," wrote Puharich, "existed in man since the Golden Age of Greece. And it exists in our frenetic age."

27 "nature of the nervous system": Ibid., n.p.

27 Joyce Borden Balokovic: LOC, Marcella du Pont Papers, "Trustees, February 8, 1947" (appears to be Puharich's handwritten notes).

28 Astor's space-traveling protagonists: John Jacob Astor, *A Journey in Other Worlds: A Romance of the Future,* 321.

29 "mother of magic": LOC, Marcella du Pont Papers, Andrija Puharich to Marcella du Pont, n.d.

29 "my great friend Admiral John Gingrich": LOC, Marcella du Pont Papers, Letter from Marcella Miller du Pont to her brother, Victor A. Miller, Esq., July 15, 1953.

29 Navy man, Rexford Daniels: Dan Hoolihan, "EMC Society History on Rexford Daniels—One of the Founders of the EMC Society," EMC.org newsletter, 50th Anniversary Edition, 2007. Daniels worked at the MIT Rad Lab Transitions Department Group 39 in the 1940s.

31 quest for the elusive sixth sense: LOC, Marcella du Pont Papers, Puharich, "Introduction to the Round Table Laboratory of Experimental Electrobiology," Camden, Maine, 1949," Appendix, n.p.; Round Table Foundation: Progress Report, 1950, n.p. Puharich's pursuits were not confined to extrasensory perception but welcomed all things parapsychological, including precognition, psychokinesis, and spirit channeling. Board meetings and weekly séances were held in the library, with subjects ranging from teleology to palm reading.

32 his eponymous torpedo: "Radio Controlled Torpedo Wins Favor of Navy and Army Experts," *Aerial Age Weekly* 3 (September 4, 1916): 744.

32 mentored by three of the most famous inventors: Tesla, unsuccessful in dealings with the military, taught Hammond about radio remote control. After the Navy endorsed Hammond's remote-controlled torpedo, Congress appropriated $750,000 ($16 million in 2016 currency) for the acquisition of what was hailed as a "wonderful invention."

32 seamlessly balanced success: "Castle Is Inventor's Vision of the Past," *New York Times,* October 9, 1988.

33 "He taught me the art of invention": LOC, Marcella du Pont Papers, Puharich Notes, n.p. Mentorship also discussed in Hermans, *Memories of a Maverick,* 48–49.

33 precedent for this idea: Alli N. McCoy and Yong Siang Tan, "Otto Loewi (1873–1961): Dreamer and Nobel laureate," *Singapore Medical Journal* 55, no. 1 (January 2014): 3–4; Banting, "The Discovery of Insulin," Nobel.org; Webb Garrison, "How to Produce New Ideas," *Popular Mechanics* (March 1954): 102–105.

33 symbol of the ouroboros: At least one historian has dedicated his research efforts to try to prove that Kekulé "may have been involved in [a] joke." Malcolm W. Browne, "The Benzene Ring: Dream Analysis," *New York Times,* August 16, 1988.

34 [Tesla] experienced extrasensory perception as a child: "Nikola Tesla," *Time, The Weekly Newsmagazine* XVIII, July 20, 1931; Andrija Puharich, "Effects of Tesla's Life and Inventions," 2–4.

35 establishment scientist and CIA asset: APS Records, Warren Sturgis McCulloch Papers, B: M139, Series 1, "Puharich, Henry K." The Macy Foundation was a CIA front, as discussed in John Marks, *The Search for the "Manchurian Candidate,"* 63, 120.

35 "metal fillings were coated with carborundum dust": Ibid., Letter to Dr. Henry K. Puharich, from Warren S. McCulloch, May 23, 1951. Puharich, "Paper No. 2," Sixth Ozone World Conference of the International Ozone Association, May 22–26, 1983, Washington, D.C.: 112–115.

36 Krock compared Puharich's quest to that of Louis Pasteur: Arthur Krock, "One Phase of the Unending Quest," *New York Times,* September 7, 1951.

36 Navy: Puharich's connection to the Navy's alleged ESP research on submarines has long since been denied, so these letters add insight to that debate. Admiral Gingrich was former chief of security and intelligence for the Atomic Energy Commission. When Marcella du Pont made the introduction, the admiral served as Chief of Naval Material, making him responsible for all Navy procurement programs. The connection between Rexford Daniels (who went on to serve as a science adviser to President Kennedy) and Andrija Puharich has also now been established.

36 new government psyops organization: Alfred H. Paddock, Jr., *US Army Special Warfare: Its Origins,* 89–90.

36 Stanley also served: Author FOIA, CIA: Memorandum for Brig. General John L. Magruder, OSD, Subject: Psychological Warfare Organization, May 28, 1951. It's worth noting that the OCPW was created on January 15, 1951, to combine propaganda—including leaflets and loudspeakers—with radical, new unconventional warfare activities.

37 "quite interested" Puharich, *Sacred Mushroom,* 5. See also LOC, Marcella du Pont Papers, Puharich personal papers (handwritten notes). Puharich writes, "Reason for securing interest of USN [U.S. Navy] in RTF [Round Table Foundation] is Electrophysical Enclosure Technique, also called treated Faraday Cage."

37 some kind of supernatural force: There are numerous YouTube video interviews of Puharich discussing his belief that there are nine principal forces overseeing reality.

38 "whistling between his teeth": Puharich, *Uri,* 13.

39 some kind of extraterrestrial intelligence: "The Nine were interested in helping mankind further evolution," Puharich believed, as per YouTube interviews cited above.

Chapter Three: Skeptics, Charlatans, and the U.S. Army

40 *Fads and Fallacies:* Martin Gardner's book was originally titled *In the Name of Science: An Entertaining Survey of the High Priests and Cultists of Science, Past and Present.* I cite the retitle as it is generally referred to this way.

40 "Since the bomb exploded over Hiroshima": Gardner, *Fads and Fallacies*, 5–7.

41 "an enormous self-deception": Ibid., 303–304, 308.

42 ESP and animals: Author FOIA, Army: "Memo, To O'Goff and O'Toole. From J. N. [sic] Rhine, Director, Duke University, Parapsychology Laboratory," July 10, 1953.

43 "an utter failure": Author FOIA, Army: Rhine Study, "Research on Animal Orientation with Emphasis on the Phenomenon of Homing in Pigeons," January 26, 1954, 11.

43 "Why do some pigeons get lost?": Ibid., 12.

43 The cat experiment was designed: Ibid., 10–11; in 1952, Osis wrote several unclassified papers on similar studies, including "A test of the occurrence of a psi effect between man and the cat," *The Journal of Parapsychology* 16, no. 4 (1952): 233.

44 After two hundred trials: Rhine Study, 13.

44 "There is a wide range of military uses of basic [research] programs": Ibid., 15. It is likely that Rhine worked on still-classified Navy programs; in numerous monographs he thanks the Navy for its support of his work—work that is never described. The Navy had reason to be involved in such research. With its revolutionary new nuclear-powered submarine, the USS *Nautilus*, Navy physiologists studied reports of anomalous perception manifested by sailors in extremely close quarters, underwater, for extended periods of time. Scientists with the Naval Submarine Medical Research Laboratory examined a variety of reported instances in which sailors experienced auditory and visual hallucinations in these extreme conditions. Of the 550 papers published by the NSMRL in the 1950s and 1960s, at least seven appear to have addressed extrasensory perception (my interpretation); all remain classified.

44 deliver a classified briefing on extrasensory perception: Author FOIA, CIA: "Henry (Andrija) Karl Puharich, Career Résumé," n.p., n.d. Puharich had been personally invited by the commandant of the U.S. Air Force School of Aviation Medicine to give a lecture on ESP. The doctors there included a large number of former Nazi doctors who were researching human physiology performance in extreme

conditions. See Annie Jacobsen, *Operation Paperclip*. These meetings are also cited in Kenneth A. Kress, "Parapsychology in Intelligence: A Personal Review and Conclusions," *Studies in Intelligence*, 21 (Winter 1977).

45 "to find [a] drug": Author FOIA, CIA: "Henry (Andrija) Karl Puharich, Career Résumé," n.p., n.d.; Puharich, *Sacred Mushroom*, 35.

45 MKULTRA Subproject 58: Marks, *The Search for the "Manchurian Candidate,"* 122. In 1973, the CIA deliberately destroyed most of the MKULTRA files on the orders of then CIA Director Richard Helms; Church Committee Hearings, Record Book I, 404. See also Puharich, *Sacred Mushroom*, 36.

45 secret to conceal: Hermans, *Memories of a Maverick*, 65.

45 Harry Stump: "Harry Stump, WWII Resistance Fighter," Associated Press, August 31, 1998. In Puharich's writings and elsewhere, Stump is given various pseudonyms. In his autobiography, published posthumously, the connection to Puharich is established. Stump was a war hero in his native Holland, honored by the Dutch government for resistance work against the Nazis. Acting as a courier, Stump, age seventeen, was captured by the Gestapo, beaten, and tortured to the edge of death.

46 "began to draw Egyptian hieroglyphs": Puharich, *Sacred Mushroom*, 15–16. All of the information about this event comes from Puharich's book; no second source was located.

47 a simple mushroom rendered with spots on the cap: Ibid., 16. Puharich wrote: "'The mushroom could take away a man's suffering,' Stump said. 'Take the skin off its neck, and the white spots too [in order] to take people out of themselves when they [can not] bear their pain.' He provided details about how to best use the potent painkiller to stimulate psychic abilities: 'The ointment is to be rubbed on the skull, on the joints, for trance.'"

48 "that a human could [psychically] travel": Ibid., 36.

49 given a higher security clearance: Author FOIA, CIA: "Henry (Andrija) Karl Puharich, Career Résumé," n.p., n.d.

49   He was told: Puharich, *Sacred Mushroom,* 26.

49   Dr. Moore, posing as a deep-pocketed professor: Author FOIA, CIA: "Appendix E. Summary of Agency Records Retrieval, Central Intelligence Agency" n.p., n.d. See also Marks, *The Search for the "Manchurian Candidate,"* 117–122.

49   "maintains the fiction": Marks, *The Search for the "Manchurian Candidate,"* 118.

50   "branded as a crackpot": Puharich, *Sacred Mushroom,* 39.

52   Flournoy's book: Flournoy, *From India to the Planet Mars.* "Fig. 21. Text No. 16; Seance of August 22, 1897. First Martian text written by Mlle. Smith (according to a visual hallucination)."

52   "Science has disclosed a hidden subliminal work": Ibid., iii. Interestingly, Hélène Smith rejected this explanation, and after the book was published never spoke to Flournoy again. In the 1910s she was embraced by the French surrealists, who declared her "the muse of automatic writing" and showcased her paintings. Despite Flournoy's intention to present a scientific alternative to psychic functioning, many of his readers decided that cryptomnesia was its own "mysterious psychic phenomena." In the introduction to the English-language edition, Flournoy's editor wrote, "An increasing number of thoughtful men are coming to believe that the hidden subliminal work within may point to an unseen spiritual world without, communication with which, if once established, could furnish us with the solution so ardently longed for."

53   Helen Keller's story: Helen Keller, *The Story of My Life,* Chapter XIV, can be read at the website of the American Foundation for the Blind.

53   the accused: *Letters from Prevorst,* written by Justinus Kerner. Kerner's book, incidentally, was a compilation of reports of occult and unexplained phenomena; the unattributed passage was a ship's log from 1686. The whole concept went around in a circle like an ouroboros.

53   He wrote to Nietzsche's sister: Paul Bishop, *The Dionysian Self: C. G. Jung's Reception of Friedrich Nietzsche,* 83–84.

Chapter Four: Quasi Science

55 "The pungency of pine and spruce": APS Records, Warren Sturgis McCullough Papers, B: M139, Series 1, "Puharich, Henry K." Round Table Foundation, letters and invitations, n.d. These documents offer insight into Puharich's elite circle of colleagues, which also included Henry Wallace, the former vice president of the United States. "Please plan a visit, you will be right at home," Puharich wrote to Wallace, whose interest in astrology, agriculture, and Freemasonry had earned him the moniker "the corn-fed mystic."

55 picnics in the blueberry fields: Andrija Puharich, *Sacred Mushroom,* 89.

56 Three chemicals: Muscarine stimulates the body's parasympathetic, or rest-and-digest, nerve endings, inducing vomiting and diarrhea. Muscarine initially produces a stimulating effect and then acts as a poison, paralyzing the nerves it previously stimulated. Atropine, a naturally occurring stimulant, increases heart rate, dilates the pupils, reduces salivation, inhibits sweating, and causes convulsions. Bufotenin is a naturally occurring psychedelic present in many species of plant and also in venom from the Colorado River toad.

56 Puharich decided to try the hallucinogenic mushroom: Puharich, *Sacred Mushroom,* 89.

57 [Huxley] wrote several letters: James Sexton, ed., *Aldous Huxley: Selected Letters,* 461, 471. The letter referenced is dated August 9, 1955. The concept of psi, which refers to the unknown element in ESP and other anomalous mental phenomena, derives from the twenty-third letter of the Greek alphabet, ψ (pronounced *sigh*) and the initial letter of the Greek word ψυχή (pronounced *psyche*), which means both mind and soul.

58 on August 7, 1955: Puharich, *Sacred Mushroom,* 97–98. Huxley's account is similar to Puharich's.

59 Stump appeared not to remember: Ibid., 98; Stump's posthumously published partial memoir, which chronicles his life starting in childhood, ends abruptly in August 1955 and does not mention

Puharich, only Huxley (see Ferriss and Stump, *Maine's Psychic Sculptor*).

60 concentration camp survivor:: Ibid., 55. Hurkos was at Vught, or Herzogenbusch, concentration camp (erroneously reported as Buchenwald). It's interesting to consider that Hurkos and Stump shared similar wartime experiences; each had worked for a resistance group during the war, each had been captured and tortured by the Gestapo.

60 Hurkos had recently solved: "The Psychic Powers of Peter Hurkos," *Paris Match,* June 14, 1952, 170.

60 Paris metro police: Browning, *Hurkos,* 74.

60 "Hurkos gave Harry [Stump] a confidence": Hermans, *Memories of a Maverick,* 67–68; interview with Stephanie Hurkos.

60 "groundbreaking results": LOC, Marcella du Pont Papers, Round Table Foundation, Progress Report, 1956, n.p.

61 "He felt the CIA was after his research": Hermans, *Memories of a Maverick*, 70-71; author FOIA, CIA: Letter to Mr. Allen W. Dulles, Director, Central Intelligence Agency, from Mary O' [illegible], Secretary to Mr. R. Gordon, Wasson, June 3, 1960. It seems that Wasson knew Moore worked for the Agency.

61 official CIA invoice: author FOIA, CIA: Memorandum for the Record, Subject MKULTRA, Subproject 58, Draft, March 21, 1956.

61 "He was like a landlubber at sea": John Marks, *The Search for the "Manchurian Candidate,"* 123. Marks interviewed Moore.

62 "remain an Agency secret": Ibid., 124.

62 drugs began to take hold: Hermans, *Memories of a Maverick,* 70-71. Hermans writes that Puharich's investors disapproved of his relationship with her. "When Joyce Balokovic found out about Andrija's and my 'sordid love-affair,' she booked passage for me on the S.S. *Rijndam*." She was sent back to Europe for several months, then returned.

62 fixated on outer space: Ibid., citing Puharich's journal.

63 Two Pentagon employees: Author FOIA, FBI: "Memorandum for the Record: Subject, Puharich, Henry K. Dr. Round Table

Foundation, Glen Cove Maine," from Special Operations Section, Federal Bureau of Investigation. (n.d.) Bureau File No. 63–4036.

64 "consultant on mushroom toxicology": Author FOIA, CIA: "Henry (Andrija) Karl Puharich, Career Résumé," n.p., n.d.

64 leapt to her death: "7-Floor Plunge Kills Mother," *Milwaukee Sentinel,* January 25, 1959.

65 threatened to leave: Hermans, *Memories of a Maverick,* 76, 78. Hermans feared the money would run out and they would have nothing to live on. Instead, with the 1959 publication of *The Sacred Mushroom,* numerous research organizations wanted to hire him.

65 sponsored by the U.S. Army Chemical Corps: Author FOIA, CIA: Puharich, Henry, and Mitchell, Edgar D., Captain. "A Research Program Whose Goal is to Unambiguously Resolve the Question as to Whether or Not Direct Brain Perception and Direct Brain Action Exist," n.d., partially paginated 54-page document.

65 fourteen-man scientific expedition: John Newland, "The Sacred Mushroom of the Shaman," *One Step Beyond,* January 4, 1961.

65 officials from the Atomic Energy Commission: Author FOIA, AEC: "Memorandum from Dr. Paul S. Henshaw," November 1, 1963.

66 "biologic memory involving information": APS Records, Warren Sturgis McCulloch Papers. "Memorandum from Paul S. Henshaw, Medical Research Branch. Subject: Observations of the Work of Henry K. Puharich, M.D." November 21, 1963, n.p.

67 secret government contracts: Author FOIA, CIA: "Henry (Andrija) Karl Puharich, Career Résumé," n.p., n.d.; Puharich, Henry, "A Research Program Whose Goal is to Unambiguously Resolve the Question as to Whether or Not Direct Brain Perception and Direct Brain Action Exist," 4.

67 quasi-science pursuits: A collection of Puharich's films and audiotapes of Arigo are available online at the University of Minnesota Duluth website, in the Sociology-Anthropology, Culture and Personality archives.

68 "psychic healing on the battlefield": Author FOIA, CIA: Puharich, Henry, "III. Research Proposal," n.p., n.d.

69   colleagues from the Round Table Foundation: Author FOIA, CIA: Henry (Andrija) Karl Puharich File, "International Conference, Exploring the Energy Fields of Man, November 19–22, 1970," program itinerary and overview, n.p., n.d.

69   Itzhak Bentov: Ibid. Bentov designed Israel's first rocket, for the War of Independence, and the steerable cardiac catheter, which paved the way for many biomedical engineering inventions.

69   escalated to . . . CIA director Richard Helms: Interview with Christopher "Kit" Green.

Chapter Five: The Soviet Threat

70   out of the public eye: Bergier, *Morning of the Magicians,* French edition. Notably, the story of the *Nautilus* was censored from the U.S. edition of the book; see also Ioan Mamulas, D.S., "Parapsychological Espionage," *Geostrategic Pulse* 45, January 5, 2009, International Institute for Strategic Studies, London.

71   condition of anonymity: Gérald Messadié, "The Secret of the *Nautilus,*" *Science et Vie* (February 1960), 509. There were no authors identified. In an interview Messadié said his information came from Bergier and "other sources."

71   Navy's response: In the September 8, 1963, issue of *This Week,* a nationally syndicated Sunday magazine supplement, U.S. Air Force Colonel William H. Bowers was quoted as saying, "The experiment in which I was alleged to have participated never took place."

71   "Soviet parapsychology research": Author FOIA: ST-CS-01-169-72, "Significance of Parapsychology in the USSR," July 1972.

72   Vasilev told a group: Ibid. As a source for this information, the analyst cites *Soviet Review 2,* no. 6, June 1961.

72   mysterious faith healer from Siberia: Malia Martin, "The Holy Devil," *New York Review of Books,* December 31, 1964.

73   "the energy underlying telepathic communication": John D. LaMothe, *Controlled Offensive Behavior— USSR (U).* Medical Intelligence Office, Office of the Surgeon General, Department of the Army, Defense Intelligence Agency, July 1972, 62; Kernbach,

"Unconventional Research in USSR and Russia," *International Journal of Unconventional Science,* Cornell University (Fall 2013): n.p.

73 "telepathic impulses": Author FOIA, CIA: ST-CS-01-169-72, "Significance of Parapsychology in the USSR," July 1972.

73 "electromagnetic, emissions from humans": Kernbach, "Unconventional Research in USSR and Russia," n.p.

74 programs stemmed from Ahnenerbe research: Ibid., n.p.

74 Demichev, to establish a special commission: Ibid., n.p.

74 had their offices: Gates, *From the Shadows,* 97.

75 Moscow Unidentified Technical Signal: Barton Reppert, "Close-up: The Moscow Signal. Zapping an embassy: 35 years later," Associated Press, May 22, 1988. Thirty-five years later, the real purpose behind the beams remains the subject of debate.

75 inside an anechoic chamber: Eugene V. Byron, "Project Pandora, Final Report," Applied Physics Laboratory, Silver Spring, Maryland, November 1966.

75 Cesaro became convinced: Author FOIA, [D]ARPA: "Memorandum to Mr. R. S. Cesaro, ARPA, from IDA Review Panel, Subject: Flash Report of Pandora/Bizarre Briefing," January 14, 1969; Minutes of Pandora Meeting of June 18, 1969;

75 produced Alzheimer's disease: Author FOIA, [D]ARPA: Minutes of Pandora Meeting of August 12 and 13, 1969. See also, Becker, *The Body Electric,* Epilogue.

76 "The actual physical results": Samuel Koslov, "Radiophobia, the Great American Syndrome," *Johns Hopkins APL Technical Digest* 2 (November 2, 1981): 102.

76 "athermal radiation on man": Paul Brodeur, *Currents of Death,* 91–92.

78 Kulagina was filmed: The declassified films are available on YouTube.

78 frog's beating heart: LaMothe, *Controlled Offensive Behavior— USSR (U),* 35.

79 wrote the Defense Department analyst: *Paraphysics R&D— Warsaw Pact.* U.S. Air Force, Air Force Systems Command, Foreign Technology Division, Defense Intelligence Agency, March 30, 1978, 8.

79 "After 5 minutes, [Dr.] Sergeyev": *Paraphysics R&D— Warsaw Pact.*
U.S. Air Force, Air Force Systems Command, Foreign Technology
Division, Defense Intelligence Agency, March 30, 1978, 8.

79 "the most significant PK test": LaMothe, *Controlled Offensive
Behavior— USSR (U),* 35.

80 four categories of existential threat: Ibid., 40.

80 "I am really disturbed": Ibid. Based on NARA records research, my
read is that it's likely that Caldwell was CIA.

Chapter Six: The Enigma of Uri Geller

85 home of Moshe Dayan: Much of this chapter comes from one of my
numerous interviews with Uri Geller. As for Geller's map-dowsing
forays with Moshe Dayan, there is no way to verify that it happened.
Dayan's pilfering of antiquities is well documented, even in his own
memoir, which includes photographs of the artifacts on display in his
home as well as maps and photographs of his digging sites.

85 "remains of ancient settlement[s]": Moshe Dayan, *Living with the
Bible,* 131.

86 Dayan was badly injured: Yael Gruenpeter, "The Israeli
Defense Minister Who Stole Antiquities," *Haaretz,* December
19, 2015.

86 massive stone artifacts: Dayan, *Living,* 31; see also Getty Images
website, where many photos of Dayan's home show his antiquities
collection.

86 "Dayan utilized my powers": Interview with Geller; Dayan, *Living,*
131–133.

86 "the matter of water-witching": Arthur J. Ellis, "The Divining Rod:
A History of Water Witching," U.S. Geological Survey, Water
Supply Paper No. 416, 1917.

87 "Far from a harmless": Gardner, *Fads and Fallacies,* 102, 113.

87 *Financial Times* of London reported: Margaret van Hatten, "A Cost-
effective Account of the Spoons," *Financial Times,* January 18, 1986.
Van Hatten confirmed Geller's £1M per job figure with Peter
Sterling, chairman of the Australian mineral company Zanex.

87 homesteaders and farmers: "Dowsing," U.S. Geological Survey, n.d.

87 U.S. forces in Vietnam: "Shades of Black Magic: Marines on Operation Divine for VC Tunnels," *Observer* 5, no. 45, March 13, 1967.

88 "In this day of nuclear powered devices": Ibid.

88 "Dowsing is human intelligence": Interview with Louis Matacia; see also Bird, *The Divining Hand,* 200–205.

89 "The cause of an effect": Bird, *Divining,* 213.

89 "legally questionable hobby": Yael Gruenpeter, "The Israeli Defense Minister Who Stole Antiquities," *Haaretz,* December 19, 2015.

89 Dayan discusses his illegally acquired collection: Dayan, *Living,* statement on jacket.

90 his mother told the BBC: Footage from Vikram Jayanti, "The Secret Life of Uri Geller, Psychic Spy," BBC.

91 "He astonished friends": Interview with Geller; Geller, *My Story,* 135–136.

91 Geller confided in Yoav Shacham: Interview with Geller; photographs from Geller's collection; Jayanti, "The Secret Life of Uri Geller," BBC.

92 Shacham had been killed: *Maariv* obituary: Yoav Shacham (Bernstein), born October 2, 1935, died November 13, 1966.

93 mesmerized by Geller's abilities: Interview with Shipi Shtrang.

94 he tested Geller: Interview with Amnon Rubinstein in Jaffa, March 2016.

95 Gamal Abdel Nasser: Interview with Sarah Zilderman, former Israel Defense Forces intelligence analyst.

95 she was quoted: Meir's exact quote was, "They say there's a young man who can foresee exactly what will happen, I can't."

96 Geller said: Puharich, *Uri,* 63; interview with Shtrang.

97 it appears in the Bible: 1 Chronicles 29:29. The passage reads: "Now the acts of David the king, first and last, behold, they are written in the book of Samuel the seer, and in the book of Nathan the prophet, and in the book of Gad the seer."

97 most nights: Interview with Gaby Berlin; interview with Sarah Zilderman.

97 "very state-of-the-art back then": Interview with Geller; also noted in Puharich's CIA file.

98 Puharich had informed the CIA: Author FOIA, CIA: Puharich, Henry, "A Research Program Whose Goal Is to Unambiguously Resolve the Question as to Whether or Not Direct Brain Perception and Direct Brain Action Exist," n.d., 19; Andrija Puharich, M.D., "Program Alpha—Phase I. Preliminary Report on DBA Effects Demonstrated by Uri Geller," August 17–25, 1971; September 20–29, 1971; November 17, 1971 to April 14, 1972.

99 Puharich as a potential liability: Author FOIA, CIA: "Memorandum for: Director of Central Intelligence, W. E. Colby; Subject: Office of Research and Development and Office of Technical Service Paranormal Perception Research Project," November 23, 1973.

Chapter Seven: The Man on the Moon

100 gave Ed Mitchell an idea: Interview with Mitchell. In 1926, Wilkins was the first man to fly from North America to the polar regions of Europe, proving that there was no continent under the Arctic ice. He commanded multiple expeditions to the Arctic and to Antarctica.

101 "These were abstruse subjects": Mitchell, *The Way of the Explorer,* 31; interview with Mitchell.

101 "I would lie awake at night": Mitchell, *Anthology of Psychic Research,* 32.

102 "how to react intuitively": Interview with Mitchell (discussion). Quote is from Alexander et al., *The Warrior's Edge,* 121, citing Deikman, "Mystical Intuition," *New Realities,* 1987.

102 "The mind has to convince the body": Interview with Mitchell.

103 rushing sounds of liquid: Shepard, et al., *Moon Shot,* Chapter Twenty-Two: Apollo 14: All or Nothing.

103 its origins: "A Planetary Science Strategy for the Moon," Lunar Exploration Science Working Group, NASA, July 1992, 2.

103 a view of the ancient aftermath: Mitchell, *Explorer,* 52.

105 Zener cards: These are among the oldest symbols known to man. The circle represents the Sun and the Moon and (much later in man's evolutionary process) the wheel and the gear. Across time, circles have been associated with infinity, perfection, and the divine. The

square is a quadrilateral, with four equal angles and four equal sides. Squares represent the four seasons, the four directions, and the four elements. The square is a symbol of civilization and of things man-made. The five-pointed star is an ideogram, a graphic symbol that, across history, has represented military power and ideas. Stars symbolize stardom. The cross, or plus symbol, with its arms of equal length, has religious and mathematical meaning. Three wavy lines is a symbol for mystery.

105 the days of cuneiform writing: Interview with Irving Finkel.

105 "This scale is so deceiving": Apollo 14 Transcript, 359.

106 Shepard opened the hatch: Ibid.

107 "Keep the mind focused": Interview with Mitchell. Further, he discusses serendipity in *Explorer* and *Anthology of Psychic Research.*

107 Believe in serendipity: Interview with Mitchell.

108 "We deceived the program by telling it": Interview with Don Eyles.

108 Mitchell entered these critical keystrokes: "Apollo 14 Lunar Surface Journal: Landing at Fra Mauro," Corrected Transcript, 1. Ed Mitchell was certain he could handle the task that lay ahead, he recalled in 2015. He had conviction. "Few astronauts knew the lunar module systems as thoroughly as I did."

110 "You are go for a landing," Apollo 14 Transcript, 449.

110 eighty-seven feet: Apollo 14, Mission Highlights, NASA (nasa.gov), July 8, 2009.

110 learn more about Earth's origins: Oldroyd, David R., ed. "The Earth Inside and Out," 17; Mitchell, *Explorer,* 52. Since the beginning of the space age, images from spacecrafts have allowed scientists to map the surface of the Moon, changing it from an astronomical object to a geological one. Every day, fifty meteorites weighing at least 100 grams each impact the Earth.

111 "I couldn't see the Earth at all": Mitchell, *Earthrise,* 110–111.

112 Disagreements followed: Apollo 14 Transcript, 132.

113 Mitchell consulted his map: Photograph, insert. There is some debate as to whether the document Mitchell is consulting in the photo is a map or a checklist. In our interview, Mitchell told me he thinks it was the map. Maps have been helping man navigate since prehistory,

painted on cave walls in Turkey and Ukraine, baked into clay tablets in Babylon.

114 "objects typically appeared one-half as far away": Mitchell, *Explorer,* 54; interview with Mitchell.

114 "We kangaroo-hopped": Mitchell, *Explorer,* 56.

115 rendezvousing with Stu Roosa: Apollo 14 Transcript, "Table 6-1, Sequence of Events."

115 "savikalpa samadhi" in space: Interview with Mitchell.

115 "Al Shepard doubled over with laughter": Mitchell, *Explorer,* 61; interview with Mitchell.

116 headline: "Captain Edgar D. Mitchell, the Uri Geller of the Astronauts," *Maariv,* February 19, 1971.

116 his worldview had shifted: Mitchell, *Anthology,* 45. "There was something wrong with ideas such as nation and state. From this point of view it is only logical to make war on other countries and on the countryside," Mitchell wrote.

117 "is the ultimate frontier": Mitchell, *Anthology,* 28.

117 The Apollo astronaut was on board: Interview with Mitchell.

Chapter Eight: The Physicist and the Psychic

118 a bit of a prodigy: Author FOIA, CIA: Puthoff Résumé, "Harold E. Puthoff, Senior Research Engineer, Electronics and Bioengineering Laboratory, Information Science and Engineering Division," submitted to the CIA October 1973.

118 unsolved questions: Interview with Puthoff.

119 "research in quantum biology": In our interview, we discussed Puthoff's paper, "CIA-Initiated Remote Viewing at Stanford Research Institute," Association of Former Intelligence Officers, *The Intelligencer: Journal of U.S. Intelligence Studies* 12, no. 1 (Summer 2001), in which the program's origins were discussed.

119 SRI performed: Author FOIA, CIA: Hal Puthoff, "Qualifications of Stanford Research Institute," circa 1973.

119 Project Lightning: Interview with Puthoff.

120 hypotheses involving a subatomic particle: Ya. P. Terletsky, "Positive, Negative and Imaginary Rest Masses," *Journal de Physique at le*

Radium 23, no. 11 (1963): 910–920; G. Feinberg, "Possibility of Faster-Than-Light Particles," *Physical Review 159* (1967): 1089–1105 (1967).

121 fear of being caught in a lie: "The Polygraph and Lie Detection," The National Academies Press, Washington D.C., 2003, 13–16.

121 Why not try to elicit: Cleve Backster, "Evidence of a Primary Perception in Plant Life," *International Journal of Parapsychology* 10, no. 4 (Winter 1968): 329–348.

121 a eureka moment for him: Backster was not the first scientist to postulate such an idea. In 1848, the experimental psychologist Dr. Gustav Theodor Fechner argued that plants grew better with affection and attention, but Backster was the first to place the story in the mainstream. Backster appeared on the TV shows of Johnny Carson, Merv Griffin, and David Frost.

122 Bird, a CIA operative: Bird's life remains a puzzle. Many sources confirm that he was CIA, as was noted in his obituary. See bibliography and also Eric Pace, "Christopher Bird, 68, a Best-Selling Author," *New York Times,* May 6, 1996.

122 plants lack a nervous system: K. A. Horowitz et al., "Plant 'Primary Perception': Electrophysiological Unresponsiveness to Brine Shrimp Killing," *Science,* August 8, 1975, 478–480; John M. Kmetz, " Plant Primary Perception: The Other Side of the Leaf," *Skeptical Inquirer* 2 (1978): 57–61.

122 Charles Darwin: František Baluška et al., "The 'root-brain' hypothesis of Charles and Francis Darwin. Revival after more than 125 years," *Plant Signaling & Behavior* 2, no. 12 (December 2008): 1121–1127. The authors discuss one of Darwin's last books, *The Power of Movement in Plants,* which is a record of the numerous experiments Darwin performed together with his son.

122 "Mother Nature": Josh Eells, "Cleve Backster, b. 1924. He talked to plants. And they talked back," *New York Times Magazine,* December 21, 2013.

123 "I'd zap one culture": Paul H. Smith, *Reading the Enemy's Mind,* 54–55; interview with Puthoff.

123 understood and accepted by his maternal grandmother: Interview with Murleen Ryder (note that Ingo changed the spelling of his name, adding a second *n*).

124 To pay the bills: Swann, "Remote Viewing, The Real Story: An autobiographical Memoir," unpublished autobiography, Chapter 4, 5.

124 high-society entertainer: "Buell Mullen, Muralist and Painter on Metals," *New York Times,* September 10, 1986.

125 Swann generally disliked: Swann, unpublished autobiography, Chapter 12, 14.

127 pursuing a related hypothesis: Interview with Puthoff; Hal Puthoff papers. Puthoff's proposal was called "The Physics of Psychoenergetic Processes Research Proposal." To his reader, Puthoff wrote: "Please note the use of the term Tachyon, from the Greek word meaning 'swift.' "

127 "Swann said": Puthoff, *The Intelligencer,* 61; interview with Puthoff.

127 a one hundred percent match: "New ASPR Search on Out-of-the-Body Experiences," Karlis Osis, *ASPR Newsletter* 14 (Summer 1972); Osis, Karlis, and Donna McCormick, "Kinetic effects at the ostensible location of an out-of-body projection during perceptual testing," *Journal of the American Society for Psychical Research* 74, no. 3 (1980).

128 "Reception for Ingo Swann": Swann, unpublished autobiography, Chapter 31. According to Swann, the week before the party, the publishing committee said it would not be publishing the results. They were, the committee said, so good that there "must be something wrong with them."

128 "The gossip line exploded": Swann, unpublished autobiography, Chapter 31.

130 "I was able to gain access": Puthoff Papers, "Words at Ingo Swann's Memorial Service," n.d.

130 Office of Naval Research: Author FOIA, CIA: H. E. Puthoff and Russell Targ, "Proposal for Research ISU 75-241, Magnetometer Stability Studies," November 14, 1975, 2.

132 "You're standing on top of it": Interview with Puthoff.

132 how the quark detector worked: Author FOIA, CIA: Puthoff and Targ, "Proposal for Research ISU 75-241," 2.

132 vocal proponent of extrasensory perception: Interview with Brian D. Josephson, June 2015, in Cambridge, UK.

134 "outside the range": Author FOIA, CIA: Puthoff and Targ, "Proposal for Research ISU 75-241," 1.

134 he hit his head: Swann, unpublished autobiography, Chapter 37.

134 "the active perturbation": Author FOIA, CIA: H. E. Puthoff and Russell Targ, "Technical Memorandum: A Progress Report on Contract Number 1471(S)73," February 23, 1973, 3.

134 ice cream to celebrate: Interviews with Hal Puthoff and Adrienne Puthoff.

135 "Their credentials": Interview with Puthoff; H. E. Puthoff, "CIA-Initiated Remote Viewing at Stanford Research Institute," Association of Former Intelligence Officers, *The Intelligencer,* 61.

135 by the standards: It appears that Ingo Swann was already on their radar. Intelligence officers had been to the offices of the ASPR, in New York City, and had questioned Dr. Osis and Janet Mitchell about Swann, per Swann's memoir; interview with Green.

137 Geller tested on behalf of the CIA: Interview with Green; interview with Mitchell. This had to be done under cover of civilian research.

137 Swann-Geller phenomena: Author FOIA, CIA: "Some Reflections on Parapsychological Phenomena in the Intelligence Community," Draft, 23 Jan 73 (n.p., 10 pages).

Chapter Nine: Skeptics versus CIA

138 "We are not in the business": Author FOIA, CIA: "Suggested PR Release in the event the DCI is queried about Agency Involvement in Paranormal Research," n.p., n.d. Underlining is in the original.

138 Those invited were told: Author FOIA, CIA: "Memorandum For (See Distribution), Subject: Proposed Investigation of Paranormal Phenomena," n.p., n.d.

139 considered becoming an Episcopal priest: Interview with Green. For Green's official government CV, see "Emerging Cognitive

Neuroscience and Related Technologies," Committee on Military Intelligence Methodology, National Research Council, National Academies Press (2008), Appendix A, 91.

139 Green wore many hats: Interview with Green. The men who had overseen the original tests with Ingo Swann were with the Office of Research and Development.

140 administration of medical tests on the psychics: Interview with Green; Author FOIA, CIA, "Summary Tests," n.p., n.d. Tests included EEGs, the Buschke Memory test, the Knox Cube test, the Thematic Apperception test, the Verbal Concept Attainment test, the Halstead-Wepman Aphasia Screening test, the Bender Gestalt Visual Motor test, the Weschler Adult Intelligence Scale, the Minnesota Multiphasic Personality and the Rorschach inkblot tests. CT scan technology combined X-ray images with a computer and was the first significant improvement on the seventy-year-old X-ray technology.

140 "brain scans": Interview with Green. Initially, Green worked from his office at CIA headquarters, analyzing reports from local physicians contracted by SRI. Later, he would travel to SRI to study the psychics.

141 Mind Science Institute of Los Angeles: Author FOIA, CIA; Puharich, Henry, and Mitchell, Edgar D., Captain. "A Research Program Whose Goal Is to Unambiguously Resolve the Question as to Whether or Not Direct Brain Perception and Direct Brain Action Exist," n.d.

141 leading up to Geller's arrival: Geller photographs; interview with Geller.

141 Geller's first meeting: Interviews with Ed Mitchell, Uri Geller, and photos in both men's private collections. The meeting with von Braun, which was arranged by Mitchell, took place in Germantown, Maryland, in the offices of Fairchild Industries, where von Braun worked.

141 one news story: Lee Rickard, "Psychics and Scientists," *Observer* 17, no. 2 (June 1, 1973); interview with Geller, March 2016, in Jaffa, Israel.

142 analysts at the Pentagon: P. T. Van Dyke and M. L. Juncosa, "Paranormal Phenomena—Briefing on a Net Assessment Study," WN-8019 ARPA, January 1973, 2.

142 "ICBM's guidance program": Ibid., 6.

142 great challenge: Ibid., 27.

143 remembers Puthoff: Interview with Puthoff.

143 "one in a million": Author FOIA, CIA: Puthoff and Targ, "Technical Memorandum: A Progress Report on Contract Number 1471(S)73, Task 3; Experimentation with Uri Geller. February 22, 1973, 10.

144 "one in a trillion": Ibid., 11.

144 "an apparent ability of Geller": Ibid., 13. In their report to CIA, the scientists noted that they made efforts to "debunk" the experiment by using magnets and discharging static electricity; in those instances the balance was not perturbed.

145 Kibler said: Cited in interview with Ray Hyman, An Honest Liar, starts at minute 20:15.

145 reported in Time magazine: Leon Jaroff, "The Magician and the Think Tank," Time, March 12, 1973.

146 ARPA's George Lawrence told Jaroff: Author FOIA, CIA: "Memorandum for C/IP&A/ORD, Subject: Briefing by Stanford Research Institute," January 24, 1973.

146 write an exposé: Leon Jaroff, "The Magician and the Think Tank," Time, March 12, 1973. Ray Hyman told Time that the SRI experiments were performed with "incredible sloppiness."

146 "Lawrence...denies having talked to TIME": Author FOIA, CIA: "Subject: More Geller Business," February 28, 1973.

146 an anti–Geller crusade: Ibid.

146 "SRI should be destroyed": John Wilhelm, The Search for Superman, 28.

146 "Geller brings disgrace": Interview with James Randi; James Randi, The Magic of Uri Geller, 5.

148 "we have no scientific explanation": Author FOIA, CIA: H. E. Puthoff and Russell Targ, "Perceptual Augmentation Techniques,"

Proposal for Research, October 1, 1973, 23: "As a result of Geller's success in this experimental period, we consider that he has demonstrated his paranormal perceptual ability in a convincing and unambiguous manner."

148 "there might be phenomena": Author FOIA, CIA: "Memorandum for the Director," January 1973.

149 internal memos for Helms: Author FOIA, CIA: Memorandum for Director of Central Intelligence: Subject: Office of Research and Development and Office of Technical Service, Paranormal Perception Research Project DD/S&T 3697-73, 1.

149 "paranormal perception phenomena": Ibid., 3.

150 a convention in Los Angeles: The convention Pat Price refers to was a Scientology gathering. I discussed this issue with Puthoff as well as with the others involved. Puthoff's written statement on this, published in the *Skeptical Inquirer* in 2007, and in response to a criticism by Martin Gardner, is as follows: "Let's take the subject of my brief involvement in Scientology in the early 1970s to which Gardner devotes considerable space. He notes, correctly enough, that I am on record as being no longer involved, but asks 'but how much of it does he still buy?' What I 'still buy' is that GSR (galvanic skin response) can be used to dredge up forgotten traumatic memories from youth, with some cathartic effect. I learned this first by accident during routine polygraphing for security purposes when I was a NSA employee in the early 1960s. It was this experience that led me out of curiosity to later investigate Scientology procedures from an empirical, firsthand viewpoint. It became obvious to me, however, that, in addition to the expected defects that accompany any circumscribed belief structure, the ethics of the organization in those years was developing some fatal flaws as well, so I severed all connections. It is ironic to me that during the time I was being accused of being a Scientology member by Martin Gardner and others, the Scientologists were picketing me for my outspoken support of those who would dare to call them to task for their activities. So it goes."

Chapter Ten: Remote Viewing

152 "a trivialization of my abilities": Targ and Puthoff, *Mind Reach,* 27.

152 in the real world of espionage: Swann was not supposed to know that the client was the CIA; in his unpublished memoir he says he knew.

153 first computerized mapping system of Mars: Interview with Vallée.

153 "I suggested he look": Interview with Vallée.

154 "Virtual addressing": Vallée, *Forbidden Science* 2, 194.

154 "a means of accessing data": Ibid., 193.

154 Puthoff remembers himself saying: Interview with Puthoff; also discussed in Puthoff, *The Intelligencer,* 63.

155 "that wasn't even his real name": Interview with Green.

155 the following address: Author FOIA, CIA: H. E. Puthoff and Russell Targ, "Perceptual Augmentation Techniques, Part One—Technical Proposal," ORD #4718-73, October 1, 1973, 7–9. GPS coordinate (latlong.net) is: 38° 34' 15.8484" N, 79° 16' 28.3836'" W.

157 "It was so odd": Interview with Puthoff.

159 classified code name: Kenneth A. Kress, "Parapsychology in Intelligence: A Personal Review and Conclusions," *Studies in Intelligence* 21 (Winter 1977): 10.

160 "This was all nonsense, he said": Interview with Green.

160 ultrasecret facility run in part by NSA: Interview with Puthoff; interview with Green.

161 "A significant investigation": Interview with Puthoff.

161 Green recalls Price saying: Interview with Green.

162 series of jobs: John L. Wilhelm, *The Search for Superman,* 208.

162 Burbank Police Commission: Interview with Burbank Police Commission, public affairs spokesperson, January 2016; Wilhelm, 229.

164 "What interested me was the nausea": Interview with Green.

165 what force: Interview with Green. In this experiment, Green had broken SRI protocol and changed the location extemporaneously, thereby reducing the opportunity for fraud to nil.

165 Berkeley police enlisted Price: Author FOIA, CIA: "Memorandum for the Record. Subject: Operational Use of Paranormals in Police Activities," n.d., 2.

166 Semipalatinsk Test Site: Star Gate Collection, CIA: "Space Nuclear Facility test capability at the Baikal-1 and IGR sites Semipalatinsk-21, Kazakhstan," n.p., n.d.

166 URDF-3: The Soviets called their site Baikal-1. It would be more than twenty years before U.S. intelligence learned that the site was in fact an underground facility used for nuclear propulsion capabilities. Like its sister site at Jackass Flats, at the Nevada Test Site, Baikal-1 was where the Soviets were working on nuclear propulsion to take men to Mars.

167 Puthoff listened and took notes: Puthoff first discussed his participation in the session in the *Intelligencer* article. For a comprehensive account, see Kress, "An Analysis of a Remote-Viewing Experiment of URDF-3," December 4, 1975.

169 Price told Kress: Star Gate Collection, CIA: Kress, 12; "An Analysis of a Remote-Viewing Experiment of URDF-3," 4, 28.

169 "The rigor of the research became a serious issue": Ibid., 11.

169 "Disinformation Section of the KGB": Ibid., 24.

170 " 'conversion' experiences": Ibid., 7.

170 "I began to doubt my own objectivity": Kress, "Parapsychology in Intelligence," 14.

170 "extrasensory perception does exist as a real phenomenon": Author FOIA, CIA: "C/AOB/OTS: Memorandum for the Record: Subject: "Parapsychology/Remote Viewing," April 20, 1975; J. A. Ball, "An Overview of Extrasensory Perception: Report to CIA." January 27, 1975.

170 "considered questionable": Kress, "Parapsychology in Intelligence," 15.

Chapter Eleven: The Unconscious

172 brain warfare: CIA (digital collection):"Summary of Remarks by Mr. Allen W. Dulles at the National Alumni Conference of the Graduate Council of Princeton University," Hot Springs, VA, April 10, 1953.

172 "mind projection": Author FOIA, CIA: "Some Reflections on Parapsychological Phenomena and the Intelligence Community"

(concerning the Swann–Geller phenomena), Draft January 23, 1973, n.p.

173 "carefully controlled experiments with Geller": Author FOIA, CIA: "Memorandum for C/IP&A/ORD," January 24, 1973.

173 "concealed in a tooth": Dr. Joseph Hanlon, "Uri Geller and Science," *New Scientist,* October 17, 1974; author FOIA, CIA: Subject, "More Geller Business," February 28, 1973.

173 the magician James Randi speculated: Author FOIA, CIA: Subject: "Special Management Guidelines for the SRI Paranormal Project," January 15, 1974.

173 "the most important consequence of the Geller craze": John Palmer, "An Evaluative Report on the Current Status of Parapsychology," Army Research Institute for the Behavioral and Social Sciences, U.S. Army, May 1986, 195. This report covered twenty years of parapsychology.

173 what happened on November 23, 1973: This radio interview is not locatable by BBC 2, so the story as it appears here is from Geller's retelling in his 1975 memoir. The CIA refers to the radio program in documents, including in a summation of the press coverage about Geller, "Geller and New Scientist," and "Geller, Dimbleby Talk-In, press conference BBC Lime Grove (London)."

175 the newspaper printed a tabulation: "Gellermania," *Sunday People,* November 1973.

176 From defense officials to religious leaders: Geller, *My Story,* 51.

176 "the rational and the irrational": Sagan, *Broca's Brain,* 72.

177 relationships between physics...and the unconscious: Wolfgang Pauli and C. G. Jung, "Atom and Archetype: the Pauli/Jung Letters."

179 "a magnetic program card was erased": R. S. Hawke, "Outline of Acoustic Emission Experiments Performed With a Person Reputed to Have Paranormal Metal Bending Abilities," Lawrence Livermore Laboratory, University of California, Livermore, California, January 11, 1979.

180 He confronted Hal Puthoff and Russell Targ: Interview with Green. There is still some debate over when this happened: some say fall 1974, others, winter 1975. See also Vallée, *Forbidden Science* 2, 291.

181 holograms: Author FOIA, CIA: "Dr. Steven A. Benton, circa 1968, and Lloyd Cross, circa 1972"; "lasers: Charles H. Townes, 1960"; "UAV, Insectothoper," 1972.

181 some kind of omen or message: Interview with Kit Green, Hal Puthoff, and Jacques Vallée. In 2016, Geller said he was not aware of this until much later.

181 "To achieve better security": Author FOIA, CIA: "OTS/SDB: Notes on Interviews with F. P. E. L. C. J. K. G., and V.C.," January 1975; Kress, "Parapsychology in Intelligence," 15.

182 all kinds of rumors: I discussed the Pat Price death with everyone who was there during this time frame, including Green, Puthoff, and Vallée.

183 "use psychokinesis to stop the human heart": John D. LaMothe, *Controlled Offensive Behavior—USSR (U),* Medical Intelligence Office, Office of the Surgeon General, Department of the Army, Defense Intelligence Agency, July 1972, 40.

183 appear to have been a heart attack: Church Committee Hearings, testimony of former CIA toxicologist Mary Embree. In its defense, the CIA insisted that it was only keeping up with what the Soviets were working on.

183 "raid against the offices of the Church of Scientology": Vallée, *Forbidden Science* 2, 392.

Chapter Twelve: Submarines

186 ELF was the only known bandwidth: Its use as a submarine transmission system had first been proposed by DARPA scientist Nick Christofilos in 1958. The highly classified project was called Project Sanguine; see also Jacobsen, *The Pentagon's Brain,* 67–71.

186 communication in a postnuclear strike environment: Dr. Jack P. Ruina, Oral History with Finn Aaserud. American Institute of Physics, August 8, 1991.

187 rabbits: Dale E. Graff, *Paraphysics R&D—Warsaw Pact,* 11–12.

187 Schwartz proposed an experiment: Interview with Schwartz.

188 Navy had spent: White House Record Office, Gerald R. Ford, Presidential Library, House of Representatives, Report No. 94-1305,

94th Congress, 2d Session, Title I—Procurement, June 25, 1976, 56–62.

188 avoid drawing attention: R. Targ, E. C. May, H. E. Puthoff, D. Galin, and R. Ornstein, "Sensing of Remote EM Sources (Physiological Correlates)," SRI International, Final Report on Naval Electronics Systems Command Project, April 1978; see also Ronald M. McRae, *Mind Wars,* 5.

188 "ELF and Mind Control": John L. Wilhelm, "Psychic Spying? The CIA, the Pentagon and the Russians Probe the Military Potential of Parapsychology," *Washington Post,* August 7, 1977, B-1.

188 Koslov lamented: Ibid., B-5.

189 beamed these signals: Author FOIA, CIA: "Project Pandora, Final Report." Applied Physics Laboratory, Silver Spring, MD, November 1966.

189 had their offices: Robert M. Gates, *From the Shadows,* 97.

190 Colby wrote to the ambassador: Star Gate Collection, CIA: "Memorandum, From Director Colby, To: [redacted]," November 26, 1975.

190 getting more potent: Yuli Vorontsov, Soviet chargé d'affaires in Washington, D.C., gave Hyland a note stating that he would take steps for the possible reduction of the EM signal. No further U.S.-Soviet negotiations on MUTS occurred, according to Robert Gates.

190 filed a formal protest: Gates, 97.

190 "Russians were using microwave beams": Paul Brodeur, *The Zapping of America,* 213.

191 also died of cancer: Obituaries for Charles Bohlen, ambassador to the Soviet Union from 1953 to 1957, who had already died of pancreatic cancer on January 1, 1974, age sixty-nine; and Llewellyn Thomas, ambassador to the Soviet Union from 1957 to 1962 and again from 1967 to 1969, who died of cancer on February 6, 1972, age sixty-seven.

192 classified and unclassified Defense Department contracts: Allan Frey, "Effects of Microwaves and Radio Frequency Energy on the Central Nervous System," Clearinghouse for Federal and Scientific Information, U.S. Department of Commerce, September 17, 1969.

For more information on Frey, see "The Work of Allan H. Frey" at the website of the Cellular Phone Task Force organization (cellphonetaskforce.org).

192 "complex electrochemical systems": Allan H. Frey, "Electromagnetic field interactions with biological systems," National Center for Biotechnology Information, National Institutes of Health, *News and Features,* 272. "In a study published in 1975 in the Annals of the New York Academy of Sciences, Frey reported that microwaves could induce 'leakage' in the barrier between the circulatory system and the brain. Breaching the blood–brain barrier is a serious matter. It means that bacteria, viruses and toxins from the blood can enter the brain. It means the brain's environment, which needs to be extremely stable for nerve cells to function properly, can be perturbed in other dangerous ways."

192 "This assumption is wrong": Frey, "Effects of Microwaves," 3.

192 atrocious translations: Ibid., 3.

193 the pulse rate of a microwave beam: Robert O. Becker, *The Body Electric,* 319.

193 microwave weapons for the Defense Department: Obituary, Dr. Robert O. Becker, *Watertown Daily Times,* May 29, 2008.

193 "he considered such work immoral": Dennis Hackett, "Sinister Signals on the Radio," *New Scientist,* September 1984.

193 "using embassy employees as test subjects": Becker, *The Body Electric,* 310.

194 "facilitate hallucinations and altered states": E. C. Wortz et al., "Novel Biophysical Information Transfer Mechanisms (NBIT)," January 14, 1976, AiResearch Manufacturing Company of California, 48.

194 "secret parapsychology laboratory": Ibid., 18.

195 "the reality of thought transference": Ibid., 3.

195 Six months earlier: Interview with Stephan Schwartz.

196 "They said that I could have her": "The Realm of the Will," *Explore* 1, no. 3 (May 2005): 204.

196 Puthoff said yes, absolutely: Interview with Puthoff; interview with Graff; Star Gate Collection, CIA, "Long-Distance Remote Viewing from a Submersible," 33, n.d.

198 Leonard Nimoy's film crew: A film of the Mobius Group event is available on YouTube, "In Search of," minute 6:23.

199 fail-safe protocols: Star Gate Collection, CIA, "Long-Distance Remote Viewing," 36–42.

199 Graff's report: Ibid. See also Puthoff, Targ, May, Swann: "Advanced Threat: Technique Assessment. Final Report, October 1978"; Jim Schnabel, *Remote Viewers: The Secret History of America's Psychic Spies,* 207.

200 Bush told Mitchell: Interview with Ed Mitchell.

Chapter Thirteen: Paraphysics

203 officially running: Author FOIA, CIA: Untitled timeline, "Secret: Date/Event/Comments," from September 1977 through January 31, 1986. See also "Memorandum for the Record," Grill Flame Briefing, December 27, 1979, in which David S. Brandwein, director of the Office of Technical Services at the CIA, discusses how the Foreign Technology Division at Wright-Patterson Air Force Base was encouraged by the CIA to carry out "the development of our program and [its] applications."

203 "Nobody wanted the job": Interview with Graff; DIA wanted the final monograph to be labeled Secret, not Top Secret, which meant that it could be shared more broadly across the Department of Defense.

204 "We had machine translators": Dale E. Graff, *Paraphysics R&D— Warsaw Pact,* 29; Interview with Graff.

204 summarized the activities: Ibid., 42. Graff paid particular attention to novel electromagnetic theories. Soviet military scientist Dr. A. V. Kogan proposed that psychic functioning was the result of "low velocity of current propagation along body nerve fibers as possibly acting like a matching antennae for detecting very long wavelengths." An alternative theory was that "naturally low EM frequencies in the brain conceive or react with natural frequencies in the environment."

204 remembers Graff: Interviews with Graff.

209 "discuss what happened": Interview with Dale Graff, interview with Barbara Graff.

213 "She'd sketched a map": Author FOIA, CIA: Rosemary Smith's map can be seen in a draft of a report, "Project Sun Streak: Psychoenergetics," #10L3162-1, 20 (n.p.).

214 "She marked a spot": Interview with Graff.

216 declassified Staff Meeting Minutes memo: Dale Graff papers, "DDO Staff Meeting Minutes #86—Parapsychology," March 28, 1979.

216 Jimmy Carter publicly confirmed: "Psychic helped locate downed U.S. plane, ex-President says," Reuters, September 21, 1995.

216 electrical signals inside the human body: Interview with Graff; Paul H. Smith, *Reading the Enemy's Mind,* 101.

217 worked like a shell game: General Allen featured on PBS, "Open Vault," February 21, 1987.

218 estimated start-up cost: "Report of Secretary of Defense Harold Brown to the Congress on the FY 1981 Budget, FY 1982 Authorization Request and FY 1981–1985 Defense Programs," January 29, 1980, 85–90. The study on mobile ICBMs started in 1971.

219 letter arrived in the mail: Dale Graff papers, "From the Director of Central Intelligence, Washington, DC 20505, To Dale E. Graff, Advanced Research Branch, Department of the Air Force, Headquarters Foreign Technology Division, Wright-Patterson Air Force Base, Ohio 45433, December 31, 1980."

220 classified program called psychoenergetics: "Grill Flame Project Report," Defense Intelligence Agency Directorate for Scientific and Technical Intelligence, October 19, 1983, 1. This was the first comprehensive overview to discuss the origins of the program as well as its initial DIA-led goals.

220 "speculative and unsubstantiated": Author FOIA, CIA: "An Overview of Extrasensory Perception," January 27, 1975.

Chapter Fourteen: Psychic Soldiers

221 to visit Army facilities: Interview with Atwater; see also Atwater, *Captain of My Ship, Master of My Soul,* 51.

223 covert infiltration techniques: Author FOIA, DIA: "Subject: Briefing Request, Major Robert E. Keenan, Chief OPSEC Spt. Division," May 15, 1978.

223 OPSEC vulnerability estimates: Interview with Atwater; interview with Graff.

224 "unique form of surveillance": Star Gate Collection, CIA: Major Murray B. Watt, "INSCOM Project Grill Flame Progress Report #1," February 21, 1979.

224 an interest in ESP and PK: Jim Schnabel, *Remote Viewers: The Secret History of America's Psychic Spies,* 14.

225 "There was evidence": Major General Edmund R. Thompson (retired), interviewed on *The Real X-Files,* Independent Channel 4, British Equinox, August 27, 1995, minutes 5–6.

225 budget request form: Interview with Skip Atwater; Atwater, "Counterspy" (available online: skipatwater.com), keyword "Opening Stargate."

225 Most of the interviewees: Interview with McMoneagle. NPIC was created in 1961 and also combined DoD assets.

226 From his perspective: Interview with McMoneagle; also see McMoneagle, *The Stargate Chronicles: Memoirs of a Psychic Spy,* 59.

226 report to a sterile room: Star Gate Collection, CIA: "Memorandum for the Record, Subject: INSCOM Project Grill Flame: Progress Report #1, Period Covered, October 1978–February 1979," February 21, 1979, 16.

227 something along the lines of: Interview with McMoneagle; also see McMoneagle, *The Stargate Chronicles,* 71.

228 The film showed: Puthoff Papers; CIA declassified film footage, as seen in "The Case of ESP," *NOVA,* WGBH, Boston, 1984.

228 he sat alone with Puthoff: Interview with Puthoff; interview with McMoneagle.

229 Others in his unit: Star Gate Collection, CIA: Kress, "Parapsychology in Intelligence," 16.

231 a terrifying situation: Interview with McMoneagle; McMoneagle, *The Stargate Chronicles,* 49.

231 "near-death experience": Interview with McMoneagle.

232 McMoneagle signed on: Star Gate Collection, CIA: "Grill Flame Project Report," Defense Intelligence Agency, Directorate for Scientific and Technical Intelligence, October 19, 1983, 6.

232 chosen for the team: Interviews with Atwater, Graff, McMoneagle. Hartleigh Trent helped run a cold-weather survival school for the Navy SEALs in Maine.

233 lots of downtime: Interview with Angela Dellafiora.
NSC gave an official request: Star Gate Collection, CIA: Subject: Transcript Remote Viewing (RV) Sessions C 54 and C 55, Summary Analysis, n.p., n.d.

233 Army memos indicated: Star Gate Collection, CIA: Subject: "Briefing to the Commander, IAGRA-OPO," Signed Major Robert E Keenan, May 15, 1978.

234 "It smells like a gas plant": Ibid., 3–5.

234 "Very much like shark fins": Ibid., 6.

234 "part of a submarine . . . huge": Star Gate Collection, CIA: Subject: Transcript Remote Viewing (RV) Session C 55, 3–5.

234 "This coffin-like thing . . . it's a weapon": Ibid., 10.

235 National Security Council for review: "Soviet anti-submarine warfare," Jimmy Carter Presidential Library and Museum, Office of Staff Secretary; Series: Presidential Files; Folder: 9/11/79; Container 129.

235 KH-9 spy satellite photographs: National Reconnaissance Office, "KH-9 Panoramic Camera Image of Typhoon Class Submarine at Severodvinsk, Mission 1217-4" (www. nro.gov).

237 one hundred photographs: Author FOIA, CIA: Photos "Iran WAC 428B, Tehran. Interior room of the US Embassy after militants seized the embassy and took 60 hostages," November 8, 1979.

237 Joint Chiefs determined: "Memorandum for LTC Watt, Subject Interim Evaluation, Grill Flame Project," March 10, 1980, signed by LTC Lenahan.

237 viewers worked to track movements: Star Gate Collection, CIA: "GRILL FLAME Evaluation in Support of Iranian Hostage

Situation," March 16, 1981; "Summary of Iranian Remote Viewing
Sessions CD-06 and CD-16, Shiraz, Qom."

238 "fire and death": Telephone interview with Fern Gauvin.

238 "Admin note 0300 Hours in Iran": Star Gate Collection, CIA:
Transcript, Remote Viewing (RV) Session CCC84, 24 April 1980.

238 McMoneagle recalls what happened: Interviews with McMoneagle,
Atwater, Graff, Gauvin.

239 So did Fern Gauvin: Interview with Gauvin.

239 Khomeini held a press conference: Rouhullah al-Mousawi
al-Khomeini, "The Failure of the U.S. Army in Tabas," April 25,
1980 [Ordibehesht 5, 1359 AHS/ Jamadi ath-Thani 9, 1400 A].

240 *What are we dealing with here?:* I asked this question of every person I
interviewed who was in a position to have an educated answer about
this, from 1972 to the present.

Chapter Fifteen: Qigong and the Mystery of H. S. Tsien

241 able to "read" with his ears: Author FOIA, CIA: "Chronology of
Recent Interest in Exceptional Functions of the Human Body in
People's Republic of China," n.p., n.d.

241 shaped Chinese philosophy, science, and statecraft: See *I Ching: Book
of Changes,* translated by Richard Wilhelm, with "Introduction to
the *I Ching.*"

242 intelligence community had a mystery: Author FOIA, CIA:
"Psychoenergetics Research in the People's Republic of China,"
October 1982, 1–5.

244 children with EHBF: Puthoff, "Psychoenergetics Research," 1.

244 government-sanctioned conference: Ibid., 2.

245 "this new power could shatter modern science": Author FOIA, CIA:
China's *Ziran Zazhi (Nature Journal)*, September 1979.

245 now including psychokinesis: Author FOIA, CIA: CIA translation of
an article in *People's Daily,* May 1979.

246 see through lead containers: Author FOIA, CIA: Dongsu, Luo,
"Discussion of Non-Visual Recognition of Images and
Electromagnetic Sensor Mechanism in the Human Body,"

Translation Division, Foreign Technology Division, Wright-Patterson AFB (January 1981).

247 Chinese health system: David A. Palmer, *Qigong Fever: Body, Science, and Utopia in China*, 33.

248 movement expanded rapidly: David Eisenberg, *Encounters with Qi: Exploring Chinese Medicine*, 154–155.

249 national qigong training course: Palmer, *Qigong Fever*, 41.

249 singled out for attack: Ibid., 43.

251 So brilliant was Tsien: "Guggenheim Jet Propulsion Center," *CALCIT: The First Twenty-five Years*, 49.

252 science adviser to Chairman Mao: Iris Chang, *Thread of the Silkworm*, 246. "Exactly what Tsien taught Mao is not known," writes the late Chang. "But it did not exactly appear to whet the latter's appetite for more education. Mao was convinced that only the working class held the key to truth." Years later, Tsien wrote that Mao's intention "was to urge me to learn from the working people, to take them as my teachers, and to make a serious effort to rebuild my world outlook."

253 director of the Fifth Academy: Chang, Ibid., 219.

254 507th Research Institute: Author FOIA, CIA: "Chronology of Recent Interest in Exceptional Functions of the Human Body in People's Republic of China," n.p., n.d. Also called the Institute of Cosmos Medicine and Engineering Research, China's Academy of Sciences, Institute of Biophysics, Unit 236 of People's Liberation Army.

254 Science returned to the limelight: Chang, *Thread of the Silkworm*, 256.

254 outer space and inner space: Author FOIA, CIA: "The Opening and Development of the Basic Research of Human Body Science, by Qian Xue Sen" (DIA handwritten translation), June 30, 1981.

255 Tsien said: Author FOIA, CIA: Ibid.; Author FOIA, CIA: "Man in Cosmic Environment–Anthropic Principle, Somatic Science and Somatology," by Qian Xue Sen, circa 1981. "Somatology," wrote Tsien, "is the synthesis of classical physiology, modern psychology, psychophysiology, neuroscience, scientific parts of Chinese

traditional medicine and Qigong (Transcendental Meditation), and other related subjects."

255 "time of war": Author FOIA, CIA: "The Opening and Development of the Basic Research of Human Body Science, by Qian Xue Sen" (DIA handwritten translation), June 30, 1981, 13.

255 "enthusiastic atmosphere": Ibid., 49.

255 scientists, and journalists traveled to China: Interview with Puthoff.

256 Puthoff prepared a sixty-page classified report: Harold E. Puthoff, "Psychoenergetics Research in the People's Republic of China," October 1982.

256 "foreign psychoenergetics achievements": "Grill Flame Project Report," Defense Intelligence Agency Directorate for Scientific and Technical Intelligence, October 19, 1983, 1, 3.

256 "elder statesman": Puthoff, "Psychoenergetics Research," 12.

256 DeLauer signed a memo: "Grill Flame Activity, Memorandum for the Asst. Sec Army for RD&A, et al.," January 19, 1983.

258 Houck recalled: Jack Houck, "PK Parties," jackhouck.com; Severin Dahlen, "Remote Annealing of High Carbon Steel Parts," *Archaeus,* February–March 1986, 3.

259 approximately one thousand individuals: International Remote Viewing Association, Jack Houck, Biography. Between 1981 and 2003, Houck collected and published data on hosted 370 PK parties (jackhouck.com).

Chapter Sixteen: Killers and Kidnappers

261 future assassination plots: "Sadat Slaying: Haig Hints Libya Plot," *New York Daily News,* October 7, 1981.

261 surface-to-air missiles: Jim Schnabel, *Remote Viewers: The Secret History of America's Psychic Spies,* 283.

262 Graff's role: Interview with Graff.

262 psychics drew sketches: Star Gate Collection, CIA: "Interim Report Given to the U.S. Secret Service on 14 December 1981," Memorandum for Commander, SRD/ITAC, From: Ltc. Robert J. Jachim, Grill Flame Project Manager.

262 Grill Flame's ancillary support: Star Gate Collection, CIA: "Grill Flame Project Report," Defense Intelligence Agency Directorate for Scientific and Technical Intelligence, October 19, 1983, 3.

263 "Pentagon official would be kidnapped": Author FOIA, CIA: "Task Identification 0049, Report Number 820116," December 15, 1981, 2.

263 Puthoff alerted Dale Graff: The chain of command was Puthoff, Salyer, Graff, Vorona.

264 Dozier recalled: Interview with Dozier in Florida. For this part of the narrative, Dozier is the primary source. See also Richard Oliver Collin and Gordon L. Freedman, *Winter of Fire: The Abduction of General Dozier and the Downfall of the Red Brigades;* Star Gate Collection, CIA, Dozier File.

265 other individuals involved: Interview with Dale Graff. The Dozier abduction was unique for the DIA. Says Graff, "At DIA, we were trying to keep track of what various organizations were finding out. We had no direct connection. The search team was an Army function. The Defense Intelligence Agency is basically an analytical organization. We didn't usually become involved in field activities. Dozier was different."

265 an Arabic speaker: McMoneagle, *The Stargate Chronicles: Memoirs of a Psychic Spy,* 123.

266 vague and disparate information: Star Gate Collection, CIA: "Special Content Report, Parapsychologists in Kent Washington," January 1982.

266 protocols SRI had developed: Star Gate Collection, CIA: Project Officer, "Coordinate Remote Viewing, Stages I–VI and Beyond," February 1985, Appendix A, Glossary. AOL is defined as, "Information produced by the conscious or unconscious which clutters the signal; noise."

268 approval of DIA director: Star Gate Collection, CIA: Routing and Transmittal Slip, "DIA/Army Grill Flame support to BG Dozier abduction," December 28, 1981.

270 Graff recalls: Interview with Graff. Another theoretical idea being considered at SRI involved the Bohm Cosmogony of Quantum

Physics, in which "time and space allow for the explicate unfolded order," and that "pre-time and space would allow for the implicate enfolded order—": "Co-ordinate Remote Viewing (CRV) 1981–1983," Briefing (SRI), August 4, 1983, Slide 4, "Is CRV comparable to other known models?"

270 find and rescue General Dozier: Author FOIA, CIA: "Memorandum for the Secretary of Defense, Subject: Special Intelligence Report Relating to the Kidnapping of BG Dozier—Information Memorandum, Jack Vorona," n.d.

271 Reagan invited him to the White House: Russ Hoyle, "Terrorism: Welcome Home, Soldier," *Time,* February 15, 1982.

273 Perry, stated in a memo: "Perry Memorandum," March 5, 1980; Smith, *Reading the Enemy's Mind: Inside Star Gate—America's Psychic Espionage Program,* 118, n479.

273 "hell of a cheap radar system": William K. Stuckey, "Psi on Capital Hill: Official Circles," *Omni,* July 1979, 24. A member of the Intelligence Committee, Rose was an early advocate of cutting-edge technology. He drove an electric car to work and was responsible for bringing computers and fiber optics to Congress when typewriters were still in use.

273 the Devil's work: Interview with Alexander.

273 "some kind of psychic powers": Turner interview, Bill Eagles (director), *The Real X-Files: America's Psychic Spies,* Independent Channel 4, British Equinox, August 27, 1995, Channel 4 documentary, 1993; Smith, *Reading the Enemy's Mind,* 117–120, n480.

275 system to train soldiers: "Co-ordinate Remote Viewing (CRV) 1981–1983," Briefing (SRI), August 4, 1983, 9. Presented as a slide show to Army INSCOM officers visiting the SRI laboratory, these stages were: "Stage 1). Ideograms and ideogram production. Signals that induce/produce ideogramic responses (gestalts); Stage 2). Sensations experienced from distant site. Signals producing tactile, sensory, dimensional estimates, directions feelings, and so forth; Stage 3). Motion and mobility (limited) at distant site resulting in primary artistic renderings. Signals producing aesthetic responses in viewer,

simple sketches and "trackers"; Stage 4). Quantitative and qualitative assessments of various distant characteristics. Signals (manifold) that induce analytic comprehensions; Stage 5). Methods of interrogating the signal line (still in R&D); Stage 6). Creating 3–dimensional models. Signals (consolidated) that yield simple replicas of distant site features." Finally, there were two stages planned but not yet developed. They were: "Stage 7). Sonics (still in R&D). Signals that induce verbal content. Stage 8). Human to human interfaces (R&D 1984/1985). Signals that imply human psychic empathy and induce/produce ideogramic responses (gestalts).'"

275 program's CRV trainers: Interview with McNear. Cowart became sick and left the program. For the next two years, Swann would train McNear in all six stages of CRV.

275 "what the enemy was doing before the enemy did it": Interview, YouTube [https://www.youtube.com/watch?v=PUrF8dQo9uc]. General Stubblebine (retired) is now a vocal member of the Agenda 21 movement. Through his attorney, he declined to be interviewed.

276 Stubblebine had a long-standing interest: "An Exclusive Interview with General Albert Stubblebine — "Men Who Stare at Scapegoats," Podcast #176, September 13, 2013, Gnostic Media, Research and Publishing. Available at gnosticmedia.com.

276 Advanced Human Technology Office: Author FOIA, Army INSCOM, "High Performance Task Force, High Performance Programs Information," 60–304.

Chapter Seventeen: Consciousness

277 not yet part of the Grill Flame program: Interviews with Colonel John Alexander (retired).

278 Anderson surmised: Jack Anderson, "Pentagon Invades Buck Rogers Turf," *Washington Post,* January 9, 1981.

281 "a major challenge": Author FOIA, Army INSCOM: "Army Science Board Report of Panel on Emerging Human Technologies," Office of the Assistant Secretary of the Army, Washington D.C., December 1983, "Abstract," n.p.

281 "strategies and actions": Ibid., i.

283 pressure was taking its toll: Interview with Fred Atwater.

284 "I thought I had killed him": Interview with Joe McMoneagle; interview with Fred Atwater. Atwater doesn't remember bleeding as badly as McMoneagle recalls. See also McMoneagle, *The Stargate Chronicles*.

285 feelings of sorrow and loss: Interview with McMoneagle; McMoneagle, *The Stargate Chronicles*, 138–139.

285 help him relax: FOIA, CIA: "Timeline, Secret: Date /Event/ Comments," Sept 77–Jan 31, 1986; interview with Atwater.

286 out-of-body experience: Star Gate Collection, CIA: "Information Paper, The Monroe Institute of Applied Sciences," January 5, 1984.

287 "second body": Robert A. Monroe, *Journeys out of the Body*, 101.

287 "unbearable ecstasy": Ibid., 197.

287 copies of her husband's journal entries: Ronald Russell, *The Journey of Robert Monroe: From Out-of-Body Explorer to Consciousness Pioneer*, 41.

287 Monroe's sexual escapades: Puharich used the pseudonym "Bob Rame" for Robert Monroe.

287 "The woolly world of consciousness": Russell, *The Journey of Robert Monroe*, 148.

288 Institute's first official U.S. Army client: Star Gate Collection, CIA: "To Det. G, Director, Individual Training Requirements–Joe, from Command Psychologist, LTC Hartzell," April 13, 1982.

289 McMoneagle recalls: Star Gate Collection, CIA: Ibid.

289 in pursuit of a new goal: McMoneagle, *The Stargate Chronicles*, 159.

289 "broaden his perception of reality": Ibid., 160–162.

289 In hindsight: Interview with Graff.

290 "improve human capability": Star Gate Collection, CIA, "Army Science Board Report of Panel on Emerging Human Technologies," Office of the Assistant Secretary of the Army, Washington D.C., December 1983, E-3, E-5.

290 "electrical effect": Ibid., E-5.

290 findings presented to Pentagon officials: Ibid., B-1.

290 Green read...[Stubblebine] disagreed and overruled: Interview with Green; interview with Alexander; Author FOIA, Army INSCOM,

"High Performance Task Force, Hemispheric Synchronization,"
294–296.

292 Human Use Review Board: Author FOIA, CIA: "Contractor
Human Use Review Board," Enclosure 2, undated. For a longer
discussion of why and how the Nuremberg Code came into effect,
see Annie Jacobsen, *Operation Paperclip.*

292 redesign the Gateway seminar: Star Gate Collection, CIA:
"Information Paper, The Monroe Institute of Applied Sciences,
Rapid Acquisition Personnel Training (RAPT)," January 5, 1984.

293 Steven Shaw walked up to the microphone: *An Honest Liar* starts at
minute 53:00.

293 "the slyest scientific hoax in years": Philip J. Hilts, "Magicians Score a
Hit On Scientific Researchers," *Washington Post*, March 1, 1983.

293 "Randi was very upset": *An Honest Liar* starts at minute 59:00.

294 Gardner...spoke out: Martin Gardner, *The New Age: Notes of a
Fringe-Watcher,* 16.

294 "gross distortions" of the facts: Author FOIA, CIA: "Defense
Intelligence Agency Background paper for Dr. Vorona, Recent
Adverse Publicity on Parapsychology Research," March 4, 1983, 1.

294 hoax did affect the INSCOM program: Interview with Alexander.

294 Doug Henning: Interview with Alexander; John Harrison,
Spellbound: The Wonder-Filled Life of Doug Henning, ii.

295 "Magic is something that happens": Myrna Oliver, "Magician Doug
Henning Dies of Liver Cancer at 52," *Los Angeles Times,* February 9,
2000.

Chapter Eighteen: Psychic Training

296 *What am I doing here?*: Interview with Graff.

298 Soviet officials became suspicious: Dusko Doder, "Soviet Stop
Building U.S. Embassy Over Use of Bugging Detector," *Washington
Post,* May 27, 1983. The story suggested that the alleged bugging
detector machine was an excuse for Soviet workers to walk off the
job over what was really a pay dispute.

299 where Graff and his team should look for bugs: Interview with
Atwater.

299 Committee on Intelligence: Elaine Sciolino, "The Bugged Embassy Case: What Went Wrong," *New York Times,* November 15, 1988.

299 Smith arrived at Fort Meade: Interview with Paul Smith.

300 symbols representing an idea: Author FOIA, CIA: Project Officer, "Coordinate Remote Viewing, Stages I-VI and Beyond," February 1985, Appendix A, Glossary.

300 thrilled with the prospect: Smith, *Reading the Enemy's Mind,* 142.

301 the Center: Dames, *Tell Me What You See,* 162–165.

302 people who were already dead: Star Gate Collection, CIA: "Advanced Training with MIAS [Monroe Institute of Applied Sciences]," January 5, 1984.

302 a trained psychologist: One of the therapists, Jan Northrup, was married to John Alexander, Stubblebine's chief of staff for esoteric technologies.

302 "The general had a lot of really far-out ideas": Interview with John Alexander.

303 "Will there be a terrorist attack": Interview with Smith; Smith, *Reading the Enemy's Mind,* 150–151.

304 One week she might be writing: Interviews with Angela Dellafiora; interview with Scott Carmichael.

304 her twin sister's astrologer: Interview with Dellafiora.

304 born in Coral: Interview with Dellafiora. See also Carmichael, *Unconventional Method*, 31–32.

305 Bordas offered adult education classes: "ESP and Parapsychology," *Indiana Gazette,* August 15, 1980.

306 "approach new technology with an open mind": Interview with Dellafiora; Author FOIA, Army INSCOM, "High Performance Task Force, High Performance Programs Information, Human Potential," I-11.

306 Dellafiora recalls: Interview with Dellafiora.

307 Court documents indicate: Smith Papers, "Summarized Record of Trial and accompanying papers of David A. Morehouse, Major, Headquarters and Headquarters Company, 82nd Airborne Division, U.S. Army, Fort Bragg, North Carolina," Cross-Examination of

Colonel Dennis Kowal, MSC, 69–71. Interview with Alexander; Smith, *Reading the Enemy's Mind,* 198.

307 "He had a lot of strange ideas": Interview with Graff.
Of Dellafiora he wrote: Smith Papers, "Summarized Record of Trial and accompanying papers of David A. Morehouse, Major," Cross-Examination of Colonel Dennis Kowal, MSC, 46–51, 73–74.

Chapter Nineteen: The Woman with the Third Eye

309 so did NSA: Star Gate Collection, CIA: Memorandum for Dr. Willis Ware, Chairman and [redacted], Member of Committee, Retired from NSA (former Crypto Manager): "NSA Scientific Advisory Committee, CIA presentation, DIA presentations, SRI presentation," n.d.

310 rounds of negotiations: Smith, *Reading the Enemy's Mind,* 227.

310 "implications are revolutionary": Star Gate Collection, CIA: Memo from Chief, POG [Redacted] to DT (Dr. Vorona), Subject: Sun Streak, Ops/Tng Objectives," September 19, 1985; Project Sun Streak: Psychoenergetics, "A Memorandum of Agreement," September 18, 1984.

311 When McMoneagle retired: Interview with McMoneagle; McMoneagle, *The Stargate Chronicles,* 189.

311 "charges of pseudoscience": Interview with Graff.

312 training protocols: "Co-ordinate Remote Viewing (CRV) 1981–1983," Briefing (SRI), August 4, 1983, 3, 9.

312 Swann's declassified summary: Star Gate Collection, CIA: "Coordinate Remote Viewing (Theory and Dynamics)," n.d., handwritten, July 14, 1988, 2.

313 Smith recalls what happened: Interview with Smith.

314 National Security Council briefings: Star Gate Collection, CIA: "Defense Intelligence Agency, Project Sun Streak, Presentation: DIA's Motivation for Pursuing this Program," Slide: Tulum Ruins, Mexico [photograph of physical site], Viewer's Response [photograph of clay model by McNear], ID.:13L3162-2; interview with Tom McNear (to verify that this was his model).

314 "he is better than me": Jim Marrs, *PSI Spies: The True Story of America's Psychic Warfare Program,* 157.

314 how-to manual: Star Gate Collection, CIA: "Coordinate Remote Viewing, Stages I–VI and Beyond," February 1985.

315 The higher-ups wanted: McMoneagle, *The Stargate Chronicles,* 172–173.

315 "tearing the unit apart": Star Gate Collection, CIA: Comments: Sun Streak Review Status, August 6, 1986 (FOIA, 5 pages); Smith, *Reading the Enemy's Mind,* 259.

315 officially transferred: Star Gate Collection, CIA: "Key Action Status, 1985, Developing Phase, Working Paper, Basic Training, 6 Stages, Drawing/Art Exercises" (undated, 12 pages); Smith, *Reading the Enemy's Mind,* 245.

316 made him and every other soldier wince: Interviews with Smith and Atwater.

317 called her a witch: Interview with Smith; Schnabel, *Remote Viewers: The Secret History of America's Psychic Spies,* Chapter 21: The Witches.

319 Great Pyramid at Giza: Star Gate Collection, CIA: Log notes, Remote Viewing Data Session, 05/10/87. Remote Viewer: GP, Interviewer, ED. CRV. Actual Site, Cheops Pyramid.

319 Madison Square Garden: Star Gate Collection, CIA: Log notes, Remote Viewing Data Session, 20/02/87. Remote Viewer: MR, Interviewer, ED. CRV. Actual Site: Madison Square Garden.

321 read the description: Star Gate Collection, CIA: Global Beacon, November 24, 1986, Viewer 079, 12 pages.

322 "Source reported": Ibid.

323 Atwater was impressed: Star Gate Collection, CIA: Global Beacon, December 22, 1986, Viewer 079, 14 pages.

324 Devil's Tower: Star Gate Collection, CIA: Global Beacon, January 30, 1987, Viewer 079, 11 pages.

326 "Soviets were pursuing": Gates, *From the Shadows,* 265.

326 "large metal structures": Smith, *Reading the Enemy's Mind,* 295.

327 Sary Shagan: Star Gate Collection, CIA: "Summary—1987, Overall Data Evaluation—Operational Projects, 8701–8719," undated; Sun

Streak Annual Report, 1987, undated; also interviews with Smith, Dellafiora, Graff; Smith, *Reading the Enemy's Mind,* 297.

328 tensions in the unit: Interview with Smith. Viewers began talking among themselves; some, including Paul Smith, wondered aloud if Angela wasn't cheating. "I don't have the records to prove it," Smith wrote of his experiences at this time, but "I suspect [she was] being frontloaded," meaning that someone was giving her information about the target before she viewed it.

328 "It can happen to anyone": McMoneagle, *The Stargate Chronicles,* 224.

328 anomaly targets: Interview with Atwater; interview with Graff.

329 "Secret Working Papers": Author FOIA, CIA: "Secret Working Papers, Psi Operational Capability," n.d, six pages. Dale Graff reviewed the papers and identified the author as Jim Salyer, who also served as the DIA's onsite contract manager at SRI.

Chapter Twenty: The End of an Era

330 Jacques Vallée resigned: Interview with Vallée, one-third of Vallée's start-ups reached the public markets. They include SangStat Medical, a biotechnology firm based in California and France; Accuray, a medical device company specializing in robotic surgery; Ixys, a power semiconductor firm; and Ubique, Inc., a web teleconferencing company (acquired by AOL).

331 "I was suicidal": Deborah Petit, "Mitchell Doubts Fathering Child, Wants Case to End," *Sun Sentinel,* August 17, 1985; Matt Schudel, "The Dark Side of the Moon: Edgar Mitchell Has Walked on the Moon and Explored Inner Space. It's Everyday Life That Gives Him Trouble," *Sun Sentinel,* January 8, 1988.

331 Randi had also fallen on difficult times: Adam Higginbotham, "The Disillusionist: The Unbelievable Skepticism of James Randi," *New York Times Magazine,* November 7, 2014.

332 "Randi resigned in fury": Ibid.; interview with Higginbotham.

332 divining information: Interview with Geller.

332 map dowsing fee: Margaret van Hatten, "A Cost-effective Account of the Spoons," *Financial Times,* January 18, 1986. Van Hatten states

that Geller's £1 million per job figure was confirmed with Peter Sterling, chairman of Zanes, the Australian mineral company. "Uri Geller's Hidden Agenda (Prospecting)," *Virgin West Coast,* April/May 1997; interview with Geller.

332 Geller and Kampelman shaking hands: Geller photos, private collection.

333 verified the story: Jonathan Margolis, *The Secret Life of Uri Geller,* 101.

333 "the state of their minds": Geller, *Geller Effect,* 157; interview with Geller.

334 Nuala Pell later said: Margolis, *The Secret Life,* 102.

334 the president said: Ronald Reagan, "Statement on Intermediate-Range Nuclear Force Reductions, March 6, 1987," Public Papers of the Presidents of the United States: Ronald Reagan, 1987.

334 top of the rotunda: Interview with Geller; interview with Alexander.

335 "In a vault in an attic of the Capitol": "Washington Whispers," *U.S. News & World Report,* May 4, 1987.

335 "What the future would bring": Interview with Geller.

335 Al Gore's house: Interview with Geller; interview with Hanna Geller, who recalled many details including the Gores' giving them a CD of the Irish singer Enya.

335 declined to comment: E-mail exchange with Rob Hamilton, Communications Coordinator, the Office of Al Gore, July 2016. John Alexander confirmed that in 1983, he taught Gore and several other members of Congress NLP skills, as part of an INSCOM training program.

335 the advice of a private astrologer: Donald T. Regan, *For the Record,* 3.

335 "President Reagan [is] deeply interested in astrology": Steven V. Roberts, "White House Confirms Reagans Follow Astrology, Up to a Point," *New York Times,* May 4, 1988; Joyce Wadler et al., "The President's Astrologers," *People,* May 23, 1988.

336 "The Scriptures say": "Reagan Wishes More Dignified Job for Son Ron," United Press International, June 30, 1986.

336 largest massed naval strength: Star Gate Collection, CIA: "Conflict in the Persian Gulf, 1987 Year in Review," United Press International, 1987.

337 "Project P": Star Gate Collection, CIA: "Sun Streak Report— Third Quarter CY 87," to Dr. Vorona, October 15, 1987.

338 alien "visitation" alleged: Star Gate Collection, CIA: "Remote Viewing Session Data," Remote Viewer: LB, Interviewer: Ed, Site 0143.

338 "possible UFO encounter": Star Gate Collection, CIA: "Remote Viewing Session Data," Remote Viewer: LB, Interviewer: Ed, Site 0234.

338 Supreme Galactic Council of Aliens: Star Gate Collection, CIA: "Description of Personnel Associated 'ET' Bases [sic]," January 28, 1987.

338 bogus targets: Smith, *Reading the Enemy's Mind*, 343.

339 "inhabitants of the distant future": Monroe, *Far Journey*, 226.

340 morale took another hit: Interviews with Atwater, Smith, Dellafiora, Graff. Ed Dames declined to be interviewed.

340 encrypted coordinates: Smith, *Reading the Enemy's Mind*, 276.

340 system being gamed: Interview with Puthoff.

341 Smith became angry: Interview with Smith; see also Smith, *Reading the Enemy's Mind*, 353.

342 "Protocol forbade me": Ibid., 303.

343 "He was clearly bored": Ibid., 304; Star Gate Collection, CIA: "Subject: SUN STREAK—Annual Report, 1987," January 19, 1988.

344 a "divine blessing": "What the Iran-Iraq War can Teach US Officials," *Middle East Forum* 20, no. 2 (Spring, 2013).

345 "some religious issues": Graff interview. This was confirmed in interviews with Dr. Kit Green, who says he encountered similar resistance. "There were individuals who were religious fundamentalists," Graff says.

345 "Remote viewing the future": Star Gate Collection, CIA: "Memo: Sun Streak Report—Third Quarter CY 87," To: DT (Dr. Vorona), Oct 15, 1987.

Chapter Twenty-One: Hostages and Drugs

346 Shiite terrorist organization, Hezbollah: U.S. District Court, District
   of Columbia, *Robin L. Higgins et al. v. Islamic Republic of Iran et al.,*
   April 21, 2008, 2–4.

347 to discuss procedures: The organization was the UN Truce
   Supervision Organization (UNTSO).

347 high-value hostage: Andrew Rosenthal, "Before His Abduction,
   Higgins Talked of Risks," *New York Times,* August 1, 1989.

347 DIAC officials asked the viewers: Interview with Graff.

347 "The nature of this operation": Interview with Louis Andre.

348 confident about the location: Interviews with Graff; interview with
   Dellafiora; interview with Smith.

349 "Higgins *had* been on water": Interview with Graff; interview with
   Dellafiora.

349 had died before he'd been hanged: Interview with Carmichael.

350 at times like this: Interview with Graff.

350 an anthology of reports: Star Gate Collection, CIA: "Site: Galactic
   Federation HQs, Coords: 1698/1009, Session 13 Jan 88." Drawings
   include UFOs, architectural plans, and robed figures.

350 received no recommendations: Smith, *Reading the Enemy's Mind,*
   382; interview with Graff. Smith writes that Dames was transferred
   into "an even more secretive unit [at INSCOM] from which he
   retired on October 1, 1991."

351 Fern Gauvin wrote: Smith Papers, "Administrative Data,
   Performance Evaluation," Morehouse, David A., Cpt." May 24, 1989
   and April 30, 1990.

351 odd behavior: Smith, *Reading the Enemy's Mind,* 390; interview with
   Dellafiora, Graff.

351 predicted by Jim Salyer: Star Gate Collection, CIA: "Secret Working
   Papers, Psi Operational Capability," 5, undated (6 pages).

352 merely office politics: Interviews with Dellafiora, Smith, Graff. In
   Smith's book, he writes that office secretary Jeannie Betters stated that
   over a two-year period Morehouse was absent from the unit "in the
   neighborhood of 150 days." Smith, *Reading the Enemy's Mind,* 390.

352 Standards of Conduct: Army Regulation 600-50, Standards of Conduct for Department of the Army Personnel, January 28, 1988; USAREC Regulation 600-25, Prohibited and Regulated Activities.

352 official performance evaluations: Smith Papers, "Administrative Data, Performance Evaluation," Morehouse, David A., Major." April 12, 1991.

352 downfall of the entire program: Interview with Dellafiora, Smith, Atwater, Graff; Smith, *Reading the Enemy's Mind,* 390. Morehouse finished training and worked for fourteen months, through December 1989.

353 "Remote Map Sensing is": Star Gate Collection, CIA: "Applied Remote Map Sensing Protocol," n.p., n.d.

353 "The Study Guide": Ibid.

353 Smith went the extra mile: Smith, *Reading the Enemy's Mind,* 355.

353 "I used my finger": Interview with Dellafiora.

353 "big loads" of cocaine: Star Gate Collection, CIA: 30 JUL 92 Task/ Target Number:-92-77-T, RV 079; and to search for and locate cocaine kingpin Pablo Escobar.

354 Switch Plate: Star Gate Collection, CIA: "Switch Plate Indoctrination, Key Security Principles," n.p., n.d.

354 "highly sensitive collection technique": Star Gate Collection, CIA: "Information about Switch Plate Tasking/Reporting/Evaluation," n.p., 5 of 7.

355 DIA advised: Ibid., 6.

356 given a prompt: Interview with Graff; interview with Dellafiora.

357 "The officials declined": Stephen Engelberg, "U.S. Says Libya Moves Chemicals for Poison Gas Away from Plant," *New York Times,* January 4, 1989.

357 Charles Jordan: Dale Graff Papers; interviews with Graff and Dellafiora.

358 Viewer 095: Star Gate Collection, CIA: [redacted] Interim report— 8916, April 26, 1989, Chief Scientists, Defense Intelligence Agency.

359 "I told Fern": Interview with Dellafiora.

360 982 counternarcotics sessions: Star Gate Collection, CIA: "Statistical Analysis – CY 90," 2 pages, n.d.

361 the most interesting: Interview with Smith.

361 "human consciousness/subconscious interaction": Star Gate
Collection, CIA: "Star Gate Summary," Enclosure to S-20, 535/
DT-S, May 15, 1991, 4.

362 "efforts by the Soviets and the Chinese": Ibid., 2.

363 only three remote viewers were left: Ed May continued to lead the
research arm of the program, with Ken Bell and Joe McMoneagle
working as his viewers. The last DIA team included Dellafiora,
Robin Dahlgren, Lyn Buchanan, and a civilian male, Greg Seward,
who signed on in November 2, 1989. Buchanan was transitioned to
computer technician and database manager, which reduced the
viewing team to three.

363 annual intelligence exchange: Graff interview; Graff e-mail, March
4, 2016.

363 future of the Star Gate program: Interview with Graff, Dellafiora,
Smith; Smith, *Reading the Enemy's Mind,* 432.

Chapter Twenty-Two: Downfall

364 Twenty-three-year history: program started in late 1972 at SRI and was
officially canceled by CIA on June 31, 1995.

364 Associated Press: "U.N. Enlists Psychic Firm to Find Iraqi's Weapon
Sites," November 19, 191.

365 legal documents: Dane Spotts, individually and assignee of PSI TECH
INTERNATIONAL, INC. a corporation, Plaintiff, vs. EDWARD
A. DAMES and JANE DOE DAMES, a marital community; and
FREDERIC M. BONSALL, a single person, In the Superior Court of
the State of Washington and For the County of King, June 15, 2001;
Smith, *Reading the Enemy's Mind,* 425.

365 "I agreed": Interview with Smith; see also Smith, *Reading the
Enemy's Mind,* 424–426.

366 fallout was tremendous: Interview with Alexander; interview with Graff.

366 Jim Marrs to write an exposé: In 1993, Joe McMoneagle published
Mind Trek, in which he disguised the government's role.

366 "way beyond his comfort level": Interviews with Dellafiora, Smith,
and Graff. Morehouse declined to be interviewed.

366 The military charges against him: Smith Papers, "Summarized Record of Trial and accompanying papers of David A. Morehouse, Major, Headquarters and Headquarters Company, 82nd Airborne Division, U.S. Army, Fort Bragg, North Carolina by General Court-Martial," convened by Commanding General, Headquarters, 82nd Airborne Division, tried at Fort Bragg, North Carolina on June 20, 1994 and August 26, 1994 and November 4, 1994.

367 "Major Morehouse is the smartest": Smith Papers, "Administrative Data, Performance Evaluation, Service School Academic Evaluation Report," Morehouse, David A., Major." June 5, 1992.

367 court-martial hearing at Fort Bragg: Ibid.; interviews with Dellafiora, Graff.

368 "The entire situation was absurd": Interviews with Dellafiora, Graff.

368 early April 1994: Smith Papers, "Summarized Record of Trial and accompanying papers of David A. Morehouse," June 20, 1994. Trial transcripts state Morehouse was "at Walter Reed Army Medical Center from about the 2d of April."

368 evil demons possessed him: Morehouse, *Psychic Warrior,* 196–197, 199.

368 Smith recalls: Interview with Smith; also see Smith, *Reading the Enemy's Mind,* 439–440.

369 Morehouse was transferred: Morehouse, *Psychic Warrior,* 228.

369 Sanity Board concluded: Smith Papers, "Summarized Record of Trial and accompanying papers of David A. Morehouse," Appellate Exhibit III, June 8, 1994.

369 *60 Minutes* producer: Howard Rosenberg, as quoted in Smith, *Reading the Enemy's Mind,* 442.

370 "Under Other than Honorable Conditions": Smith Papers, "Memorandum for Commander, 82nd Airborne Division, Fort Bragg, NC. Subject, Dismissal of Charges – U.S. v. Maj. David A. Morehouse, HHC, 82nd Airborne Division, Fort Bragg, NC." Department of the Army, January 2, 1995.

370 "sources or origins of the phenomenon": Star Gate Collection, CIA: "An Evaluation of the Remote Viewing Program: Research and

Operational Applications," Draft report, prepared by the American Institutes for Research, September 22, 1995, E-4.

370 "One must question": Ibid., E-4, E-5.

370 psychologist Ray Hyman: Hyman declined to be interviewed.

371 randomly chosen remote viewers: Smith, *Reading the Enemy's Mind,* 449.

371 to travel to CIA headquarters: Interview with Dellafiora.

371 "It just didn't feel appropriate": Gilbert A. Lewthwaite and Tom Bowman, "Pentagon employed psychic spy unit: Fort Meade program sought to 'divine' intelligence data," *Baltimore Sun,* November 30, 1995.

372 filth and feral cats: "Elderly Scientist Ordered Evicted from Reynolds Estate Dies in Fall," *Winston-Salem Journal,* January 4, 1995.

Chapter Twenty-Three: Intuition, Premonition, and Synthetic Telepathy

377 Wolfgang Pauli and the psychiatrist Carl Jung: C. J. Jung, *Synchronicity,* 19.

378 the CIA concluded in 1975: Author FOIA, CIA: "An Overview of Extrasensory Perception," January 27, 1975.

378 "paranormality could be rejected a priori": Star Gate Collection, CIA: John Palmer, "An Evaluative Report on the Current Status of Parapsychology, Army Research Institute for the Behavioral and Social Sciences," May 1986.

378 "Remote viewing is vague and ambiguous": Star Gate Collection, CIA: "An Evaluation of the Remote Viewing Program: Research and Operational Applications: Draft Report, American Institutes for Research, September 22, 1995. Conclusion, E-4.

379 first began researching ESP: Since then, discoveries in the electromagnetic spectrum have included space communications (1960), lasers (1957), fiber optics (1980), and compact terahertz radiation devices (2007). Terahertz radiation was discovered in 1896.

379 Copernican heliocentrism: NASA says Aristarchus of Samos was the first known person to propose that the Sun was the center of the universe, which he did in the third century BC.

380 "Spidey sense": Eric Beidel, "More than a Feeling: ONR Investigates 'Spidey Sense' for Sailors and Marines," Office of Naval Research, Corporate Strategic Communications, March 27, 2014.

381 "preempt snipers, IED emplacers": Joseph Channing, "U.S. Navy Program to Study How Troops Use Intuition," *New York Times,* March 27, 2012. Note: Richburg sensed that a man had planted a bomb and evacuated the area before the explosion. "The bomb definitely would have killed some people," said Maj. John Stark, a liaison officer to the Iraqi army.

381 the stigma of ESP and PK: The British journalist Jon Ronson's satirical book, *The Men Who Stare at Goats* (2005), and the movie of the same name (2009) enhanced negative perception of remote viewing.

381 "sensemaking": Office of Naval Research Warfighter Performance Department, Exhibit Fact Sheet: Combat Hunter Computer-Based Trainer; ONR Exhibit Fact Sheet: Virtual Observation Platform: Enhanced Perceptual Training. Sensemaking is also called anticipatory thinking.

381 followed McMoneagle's lead: Kress, "Parapsychology in Intelligence," *Studies in Intelligence* 21 (Winter 1977): 8.

382 Power Dreaming session: The Power Dreaming tour can be seen on YouTube. Power Dreaming software, developed by Naval Hospital Bremerton and ICF International, is designed to help sufferers of post-traumatic stress disorder deal with emotional stressors by creating a sense of control within a virtual reality setting. The Power Dreaming creed reminds the warrior trainee of their code: "There is profound honor in confronting the pain the mind must endure that is born of a warrior's sacrifice."

383 Can humans alter: E-mail correspondence with Kit Green: "one can also clearly argue that even the resulting electrical, and adjacent modulation of tissues even not physically connected to a network are thus influenced by 'ephaptic' currents...are matter...even the electrons."

383 qigong "unproven as medicine": Roger Jahnke et al., "A Comprehensive Review of Health Benefits of Qigong and Tai Chi,"

National Center for Biotechnology, National Institutes of Health, July–August, 2010.

384 Scientific skeptics: Peter Huston, "China, Chi, and Chicanery: Examining Traditional Chinese Medicine and Chi Theory," *Skeptical Inquirer* 19, no. 5 (September–October 1995).

384 *Dictionary*'s author: Robert T. Carroll, "Transcendental Meditation," *The Skeptic's Dictionary,* available online. The "one study" Carroll cites is listed as Alberto Perez-De-Abeniz and Jeremy Holmes, "Meditation: Concepts, Effects and Uses in Therapy," *International Journal of Psychotherapy* 5, no. 1 (March 2000): 10, 49.

385 "soldiers [to] communicate by thought alone": Jacobsen, *The Pentagon's Brain,* 311–312; "Statement of Dr. Eric Eisenstadt, Defense Sciences Office (DSO), Brain Machine Interface," DARPATech '99 Conference.

385 "tell machines": Eko Armunanto, "Artificial telepathy to create Pentagon's telepathic soldiers," *Digital Journal,* May 10, 2013.

385 says program director Michael D'Zmura: "Scientists to study synthetic telepathy," Phys.org, August 13, 2008.

385 "brainwave control device": Edmond M. Dewan, "Occipital Alpha Rhythm Eye Position and Lens Accommodation," *Nature* 214, (June 3, 1967): 975–977.

386 "Man's Brain Waves Can 'Talk'": Howard Simons, "Man's Brain Waves Can 'Talk' Overcoming Speech Barriers," *Washington Post,* October 21, 1964.

386 similar studies are under way: Correspondence with Andrea Stocco; R. Rao, et. al., "A Direct Brain-to-Brain Interface in Humans," PLUS One, November 5, 2014.

386 "Evolution has spent": Deborah Bach, "UW team links two human brains for question-and-answer experiment," *UW Today,* September 23, 2015.

387 "involved technology, not ESP": Interview with Dr. Alvaro Pascual-Leone.

387 Dr. Pascual-Leone said: "Direct brain-to-brain communication demonstrated in human subjects," Beth Israel Deaconess Medical Center, Press Release, September 3, 2014.

Chapter Twenty-Four: The Scientists and the Skeptics

388 100-Year Starship project: Interviews with Hal Puthoff, Eric Davis; Sharon Weinberger, "100 Year Starship: An interstellar leap for mankind?," BBC Future (BBC.com), March 22, 2012.

389 fighting claims by skeptics: Interview with Lawrence Krauss, astrophysicist, who labeled Puthoff a "fringe scientist."

389 whether it can be harnessed: This section is from interviews with Puthoff, as well as his essay "Physics and Metaphysics as Co-emergent Phenomena," published as a chapter in S. Savva, ed., *Life and Mind,* Trafford Publishing, Victoria, BC, Canada, 2006.

389 "the 'Holy Grail' of energy research": H. E. Puthoff, "SETI, the velocity-of-light limitation, and the Alcubierre warp drive: An integrating overview," *Physics Essays* 9 (1996): 156; H. E. Puthoff, "Space propulsion: Can empty space itself provide a solution?" *Ad Astra* 9 (1997): 42; H. E. Puthoff, "Can the vacuum be engineered for spaceflight applications? Overview of theory and experiments," *Journal of Scientific Exploration* 12 (1998): 295; H. E. Puthoff, "Engineering the zero-point field and polarizable vacuum for interstellar flight," *Journal of the British Interplanetary Society* 55 (2002): 137.

389 a trip to Mars: William B. Scott, "To the Stars: Zero-point energy emerges from realm of science fiction, may be key to deep-space travel," *Aviation Week & Space Technology,* March 1, 2004.

389 NASA's current figure: "Mars Program Planning Group Frequently Asked Questions," nasa.gov.

390 Krauss called Puthoff a "crackpot": Interview with Lawrence Krauss. It's worth noting that Krauss himself has plenty of critics. In *Scientific American,* in a November 20, 2015, article titled "Is Lawrence Krauss a Physicist, or Just a Bad Philosopher?" John Horgan interviewed physicist George Ellis (who co-wrote with Stephen Hawking the classic work *The Large Scale Structure of Space-Time*) about Krauss's work: "What he is presenting is not tested science," said Ellis. "It's a philosophical speculation, which he apparently believes is so compelling he does not have to give any specification of evidence that would confirm it is true."

390 "pre-scientific concept of a cosmic energy": H. E. Puthoff, "Physics and Metaphysics as Co-emergent Phenomena," in Savva, *Life and Mind;* H. E. Puthoff, "Source of vacuum electromagnetic zero-point energy," *Physical Review* A, Vol. 40 (1989): 4857.

390 In pursuit of this theory: Interview with Puthoff; interview with Davis. Davis has been at the lab since he completed a Teleportation Study for the Defense Department. Of his work, he says: "All of my work for Hal since late 2004 has been on further developing the Einstein general relativistic theory and the quantum field theory (per the physics of the quantum vacuum) for faster-than-light space propulsion via warp drives and traversable wormholes. This research portfolio also includes the study of time machines, alternatives to black holes, quantum vacuum zero-point fluctuations and their manifestations and impact on the universe, and the impact of quantum entanglement and teleportation on the structure of space-time (and eventually its role on consciousness). So the physics of consciousness and psychic phenomena are super interesting to me, though low on my research priorities because my faster-than-light interstellar flight studies are very high priority right now due to my connections to NASA and the DoD."

391 Tsien's primary role: "Tsien Hsue-shen, 2007 Person of the Year," *Aviation Week & Space Technology,* January 7, 2008.

391 *New Scientist* named Tsien: Top Ten Influential Space Thinkers, *New Scientist,* September 5, 2007.

392 Kaku explains quantum entanglement: Brent Baughman, "Scientists Take Quantum Steps Toward Teleportation," NPR, *All Things Considered,* August 1, 2010.

392 "the nature of this profound phenomenon": "The Experiment That Will Allow Humans to 'See' Quantum Entanglement," *MIT Technology Review,* February 17, 2016.

393 He discussed the data: Graff, remarks at the Quantum Retrocausation III symposium at the University of California, San Diego, June 15–16, 2016; interview with Graff. Each day an Associated Press photograph appears on page A6 in Graff's local paper, the *Reading Eagle.* On the top half of that page the paper runs

"News across the Nation," and on the bottom half runs "News across the World." In the lower right-hand corner is the photograph. Graff confirmed with the editor that the photo has nothing to do with either local or world news; it's arbitrarily selected from the AP pool.

394 "There is an underlying reality": Interview with Graff.

395 an active military and intelligence science adviser: Interview with Green; Biographical Sketch of Committee Members, National Academies Press.

395 examine the future of military science and brain research: Green et al.,"Emerging Cognitive Neuroscience and Related Technologies of the Committee on Military and Intelligence Methodology for Emergent Neurophysiological and Cognitive/Neural Research in the Next Two Decades," (2008) 15–51.

395 asked to join a classified science advisory board: Interview with Green. Clapper, a retired general, served as the director of the Defense Intelligence Agency during the last four years of the remote-viewing program.

396 Hillary Clinton spoke of UAPs: Al Vicens, "Hillary Clinton Is Serious About UFOs," *Mother Jones,* March 25, 2016. Clinton told Jimmy Kimmel, "There's a new name—it's 'unexplained aerial phenomenon'. UAP, that's the latest nomenclature."

396 when working with Uri Geller: Interview with Green; interview with Vallée. There are some issues involving when, exactly, this happened. The LLNL physicist Ron Hawke says it occurred in late 1974; Vallée (not present, but privy to info) writes about it in his journal in March 1975.

397 "Common injuries": Green has publicly referred to his pro bono work in only one place, as one line in his biography at the International Remote Viewing Association (IRVA) website.

398 run by Garry Nolan: Information about the Nolan Lab and Garry Nolan is available at the Stanford University website. Nolan is presently the Rachford and Carlota A. Harris Professor in the Department of Microbiology and Immunology at Stanford University School of Medicine.

401 "I believe in a personal God": Alexander Carpenter, "Martin Gardner on Philosophical Theism, Adventists and Price," *Spectrum,* October 17, 2008. This interview with Gardner is available online courtesy of Cambridge University Press (spectrummagazine.org).

401 "God is the Great Magician": Martin Gardner, *The Whys of a Philosophical Scrivener,* 184.

401 hoax involved a federal crime: Interview with Adam Higginbotham; Higginbotham, "The Disillusionist: The Unbelievable Skepticism of James Randi," *New York Times Magazine,* November 7, 2014.

402 "I felt like a phony": Justin Weinstein and Tyler Measom, *An Honest Liar* documentary.

402 "Never!" he shouted: Interview with James Randi; Geller's ashes: Michael J. Mooney, "The God of Skeptics," *Miami New Times,* August 27, 2009.

Chapter Twenty-Five: The Psychic and the Astronaut

403 Netanyahu said: TV Interview with Prime Minister Netanyahu, Ukrainian TV. This is footage in Geller's private collection.

406 suggested as its central thesis: Vikram Jayanti, *The Secret Life of Uri Geller—Psychic Spy?* BBC Two documentary.

406 I record interviews: Interviews with Uri Geller, Hanna Geller, Shipi Shtrang.

409 Geller's ESP and PK abilities: Interview with Amnon Rubinstein in Tel Aviv. Rubinstein was a member of the Knesset, the legislative branch of the Israeli government, between 1977 and 2002.

409 a violent time in Israel: Diaa Hadid, "American Graduate Student Killed in Stabbing Rampage Near Tel Aviv," *New York Times,* March 8, 2016; Oren Liebermann, "American fatally stabbed in Israel terror attack that wounds ten others," CNN, March 9, 2016.

413 Netanyahu was quoted as saying: Isabel Kershner, "Israelis Find New Tunnel from Gaza into Israel," *New York Times,* April 18, 2016.

413 "My gut tells me": Interview with Dan Williams. In my 2016 interview with map dowser Louis Matacia, the former Army surveyor who famously taught Marines how to dowse for Viet Cong

tunnels during the Vietnam War, Matacia told me that in 2005, he'd gone to Israel to help security forces dowse for tunnels along the southern border with Gaza. I confirmed this with a former Air Force colonel named Ron Blackburn, who was also on the mission. Terrorist organizations like Hamas regularly dig tunnels from the Gaza Strip into Israeli territory, and now ISIS is reportedly doing the same thing in Syria.

415 Mitchell explains: Interview with Mitchell.

418 map on the Moon: United States Geological Survey map, 2-LS-1/ EVA-2, Apollo 14 Image Library, Landing Site Maps (hq.nasa.gov). Looking at this map, on the Moon, Mitchell said: "No, I think we're coming out of that swale, that valley. As a matter of fact, it's on this map. This darkness in here [east of the crater labeled '720' in the USGS map] is what we were calling (the eastern wall of) that valley. That was a very good depression. And that's where Al's saying it's up the hill. See, there's another one over here, and then we really started up the flank of Cone Crater." From "Climbing Cone Ridge – Where Are We?", Corrected Transcript and Commentary, by Eric M. Jones, NASA, 1995.

418 "I'm in the final stages of my life": Interview with Mitchell.

LIST OF INTERVIEWS AND WRITTEN CORRESPONDENCE

Colonel John B. Alexander, Ph.D. (retired): soldier, scientist; former Green Beret and Special Forces commander, U.S. Army; former director, Advanced Human Technology Office, U.S. Army Intelligence and Security Command (INSCOM); former director of nonlethal weapons, Los Alamos National Laboratory, Los Alamos, NM

Louis Andre: former research director for the Directorate for Intelligence Production, Defense Intelligence Agency

Captain Fred "Skip" Atwater (retired): former operations manager, 902nd Military Intelligence Group, Detachment-G [remote viewing], U.S. Army, INSCOM

Michael Bigelow: Historian, U.S. Army, INSCOM

Hugh Bowden: Head of Department, Department of Classics, Kings College London, London, UK

Deepak Chopra: author, physician; former chief of staff, New England Memorial Hospital, director, the Chopra Center

Eric W. Davis: astrophysicist; scientific consultant, NASA Breakthrough Propulsion Program; consultant, Department of Defense; member, Association of Former Intelligence Officers; fellow, British Interplanetary Society

Brigadier General James L. Dozier (retired): U.S. Army, Deputy Chief of Staff, NATO Southern Command

Don Eyles: engineer; Apollo computer guidance systems, NASA, Charles Stark Draper Laboratory, Cambridge, MA

Irving Finkel: Assistant Keeper of the Ancient Records [Sumerian, Babylonian, and Assyrian script, languages, and cultures], British Museum, London, UK

Angela Dellafiora Ford: civilian intelligence analyst U.S. Army, INSCOM, and Defense Intelligence Agency (retired); remote viewer

Fernand Gauvin: civilian counterintelligence officer, U.S. Army (retired); branch chief, Sun Streak Program, Defense Intelligence Agency

Uri Geller: telepath; research subject: CIA, Department of Defense, Lawrence Livermore National Laboratories

Dale E. Graff: physicist, aeronautical engineer; former chief of the Advanced Missile Systems Forecast Section Wright-Patterson Air Force Base, U.S. Air Force; former director of Advanced Concepts Office, Directorate of Science and Technology, Defense Intelligence Agency; former director of Star Gate Program, Department of Defense

Christopher "Kit" Green: physician, neurophysiologist, CIA (retired); former chairman of the National Academy of Sciences; former chairman of the board, Army Science and Technology Committee; founding member, Defense Intelligence Agency Technology Insight–Gauge, Evaluate, and Review (TIGER) Committee

Brian D. Josephson: physicist, Nobel Laureate (1973); Cavendish Laboratory, University of Cambridge, UK

Serge Kernbach: technologist; director, Research Center of Advanced Robotics and Environmental Science, Stuttgart, Germany; member, Academy of Natural Sciences, Germany

Robert Knight: photographer

Lawrence M. Krauss: theoretical physicist and cosmologist

Louis J. Matacia: dowser; topographical surveyor, U.S. Army (retired)

Chief Warrant Officer Joseph McMoneagle (retired): remote viewer; former senior projects officer, Signals Intelligence and Electronic Warfare, U.S. Army, INSCOM

Lieutenant Colonel Thomas McNear (retired): former counterintelligence officer U.S. Army, remote viewer

Richard Allen Miller: physicist; former consultant, Office of Naval Intelligence

Captain Edgar Mitchell (retired): Apollo 14 astronaut, aeronautical
    engineer; founder, Institute of Noetic Science, Petaluma, CA

Garry Nolan: geneticist, immunologist, biotechnologist; founder and
    chief scientist, Nolan Lab, Stanford University, Stanford, CA

Dr. Alvaro Pascual-Leone: professor of neurology and associate dean for
    Clinical and Translational Research, Harvard Medical School,
    Cambridge, MA

Harold Puthoff: physicist, former scientist, NSA; former chief scientist,
    Biofield Measurements Program [Remote Viewing], Stanford,
    Research Institute, Stanford, CA; former consultant, CIA; chief
    scientist, Institute for Advanced Studies at Austin, TX

James Randi: Canadian-American retired stage magician; scientific
    skeptic

Amnon Rubinstein: law scholar, politician, Israeli government official;
    Minister of Communications, Minister of Science and Technology
    and Space

Jack Sarfatti: theoretical physicist; consultant, 100 Year Starship project,
    DARPA

Caleb A. Scharf: astrobiologist; director of the Astrobiology Center,
    Columbia University, NY

Harrison Schmitt: Apollo 17 astronaut, geologist; U.S. senator, New Mexico

Stephan A. Schwartz: research scientist; former special assistant for
    research and analysis to the Chief of Naval Operations, former
    consultant to the Oceanographer of the Navy

Angela Thompson Smith; former researcher, Princeton Engineering
    Anomalies Research Laboratory, Princeton University, Princeton,
    NJ; remote viewer

Major Paul H. Smith (retired): remote viewer; former electronic warfare
    operator, strategic intelligence officer, U.S. Army, INSCOM; former
    intelligence analyst, Defense Intelligence Agency

Winston Smith: remote viewer

Andrea Stocco: cognitive neuroscientist, Institute for Learning and Brain
    Sciences (I-LABS), University of Washington

Russell Targ: physicist; former codirector, Biofield Measurements
    Program [Remote Viewing], Stanford Research Institute, Stanford,

CA; former consultant, CIA; former senior staff scientist, Lockheed–Martin

Charles T. Tart: psychologist

Jacques Vallée: astrophysicist; venture capitalist; former assistant researcher, Project Blue Book, U.S. Air Force; former principal investigator, (D)ARPA, Department of Defense; former consultant to SRI on Project Grill Flame

Jack Vorona: physicist; former chief scientist for the Directorate of Science and Technology, Defense Intelligence Agency

Dan Williams: journalist; Thomson Reuters senior correspondent for Israel and the Palestinian Territories

Interviews and Discussions with Family Members of Principal Sources

Hanna Geller

Shipi Shtrang

Ginette Matacia Lucas

Stephanie Hurkos

Murleen Ryder

Andrew Puharich

Adrienne Puthoff

Books

Alexander, John B. *Future War: Non-Lethal Weapons in Twenty-First-Century Warfare*. New York: St. Martin's, 1999.

———. UFOs: Myths, Conspiracies, and Realities. New York: St. Martin's, 2011.

Alexander, John B., Richard Groller, and Janet Morris. *The Warrior's Edge*. New York: William Morrow, 1990.

Astor, John Jacob. *A Journey in Other Worlds: A Romance of the Future*. New York: D. Appleton, 1894.

Atwater, F. Holmes. *Captain of My Ship, Master of My Soul: Living with Guidance*. Charlottesville, VA: Hampton Roads Publishing, 2001.

Becker, Robert O., and Gary Selden. *The Body Electric: Electromagnetism and the Foundation of the Life*. New York: Morrow, 1985.

Bird, Christopher. *The Divining Hand: The 500-Year-Old Mystery of Dowsing*. New York: Dutton, 1979.

Bishop, Paul. *The Dionysian Self: C. G. Jung's Reception of Friedrich Nietzsche*. Berlin, New York: W. de Gruyter, 1995.

Bohm, David. *Thought as a System*. New York: Routledge, 1994.

———. *Wholeness and the Implicate Order*. New York: Routledge, 1980.

Bowden, Hugh. *Classical Athens and the Delphic Oracle: Divination and Democracy*. New York: Cambridge University Press, 2007.

Brodeur, Paul. *The Zapping of America: Microwaves, Their Deadly Risk, and the Coverup*. New York: Norton, 1977.

Broughton, Richard S., Ph.D. *Parapsychology: The Controversial Science*. New York: Ballantine, 1991.

Browning, Norma Lee. *Peter Hurkos: I Have Many Lives*. Garden City, NY: Doubleday, 1976.

———. *The Psychic World of Peter Hurkos*. Garden City, NY: Doubleday, 1970.

Carmichael, Scott W. *Unconventional Method*. Seattle, WA: Amazon Digital Services, LLC, 2014.

Chang, Iris. *Thread of the Silkworm*. New York: Basic Books, 1995.

Collin, Richard Oliver, and Gordon L. Freedman. *Winter of Fire: The Abduction of General Dozier and the Downfall of the Red Brigades*. New York: Dutton, 1990.

Dames, Major Ed. and Joel Harry Newman. *Tell Me What You See: Remote Viewing Cases from the World's Premier Psychic Spy*. Hoboken, NJ: John Wiley & Sons, Inc., 2011.

Dayan, Moshe. *Living with the Bible*. New York: William Morrow & Company, Inc., 1978.

Dong, Paul. *China's Major Mysteries: Paranormal Phenomena and the Unexplained in the People's Republic*. San Francisco: China Books and Periodicals, 1996.

Eisenberg, David, M.D., with Thomas Lee Wright. *Encounters with Qi: Exploring Chinese Medicine*. New York: W. W. Norton, 1999.

Epstein, Fritz T. *War-Time Activities of the SS-Ahnenerbe*. London: Vallentine, Mitchell, 1960.

Ferriss, Lloyd, and Rita Harper Stump. *Harry Stump, Maine's Psychic Sculptor*. Rockland, ME: Maine Author's Publishing, 2012.

Flournoy, Theodore. (Translated by Daniel B. Vermilye) *From India to the Planet Mars: A Study of a Case of Somnambulism with Glossolalia*. New York, London: Harper and Brothers Publishers, 1900.

Flowers, Stephen E., Michael Moynihan, and Karl Maria Wiligut. *The Secret King: Karl Maria Wiligut, Himmler's Lord of the Runes*. Waterbury Center, VT: Dominion Press; Smithville, TX: Rûna-Raven Press, 2001.

Gardner, Martin. *Fads and Fallacies in the Name of Science: The Curious Theories of Modern Pseudoscientists and the Strange, Amusing and Alarming Cults that Surround Them. A Study in Human Gullibility*. New York: Dover, 1957.

————. *The New Age: Notes of a Fringe-Watcher*. Buffalo, NY: Prometheus Books, 1988.

Gates, Robert Michael. *From the Shadows: The Ultimate Insider's Story of Five Presidents and How They Won the Cold War*. New York: Simon & Schuster, 1996.

Geller, Uri. *My Story*. New York: Praeger, 1975.

Geller, Uri, and Guy Lyon Playfair. *The Geller Effect*. New York: H. Holt and Co., 1986.

Goudsmit, Samuel A. *The History of Modern Physics, 1900–1950: Volume I: Alsos*. Los Angeles, CA: Tomash Publishers, 1983.

Graff, Dale E. *River Dreams: The Case of the Missing General and Other Adventures in Psychic Research*. Boston: Element Books, 2000.

————. *Tracks in the Psychic Wilderness: An Exploration of Remote Viewing, ESP, Precognitive Dreaming, and Synchronicity*. Boston: Element Books, 1998.

Harrison, John. *Spellbound: The Wonder-filled Life of Doug Henning*. New York: BoxOffice Books, 2009.

Hermans, H. G. M. *Memories of a Maverick, Andrija Puharich M.D., LL.D.* Drukgroep Maassluis, The Netherlands: Pi Publications, 1998.

Higgins, Robin. *Patriot Dreams: The Murder of Colonel Rich Higgins*. Quantico, VA: Marine Corps Association, 1999.

Jacobsen, Annie. *Operation Paperclip: The Secret Intelligence Program that Brought Nazi Scientists to America*. New York: Little, Brown and Company, 2014.

————. *The Pentagon's Brain: An Uncensored History of DARPA, America's Top Secret Military Research Agency*. New York: Little, Brown and Company, 2015.

Johnston, Sarah Iles. *Ancient Greek Divination*. West Sussex, UK: Wiley-Blackwell, 2008.

Jung, C. G. *Synchronicity: An Acausal Connecting Principle*. Princeton, NJ: Princeton University Press, 1973.

Kelleher, Colm, Ph.D., and George Knapp. *Hunt for the Skinwalker: Science Confronts the Unexplained at a Remote Ranch in Utah*. New York: Paraview Pocket Books, 2005.

Leek, Sybil. *Telepathy: The Respectable Phenomenon*. New York: Macmillan, 1971.

Margolis, Jonathan. *The Secret Life of Uri Geller: CIA Masterspy?* London, UK: Watkins, 2013.

Marrs, Jim. *PSI Spies: The True Story of America's Psychic Warfare Program*. Franklin Lakes, NJ: The Career Press, Inc., 2007.

Marks, John. *The Search for the "Manchurian Candidate": The CIA and Mind Control, The Secret History of the Behavioral Sciences*. New York: W. W. Norton, 1991.

Mars: Science Fiction to Colonization. Berkeley, CA: Lighting Guides, 2015.

May, Edwin C., Ph.D., Victor Rubel, Ph.D., and Lloyd Auerbach, M.S. *ESP Wars: East & West: An Account of the Military Use of Psychic Espionage as Narrated by the Key Russian and American Players*. Palo Alto, CA: Laboratories for Fundamental Research, 2014.

McMoneagle, Joseph. *Mind Trek: Exploring Consciousness, Time, and Space Through Remote Viewing*. Charlottesville, VA: Hampton Roads Publishing Company, Inc., 1993.

———. *The Stargate Chronicles: Memoirs of a Psychic Spy*. Hertford, NC: Crossroad Press, 2006.

McRae, Ronald M. *Mind Wars: The True Story of Government Research into the Military Potential of Psychic Weapons*. New York: St. Martin's, 1984.

Miller, Richard Alan, Ph.D. *Power Tools for the 21st Century*. Grant's Pass, OR: OAK Publishing, 2013.

Mitchell, Edgar D. *Earthrise: My Adventures as an Apollo 14 Astronaut*. Chicago: Chicago Review Press, 2014.

———. *Psychic Exploration: A Challenge for Science*. New York: G. P. Putnam's Sons, 1974.

———. *The Way of the Explorer: An Apollo Astronaut's Journey through the Material and Mystical Worlds*. New York: G. P. Putnam's Sons, 1996.

Monroe, Robert A. *Far Journeys*. Garden City, NY: Doubleday, 1985.

———. *Journeys out of the Body*. New York: Harmony, 2001.

Morehouse, David. *Psychic Warrior: Inside the CIA's Stargate Program: The True Story of a Soldier's Espionage and Awakening.* New York: St. Martin's, 1996.

Murphy, Gardner, M.D., and Robert O. Ballou, eds. *William James on Psychical Research.* New York: Viking, 1960.

Ostrander, Sheila, and Lynn Schoeder. *Psychic Discoveries.* New York: Marlowe & Company, 1997.

Palmer, David A. *Qigong Fever: Body, Science, and Utopia in China.* New York: Columbia University Press, 2007.

Pauli, Wolfgang, and Jung, C. G. "Atom and Archetype: the Pauli/Jung Letters, 1932–1958." Edited by C. A. Meier. Princeton, NJ: Princeton University Press, 2001.

Pauwells, Louis, and Jacques Bergier. *The Morning of the Magicians: Secret Societies, Conspiracies, and Vanished Civilizations.* Rochester, VT: Destiny Books, 2009.

Puharich, Andrija. *Beyond Telepathy.* Garden City, NY: Anchor Books, 1973.

———. *The Sacred Mushroom: Key to the Door of Eternity.* Garden City, NY: Doubleday, 1959.

———. *Uri: A Journal of the Mystery of Uri Geller.* Garden City, NY: Anchor, 1974.

———, ed. *The Iceland Papers: Select Papers on Experimental and Theoretical Research on the Physics of Consciousness.* Amherst, WI: Essentia Research Associates, 1979.

Quigley, Joan. *"What Does Joan Say?": My Seven Years as White House Astrologer to Nancy and Ronald Reagan.* New York: Birch Lane, 1990.

Randi, James. *The Magic of Uri Geller.* New York: Ballantine Books, 1975.

Regan, Donald T., *For the Record: From Wall Street to Washington.* United States: Harcourt Brace Jovanovich, 1988.

Russell, Ronald. *The Journey of Robert Monroe: From Out-of-Body Explorer to Consciousness Pioneer.* Charlottesville, VA: Hampton Roads Publishing, 2007.

Sagan, Carl. *Broca's Brain: Reflections on the Romance of Science.* New York: Random House, 1979.

———. *The Demon-Haunted World: Science as a Candle in the Dark*. New York: Ballantine, 1996.

Schmitt, Harrison H. *Return to the Moon: Exploration, Enterprise, and Energy in the Human Settlement of Space*. New York: Praxis, 2006.

Schnabel, Jim. *Remote Viewers: The Secret History of America's Psychic Spies*. New York: Dell, 1997.

Schoch, Robert M., and Logan Yonavjak. *The Parapsychology Revolution*. New York: Jeremy P. Tarcher/Penguin, 2008.

Sexton, James, ed. *Aldous Huxley: Selected Letters*. Chicago, IL: Ivan R. Dee, 2007.

Shepard, Alan B., Donald K. Slayton, Jay Barbree, Howard Benedict, and Neil Armstrong. *Moon Shot: The Inside Story of America's Race to the Moon*. Atlanta, GA: Turner Publishing, Inc., 1994.

Sklar, Dusty. *The Nazis and the Occult*. New York: Dorset Press, 1977.

Smith, Paul H. *The Essential Guide to Remote Viewing: The Secret Military Remote Perception Skill Anyone Can Learn*. Las Vegas: Intentional Press, 2015.

———. *Reading the Enemy's Mind: Inside Star Gate—America's Psychic Espionage Program*. New York: Tom Doherty Associates, 2005.

Speer, Albert. *Inside the Third Reich: Memoirs*. New York: Galahad Books, 1995.

Stephenson, William. *A Man Called Intrepid: The Secret War*. New York: Harcourt Brace Jovanovich, 1976.

Targ, Russell. *Do You See What I See?: Memoirs of a Blind Biker*. Charlottesville, VA: Hampton Roads Publishing, 2008.

———. *The Reality of ESP: A Physicist's Proof of Psychic Abilities*. Wheaton, IL: Quest, 2012.

Targ, Russell, and Harold E. Puthoff. *Mind Reach: Scientists Look at Psychic Ability*. New York: Delacorte Press/Eleanor Friede.

Tart, Charles T., ed. *Altered States of Consciousness: A Book of Readings*. New York: John Wiley & Sons, 1969.

Thomas, Keith. *Religion and the Decline of Magic: Studies in Popular Beliefs in Sixteenth- and Seventeenth-Century England*. London, UK: Penguin Books, 1971.

Tompkins, Peter, and Christopher Bird. *The Secret Life of Plants: A Fascinating Account of the Physical, Emotional, and Spiritual Relations between Plants and Man*. New York: Harper, 2002.

Vallée, Jacques. *Forbidden Science: Volume Two*. San Francisco, CA: Documatica Research, LLC, 2014.

———. *Forbidden Science: Volume Three*. San Francisco, CA: Documatica Research, LLC, 2014.

Wilhelm, John L. *The Search for Superman*. New York: Pocket Books, 1976.

Wilhelm, Richard and Cary F. Baynes. *The I Ching, or, Book of Changes*. Princeton, NJ: Princeton University Press, 1967.

Wilkins, Sir Hubert, and Harold M. Sherman. *Thoughts Through Space: A Remarkable Adventure in the Realm of Mind*. Charlottesville, VA: Hampton Roads Publishing, 2004.

Wulff, Wilhelm. *Zodiac and Swastika: How Astrology Guided Hitler's Germany (Tierkreis und Hakenkreuz)*. Gütersloh, Germany: Bertelsmann Sachbuchverlag Reinhard Mohn, 1968.

Monographs and Reports

Advanced Research Projects Agency. "Paranormal Phenomena—Briefing on a Net Assessment Study." RAND Corporation, Santa Monica, CA, January 1973.

American Institutes for Research. "An Evaluation of the Remote Viewing Program: Research and Operational Application." Draft Report, September 22, 1995.

Army Science Board. "Report of Panel on Human Technologies." Department of the Army, Assistant Secretary of the Army Research Development and Acquisition, Washington, D.C., December 1983.

Byron, E.V. "Operational Procedure for Project Pandora Microwave Test Facility," The Johns Hopkins University Applied Physics Laboratory, Silver Spring, MD, October 1966.

———. "Project Pandora, Final Report." The Johns Hopkins University Applied Physics Laboratory, Silver Spring, MD, November 1966.

Committee on Assessing Foreign Technology Development in Human Performance Modification; Board on Behavioral, Cognitive, and

Sensory Sciences; Division on Engineering and Physical Sciences; Division of Behavioral and Social Sciences and Social Sciences and Education; National Research Council. "Human Performance Modification: Review of Worldwide Research with a View to the Future." The National Academies Press, Washington, D.C.

Davis, Eric W. "Teleportation Physics Study." Warp Drive Metrics for the Air Force Research Laboratory (AFMC), Edwards Air Force Base, CA, August 2004.

Davis, Jack. "Defining the Analytic Mission: Facts, Findings, Forecasts, and Fortune-telling. Central Intelligence Agency." Volume 38, Number 5, 1995.

Druckman, Daniel, and John A. Swets, eds. "Enhancing Human Performance. Issues, Theories, And Techniques." Committee on Techniques for the Enhancement of Human Performance, Commission on Behavioral and Social Sciences and Education, National Research Council. National Academy Press, Washington, D.C., 1988.

Foreign Broadcast Information Service. "USSR Report: Life Sciences, Biomedical and Behavioral Sciences." April 19, 1984.

Frey, Allen H. "Effect of Microwaves and Radio Frequency Energy on the Central Nervous System." Clearinghouse for Federal and Scientific Information, U.S. Department of Commerce, September 17, 1969.

Kress, Kenneth A., Ph.D. "An Analysis of a Remote-Viewing Experiment of URDF-3," Central Intelligence Agency [redacted], December 4, 1975.

——— [redacted]. "Parapsychology in Intelligence: A Personal Review and Conclusions." *Studies in Intelligence,* Volume 21, Winter 1977.

Jones, Eric M. "Landing at Fra Mauro, Corrected Transcript," Apollo 14 Lunar Surface Journal, National Aeronautics and Space Administration, June 20, 2014.

LaMothe, John D. "Controlled Offensive Behavior—USSR (U)." Medical Intelligence Office, Office of the Surgeon General, Department of the Army, for the Defense Intelligence Agency, July 1972.

Maire, Louis F. III, and J. D. LaMothe. "Soviet And Czechoslovakian Parapsychology Research (U)." U.S. Army Medical Intelligence and Information Agency, Office of the Surgeon General for the Defense Intelligence Agency, September 1975.

May, Edwin C., Ph.D. "Enhanced Human Performance Investigation." SRI Project 1291, SRI International, Final Technical Report, December 1986.

McKelvy, Dolan M. "Psychic Warfare: Exploring the Mind Frontier." Air War College Research Report, Air University, U.S. Air Force, Maxwell Air Force Base, Alabama, 1988.

Mumford, Michael D., Ph.D., Andrew M. Rose, Ph.D., and David A. Goslin, Ph.D. "An Evaluation of Remote Viewing: Research and Applications." American Institutes for Research. Washington, D.C., September 29, 1995.

National Research Council of the National Academies. "Avoiding Surprise in an Era of Global Technology Advances." The National Academies Press, Washington, D.C., 2001.

———. "The Polygraph and Lie Detection." The National Academies Press, Washington, D.C., 2003.

Office of Scientific Intelligence. "The Soviet Bioastronautics Research Program." Central Intelligence Agency, February 22, 1962.

Oldroyd, David R., ed. "The Earth Inside and Out: Some Major Contributions to Geology in the Twentieth Century." Geological Society Special Publication No. 192, The Geological Society of London, England, 2002.

Paddock, Alfred H. Jr. "U.S. Army Special Warfare, Its Origins: Psychological and Unconventional Warfare, 1941–1952." National Defense University Press, Washington, D.C., 1982.

Palmer, John. "An Evaluative Report on the Current Status of Parapsychology." Parapsychology Laboratory at the University of Utrecht for the U.S. Army Research Institute for the Behavioral and Social Sciences, Alexandria, VA, May 1986.

Puharich, Henry K. "Introduction to the Round Table Laboratory of Experimental Electrobiology." Round Table Foundation, Camden, Maine, 1949.

Puthoff, Harold E. "Psychoenergetics Research in The People's Republic of China (1982)." SRI International, Menlo Park, CA. Defense Intelligence Agency, October 1982.

Puthoff, H.E., I. Swann, and G. Langford. "NIC Techniques (U)." SRI International Project 7560, Menlo Park, CA. Defense Intelligence Agency, January 2000.

Rhine, J. B. "Final Report, ESP (Extrasensory Perception)." Engineer Research and Development Laboratories, Fort Belvoir, VA, July 10, 1953.

————. "Research on Animal Orientation with Emphasis on the Phenomenon of Homing in Pigeons," Engineer Research and Development Laboratories, Fort Belvoir, VA, January 26, 1954.

U.S. Air Force, Air Force Systems Command, Foreign Technology Division. "Paraphysics R&D—Warsaw Pact (U)." Defense Intelligence Agency, March 30, 1978.

United States Army Intelligence and Security Command. "High Performance Task Force Report: An Inscom Beyond Excellence." Arlington Hall Station, Arlington, VA, March 1983.

U.S. Government. "Coordinate Remote Viewing Stages I-VI and Beyond," February 1985.

U.S. Joint Publications Research Service. "Bibliographies on Parapsychology (Psychoenergetics) and Related Subjects—USSR." March 28, 1972.

————. "Translations on USSR Science and Technology Biomedical Sciences, No. 2," U.S., Arlington, VA, March 8, 1977.

Weybrew, Benjamin. "History of the Military Psychology at the U.S. Naval Submarine Medical Research Laboratory." Report Number 917. Naval Submarine Medical Research Laboratory, Submarine Base, Groton, CT, August 31, 1979.

Wortz, E.C. et al. "Novel Biophysical Information Transfer Mechanisms (NBIT)." AiResearch Manufacturing Company of California. Torrance, CA, January 14, 1976.

Zhongguo, Renti, and Kexue. "Chinese Journal of Somatic Science." Defense Intelligence Agency, Washington, D.C., July 1990.

BIBLIOGRAPHY

Articles and Press Releases

Alexander, Lieutenant Colonel John B. "The New Mental Battlefield: Beam Me Up, Spock," *Military Review*, No. 12. December 12, 1980.

Anderson, Jack. "Pentagon Invades Buck Rogers Turf," *Washington Post*, January 9, 1981.

Armunanto, Eko. "Artificial telepathy to create Pentagon's telepathic soldiers," *Digital Journal*, May 10, 2013.

Bach, Deborah. "UW team links two human brains for question-and-answer experiment," *UW Today*, September 23, 2015.

Backster, Cleve. "Evidence of a Primary Perception in Plant Life," *International Journal of Parapsychology* 10, no. 4 (Winter 1968): 329–348.

Baluška, František et al. "The 'root-brain' hypothesis of Charles and Francis Darwin. Revival after more than 125 years," *Plant Signaling & Behavior*, December 2008.

Baughman, Brent. "Scientists Take Quantum Steps Toward Teleportation," NPR, *All Things Considered*, August 1, 2010.

Beidel, Eric. "More than a Feeling: ONR Investigates 'Spidey Sense' for Sailors and Marines." Office of Naval Research, Corporate Strategic Communications, March 27, 2014.

Bordas, Coleman C. "ESP and Parapsychology," *Indiana Gazette*, August 15, 1980.

"Buell Mullen, Muralist and Painter on Metals," *New York Times*, September 10, 1986.

"Captain Edgar D. Mitchell, the Uri Geller of the Astronauts," *Maariv*, February 19, 1971.

"Castle Is Inventor's Vision of the Past," *New York Times*, October 9, 1988.

Channing, Joseph. "U.S. Navy Program to Study How Troops Use Intuition," *New York Times*, March 27, 2012.

Dahlen, Severin. "Remote Annealing of High Carbon Steel Parts," *Archaeus* (February–March 1986): 3.

Doder, Dusko. "Soviets Stop Building U.S. Embassy Over Use of Bugging Detector," *Washington Post*, May 27, 1983.

"Elderly Scientist Ordered Evicted from Reynolds Estate Dies in Fall,"
Winston-Salem Journal, January 4, 1995.

Ellis, Arthur J. "The Divining Rod: A History of Water Witching," U.S.
Geological Survey, Water Supply Paper No. 416, 1917.

Emerging Technology from the arXiv, "The Experiment That Will
Allow Humans to 'See' Quantum Entanglement," *MIT Technology
Review,* February 17, 2016.

Engelberg, Stephen. "U.S. Says Libya Moves Chemicals for Poison Gas
Away from Plant," *New York Times,* January 4, 1989.

Feinberg, Gerald. "Possibility of Faster-Than-Light Particles," *Physical
Review* 159 (1967): 1089–1105.

"Gellermania," *Sunday People,* November 1973.

C. Grau, et al. "Conscious Brain-to-Brain Communication in Humans
Using Non-Invasive Technologies," *PLOS One*, August 19, 2014.

Gruenpeter, Yael. "The Israeli Defense Minister Who Stole Antiquities,"
Haaretz, December 19, 2015.

Hackett, Dennis. "Sinister Signals on the Radio," *New Scientist,*
September 1984.

Hadid, Diaa. "American Graduate Student Killed in Stabbing Rampage
Near Tel Aviv," *New York Times,* March 8, 2016.

Horowitz, K. A., D. C. Lewis, and E. L. Gasteiger. "Plant 'Primary
Perception': Electrophysiological Unresponsiveness to Brine Shrimp
Killing," *Science,* August 8, 1975, 478–480.

Hoyle, Russ. "Terrorism: Welcome Home, Soldier," *Time,* February 15,
1982.

Iozzio, Corinne. "Scientists Prove That Telepathic Communication Is
Within Reach: An international research team develops a way to say
'hello' with your mind," Smithsonian.com, October 2, 2014.

Jaroff, Leon. "The Magician and the Think Tank," *Time,* March 12, 1973.

Kernbach, Serge. "Unconventional Research in USSR and Russia,"
International Journal of Unconventional Science (Fall 2013): 1–23.

Kershner, Isabel. "Israelis Find New Tunnel from Gaza into Israel," *New
York Times,* April 18, 2016.

Kmetz, John M. " Plant Primary Perception: The Other Side of the
Leaf," *Skeptical Inquirer* 2 (1978): 57–61.

Lewthwaite, Gilbert A., and Tom Bowman. "Pentagon employed psychic spy unit Fort Meade program sought to 'divine' intelligence data," *Baltimore Sun,* November 30, 1995.

Liebermann, Oren. "American Fatally stabbed in Israel terror attack that wounds ten others," CNN, March 9, 2016.

Martin, Malia. "The Holy Devil," *New York Review of Books,* December 31, 1964.

Messadié, Gérald. "The Secret of the *Nautilus,*" *Science et Vie,* no. 509, February 1960.

Mooney, Michael J. "The God of Skeptics," *Miami New Times,* August 27, 2009.

"Nikola Tesla," *Time, The Weekly Newsmagazine,* Volume XVIII, July 20, 1931.

"Obituary: Dr. Robert P. Becker," *Watertown Daily Times,* May 29, 2008.

Osis, Karlis. "New ASPR Search on Out-of-the Body Experiences," ASPR Newsletter, no. 14, Summer 1972.

Osis, Karlis, and Donna McCormick. "Kinetic effects at the ostensible location of an out-of-body projection during perceptual testing," *Journal of the American Society for Psychical Research* 74, no. 3 (1980).

Pace, Eric. "Christopher Bird, 68, a Best-Selling Author," *New York Times,* May 6, 1996.

Petit, Deborah. "Mitchell Doubts Fathering Child, Wants Case to End," *Sun Sentinel,* August 17, 1985.

Puthoff, Harold. "CIA-Initiated Remote Viewing at Stanford Research Institute," Association of Former Intelligence Officers, *The Intelligencer: Journal of U.S. Intelligence Studies* 12, no. 1 (Summer 2001).

Rao, R., et. al. "A Direct Brain-to-Brain Interface in Humans," PLUS One, November 5, 2014.

"Reagan Wishes More Dignified Job for Son Ron," *United Press International,* June 30, 1986.

Reppert, Barton. "Close-up: The Moscow Signal. Zapping an embassy: 35 years later," Associated Press, May 22, 1988.

Roberts, Steven V. "White House Confirms Reagans Follow Astrology, Up to a Point." *New York Times,* May 4, 1988.

Rosenthal, Andrew. "Before His Abduction, Higgins Talked of Risks," *New York Times,* August 1, 1989.

Scharf, Caleb A. "The Panspermia Paradox," *Scientific American,* October 15, 2012.

Schudel, Matt. "The Dark Side of the Moon: Edgar Mitchell Has Walked on the Moon And Explored Inner Space. It's Everyday Life That Gives Him Trouble," *Sun Sentinel,* January 8, 1988.

Schwartz, Stephan. "The Realm of the Will," *Explore: The Journal of Science and Healing* 1, no. 3 (May 2005): 198–207.

Sciolino, Elaine. "The Bugged Embassy Case: What Went Wrong," *New York Times,* November 15, 1988.

"Shades of Black Magic: Marines on Operation Divine for VC Tunnels," *Observer* 5, no. 45 (March 13, 1967).

Simons, Howard. "Man's Brain Waves Can 'Talk' Overcoming Speech Barriers," *Washington Post,* October 21, 1964.

"Sybil Leek, The South's White Witch," *BBC Home,* October 28, 2002.

Tesla, Nikola. "My Inventions," *Electrical Experimenter,* June 1919.

"Top Ten Influential Space Thinkers," *New Scientist,* September 5, 2007.

"Tsien Hsue-shen, 2007 Person of the Year," *Aviation Week & Space Technology,* January 7, 2008.

"U.N. Enlists Psychic Firm to Find Iraqi's Weapon Sites," Associated Press, November 19, 1991.

Van Hatten, Margaret. "A Cost-effective Account of the Spoons," *Financial Times,* January 18, 1986.

Vicens, A. J. "Hillary Clinton Is Serious About UFOs: The Democratic front-runner's talk of extraterrestrials is the least bizarre part of this election," Mother Jones.com, March 25, 2016.

Wadler, Joyce et al. "The President's Astrologers," *People,* May 23, 1988.

"Washington Whispers." *U.S. News & World Report,* May 4, 1987.

"What the Iran-Iraq War Can Teach US Officials," *Middle East Forum* 20, no. 2 (Spring 2013).

Wilhelm, John L. "Psychic Spying? The CIA, the Pentagon and the Russians Probe the Military Potential of Parapsychology," *Washington Post,* August 7, 1977.

BIBLIOGRAPHY

Personal Papers, Photographs, and Unpublished Manuscripts

Uri Geller

Dale Graff

Dr. Christopher "Kit" Green

Edgar Mitchell

Harold Puthoff

Andrew Puharich

Paul Smith

Jacques Vallée

Documentary Films

An Honest Liar. Produced and directed by Justin Weinstein and Tyler Measom. Abramorama Films, 2014.

Psychics, Saints and Scientists. Narrated by Dr. Thelma Moss. Record Group 306, National Archives and Records Administration, U.S. Information Agency, 1972.

The Real X-Files. Produced and directed by Jim Schnabel. Waking Times Films, Independent Channel 4, England, UK, 1995.

The Secret Life Of Uri Geller— Psychic Spy? Directed by Vikram Jayant. BBC Two, 2013.

Uri Geller: A Life Stranger Than Fiction. Produced and directed by Simon Cowell. Indigo Films, 2009.

INDEX

"ESP—Fact or Fancy?"
  (McConnell), 377
Espionage Act of 1917, 161, 369
EST (Erhard Seminars Training),
  245
European Commission Future and
  Emerging Technology Program,
  386–87
"Evidence of Primary Perception in
  Plant Life" (Backster), 122
"Exploring the Energy Fields of
  Man" (conference), 68
extraordinary human functioning,
  102, 104, 137, 194, 416;
  Extraordinary Human Body
  Function (EHBF), 244, 250, 254,
  276, 362, 391; Extraordinary
  Powers Craze, 244, 254
eyeless sight, 63, 97, 244, 246
Eyles, Don, 108

*Fads and Fallacies in the Name of
  Science* (Gardner), 40–41, 86, 146
Faraday cage, 34, 185–86
Faurer, Lincoln D., 274
FBI (Federal Bureau of
  Investigation), 54, 63, 183, 251,
  261, 265, 283, 332, 357–58, 360
Fechner, Gustav Theodor,
  444n(121)
Feinberg, Gerald, 120
First Sacred War, 341, 373
First Science Symposium (Beijing),
  246
First Science Symposium of the
  Extraordinary Function of the
  Human Body (Shanghai), 244
Fitzwater, Marlin, 335–36
Flournoy, Théodore, 51–52,
  433n(52)
Force, Taylor, 410
force powering anomalous mental
  phenomena, 73, 149, 165, 184,

216, 246, 361–62, 370, 378, 412,
  428n(26); and modern
  technology, 373, 381, 419
forensic medicine, 139–40, 394–95,
  397
Förster-Nietzsche, Elisabeth, 53
Fostervoll, Alv Jakob, 176
Freud, Manzy, 90
Freud, Sigmund, 56
Frey, Allan H., 191–93, 455n(192)
From India to the Planet Mars
  (Flournoy), 52
From the Shadows (Gates), 190
Frost, David, 444n(121)
"Frost Fairies, The" (Canby), 53
"Frost King, The" (Keller), 53
Frye, William J., 64
Fundamentals of Quantum Electronics
  (Puthoff), 118

Gaddafi, Muammar, 261
Gardner, Martin, 40–42, 86,
  145–46, 176, 293–94, 400–402,
  449n(150)
Garrett, Eileen, 34, 37
Gates, Robert M., 189–90, 235,
  326, 371, 454n(190)
Gauvin, Fernand, 232–33, 238–39,
  340, 351, 358–59, 361
Geller, Hanna, 405–6, 409, 412
Geller, Uri, 69, 89–99, 164, 239,
  400, 403–13; and ARPA,
  145–46, 371; and CIA, 98–99,
  137, 140–49, 172–73, 176–79,
  404, 448n(144); and Kit Green,
  99, 140, 142, 147–48, 178–79,
  291; and LLNL, 176–81; and map
  dowsing, 85–87, 89, 95, 197, 332,
  409, 439n(85); and mind
  projection, 408–9; and Mitchell,
  141–42, 414–15, 447n(141); and
  Mossad, 91–92, 94, 178, 183, 406,
  408–12; as performer, 93–94, 96,

ABOUT THE AUTHOR

ANNIE JACOBSEN is the author of the *New York Times* bestsellers *Area 51* and *Operation Paperclip,* and the Pulitzer Prize finalist *The Pentagon's Brain.* She was a contributing editor at the *Los Angeles Times Magazine.* A graduate of Princeton University, she lives in Los Angeles with her husband and two sons.